Government Violence
and Repression

Recent Titles in
Contributions in Political Science
Series Editor: Bernard K. Johnpoll

A Political Organization Approach to Transnational Terrorism
Kent Layne Oots

Individualism and Community: The State in Marx and Early Anarchism
Jeffrey H. Barker

Sentinels of Empire: The United States and Latin American Militarism
Jan Knippers Black

Portugal in the 1980's: Dilemmas of Democratic Consolidation
Kenneth Maxwell, editor

Dependency Theory and the Return of High Politics
Mary Ann Tetrault and Charles Frederick Abel, editors

Ban The Bomb: A History of SANE, the Committee for a Sane Nuclear
Policy, 1957–1985
Milton S. Katz

Republicans and Vietnam, 1961–1968
Terry Dietz

The Politics of Developed Socialism: The Soviet Union as a
Postindustrial State
Donald R. Kelley

Harry S. Truman: The Man from Independence
William F. Levantrosser, editor

News from Somewhere: Connecting Health and Freedom at the Workplace
Gary A. Lewis

"Pursuing the Just Cause of Their People": A Study of Contemporary
Armenian Terrorism
Michael M. Gunter

When Marxists Do Research
Pauline Marie Vaillancourt

GOVERNMENT VIOLENCE AND REPRESSION

An Agenda for Research

EDITED BY
Michael Stohl and George A. Lopez

Contributions in Political Science, Number 148

Greenwood Press
New York · Westport, Connecticut · London

To Catherine Burke Lopez
who endures, inspires and continues to love
throughout adversity

and

to my aunt and uncle
Florence and Max Epstein
with love and appreciation for their love of ideas

Library of Congress Cataloging-in-Publication Data
Main entry under title:

Government violence and repression.

 (Contributions in political science, ISSN 0147–1066 ;
no. 148)
  Bibliography: p.
  Includes index.
  1. Political persecution—Addresses, essays, lectures.
2. Civil rights—Addresses, essays, lectures.
3. Terrorism—Addresses, essays, lectures. I. Stohl,
Michael, 1947– . II. Lopez, George A. III. Series.
JC571.G69 1986   323.4′9   85–24741
ISBN 0–313–24651–3 (lib. bdg. : alk. paper)

Library of Congress Catalog Card Number: 85-24741
ISBN: 0–313–24651–3
ISSN: 0147–1066

First published in 1986

Greenwood Press, Inc.
88 Post Road West, Westport, Connecticut 06881

Printed in the United States of America

The paper used in this book complies with the
Permanent Paper Standard issued by the National
Information Standards Organization (Z39.48–1984).

10 9 8 7 6 5 4 3 2 1

Contents

Preface   vii

1. State Terrorism: Issues of Concept and Measurement
   Christopher Mitchell, Michael Stohl, David Carleton, and
   George A. Lopez   1

2. Conceptual Problems of Studying State Terrorism
   Michael Nicholson   27

3. The Political Origins of State Violence and Terror: A
   Theoretical Analysis
   Ted Robert Gurr   45

4. National Security Ideology as an Impetus to State
   Violence and State Terror
   George A. Lopez   73

5. State Terrorism and Repression in the Third World:
   Parameters and Prospects
   Miles Wolpin   97

6. Genocide as State Terrorism
   Barbara Harff   165

7. Terrorism, Counter-Terrorism, and the Democratic
   Society
   Grant Wardlaw   189

8. The Superpowers and International Terrorism
   Michael Stohl   207

9. The Implausible Dream: International Law, State
   Violence, and State Terrorism
   Robert A. Friedlander   235

   Bibliographic Note   269

   Index   271

   Contributors   277

Preface

Our first volume for Greenwood Press, *The State as Terrorist: The Dynamics of Governmental Violence and Repression*, presented a collection of essays focused on the extent to which political terror and repression were consciously employed tactics or "rationally" selected policies of governments in contemporary affairs. One deliberate goal of that work was to bridge scholarship examining insurgent terror with the human rights literature, which explores state violence inflicted against its own citizens. Since the publication of that volume eighteen months ago, global politics are no less concerned with acts of political terrorism within and between states. But the policy and scholarly discussion still appears to move overwhelmingly in the direction of studying only insurgent or revolutionary terror. So, too, scholarly examination of gross violations of human rights appears bogged down either in counting particular violations or in debating different conceptions of the primacy of diverse human rights, specifically economic and social rights versus civil and political rights.

Certainly each of these themes warrants the attention they are receiving, however disjunctured that attention may proceed. In this volume, we have assembled contributions that move to further define the study of terror violence employed by government. Each chapter attempts a delineation of a particular aspect of government violence in our time and postulates how social science inquiry might proceed more systematically in the future.

In the first chapter, with collaborators Chris Mitchell and David Carleton, we examine the diverse conceptual dimensions of government violence that pose unique problems to the study of state terrorism and repression. Our essay concludes with an outline of a data-gathering strategy for such study. In the second chapter, Michael Nicholson struggles with the cumbersome epistemologial issues associated with the study of government terror. His assessment that the pitfalls which exist in the study of this phenomenon do not pose extreme difficulties to the careful social scientist are critical to future research.

In chapters three through eight each contributor examines a particular aspect of government violence about which we need to learn more in order to claim accurately that we have a social science knowledge base about this phenomenon. In the third chapter, Ted Robert Gurr develops an integrated set of propositions about the conditions under which national elites will resort to repression and terror violence. Gurr's initial claims about the extent to which government may be reacting to "challengers" provides linkages between the study of government terror and the literature of insurgent terror and comparative revolutions. George Lopez dissects the National Security Ideology prevalent in Latin America as an example of the shared mindset necessary for leaders to elect terror violence. In the chapter that follows, Miles Wolpin provides a data-based analysis of the correlates of repression in the Third World. After comparing the characteristics and processes of numerous genocides in her chapter, Barbara Harff then prescribes the future contours of research in this most extreme form of government terror violence.

The final three chapters of the volume explore the policy actions and reactions of nation states in coping with insurgent terror or in executing terror as a foreign policy. Relying primarily on an analysis of the British experience of coping with factional violence and insurgent terror, Grant Wardlaw emphasizes that the greatest danger posed to governments by internal terror and violence rests in the temptation of overreaction in the use of force. In chapter eight, Michael Stohl scrutinizes the patterns of the United States and the Soviet Union as they employ various forms of terrorism to execute their foreign policy strategies. Finally, Robert Friedlander details the long tradition of international law that has attempted to keep pace with the changing contours of government violence.

No volume of separately developed papers that aims to set the research directions for future scholarship can have any hope of doing so unless participants in the project meet deadlines and work collegially with critiques provided of initial drafts. We have found this group of scholars, despite their geographic dispersion, to have performed exceptionally well in this regard. Thus, whatever contribution to the field that the volume may make clearly reflects their individual and corporate dedication to it. We thank them one and all, as we do Marta Rose of Earlham College, who provided invaluable research and editorial assistance as the volume neared completion.

George A. Lopez
Michael Stohl

Government Violence
and Repression

1

State Terrorism: Issues of Concept and Measurement

Christopher Mitchell, Michael Stohl, David Carleton, and George A. Lopez

Amnesty International is often asked to compare and contrast the human rights record of different countries or of successive governments. It does not and cannot do this. Government secrecy and intimidation from many countries can impede efforts to corroborate allegations; this fact alone makes it impossible to establish a reliable and consistent basis for comparison. Furthermore, prisoners are subjected to widely differing forms of harassment, ill-treatment and punishment, taking place in diverse contexts and affecting the victims and their families in different ways; this fact would render any statistical or other generalized comparison meaningless as a real measure of the impact of human rights abuses.[1]

It is increasingly accepted among scholars that it is inappropriate and misleading to use the term "terrorism" solely in cases where the behavior in question is carried out by some non-state organization [such as the Irish Republican Army (IRA) or the Palestine Liberation Organization] against a government, its agents, or the general citizenry of the state. We have relearned the lesson that it is perfectly reasonable to use the term "terrorism" for certain actions of the state itself, either using its official functionaries or using deniable surrogates.[2] Hence, the study of the state's use of terror against some or all of its own citizenry has recently ceased being a matter of concern solely for historians' consideration of Jacobin actions in revolutionary France or of Josef Stalin's "Great Terror." It has once again become the subject matter of sociologists and political scientists, with their aim to develop general explanations and theories about recurrent social and political phenomena.[3]

Any effort to explain and generally account for the phenomenon of state terrorism implies three initial requirements:

1. An unambiguous frame of reference to tell when we are, or are not, observing the phenomenon under analysis; that is, we need a clear definition of the nature of terrorism in general and state terrorism in particular

2. A comprehensive data set, which, following the definitional requirements enunciated above, provides information sufficient to make judgments about the phenomenon itself and its relationship to other aspects of the political process

3. Some way of indicating variations in the intensity of the phenomenon so that we can make comparisons (a) between cases, for example, states that employ terrorist strategies, (b) within the same case over time, and (c) between events from case to case both within and between states that employ terrorist strategies

In short, we need to establish clear conceptual and operational definitions, collect the data, and create scaling procedures that will allow proper social science analysis and comparison. While the epistemological requirements for building a data-based theory of state terrorism are no different in principle from those of any other area of social science research (see Nicholson's chapter in this volume), that task still remains incomplete.

We believe an encouraging start has already been made toward tackling the first of these problems. A beginning has been made in disentangling the defining attributes that distinguish state terrorism from other forms of behavior by organs of the state that may resemble it.[4] The literature on the nature of state terrorism is growing, even if no generally accepted definition has yet emerged. In contrast, the matter of gauging the *degree* of state terrorism at any point in time has been relatively neglected. This chapter is intended to be an initial contribution to addressing this problem. Hence, the main focus is on the possibility of developing measures of state terrorism to enable researchers to fulfill the three requirements for empirical investigation indicated above.

In undertaking this task, we recognize two distinct types of problems. The first of these is the obvious practical problem that we are attempting to study a phenomenon for which accurate data are difficult, if not impossible, to obtain. While there are times when the state and its agents find it useful to advertise their terrorist intent (as do non-state actors), this occurs infrequently. As Raymond Duvall and Michael Stohl argue, "Governments often do not permit their terrorist actions to be widely publicized."[5] State authorities can hardly be expected to admit that they are pursuing a strategy of repression or state terrorism (even against an unpopular minority), even if the strategy is characterized more benignly as, perhaps, a simple "police action."[6] Government concealment of the extent to which it practices terrorist strategies can thus be taken for granted in most cases, as can government denials of responsibility for terrorist actions and government justifications of "necessary measures" when these prove impossible to conceal from domestic (or international) publics. Frequently, it is possible to recognize the scale of a state's terrorism only once the cells have been opened and the graves dug up by a new regime. Apart from being a *post hoc* revelation, it is also infrequent, so that any sustained contemporary monitoring, whether quantitative or qualitative, is usually impossible on any reliable basis, even if some rough indications can be gained through the activities of organizations such as Amnesty International.[7]

The practical difficulties of obtaining even semi-reliable data on a clandestine activity practiced in the half-world of state security would seem to make the idea of being able to compare degrees of state terrorism an exercise in futility, and one that cannot and indeed should not be attempted, as the quotation from Amnesty International that opens this chapter asserts. However, we would argue that the practical difficulties can be overcome if proper theoretical care is invested at the outset, and, further, that, as has already been shown through the propaganda and public relations activities of opposition groups in many settings, monitoring the incidence of state terrorism is not impossible.[8] These prior intellectual and conceptual problems must be considered before the practicalities of access to accurate information and reliable quantitative data may be confronted. These problems center mainly around problems of (1) comparability—are we measuring the same behavior from case to case if what is ostensibly the same act occurs in a completely different environment with very different effects? and (2) inference—can we infer that the same action indicates the same intention on the part of two different actors? In other words, in comparing and scaling state terrorism, we confront the familiar difficulties of the validity and reliability of indicators, as well as that of indirect measurement of phenomena inaccessible to direct observation. Only when these tensions are overcome may we move ahead and attempt to solve the problem of practical data gathering and analysis.[9]

DELINEATING STATE TERRORISM: SOME PROBLEMS

As a result of recent scholarly work to delineate the nature of "terrorism" and of "state terrorism," and to distinguish "terrorism" from other aspects of governmental behavior of a repressive or coercive nature, it is increasingly accepted that not all repressive measures are, by definition, state terror.[10] As with non-state terrorism, there are both emotional and instrumental aspects to a state's use of different forms of terror against targets among its citizenry. Hence, many writers emphasize that the term "terrorism" should most usefully be reserved for those occasions on which some actor (whether governmental or non-governmental) attempts to achieve some response (active or passive) from its

target population through the creation of extreme fear within that population. For an act to be considered terrorism, then, the creation of fear
must be a means toward an end. The act of violence therefore does not
actually have to be directed at the target population. The population,
however, must perceive themselves at risk and as the ultimate target of
the act.

This argument constitutes the foundation for the work of Duvall and
Stohl who assert that terrorism is "action intended to induce sharp fear
and *through that agency* to effect a desired outcome to a conflict situation."[11] Hence, all violence on behalf of the state is not necessarily terrorism, although terrorism involves the actual use of violence or the
believable threat of its use. Alexander Dallin and George Breslauer argue
that state terrorism is the arbitrary use, by organs of political authority,
of severe coercion against individuals or groups, the credible threat of
such use, or the arbitrary extermination of such individual groups."[12]
However, as George Lopez has argued, even the harming of one particular group in a society must partly be aimed at inducing fear-deter-
mined behavior on the part of others to count as state terror. As a good
example of state terrorism in action, Lopez indicates the arrest of union
leaders in order to break the power of the unions, but also to show others
that they are liable to similar treatment unless their behavior changes.[13]
Thus, to count as a terrorist action, an event must have an element of
demonstration effect in the minds of the perpetrators. The action is undertaken *pour encourager les autres,* or to discourage them if the terror
inspired in the target is intended to act in a deterrent manner.

At this point, it should also be noted that to fall into the category of
behavior that we are calling terrorism there must be an essentially instrumental element of affecting the behavior of some target group. If
the "mere" removal of the victims comprises the end of the strategy,
then the behavior falls outside the category of terrorism. As in the case
of the Nazi strategy toward gypsies, Jews, and homosexuals, if the aim
includes (or becomes) the destruction of a nation, people, or ethnic
group, then the term "genocide" is appropriate. In such cases, the objective appears to be the physical destruction of a category of individuals,
not the influencing of other persons or the influencing of other social
groups through the terror inspired by the strategy (although this may
have been a secondary result). Thus, when Dallin and Breslauer discuss
the arbitrary extermination of groups,[14] we would consider them to be
off the mark if they were to include such groups when the intention was
merely to eliminate them and influence no others. For a more thorough
discussion of genocide and its relation to state terror, see the essay by
Barbara Harff in this volume.

Two additional key aspects can be discerned from the above discussion.
The first is that terrorist actions or strategies frequently involve two

distinct targets: those who compose the actual targets of the coercive violence, and those who observe the effects of the violence and whose fear the perpetrator intends to arouse or increase. In other words, terrorism serves as an example of what C. Mitchell has elsewhere termed an *indirect* form of conflict behavior.[15] However, it constitutes an unusual form of such behavior, in that the final target of the action is often some general category of individuals rather than a specific organization or set of individuals. This aspect of terrorism has often led analysts to characterize it as "indiscriminate" or "arbitrary." But, in fact, terrorism is neither, unless it has been so badly organized or perpetrated as to be ineffective. The ultimate targets of terrorist strategies are people who can recognize themselves as potential victims because they are members of a social group selected by the terrorist actors, such as members of an ethnic community, a class, or a profession, members of a tribal or linguistic group, or members of a political movement. Thus, in many cases, targets of both state and non-state terrorism become targets simply because they are members of some ascribed or achieved category, rather than for anything they have done personally. Hence, while terrorism is not arbitrary or indiscriminate, it may certainly be *impersonal*, although this distinction may seem unnecessarily scholastic to any member of a target category!

In sum, terrorism by the state (or non-state actors) involves deliberate coercion and violence (or the threat thereof) directed at some victim, with the intention of inducing extreme fear in some target observers who identify with that victim in such a way that they perceive themselves as potential future victims. In this way, they are forced to consider altering their behavior in some manner desired by the actor. From this conceptualization emerge the key ideas of

1. Purposive behavior or intention on the part of the "terrorist actor"
2. The act or threat of violent harm to a victim(s)
3. Observation of the effects of the act or harm by some ultimate target(s)
4. Identification by the target with the victim
5. Some degree of terror induced in the target(s) through a "demonstration effect" and the act of identification
6. Altered behavior ("compellence") or abandoned behavior ("deterrence") as a direct result of the terrorist demonstration[16]

Stripped to its bare essentials, this definition of terrorism involves Actor A striking at Victim B with the intention of affecting the emotional state of Target C to such a degree that Target C changes behavior. In this, the key elements include the intention of Actor A to create an appropriate emotional response in Target C; the nature of the emotion experienced by Target C (for example, "sufficient terror"); and the altered behavior of Target C as a result of Actor A's behavior toward Victim B. Unfortunately, these elements are the most problematical when it comes to distinguishing terrorism from other categories of behavior, and hence the most difficult to use as a basis for developing means of measuring and comparing.

Intentions

In the above formulation, we distinguished terrorism from other forms of coercion and violence by the intention of the actor and the direction of the influence attempt. Thus, any actor employing that particular strategy must have the intention of inducing extreme fear in some population of observers as the main objective for the strategy to count as "true" terrorism. The actual effect on the victim (neutralization, death) may be a secondary objective, but the effect of observing others must be *primary*. A clear distinction must therefore be made between policies that "simply" aim at genocide or the destruction of a particular class within society, as in Cambodia, and those that aim at terrorizing others associated with the victims, such as the U.S. Operation Phoenix campaign in South Vietnam, which sought to "neutralize" National Liberation Front (NLF) support in rural areas. In the first example, the intentions of the Khmer Rouge government seem to have been the removal of class enemies and the "re-education" of those capable of learning from their past "crimes," but not the direct terrorizing of defined parts of the Khmer population, though it clearly had this effect.[17] In the second example, the purpose of the Phoenix program was the reduction of NLF support in rural villages. In effect, the village intelligence officers were given license and justification to arrest, torture, and kill those they identified as a threat. As Frances Fitzgerald has noted, "The true destructiveness of the program came from the very structure of the program itself. Like any stranger to the village, the district intelligence officer, were he a model of probity, would of necessity have some difficulty distinguishing between the 'hard-core' Front cadres, the marginal Front supporters, and the people who went along with the NLF for the sake of survival."[18] But, of course, not all officials were models of probity, and the program was clearly used to terrorize all potential NLF supporters.[19]

Similarly, we must be clear that cases that *inadvertently* terrorize some group or category within a population do not count as "true" terrorism if the effect of inducing extreme fear in that population was not an intention of the perpetrators. In many ways, this situation illustrates how the generally accepted view of the nature of terrorism is closely related to familiar Thomist doctrine of the "law of double effect." Although Thomist ideas are concerned with the moral questions of the justifiable, and hence just, action, rather than the definitional question of the essential nature of certain kinds of action, they are similarly based upon the conception of making distinctions between acts according to the *intentions* of the actor.

Here, however, definitional problems arise. First, it is frequently impossible to tell what intentions underlie an observable act from the mere observation of the act itself. Is the disappearance, arrest, or deportation of a journalist by a government or its agents intended to intimidate other journalists or to remove a specific annoyance from the country in question? Unfortunately, one cannot judge from the mere occurrence of a single specific action. Moreover, observation of the fact that other journalists are indeed intimidated does not clarify the intentions of the government in question. One can infer that, in many cases, such was the government's intention. Using such an inference, one can thus regard *all* such acts as having the necessary element of intention to induce fear, thus using the action itself as an indicator of state terrorism. There are, however, justifiable residues of doubt in adopting this strategy. The doubts lessen if and when information becomes available from other sources and if at later dates intentions of the authorities are confirmed. At the present stage of collecting such information, the feeling of unease is greatest. But while there will always be doubt and uncertainty with this approach, it may be reduced by gathering data within a context-specific collection effort.

Second, the problem of mixed motivations underlying actions and policies emerges in two forms. The first is the simple fact that both policies and individual actions are normally taken in order to achieve a variety of objectives, so that intentions become mixed. A government may undertake a massive and violent relocation of the population in a region and engage in search-and-destroy operations in the cleared areas, as the Kenyan government did in the northeastern region of that country in 1966–1967. However, it may do so with a wide variety of objectives, some concerned with the easing of the tasks of the security forces in the area, others with simplifying the administration of the local population, and still others with land reform and resettlement. Only incidentally might such a policy be regarded as a way of cowing and instilling fear in the dissident population, and the realization that this has, indeed, been the effect arises only at a subsequent stage of the operation. Should we consider such a relocation an act of state terrorism, or does it become so in the latter stages of the operation when (possibly) the anti-guerrilla or logistical objectives have been either achieved or judged to have been a failure and the security forces continue or expand the operation?

Another aspect of mixed motivations and objectives concerns the equally simple fact that different parts of "the state" and different state agents may have different objectives in implementing a repressive or coercive policy. Only some of these may involve the intention to terrorize. This problem might arise when the terrorist campaign becomes lengthy, so that the actual agents carrying out the activity begin to develop objectives of their own, such as their own survival or aggrandizement, which can diverge from those of their superiors in the state apparatus that decided upon the initial action. The question then emerges: Whose intentions are important for determining whether actions constitute state terrorism or not? A clue to this type of problem might be found in the attempts of superiors to regain control of their policies in the face of evidence of terrorist activity that was not ordered. The longer such a policy is allowed to continue, however, the less willing we should be to believe that, whatever its true origins, "the state" is troubled to have its agents act in such ways *in its name*. It will obviously be difficult to make an absolute determination in such cases, but the important point is that the longer abuses occur without corrective state actions, the more confident we may be in attributing the violence to the upper echelons of the state. The last five years of death squad activity in El Salvador serves as a case in point. At least until the latter half of 1984, the death squads were serving the wishes of the Salvadoran government, and the lack of progress made by the judicial and executive system in curbing their "excesses" was related to the belief by the Salvadoran "state" that their interests were being served. Since the election of Duarte, it has become obvious that he himself does not direct the death squads and that they do not act in his name; yet it is also the case that the death squads continue to operate and from all reports do so with the continued connivance of senior state officials.[20] They still, therefore, are able to terrorize the population in the name of "the state," even if some of the more important members of "the state" are opposed to their activities. Such cases serve to highlight the difficulty of analyzing "state" terrorism when the state itself is a multi-faceted institution with competing sources of authority.

As with all criteria that rely upon actor intentions, those that distinguish terrorist strategies from "mere" coercion or repression are fiendishly difficult to observe or infer with any certainty. If this "intentions" approach is to be used as a basis for indicating the existence of a policy of terrorism by the state and its agents (as with non-state actors as well), then we are confronted with the problem of inferring intention from particular categories of action within a given context; so that the action itself becomes the indicator of terrorism and the frequency and extent of that action a measure of the degree of terrorism in practice. This is a difficult compromise, but one that can be found in other fields where the issue of intentionality is important.[21] When we reconsider the nature of the intervening variable in the causal chain, the sense of terror experienced by the target(s), the resolution of this problem is further complicated.

Fear and Terror

The essence of state (and other) terrorism is that it achieves its obsjesctive by inducing "extreme fear" within a target population by some means. While this is a common-sense view of the nature of the strategy, it clearly raises some issues regarding the boundary between terrorist tactics and those that seek to succeed by arousing lesser emotions in the minds of the target population. If we are seeking to measure and make comparisons of degrees of state terrorism, it may be more than a semantic quibble to ask about the nature of "being terrified" as opposed to merely "being afraid" or "being slightly worried." Before going further with this discussion, we should recognize that this question of varying levels of anxiety remains a legitimate point of contention among scholars studying terrorism. If the intentions of state actors are the key defining characteristics of state terrorism, what may be important is not whether extreme fear or terror was actually induced, but whether the state actor intended to create such fear. Ignoring this point may reduce the measurement process to one of measuring only effective state terror while ignoring the actions of ineffective or inefficient states. The effective and the ineffective state may share the same willingness and propensity to abuse part or all of their citizenry. This will remain a legitimate and important area of contention in the questions of both definition and measurement. Beyond these concerns, the question of extreme fear is also important for any examination of either the effect or the effectiveness of state terrorism.

The problem is that much state activity is directed toward affecting a population's behavior by making it afraid to do some things and afraid not to do others. Much of crime control is based upon this principle, but so is tax paying. In most cases, the target population does not therefore experience "extreme" fear, but some milder form thereof. In this discussion, it is useful to be reminded that we are interested in those cases where the state is attempting to induce such fear and also is doing so by threatening violence or actually employing it. However, this does raise the possibility that there are varying degrees of fear that might be experienced by a target and also the problem of observing when fear ceases to become mild and becomes extreme.

This point may be illustrated by noting that the present British government under Prime Minister Margaret Thatcher has been pursuing a strategy of using (some would say misusing) the Official Secrets Act with maximum severity against members of the state bureaucracy who have leaked confidential or politically embarrassing documents to the media or even to members of Parliament. "Leakers" have been charged under the more "serious" sections of the Act, which enable more severe penalties to be inflicted, and have been sentenced under such sections by a judiciary that seems to share the government's view that efforts to make government more accessible fall only a little short of treason. It is undoubtedly the case that the intention of such activity is to discourage future leaks that embarrass the government and to do so by inducing fears of imprisonment, disgrace, and loss of employment within the national bureaucracy. However, it can hardly be argued that such a strategy induces "extreme fear" in the same sense as a campaign of indiscriminate imprisonment or assassinations and disappearance such as that employed by Idi Amin against his own bureaucracy and henchmen.[22] We are apt to hear more about the recklessness of Mrs. Thatcher in this case and to learn of the state of mind that this has created in her bureaucracy; but nonetheless we recognize that descriptions of this "state" as exteme fear may be mere rhetoric, which is not, in any case, the result of a campaign of terror. We have thought very little about the state of mind that is created in those working under the conditions of state terror, but that state of mind is an important component of "the terror."

At one level, the aims become to gauge and scale the intensity of the human emotional experience—a difference in degree indicated by our use of such terms as "fearful" and "terrorized." Using the vernacular, we recognize a great difference between a target population (or individual) being slightly worried, afraid, fearful, and terrified out of their wits by some government activity. However, it becomes more difficult, once such a continuum has been established, to place even an arbitrary cutoff point somewhere near the high-intensity end of such a continuum, to identify a threshold between fear and terror. In addition, we must remember that the population may not react with "extreme fear" to activities that we, as outside observers, believe they should. Again, should acts that are intended to generate terror by their agents, but do not, be counted as terrorism?

At another level, the intensity of the emotion experienced might be examined by asking the nature of the fear being experienced as a result of government activity. Fear of what, or fear for what? Again, one can envisage some continuum of perceived threat that begins with the kind of milder fear discussed in the U.K. context—fear for one's job or one's livelihood, which can be a major deterrent or compellent force if used systematically by a government[23]—and ends with the fear for one's life or the lives of one's family. At this point, we return to the list of alternatives that a state may operationalize against its population as developed by Lopez.[24] The state employs information control, law enforcement techniques that go beyond normal legal limits, economic coercion, and finally life-threatening strategies to carry out its terrorist aims. The level of state coercion can intrude deeply into a person's life depending not only on the intention of the state but also the position of the targets and their condition at any moment in time. Although both Jews and union workers were, in fact, targets of terror in these cases, the nature of the fear for a Jew in Germany and Eastern Europe in the 1930s and Argentina in the 1970s is different from the fear experienced by non-Jewish union workers. The nature of an individual's fear intervenes with the question of how one perceives oneself within the socio-political context and with the issues related to the state coercive and terror targets.

The critics of this line of argument claim that by making state terrorism merely the most extreme form of state coercion (defined as those state activities intended to obtain conformity by inducing some level of fear deemed appropriate in a target population), we are confusing the relatively clearly defined phenomenon of terrorism and making its analysis more difficult. Unfortunately, this seems an inevitable result if we choose to define the phenomenon partly by its ultimate effect on people. There seems to be no clear way of distinguishing between those targets who are terrified and those who are fearful. A clear boundary must be established, or we are left to treat state terrorism as only the extreme range of state activities intended to achieve desired results by inducing varying levels of fear in some target.[25]

Longevity

Our discussion to this point requires developing some means of comparing levels of state terrorism that rely on the observable activity of state agents, plus inferences regarding underlying intentions, and upon the reasonable arousal of high levels of fear (again to be inferred) for salient values (life, freedom) among a target population. In other words, varying levels of state terrorism can be inferred from observing state activities at a given point in time and also by observing the actions of the target population, both behavioral and attitudinal.

Unfortunately, as the Amnesty International report excerpted at the head of this chapter and Duvall and Stohl make clear, the absence of actual behavioral indicators at a given point in time might not be a reliable indicator of the absence of state terror in a particular country because of the longevity of the impact of a successful campaign of state terror.[26] In this aspect, state terror (even more so than non-state terror, since until the regime is replaced there can be no effective mythology that law and order have been "restored") may have a kind of "half-life" of its own, which lingers and has effects for some time after the observable use of terror by state agents, quite apart from the physical removal of "troublemakers" who no longer have to be observably coerced, arrested, or killed. The observing target population may have been intimidated to such an extent that, at least for a time, there is no overt demonstration of state power by state agents. The threat remains implicit because a general learning process has taken place. In many ways, the most effective use of coercion reveals itself by its apparent absence. Conflict has been suppressed. People know what they can and cannot do. In essence, the behavioral terror process has become a part of the political structure. As structure it is no longer observable as a behavioral event, except at those times that lessons are forgotten or the regime decides that greater numbers of people or additional categories of persons need to be more tightly controlled.

In many ways, this aspect of state terrorism links directly to the work of P. Bachrach and M. S. Baratz[27] and S. Lukes,[28] and to the conception of "non-decisions" in situations where people refrain from activity for fear of consequences or from recognition of the futility of trying. One of the reasons for inactivity highlighted by work on the exercise of community power is the fear that, by acting, one will draw some form of unwanted reprisal by the powerful within society. Hence, it is safest not to act.

The argument about the long-term effects of state terrorism and the exercise of "implicit" power is to us a convincing one, and Duvall and Stohl give sufficient examples of the long-term effects of sustained campaigns of state terrorism to demonstrate that the phenomenon is by no means a rare one.[29] However, the longevity argument is yet another aspect of any analysis of state terrorism that complicates the task of measuring and comparing different levels of terrorism in different situations. In a particular case, where no apparent terrorist actions are being carried out by the state, its agents, or surrogates, do we confront a situation where there *is* no state terror and has been none for some time, or are we seeing merely the results of a relatively recent and successful campaign of state terror on an intimidated population? The two situations are quite different, and they may be effectively considered only if we do not divorce events analysis from structural analysis and conduct our research within a framework cognizant of historical development. This is no small task as the basis of the foundation of measurement of any concept, but it cannot be avoided.

In addition, in any analysis that attempts to investigate political relationships across systems, factors that distinguish those political systems from each other must also be considered if they might influence our understanding of the particular concept under investigation. Stohl discusses three aspects of political systems that would influence the magnitude and the types of terrorism that occur within these systems.[30] These three factors, vulnerability, manageability, and effectiveness, would suggest that the concerns raised above concerning longevity would be affected by the basic political structures that serve to distinguish political systems.

Legitimacy and Legality

One final aspect of the essential nature of state terrorism is the question of its arbitrariness or illegality. Many writers argue or imply that an essential quality of state terrorism is that it is either arbitrary in that it does not conform to the due process of the law, or illegal in that it is carried out in the face of clear legal prohibitions against such measures. The latter is certainly more frequent when the state is using surrogate agents to carry through a campaign of terrorism.

It may, indeed, be the case that, in many instances of state terrorism, the agents of the state frequently break or ignore their own laws, so that the security organs of the state can be said to be acting illegally. However, this is not always the case, and there are many ways in which state policies involving the creation of extreme fear or terror can be made to conform to the country's legal code (or vice versa). Thus, any definition of state terrorism that included the attribute of illegality would probably create more problems than it solved.

For example, it is usually a simple matter for state authorities, even in relatively open and accountable systems, to introduce "temporary" or "emergency" legislation to provide legal backing for "security" actions. The experience of the United Kingdom in dealing with the IRA, Irish National Liberation Army (INLA), and Protestant para-military forces in Northern Ireland is instructive in this regard. Alternatively, the whole apparatus of terrorizing might be built into the legal system of particular societies, so that actions that essentially involve affecting people's behavior by inducing high levels of fear could easily have the backing of the law and in this sense be completely non-arbitrary. Good examples of this include the system of state security pass laws, residence qualifications, and anti-terrorist legislation used to support the apartheid system of the Republic of South Africa where much of the state apparatus and the legal system has been structured to legalize the widespread threat and use of state terror to maintain the system of racial separation. In a less structured way, the introduction of "Islamic justice" into such countries as Iran and the Sudan in recent years appears suspiciously to resemble an effort by the state to affect behavior by inducing extreme fear of non-conformity, yet to be wholly "legal."[31] Thus, if legality is presumed to simply imply actions authorized by the legal system, there is not necessarily any advantage from a conceptual standpoint of introducing the term into a discussion of state terrorism.

In short, the complications involved in using the legal/illegal or arbitrary/non-arbitrary criteria for distinguishing "state terrorism" from the "legitimate use of the state's coercive sanctions" seem considerable. Hence, we would argue that it would be a mistake to use such characteristics to distinguish the "state-as-terrorist" from the "state-as-something-else."

MEASURING STATE TERRORISM: ALTERNATIVES
AND PROBLEMS

Essentially, our discussion thus far has attempted to elaborate on the question, What is state terrorism and how do we recognize its presence? Answers to this basic question may be summarized to state that state terrorism is present when

1. An actor intends to influence the behavior of a target population.
2. The means of influence involve the act or threat of violence on some victims with whom the target will identify.
3. The deliberate effects of such actions are to induce a condition of extreme fear or terror in the target population.
4. The actor is the state, its agents, or some approved surrogate group.

While relatively easy to explicate the requirements, how will we achieve such a data set? To answer this, we propose to return to the conceptual and measurement questions with which we began. This leads us to focus on three dimensions of terrorism to begin to measure the level of state terrorism in a country at a given time, and to continue to illustrate the problems involved in such measurement.

Scope

The "scope of terrorism" refers to the nature of the activity indirectly aimed at the target population by the state authorities or their surrogates, and particularly the degree of harm directly inflicted upon the victims in order to create the required level of fear in the target. "Scope" indicates the level of state terrorism by asking what might happen to victims of the terrorist activity. "Increasing the scope" involves increasing the kinds of harm that can be inflicted. The lowest level might thus involve the infliction of some symbolic humiliation upon a victim or a deprivation of livelihood, while the highest could involve deliberate physical injury or loss of life through assassination or some lethal campaign of violence. The crucial characteristic is thus the degree of potential harm inflicted, which in everyday language might range from systematic inconvenience to injury and death.

Intensity

Like scope, "intensity" refers to the nature of the activity *directed at the victim*, in terms of the harm inflicted. "Intensity" refers merely to the frequency of occurrence of the various types of terrorist behavior during a given time period. Arbitrary imprisonment without trial would represent a different level of intensity of state terrorism depending upon whether it was an isolated occurrence, affecting only a few people each year, or a regular feature of the activities of the state security forces, such that large numbers of people were detained without trial for political reasons or for "offenses against the state." Quite simply, the intensity of state terrorism refers to how frequently particular activities are utilized.[32] It might be that, in one instance, the scope of state terrorism is limited to activities stopping short of deliberate physical injury, but that it frequently takes place stopping short of deliberate physical injury, *or* that it takes place frequently, affecting large numbers of victims. This might be contrasted with another case where assassinations are carried out but infrequently. At the same time, it is important to keep in mind that state terror regimes often alter their strategies with the resultant appearance of a lessening of intensity (and/or scope) when that conclusion is actually unwarranted. M. Berman and R. Clark report:

A decline in reported instances of torture in the Philippines in 1977 was explained by opponents of the Marcos regime as representing a trend on the part of officials to move away from detaining prisoners who could provoke criticism of the government towards the practice of arranging the disappearance of opponents.[33]

Unfortunately, this relatively simple extension of the scope of state terrorism is complicated by the fact that certain kinds of actions are more extensive than others, quite apart from the question of intensity. In simple terms, certain types of terrorist events, by their nature, affect a number of people. For example, a single event such as arbitrary arrest might affect only a single individual. In contrast, another single event such as the use of automatic weapons against a procession or a bomb attack on a bar might involve large numbers of casualties. One needs to consider whether the single events should be regarded as equivalent, in some sense, or whether it is possible to weight events for numbers harmed at the given level of "harm."

Finally, there is the meaning of intensity in the sense of concentration. It is not unreasonable to argue that there is a marked difference between situations involving state terrorism where such activities are confined to the major cities and others in which they are confined to a particular region of the country as a whole. The latter would plausibly indicate a "higher" level of state terrorism, but there are obvious problems in making decisions about the relative levels of state terrorism indicated by the two other situations.

Range

Finally, we can ignore the impact of actions on those directly affected, and argue that state terrorism can differ in level according to the size and type of the target population itself. It obviously makes a difference whether the state's agents are trying to arouse a condition of extreme fear within a professional group, within a particular socio-economic class, within the rank-and-file members of some mass organization, or within the members of a religious or linguistic community such as the Catholics in Northern Ireland. In many ways, this concept of a different range for state terrorism is quite distinct from the other dimensions discussed above. It comes nearest to dealing with the question of who it is intended to terrorize, even if it wholly ignores the question of the degree of fear experienced by the target population and relies instead on the aggregate numbers of the target population (much of which might remain unaffected by the state's terrorism or respond by rage and retaliation rather than fear and compliance). However, it again seems to be an important dimension in considering degrees of state terrorism. It does make a difference whether the state is attempting to terrorize a small elite or a total community.

On this basis, it is now easier to proceed to our second question concerning state terrorism: How might one be able to measure the level of state terrorism present in a country at any point in time so that comparison can be made with other countries? The most immediately obvious answer to this question, given the characteristics of state terrorism outlined above, is "Indirectly." This response is almost inevitable, given the fact that the definition involves the presence or absence (or presence in varying degrees) of actor *intentions*, rarely directly or reliably observable; target *emotions* of worry, fear, or terror, which are equally elusive; and means or *actions* intended to provoke terror, which are in principle observable and hence countable, but which may be confused with other similar events not informed by the same intentions or producing the same results, either in nature or in degree.

The necessity of indirect measurement is generally accepted in social science research where intentions are involved. "The most obvious instances of indirect measurement are those that arise whenever we are attempting to infer a postulated internal state, such as an attitude or a utility, on the basis of behavior of various kinds."[34] The concept of aggression serves to illustrate much of H. Blalock's discussion of the problems inherent in indirect measurement. He categorizes attempts to measure these behaviors by defining them in terms of (1) internal states, (2) consequences, (3) standards, and (4) replications. Five "simplifications" are common in social scientists' inclusion of internal states as part of the definition of concepts. Each of these simplifications creates new pitfalls. The most germane to the study of state terrorism are those attempts to link the concept with some form of "master motive" (some form of the realist concern with power, for example) and to use clues based on past behavior to infer motivation unless it is linked to a falsifiable theoretical framework. Focusing on the consequences of behavior allows the side-stepping of measuring internal states. Blalock cautions that this strategy may "tempt one to ignore all sorts of intervening and conditioning variables,"[35] and this oversimplification may create false causal connections. Defining behaviors in terms of deviations from standards relies on accepting definitions of social standards that are themselves frequently vague and contentious. As Blalock points out, "The temptation, here, is to substitute more precise standards for the true but fuzzy ones."[36] The problem of replications as defined by Blalock need not concern us as it relates primarily to experimental situations. The essential point "is not that assumptions can or should be avoided but that they need to be made explicit. Furthermore, we see that each measurement strategy requires the use of theoretical assumptions, only some of which can be tested."[37]

Thus, accepting the principle that only indirect measurement of the phenomenon of state terrorism is likely to be possible is just the first basic step. Even within the limits of the definition suggested above, it will be immediately apparent that state terrorism is a complex multidimensional phenomenon that may require a number of distinct indicators, each with its own definitional baggage and theoretical assumptions and not all of which will necessarily correlate highly. It may even be necessary to try to develop a number of scales for each subcategory of terrorism, given that the instruments available to create a sense of terror in a target population vary according to the specific type of actor involved in the attempt. Means available to the security forces of the state differ considerably from those available to surrogate agents acting on behalf or with the tacit approval of state authorities. In some Latin American countries, of course, the line between the army and the death squads is extremely hard to draw. Similarly, for a member of the Catholic community in Northern Ireland, the para-military "B-Special" Royal Ulster Constabulary probably looks suspiciously like Protestant terrorists in the uniform of the state. In effect, the tactics open to surrogate state terrorists resemble those open to anti-state terrorists rather more than those available to the official security forces of the state. As a preliminary step, it might therefore be useful to divide the whole range of possible "terrorisms" into subcategories, and then devise distinct scales of intensity for surrogate and official state terrorism for each of these.

Existing Data Sets

At present, there is no comprehensive state terrorism data set. Even if we begin from the assumption that state terrorism is a subcategory of state violence, there is still no data set upon which to draw, as there is no single comprehensive state violence data set either. There is, however, at least a partial data set on state violence contained in the *World Handbook of Political and Social Indicators III*. Further, if we were to define state terrorism as a deviation from pre-defined standards of behavior and we were willing to begin with a data set based on state violation of human rights, we could also use the data set constructed by Freedom House. Before moving on to a discussion of what would be required for an ideal adequate data set and to indicate possible steps toward that ideal, it is useful to briefly examine these existing efforts to illustrate some of the pitfalls and requirements of an adequate data set on state terrorism.

The World Handbook of Political and Social Indicators III is an attempt to provide a comprehensive data set for a wide variety of political and social indicators. One subset of these indicators concerns what the handbook editors refer to as State Coercive Behavior. The major subset within this category is labeled "government sanctions" and is defined as follows: "A governmental sanction is an action taken by the authorities to negotiate or eliminate a perceived threat to the security of the government, the regime, or the state itself."[38]

The *World Handbook* distinguishes three types of governmental sanctions: (1) censorship, (2) restrictions on political behavior, which includes everything from imposing curfews, banning a political party and harassing its members, to the imposition of martial law, and (3) arrests. These events are available in a daily file and are coded as imposed or relaxed. They are aggregated on a yearly basis and are combined into one index. In addition to these sanction variables, the *World Handbook* also includes a measure of political executions, which are defined as

an event in which a person or group is put to death under orders of the national authorities while in their custody. Excluded are assassinations, even if known to have been arranged by the authorities, and persons killed in riots, armed attacks and the like. Also excluded are executions for criminal offenses, such as murder, that are not reported to have political significance.[39]

As Taylor and Jodice note: "What the sanctions measure attempts to indicate is merely the frequency and concentration of sanction events. The expectation is that the relations between these twitches of government activity and the pattern of protest will prove interesting for comparative analysis."[40] In other words, these data were collected because of an underlying theoretical premise regarding the nature of anti-regime violence. They were not collected for theoretical concerns connected to the violence of the state, and, as such, illustrate the problem of using data collected for both "other" theoretical purposes in general and the case of state terrorism in particular.

If we begin from a perspective that the general category "governmental violence" is interesting because we might learn something about the pattern of protest, we essentially assume a theoretical framework in which governmental violence is reactive to anti-state activity. This assumption makes it less likely that we will be able to employ such a data set for behavior that is defined as intentional and instrumental. Further, those aspects of the behaviors that are considered in this light are defined within a "law-and-order" framework that assumes that the purpose of such activity is to restore some undefined equilibrium. Finally, it should be clear that much of what is central in the *World Handbook* are legal actions by the state, such as, censorship, curfews, and the banning of political parties. Indeed, even the political execution variable focuses on those individuals who are executed after having been processed in the legal system (however fraudulently). Most (if not all) executions not officially recognized or claimed by the state are not counted. Thus, the *World Handbook* data clearly suffer from the problems we associated above with a reliance on the legal/illegal distinction in defining state terrorism.

When we examine the data more closely, we find that the problems indicated at the opening of this chapter by the authors of the Amnesty International report have obviously made their presence felt. Despite an impressive array of sources, there is questionable face validity in some of these measures when individual nations are examined. For example, Guatemala, which has experienced thousands of political murders by the government in the last thirty years, is reported as having had thirty-five political executions from 1948 to 1975. El Salvador had none. Guatemala is listed as imposing sanctions only a total of 5 times in the period of 1970–1977, while the United States is recorded as having imposed such sanctions 295 times in the same period. It is clear, then, that the *World Handbook* is not a useful place to begin. Despite extensive sources and resources, the theoretical orientation, combined with an events-based approach that apparently was insensitive to the difficulty of acquiring data on these types of governmental activities, cripples the data set for our purposes.

The Freedom House data set illustrates the use of standards-based data collection efforts and also the difficulty of social scientists attempting to employ data gathered by non-social scientist advocacy organizations. Every year since 1973, Freedom House has ranked each country in the world on a political and a civil rights scale. The civil rights scale is potentially quite useful for our purposes because it purportedly takes into account the major aspects of the security of the person. The bases for the scale are clearly discussed, and empirical referents are specified for each point on the scale. The data thus appear to represent a fine source of systematic data. Unfortunately, upon closer examination, they exhibit serious limitations.

Although these data have been discussed in depth elsewhere,[41] it will be useful to review the shortcomings here. H. Scoble and L. Wiseberg demonstrate quite convincingly that the rankings suffer from clear cultural and ideological biases. In effect, the scales measure little more than the extent to which a country mirrors the American political system and the extent to which it adheres to capitalist economic principles. They also point out that the make-up of the scales has changed over time. On several occasions, Raymond Gastil, the chief investigator, has added new concerns to the scale. Thus the rankings are not equivalent over time. Nor is it clear upon what sources of information the scales are based. Freedom House is not a research organization, and thus does not have its own data base. As consumers of the data, we know nothing about the extent or reliability of the data base they have employed.

The most serious problems with the data appear to derive from the apparent lack of social science expertise in the construction of the data set and the derivation of the scales. As John McCamant has indicated, the various dimensions of the scales are never disaggregated. Rather, these dimensions, such as the holding of political prisoners, the freedom of assembly, media independence and so on, are simply presented as a single variable. The range of each dimension, the weighting system employed, and how these different dimensions are brought together to produce a single ranking are never discussed. Further, the operationalizations of the scale ranks are quite vague and appear, in fact, rather arbitrary. As McCamant explains:

To test the adequacy of these criteria, I removed the rankings, scrambled the order, and asked five students to rank the criteria according to the seriousness of the violation of civil rights. No one came close to the order given by Gastil. ...If it is impossible to even know which criteria represent more serious violations, it is certainly impossible to use them for evaluating information on different countries.[42]

The result of these problems, of course, is that the Freedom House scales lack all semblance of reliability. They simply represent the organization's assertions. These assertions are based on as-yet-unknown data and uncertain criteria. Thus, it is doubtful that anyone could ever replicate the scales. Lacking replicability and reliability, they are quite inappropriate for analytical inquiry.

The most well-known attempts to measure various aspects of state terrorism and government violence have relied on impressions of expert judges. This method has been a particular favorite of students who have approached the problem from a human rights perspective. In this approach, the researcher may begin with a number of recognized "experts" on the geographical region in question and ask them to rank the country's human rights behavior. The results are then averaged across the respondents. This approach was first employed by Russell Fitzgibbon and Kenneth Johnson and more recently by Lars Schoultz.[43] The problems with the approach are both obvious and well known. The actual expertise of the chosen "experts" is bound to vary. The experts may employ somewhat different conceptions of human rights (or whatever else they are judging) and then may also have very different definitions of what constitutes "high" and "low" levels of abuse. In short, the researcher may be the unwitting recipient of scales that are based on a different measurement scheme from each of the so-called experts. Clearly, an acceptable measure requires greater internal consistency than a set of impressions derived without clear coding guidelines.

Recently, two of us have collaborated on a research project that employed a procedure designed to solve some of the aforementioned problems with standards-based scales.[44] Two parallel indexes were constructed from the information presented in the annual reports of the U.S. Department of State and Amnesty International. A political terror scale published in the 1980 *Freedom House Yearbook* was employed as a basis for the scaling.[45] The information in the annual reports was used to rank countries on this five-point ordinal scale:

Level A: Countries live under a secure rule of law, people are not imprisoned for their views, and torture is rare or exceptional ... Political murders are extremely rare ...

Level B: There is a limited amount of imprisonment for nonviolent political activity. However, few persons are affected, torture and beating are exceptional ... Political murder is rare ...

Level C: There is extensive political imprisonment or a recent history of such imprisonment. Execution or other political murders and brutality may be common. Unlimited detention, with or without trial, for political views is accepted ...

Level D: The practices of Level C are expanded to larger numbers. Murders, disappearances, and torture are a common part of life ... In spite of its generality, on this level terror affects primarily those who interest themselves in politics or ideas.

Level E: The terrors of Level D have been extended to the whole population ... The leaders of these societies place no limits on the means or thoroughness with which they pursue personal or ideological goals.

It should be clear that the levels of the scale are distinguished according to the use of political killings, torture, and imprisonment. With this scale as a guide, we used the Amnesty International and State Department information as raw data and ranked the fifty-nine countries included in our analysis for each year the reports were available (1977–1984). In the construction of each index, we scaled the data presented in the reports as if they were accurate and complete. We thus produced two different scales for the same countries and years—two views of "reality" that measured deviations from the standards established by the collators of the reports and reflective of their biases. While the scales may be criticized for a lack of precision, they did appear to usefully distribute countries from best to worst, and thus were employed in analyses appropriate to ordinal data. However, despite high levels of inter-coder reliability, we were confident only that the scales could be replicated from our existing data, not that the data themselves were valid and reliable.

Each of the original data sources had been constructed for other purposes. The State Department's report on human rights conditions is clearly a political document designed for the purpose of minimizing the abuses of friends and aggressively pursuing the violations of adversaries (see the yearly critiques of the Americas Watch organization). On the other hand, Amnesty International, while not legitimately susceptible to the charge of a clear political bias (although subject to a "Western Liberal Bias" according to one recent critique), has a clearly anti-social science bias. Amnesty International has consciously reported its findings in such a way that social science reconstruction of yearly reports could not yield a document that could be comparative across countries within a single year or by country across the years. The organization believes not only that it is impossible to create such accurate reporting but that to do so would be politically unwise.[47] The current situation, then, is that the major, reliable organization that has been collecting information considered to be very useful as a data base has consciously and successfully prevented its information from being employed for social science purposes.

The core conclusion of this brief survey of available methods and resources shows that there exist little useful data at present. But, we contend, with theoretical care, we can build upon the shortcomings of these previous efforts to construct a data set that will (1) have broad coverage across countries and time, (2) be based on multiple sources, (3) be reliable and valid, (4) have intensiveness (depth of coverage), (5) have extensiveness of coverage (multiple indicators), and (6) be sensitive to differences across countries and time.

CONCLUSION

On the basis of the foregoing discussion, it might be argued that efforts to treat state terrorism as a multi-dimensional phenomenon requiring multiple means of measurement are overly complex and hence doomed to failure. But that would miss, we believe, the major thrust of the preceding discussion. It is not our intention to argue that the measurement need be overly complex, but rather that when attempting to simplify the measurement process, particularly in the early stages of the research endeavor, simplification not be at the expense of the theoretical content and distinguishing features of terrorism as a political process. What are required are some simple indicators of differing levels of state terrorism by which different examples can be categorized in a more/less fashion and which reflect, roughly, the level achieved in a given year. At this stage in our ability to both collect and classify such information, it should be apparent that events data-based collections will be more difficult to establish and justify without enormous investments of resources at both the measurement and the collection stages. Standards-based assessments of violations will be more useful if there are fewer resources to expend. Ultimately, however, an events-based analysis should be developed because the phenomenon of terrorism requires knowledge of the impact of structures of terrorism and the impact of particular events on those structures and the rest of the political system.

NOTES

1. *Amnesty International Report 1984* (London: Amnesty International, 1984), p. 4.
2. Michael Stohl, "International Network of Terrorism," *Journal of Peace Research* 20, no. 1 (1983), pp. 87–94.
3. On the difference in perspective between historians and social scientists, see Peter Winch, *The Idea of a Social Science* (New York: Humanities Press, 1958); Vernon Van Dyke, *Political Science: A Philosophical Analysis* (Stanford, Calif.: Stanford University Press, 1960); and Walter Laqueur, *Terrorism* (Boston: Little, Brown, 1979).
On the reintroduction of state terrorism as a "legitimate" subject, see also the never-interrupted work on totalitarian and authoritarian states of scholars such as Hannah Arendt, *The Origins of Totalitarianism* (New York: Harcourt, Brace, and World, 1968); Barrington Moore, *Terror and Progress: U.S.S.R.* (Cambridge, Mass.: Harvard University Press, 1954); I. L. Horowitz, *Taking Lives: Genocide and State Power*, 3d ed. (New Brunswick, N.J.: Transaction Books, 1980); and Eugene V. Walter, *Terror and Resistance* (New York: Oxford University Press, 1969).
4. Raymond Duvall and Michael Stohl, "Governance by Terror," in Michael Stohl, ed., *The Politics of Terrorism* (New York: Marcel Dekker, 1983), pp. 179–219; and George Lopez, "A Scheme for the Analysis of Government as Terrorist," in Michael Stohl and George Lopez, eds., *The State as Terrorist: The Dynamics of Governmental Violence and Repression* (Westport, Conn.: Greenwood Press, 1984), pp. 59–82.
5. Duvall and Stohl, "Governance by Terror," p. 181.
6. The admission by Major Mengistu, the head of the Ethiopian Armed Forces Committee (the Derg), in 1976 that his regime was having to counteract

the "red terror" practiced in Addis Ababa and elsewhere by the Ethiopian People's Revolutionary Party with a government "socialist terror" was a rare moment of candor by a head of government.

7. The Argentine government's receipt of a 50,000-page report on army–government-inspired and -organized terror within that country in the period of military rule during 1976–1983 is a rarity bordering on the unique.

8. See, for example, the work by the Anti-Apartheid Movement in revealing and documenting South African terrorist strategies in Namibia, and the work of journalists in revealing the magnitude of mass killings in Dr. Milton Obote's Uganda and in Matabeleland.

9. For a discussion of the problem of comparability across political systems, see A. Przeworski and H. Teune, *The Logic of Comparative Social Inquiry* (New York: Wiley-Interscience, 1970).

10. Michael Stohl and George Lopez, "Terrorism and the State," in Stohl and Lopez, *State as Terrorist*, pp. 3–9.

11. Duvall and Stohl, "Governance by Terror," p. 182, emphasis added.

12. Alexander Dallin and George Breslauer, *Political Terror in Communist States* (Stanford, Calif.: Stanford University Press, 1970), p. 1.

13. George Lopez, *Terrorism and World Order*, The Whole Earth Papers, no. 18 (New York: Global Education Associates, 1983), p. 5.

14. Dallin and Breslauer, *Political Terror*, p. 1.

15. C. Mitchell, *Peacemaking and the Consultant's Role* (New York: Nichols, 1981), pp. 134–135.

16. See Thomas Schelling, *Arms and Influence* (New Haven, CT: Yale University Press, 1966), for the distinction between compellance and deterrence.

17. Francois Ponchaud, *Cambodia: Year Zero* (New York: Holt, Rinehart and Winston, 1978).

18. Frances Fitzgerald, *Fire in the Lake* (New York: Random House, 1973), p. 550.

19. Noam Chomsky and Edward Herman, *The Political Economy of Human Rights*, vol. 1: *The Washington Connection and Third World Fascism*, vol. 2: *After the Cataclysm: Postwar Indochina and the Reconstruction of Imperial Ideology* (Boston: South End Press, 1979).

20. *Amnesty International Report 1983* and *Amnesty International Report 1984* (London: Amnesty International, 1983 and 1984).

21. H. Blalock, "Measurement and Conceptualization Problems: The Major Obstacle to Integrating Theory and Research," *American Sociological Review* 44 (1979), pp. 881–894.

22. As described by Henry Kyemba in the aptly titled *State of Blood* (London: Transworld Publishers, 1977).

23. Blacklisting may not appear to resemble the more extreme types of deterrence via induced terror, but the fear of losing one's livelihood appears to have had a major impact upon people's behavior during the McCarthy period in both the United States and Australia. Such a threat would, of course, be an example of state repressive policies rather than terrorism.

24. Lopez, "Scheme for the Analysis."

25. Giovanni Sartori, "The Tower of Babel," in Giovanni Sartoni, Fred W. Riggs, and Henry Teune, eds., *Tower of Babel: On the Definition and Analysis of*

Concepts in the Social Sciences, International Studies Association Occasional Paper No. 6, 1975, pp. 7–38.

26. Duvall and Stohl, "Governance by Terror."

27. P. Bachrach and M. S. Baratz, "Decisions and Non-Decisions: An Analytical Framework," *American Political Science Review* 51 (1963), pp. 632–642.

28. S. Lukes, *Power: A Radical View* (New York: Macmillan, 1974).

29. Duvall and Stohl, "Governance by Terror."

30. Michael Stohl, "The Three Worlds of Terrorism," *TVI: Terrorism, Violence, Insurgency* 3, no. 6 (1982), pp. 4–12.

31. See also the discussion of Algeria by D. Strickland and P. Kauss, "Political Disintegration and Latent Terror," in Stohl, *Politics of Terrorism*, pp. 77–118.

32. Another possible indicator of the degree of state terrorism might be the actual effort a state puts into terror and repression, as indexed by the numbers of police and security forces as a percentage of overall population or national budget devoted to police and internal security affairs.

33. M. Berman and R. Clark, "State Terrorism: Disappearances," *Rutgers Law Journal* 13 (Spring 1982), pp. 531–577.

34. H. Blalock, *Conceptualization and Measurement in the Social Sciences* (Beverly Hills, Calif.: Sage Publications, 1982).

35. Ibid., p. 886.

36. Ibid., p. 887.

37. Ibid., p. 888.

38. C. Taylor and D. Jodice, *World Handbook of Political and Social Indicators III* (New Haven, CT: Yale University Press, 1983), p. 62.

39. Ibid., pp. 62–63.

40. Ibid., p. 76.

41. H. Scoble and L. Wiseberg, "Problems of Comparative Research in Human Rights," and John McCamant, "A Critique of Present Measures of 'Human Rights Development' and an Alternative," both in V. Nanda, James Scarritt, and George Shepherd, eds., *Global Human Rights: Public Policies, Comparative Measures, and NGO Strategies* (Boulder, CO: Westview Press, 1981).

42. McCamant, "Critique of Present Measures," p. 132.

43. R. Fitzgibbon and K. Johnson, "Measurement of Latin American Political Change," *American Political Science Review*, 55 (1961), pp. 515–526; and Lars Schoultz, "U.S. Foreign Policy and Human Rights Violations in Latin America: A Comparative Analysis of Foreign Aid Distributions," *Comparative Politics*, 13 (1981), pp. 149–170.

44. Michael Stohl, David Carleton, and Steven E. Johnson, "Human Rights and U.S. Foreign Assistance: From Nixon to Carter," *Journal of Peace Research* 21, no. 3 (1984), pp. 215–226; and David Carleton and Michael Stohl, "The Foreign Policy of Human Rights: Rhetoric and Reality from Jimmy Carter to Ronald Reagan," *Human Rights Quarterly* 7, no. 2 (May 1985), pp. 205–229.

45. Raymond Gastil, *Freedom in the World* (New York: Freedom House, 1980), p. 37.

46. C. Desmond, *Persecution: East and West* (New York: Penguin Books, 1983).

47. *Amnesty International Report 1984.*

2

Conceptual Problems of Studying State Terrorism

Michael Nicholson

Terrorism of all sorts, whether practiced by states, inspired by states, or completely within the province of some non-state group, is a topic that arouses the most passionate concern. Because of this, it is also an issue that arouses a great deal of confusion and hence requires more than usual care in sorting out the epistemological, methodological, and moral problems. Given that behind the condemnation of terrorism there is often the tacit advocacy of certain points of view, and that condemnation often varies in strength according to the identity of those who initiate terrorism, the need for dispassionate analysis is emphasized.

The problem I wish to address is whether the phenomenon of state terrorism can be studied by the empiricist methods of the social sciences or, whether due to some curiosity of its nature, it requires some different methodology. I have a conventional conception of "social science methodology" that is basically a formulation of the empiricist conception of the philosophy of science.[1] The development of a social science, according to this view, involves the attempt to formulate theories of processes, where these theories are sets of logically inter-related statements that can be subjected as a set, if not always individually, to observational testing. "Testing" means the confrontation with empirical evidence such that we can conceive of what evidence would be relevant for the statements to be true and also false. The propositions of a social science are therefore not just particular statements about singular and unique events, but involve general statements about classes of events. In the case of state terrorism, we aim to make statements about when states involve themselves in terrorism, and when they do not, and what forms it takes. We then discuss particular cases with reference to these more general principles. In fact, I would contend that, as a general procedure, when we make statements about particular events, we commonly have in mind intuitive concepts of general patterns of events that are implicit. For an explanation we need to have such generalizations. It is the job of the social scientist to make them explicit.

A common diagrammatic description of this is a slightly modified version of C. G. Hempel's diagram:[2]

General propositions about state terrorism: $P_1, P_2, \ldots, P_n$.

Specific propositions about a case: $C_1, C_2, \ldots, C_m$.

Specific propositions about the case in hand deduced
for the P's and the C's: $E_1, E_2, \ldots, E_g$.

We then claim we have an explanation of the E's in terms of the specific propositions, the C's, and the general propositions, the P's, which constitute our theory. Needless to say, in our present state of knowledge, few aspects of the social sciences and certainly not the study of terrorism can claim to have achieved such a level of rigour. All we can seriously hope to have is what Hempel calls "explanation sketches," namely, outlines of rigorous explanations. However, there is an important assertion that explanations rely on generalizations even if they cannot be traced out in their full rigour.

Such methodologies are widely used in social science, including political science. The validity and usefulness (not quite the same thing) of such methods in the social sciences are disputed by many, though they have a wide following, particularly in the United States. I shall not, however, discuss the general question of whether an empiricist methodology is useful in the analysis of social science and hence whether a political science itself is possible, but shall assume that it is.[3] However, is there something specific about state terrorism, or perhaps any other form of terrorism, that, perhaps with some other forms of political activity, make it immune from this sort of analysis? My argument is that there is not.

It is my contention that we can evolve theories of state terrorism that are of the same epistemological status as other theories of human behaviour. However, there are some specific issues and indeed specific problems that should be noted. They appear in one form or another in many branches of the social sciences and are not original. However, they deserve special attention in this context and fall into two classes.

First, there are the problems that are familiar within many different guises associated with the concept of the "state-as-actor" and specifically the "state-as-unitary-actor." Second, there are problems deriving from the extremely emotive nature of the subject matter, which should lead us into unusual prudence in our usage of words and concepts. In many ways, this leads us back to the sort of concerns of the much maligned linguistic philosophers of the 1950s, though my discussion will be of a profound triviality compared with their analyses of questions.[4]

First, let us look at the "state-as-unitary-actor" problem and any special peculiarities that this may raise in the context of terrorism. In talking of "the state" we must ask, which people or groups are in the state apparatus. This applies to whatever policy we are considering. If we say, "The British government has a restrictive monetary policy"—something far removed from terrorism (except perhaps in the more extreme and fanciful of political rhetoric), we need to learn what groups actually make the decision, in the sense that they could have done something different; what groups may not initiate the decision, but have some veto over it; and what groups tacitly support it, where their tacit support is required.

"The Government," and even less "the state," is not a single decision maker, nor even a nearly homogeneous group, but a complex and often not easily identifiable set of groups and coalitions. Though the precise manifestations are different, this is true of all societies whether authoritarian, libertarian, democratic, or whatever. For some sorts of policy, it might be an appropriate simplification to assume that the government or state is a unitary decision maker. While the detailed study of monetary policy in a capitalist or mixed economy would require analysis of the different groups involved, a general picture using the unitary decision maker as a model is a simplification that frequently leads to little distortion. It depends on the detail required in the answer.

I would hypothesize that this is less often true in the case of state terrorism. Commonly the institutions of state terrorism are more loosely controlled by any central governmental authority than those of monetary policy. The various terror squads that have operated on El Salvador, or Argentina prior to the change in regime, were fairly loosely under the control of the official governmental authorities and obviously had a great deal of autonomy. Under the Nazi regime in Germany, particularly in the 1930s, there were various competing and warring groups that were, more or less, all agents of state terrorism, but by no stretch of the imagination were they part of a coherent plan of state terrorism.[5] Bureaucratic infighting might be regarded as an almost universal characteristic of government administrations, but the Rohm purge (1934) might be regarded as something more than an extreme form of the phenomenon. I am thus suggesting an added caution in the analysis of state terrorism in the use of the word "state" or "government" in any sort of sentence in which these words appear. Strictly, it involves no more of an epistemological warning than is raised whenever we talk of groups acting whether they are small or large groups. The degree to which it is a special problem for the analyst of state terrorism is worthy of note.

The second problem worthy of special note is the frequent use of emotive definitions and the difficulty of analysing highly emotive subject matter in an analytical way. Logically there is no special problem in distinguishing factual from value positions in this matter; psychologically it is very difficult. A lot of the problem stems from the fact that most people are much more sympathetic to some governments than they are to others. Most writers deplore state terrorism, but are a great more "understanding" to the "need" for it when practiced in some countries than they are of others. Neither moral nor scientific impartiality is commonplace. It is always fairly safe to quote Nazi Germany (as I have done) and safe enough to quote Stalin's Soviet Union. More recently Idi Amin is almost universally regarded as a safe object of obloquy. However, almost every other form of state terror has its defenders. The defense stems either from a general sympathy with the long-run political ideals of the government in question or because of the strategic significance of the area, and often both. The Pol Pot regime, which uses what most people would regard as state terror on an extreme scale, arouses relatively little objection because of the strategic usefulness of the regime.

For much the same sort of reasons, the Shah of Iran managed the support of many governments in the West who were in principle opposed to state terrorism (the successor regime is not, of course, any better—arguably worse). Many South American states have "authoritarian" (acceptable) and not "totalitarian" (not acceptable) governments, which makes commentators from the political Right accept acts that they would not accept in other regimes. (I do not dispute that a distinction can be made between authoritarian and totalitarian, though one would be intrigued to hear the uncoached efforts of many senior U.S. government politicians to formulate these differences.) The Republic of South Africa is fairly widely condemned by the political Left and Centre, though even the Far Right express their understanding of South Africa's problems with caution and diffidence. Apart from Amin, state terrorism in Black Africa is regarded with "understanding," except from some of the political Right (who can scarcely conceal their delight) and some maverick liberals.

The problem is therefore a common one. People are more sympathetic toward some regimes than others and in their moral judgements are apt to treat them more leniently. Coupled with this is that some regimes are genuinely under threat from either internal or outside forces and use authoritarian methods to defend themselves (though these need not be terroristic, though they commonly seem to degenerate into such). Thus, the Swedish government is not faced with as many problems as, say, the Yugoslavian government, in that there is very little danger of violent overthrow and it can be said to have taken a good liberal attitude toward dissent. This is not true of, say, most African governments and leads to authoritarian methods and the danger of state terrorism.

My argument, then, is that because of the emotional significance of terrorism, whether state or non-state, and the strong reasons we often have for favouring one sort of government rather than another, we have to be extremely careful with definition. This is the case in all science, whether natural or social. It is particularly the case in the social sciences where political and ethical factors intrude into almost all aspects of study, and it is even more true when the very terms we use (such as "terrorism") are themselves emotionally charged. Thus, in the last analysis I am making only the fairly obvious injunction of the philosopher of science to the scientist, which is "define with care," but I am emphasizing it to the greatest degree possible owing to the grave danger in this field of defining our terms such that we get the "correct" answers from whatever political perspective we operate.

There is a further practical problem that has to be faced by the investigator of state terrorism. Governments often deny that they do it, or when it is admitted they claim unusual provocation. Thus, they deliberately try to conceal the facts and mislead investigations in a way that they are less likely to do when discussing, say, monetary policy. Hence, we are faced not merely with an absence of data, but with a deliberate attempt to falsify data to give the wrong impression. This has the added problem that because data on all the countries are unreliable if the government can make them so, then one's ideological enemies can be accused of a greater degree of state terrorism than they might in fact be pursuing. Again, this is a problem that the social scientist comes across not infrequently, and we are talking of degree, not a novel problem. Nevertheless, the monetary theorist less often complains of actual deception by the providers of data.

Having used them loosely, I now wish to clarify the use of the terms "terrorism" and "state terrorism," though not, I think, in a manner that will cause any undue surprise. By terrorism I mean the use of acts that induce fear amongst some social group or a whole population, so as to induce them to act in a way they would otherwise not have. The number of people who are direct victims of terrorist acts might be quite small (though not always, as under Stalin's regime), but its purpose is to induce in the rest of the population the awareness that they might be victims, even if statistically the chances are fairly small. This form of definition of terrorism covers all sorts of terrorism. It was conventionally used for non-state actors, and in much journalistic writing often still is. In such writings, it is also employed to mean terrorist groups of whom the writer disapproves, and is hence used prejoratively, though the same sorts of acts are often approved of when performed by politically congenial groups. However, it quickly becomes clear that the above definition of terrorism includes a number of acts conducted by governments in a number of different circumstances. Several rather different types of acts, with different sorts of goals, can properly be regarded as state terrorism.

I suggest the following fourfold categorization as convenient. First is the control by a state of its own citizens by methods of terror. Second is its use in colonial situations. Third is the use of terror as a means of prosecuting war, and fourth is the use and support of terror as a form of surrogate war. A point I would re-emphasize, though, is that I am regarding terrorism as a form of coercion, but not the only form. The actual act of terror is perpetrated against only some, possibly a small minority, of the potential victims in order to frighten them into compliance. Thus, the concentration camp policy of the British in the Boer War was coercion (but deplorable) but not, as such, terrorism.[6] More extremely, under these definitions, the Holocaust of the Jews was not terrorism. Its aim was not to secure the compliance of survivors (or anyone else). It was to eliminate the Jews, namely, a deliberate act of genocide.

The first form of state terrorism hardly needs comment, as terror has been widely used as a tool of social control in all but those few historical cases of open societies. Physical fear has always been known as a powerful tool for inducing compliance. Some subgroups formed by the state, such as armed forces, have used hideous physical punishments until well into the nineteenth century, and execution well into the twentieth. This is still the case in many societies. Terror is used in colonial situations and in many ways has some similarity to physical terror over a domestic population. Definitional difficulties quickly arise as to what a colonial situation is and, at least in some states of colonialism, what the "state" exercising the terror is.

Further, terror is not a day-to-day instrument of social control in colonial situations (exept in a very extended concept of the notion of terror, but I do not want to get embroiled in the question of whether all social control involves violence). It is more commonly used after some uprising such as reprisals after the Indian Mutiny of 1856 (remarkably vicious even on both sides).[7]

A definition of "colonial" is notoriously difficult. "Internal colonialism," such as can plausibly be mentioned about the north of Scotland vis-à-vis the rest of Britain,[8] raises a variety of issues that are peripheral to this chapter. Here I am referring to unambiguous colonialism where people are ruled over an extended period by a clearly external power, such as the European colonization of most of Africa in the nineteenth and first half of the twentieth century. When state terrorism was used, it could be employed in a less inhibited manner than domestically, for the dual reason that it was out of the public eye of any domestic re-straining influences and, perhaps more critically, because colonial peoples were deemed inferior. Thus, cruelty against them was more acceptable.

The use of terror as an instrument of overt warfare is again widespread and probably always has been, though two forms can be usefully distinguished. The first is terror to induce compliance among an occupied population. This can take much the same form as terror against one's own population except, perhaps, that greater public brutality can conveniently be exhibited. Reprisals against admittedly innocent people can be, and often are, used to dissuade people from hostile acts toward an occupying force. Other methods in war are such things as bombing to break the morale (an antiseptic phrase for "frighten") of civilian populations, so as to destroy the support for a war. Bombing does not seem to have been very effective in practice for this purpose, as witness both Britain and Germany in World War II.[9] These forms of terror have been widely used historically and can almost be regarded as part of the standard equipment of the state in its coercive role.

It is the fourth category that deserves more attention. Ever since political societies have existed, it has been the case that they have tried to coerce each other into doing things that they would otherwise not have done. This is as true today about states as it ever was. One important device is to replace an existing set of rulers who seem inimical to one's cause with another more compliant set. Defeat in battle and the replacement of the government are, of course, common, but another way is to assist disaffected members of a society themselves to overthrow the offending government. This can be done by relatively benign and nonterroristic methods such as influencing elections to less benign methods such as supporting guerrilla groups or providing the means and training for terrorists to flourish and operate more successfully. In effect, this is pursuing warfare by other means. If one neglects moral factors, then this might seem to be an appropriate thing for a government to do. Whether to adopt it in an attempt to alter the complexion of another government of which it disapproves would simply seem to be a matter of whether it was deemed to be more efficient or not.

Now we come to a matter of some embarrassment for many people. There is little doubt that governments of many ideological complexions pursue, or at least condone, terrorism. Apologists for the Soviet Union as well as for the United States invent ingenious sophistries for their leaders to utter, and perhaps believe, but the crude realities remain. Zionists and anti-Zionists alike are strong on accusation but weak on justification. The tacit, if not active, support of terror is not the preserve of a few irresponsible fanatics, but is connived in, at least, by a great many "respectable" governments. However, few governments or their apologists are likely to admit to this, as there is always, or nearly always, an interest by governments in deploring terror as a political method. In part this is because of a general feeling of abhorrence of terror as a technique of violence, believing that the deliberate, as distinct from the incidental, killing of people who bear no responsibility for a conflict is outside the domain of honourable warfare.

While this concept does not seem to me to survive much scrutiny of any actual warfare, the deliberate use of terror does raise feelings that "proper" warfare does not. Even in an era where the general concept of warfare was regarded as a more appropriate form of conduct than it is today—namely, 1914—the terror that was used by the Germans in subduing the Belgian civilian population aroused strong feelings that cannot all be blamed on general war hysteria.[10] Thus, governments might refrain from using terror, or if they do deny it, simply because it is likely to be regarded as unacceptable by many of their own citizens even if they accepted the general hostility toward the other state.

The other reason why states are unwilling to accept terrorism as a legitimate tool officially, whatever they might do privately, is that they themselves might become the object of it. It is very difficult for a state, however strong and however efficient its internal security forces, to remain invulnerable to some acts of terror. Therefore, they are likely to raise a moral standard against it, which, of course, makes it embarrassing if it is found that the government is aiding and abetting similar activities elsewhere. While it is probable that there are secret reports in many well-locked filing cabinets on the relative efficiency of supporting terrorists as distinct from other forms of activity, along with evaluations of the efficiency of different terrorist groups with recommendations about who to support, this is rarely a publicly admitted activity. This, then, inhibits the sort of analysis of it that one might get in public about the issues of, say, conventional compared with nuclear war, which are publicly discussed.

Now this alone goes a long way to explain the relative neglect of scholars of state terrorism. People are simply embarrassed. The implicit question behind a lot of work on terrorism is, How do we protect ourselves from terrorism? This is perfectly natural. Few scholars themselves are proposing to be terrorists, while there is always some sort of possibility of being a victim of terrorism or finding oneself bereaved because of it. The effects of terrorism (though not particularly state terrorism) impinge on many people if only at the checkpoints in airports. If the question could be re-interpreted to be, "When do states we dislike from an ideological point of view promote terrorism? then we might approach the subject without embarrassment. However, terrorism is something about which it is difficult to remain dispassionate, much more so than "proper" warfare. Yet many states appear, even from the necessarily misleading evidence, to take part in it, such that only by the most ingenious acts of self-deception can individuals disguise from themselves that some regime for which they have an ideological partiality has some responsibility somewhere or another for such acts. Thus, it is psychologically more secure to leave things on one side of criteria that indicate to a scholar whether some problem is interesting or not.[11] The first is the problem of ideology and political or moral concern. We are interested in problems because we see them as important from a moral or ideological point of view. The second is the way we divide society up into different social groupings, classes, or whatever, in order to conduct a social analysis. I shall discuss these in turn.

It is not surprising that scholars in international relations are particularly interested in war. Not only is it a particularly spectacular event in the international scene, it is also one about which scholars have strong moral convictions. Some believe it to be inherently wrong. However, perhaps necessary under some circumstances though, this is a relatively modern idea. The concept of war as glorious and perhaps also purifying has a long history, probably longer than that of war as morally wrong. Similarly, such things as economic under-development are matters that concern many people for obvious moral reasons. Others are more concerned with the problem of attaining an orderly society and one that moves sedately on, in a full consciousness of its past. Thus, many supporters of the maximum possible use of the market mechanism as the best way of operating economic systems, which is now such a fashionable point of view, do so because of a view that this maximizes individual liberty.[12] The implication, at least, is that the moral premise is individual liberty, and, then, purely as a technique, it is thought that a market mechanism produces this. If some other method of economic organization appeared to give a greater scope to individual liberty, or if, as many contend, there are aspects of a market system that lead it to develop in ways inimical to individual liberty, then presumably, if convinced of the force of the argument, such a person would alter his views. However, there are people who seem to believe that capitalism is in itself a more virtuous way of operating an economic system, and prefer it to another system even in situations where it is not conducive to individual liberty. Ideologies are complex phenomena, and what, for an individual, is a basic premise and what is deduced are not always easy to discern.

However, given an ideology, this leads to certain questions being asked and certain ones being avoided. For example, the market mechanism is generally regarded as most justifiable if we have something approximating perfect competition where firms as entities maximize profits. This is not conducive to a careful examination of a theory of bribery despite the fact that bribery is probably a significant feature of the economic system.[13] It is difficult, of course, to know just how signifiant it is, as by its nature a bribe is an economic act that is conducted out of the public eye; but even from the cases we know it cannot be neglected and may significantly affect the operation of the economic system away from the direction that would be indicated by the proponents of the perfect market. Bribery is not a characteristic of capitalism alone, and the eager proponent of the market mechanism will rush forward to allege that it may well be more widespread in socialistic or indeed any other system. This is, of course, why it is such an embarrassment to everyone of more or less any ideological persuasion and probably accounts for the relative absence of a serious theory of bribes in the economic theory of either socialist or capitalist economies. It is hopefully dismissed as "friction."

The parallel with state terrorism is clear. It fits in conveniently with no majority ideological view, in that states of most political complexions use it, however censorious they may be in theory, particularly when practised by other states. In consequence, the theory of state terrorism is not as well analysed as it might be. This, however, is not because there is anything about state terrorism as such that makes it unanalysable by conventional social science methods, any more than bribery is unanalysable by conventional economic methods. It is because of the unwelcome conclusions to which our analysis might lead us.

The second factor that turns a social scientist's attention toward certain sorts of problems and away from others is the issue of what social groups or divisions one accepts categories with which to analyse social behaviour. Thus, if in the analysis of the international system one adopts states as the basic unit, then certain sorts of problems become central and others peripheral. Again, if one takes social class as the basic unit in society, then some problems become dominant and others can be put on one side. The issue raised by feminists of all shades has been that the neglect of women as a grouping has led to the omission of the analysis of many important questions. Now the problem of what to take as the group whose behaviour one is going to analyse is dependent in part on a number of factors, some scientific, some not. One may take a grouping because one sympathizes with some of the interest of that group, and analyse the effectiveness of a theory of society in which that group is identified as such and separate from other groups. Two issues here seem to be distinguished, though the danger of confusion is both obvious and serious. I may have very much to heart the interests of certain social groups—say, groups of people over seventy years of age. However, this would not mean that dividing people up into age groups for the purpose of analysing society would answer more than a very few questions. My problem would be how to aid the over-seventies and not use them as some explanatory variable.

However, other groups, for example, an economic group such as small farmers, with whom I may or may not have sympathy may act as a social group, and an analysis of society based on economic grouping around industries and classes of industries might answer a number of questions very satisfactorily. Indeed, a great deal of economic bargaining between states can be properly understood only if one takes very seriously industrial groupings within a state as significant actors within the analysis. The history of the Common Agricultural Policy of the European Economic Community provides more illustrations than one could wish. Thus, while our initial choice might be based on such issues as sympathies with a social group (or hostility to a group), or simply a guess that it might be a fruitful grouping for the development of a theory of certain forms of social behaviour, whether it turns out to have payoffs in terms of theoretical power depends on the degree to which we can develop testable theory from such an assumption. Effectively these are "research programs,"[14] using the term in a small-scale sense.

A Marxist can ask what significant questions can be answered by using class as the basic unit of social analysis. Even within a Marxist perspective one can ask whether this is sufficient, as Marxist feminists do, while the non-Marxist or the sceptical Marxist might ask whether a whole range of significant questions from some ethical point of view are left unanswered by this sort of analysis. Thus, in a crude and over-simplified way, a Marxist would analyse the conflict in Northern Ireland as primarily a class conflict that has been muddied by bringing in religious, ethnic, and nationalist issues to the advantage of the capitalists (or in many versions colonialists). Most non-Marxists would argue that the religious–ethnic issue is, in fact, dominant and that the problem could be satisfactorily analysed (if not regrettably solved) without bringing in social class at all (or if so very much as a minor variable). That it is not clearly decidable testifies to the difficulty of social science. Nevertheless, deciding which classifications lead to the most powerful theories is in principle a resolvable problem.

What, if any, are the methodological or epistemological objections to producing a theory in which state terrorism is conceived of as a goal-directed model where a state endeavours to obtain certain ends and chooses this as a means.[15] Goal-directed models are common in the social sciences. Indeed, all decision theory models that are descriptive as opposed to prescriptive are of this form. In essence, such a theory posits that a decision maker or decision-making group aims to achieve some desired state of affairs (which could be maximizing profit for a business firm, power for a state, "utility" for practically everybody). Various initial conditions and constraints are given. From these circumstances the behaviour of the actor in pursuance of these goals can be analysed on the assumption that, on some set of criteria, its behaviour is "efficient." These are widely used and accepted in many branches of the social sciences, and indeed micro-economic theory (that is, the theory of the individual economic agent, whether producer or consumer) consists primarily of goal-directed models.

Occasionally qualms are expressed about this sort of analysis in that the actors in social science are conscious, thinking beings. Now, teleological or goals-seeking models are common enough in the natural sciences, in particular in biology. While these raise some problems, I think that they can be fairly regarded as little more than complex linguistic confusions.[16] Thus, if we say that a plant "searches for the light," it would not normally be regarded as some conscious act on the part of the plant, though in the case of a higher mammal such as a dog it might well be. However, neglecting any philosophical issues raised by dogs, it is undoubtedly the case that human beings do have conscious goals that they pursue, and thus our goal-directed theories are not merely a matter of posing a set of laws and a set of initial conditions from which we can deduce, at least in principle, what the consequences will be. Even if we could restate goal-seeking behaviour without mentioning the goal, to do so would be misleading and miss some essential important characteristics of the problem.

But does this then mean that because we have introduced conscious mental processes into the picture, we have in some sense made the analysis less scientific? The question is purely rhetorical. The assumption that a state or any other social group is pursuing certain goals implies that from certain initial and observable conditions, certain observable actions will occur. Whether or not the observable actions take place provides the test of the theory. It is admittedly the case that laws express goal seeking but they are still the subject of empirical verification or refutation in much the same manner. There are, of course, complications about goal-seeking models, particularly about the direct testability of the goals themselves. As I have posed the procedure, this is unnecessary. A goal is "correct" if it yields correct predictions or descriptions of the relevant events. Thus, a direct testing of the goals is superfluous, though it might be interesting for other purposes.

An extreme variant of this view, expessed by Milton Friedman,[17] is that it does not matter if the goal is in fact false (presumably on the basis of some direct questioning) provided that the predictions are correct. I have argued against this extreme position elsewhere.[18] Particularly, in the study of a subject such as state terrorism, a closer examination of the goals is likely to repay some closer scrutiny. It is a field where hypocrisy abounds. If we are to explain state terrorism by means of explicitly articulated goals, we will commonly get the wrong answer. To analyse the system, we have to posit what we think are the goals of the states in question, and then see whether that actual facts match up with these assumed goals, and if not, try some other set of assumptions in the approved scientific manner. However, the comparison between the goals that give the correct predictions and the supposed goals of the decision makers as they are articulated is itself an interesting and possibly fruitful study, though the gathering of the evidence is by its nature very difficult. Some discrepancy is attributable to direct lying, to deceive either other governments or a domestic constituency. While political scientists might deplore this, they can hardly be surprised by it.

More intriguing are the cases where decision makers delude themselves about the nature of their behaviour. The delusions might take the form of not asking awkward questions to various branches of government and endeavouring to forget that they perhaps should be asked. They might involve general intellectual confusions and inconsistency. The degree to which people can act in contradiction to articulated beliefs, without apparently being aware of the contradictions, is an intriguing psychological problem and one of particular importance for a topic such as student of political behaviour. Though complex, it is, of course, an issue that is perfectly amenable at least in principle to scientific investigation. It should not be concluded from this that because of the apparent incoherence of the goals a goal-directed analysis is impossible. The actual goals may be perfectly coherent—in fact, I suspect they normally are. It is merely that they commonly conflict the articulated goals.

I am suggesting, therefore, that goal-directed models are perfectly legitimate ways of analysing the phenomenon of state terrorism; indeed, if we do not use theories of this kind, then we are probably not going to be able to say anything about state terrorism beyond telling stories of particular incidents or making rather vague and almost empty generalizations.

First, to delimit the field a little: Governments often want to coerce other governments in various different ways. Crudely, there are three methods. The coercing government might accept the essential structure of the rival, but wish to influence it in some particular way. One such reason for coercion may, of course, be to compel it to retain its existing form of government or alliances in the face of internal pressure to alter them, a pattern familiar to us in Eastern Europe amongst many other places. The second is for the coercer still to accept the essential existence of the state, but to very seriously wish to affect its policies. This might come about by defeating it in war and giving it little alternative but to comply, such as Germany in 1918 and 1919. Alternatively, it might attempt to replace the government by something more congenial. This is a pattern familiar to us in recent years in South America. The third, which is less common, is to deny the legitimacy not just of the government of a state but of the very existence of the particular state itself. The most conspicuous example of this in recent decades is Israel. It is the second and third of these where state-sponsored terrorism is of most significance. I shall concentrate on the second for the purposes of the exposition of my case.

A government, for whatever reason, wishes to replace the government of another state by one that it hopes will follow policies that favour it. There are many reasons why this should be so. It might perceive the existing government as posing some strategic threat to its security either directly or by the alliances it forms with hostile powers. It might wish

for more favourable trading and investing conditions; it might find it
ideologically unprepossessing; indeed, it might well find it to be a mixture
of all three. Theoretically, most governments hold to the view that intervention in the affairs of other states is improper, though this does
not, in practice, seem to deter them greatly; it simply makes them more
ingenious in thinking of excuses. There is therefore a choice of methods
including, for example, outright attack, if this is militarily feasible and
the victim is not the client state of another who is in a position to intervene. Alternatively, it might impose economic sanctions of various sorts;
it might support guerrilla groups; or it might support simple terrorists,
providing training, equipment, money, and so on in an attempt to overthrow the government. Sanctions might be regarded as a proper form
of coercion. It is certainly not a terroristic act. The second two frequently
involve what I would describe as terrorism.

Another version of this might be if a government, a repressive government, itself uses state terrorism against its citizens. Again, a number
of South American governments come to mind. Then an outside power
might support the regime both in materials and in diplomacy, again
because of it prefers its stance to that of the possible alternatives. Again,
because of the moral problems, many ingenious excuses are brought out
to justify the propriety of this by governments ostensibly in favour of
peaceful societies.

Faced with this situation, a government can simply choose which is
the most efficient way of pursuing its goals. "Efficient" here means simply
pursuing the policy that will maximize the probability of achieving its
goals with the minimum of expenditure. Various forms of models might
be tried, such as an expected utility model. This is not, despite what may
be thought, the only choice model. However, some sort of theory that
supposes that the government looks at a variety of alternatives and chooses
that which is most effective according to some discoverable criterion is
surely applicable. It may be more difficult, but in principle it seems to
be conceptually (if not morally) exactly the same class of problem as
analysing the case of a state that has decided to impose economic sanctions on some other state and is considering which of the different types
of economic sanctions to impose. Alternatives are an import ban, an
export ban, limitations on credit, blocking of accounts, and direct prohibition of particular forms of equipment—all, of course, with or without
the attempt to induce its allies to carry out similar sorts of activity. A
country might like to impose all simultaneously or just some. Its choice
will be dictated by a mixture weighing the costs of imposing some sanction along with the effectiveness of the sanction in inducing compliance
by the other state.

The point is that one can analyse this sort of problem systematically
and offer explanations of why particular sorts of sanctions are or are

not employed in particular circumstances. In principle, an economic theory of sanctions is not difficult to produce, though there may be practical problems. I think few people would suppose that it is epistemologically improper, whatever practical difficulties may be involved. Again, I repeat, I can see no epistemological differene between a theory of how a state chooses between other forms of coercive action including state terrorism.

There are, of course, moral issues involved, and here again we have to be careful to avoid confusion. Terrorism, whether state inspired or not, is regarded with moral repugnance by many people who are nevertheless not pacifists. Hence, while they might approve of overt military action against a regime, even if it involved the loss of civilian lives, they would nevertheless strongly disapprove of actions intended to instill terror into the population. This has two consequences. First, some members of some governments are also likely to share these feelings and would be unwilling to sanction terrorism even if it could be demonstrated as being more efficient than other methods from all other points of view. While it seems unlikely that the members of the operating forces would share these feelings—someone who chooses a career in "covert operations" is unlikely to be a person of delicate moral sensibility—the political masters might impose constraints such that an operation becomes infeasible. Similarly, members of the public are likely to disapprove of and, at least in open societies, to put some constraints on the use of terror by the governments and make it inexpedient for them to use it too openly. Examined from the point of view of the cynical amoral decision maker, this issue would be regarded as a cost. The analyst, also in a cold-blooded frame of mind, must consider the problem of when moral attitudes, either on the part of the government itself or on the part of the citizens, become an issue in the analysis. The issue of when people act in accordance with expressed moral values and when they act contrary toward them, and indeed what moral attitudes are held in a society of a particular sort and at a particular time, are, of course, subjects for social scientific analysis, as distinct from the content of the moral codes, which is the subject matter of the moral philosopher.

The analyst also has moral attitudes toward state terrorism and indeed any other form of terrorism. In public, few analysts, whether of the political Right or Left, would support terrorism. In private, they mostly do. Excuses can, of course, be made. Some state terrorism might be regarded as "defensive" or possibly "preemptive." A government takes part in terroristic activities because it argues (and doubtless there are many cases with justification) that if it did not, the fabric of the state would be subverted either in the interest of some group within the state or in the interest of some other state. Thus, state terrorism might be regarded as many people regard war, a deplorable necessity but a necessity nonetheless, if the societies of which we are members are to survive.

Let us suppose that such instances arise. A state is threatened by terrorism supported by an external power. That is, it is threatened by my second sort of terrorism—Nicaragua today might be an example. Is such a state justified in using terrorism in response? I emphasize *terrorism* in the sense of deliberately inducing fear, perhaps in completely innocent people, in order to eliminate or at least reduce non-state terrorism. In other words, is terrorism ever a legitimate tool of policy, in particular when it is used against non-state terrorists? Obviously the opposite question can also be asked. Is non-state terrorism ever justified (to clarify the mind on this question—and upset the emotions, which often comes to the same thing—the reader is recommended to reflect on the various acts carried out by resistance movements in Europe during the German occupations during the Second World War)?

A "pure" defense against non-state terrorism without resort to some terror is difficult when the terrorists have the support of a community. I suggest that these questions are normally extremely difficult to answer except for the total pacifist. If physical violence is ever justified, we must seriously consider the possibility that terror, state or otherwise, is also justified. We anaesthetize the moral problem by calling state terrorism "internal defense" and non-state terrorism "freedom fighting." The strict epistemologist can let the problem slumber, but it is the moral philosopher's job to wake it up.

Even though many would accept the above argument and resultant dilemma, few would actually maintain that terror in order to "destabilize" another government is justified. However, there must be a considerable number of people in various governments who believe that it is, otherwise it would not happen. Tucked away in the bureaucracies, there are doubtless many people who would admit this. What timorous liberal academics such as the author of this piece would regard as unbearably cynical is seen as legitimate behaviour by many hardier spirits. However, few politicians would admit to it in public, but it is at this point that the moralist must object. As epistemologists we must ask for precise definitions and consider what problems can properly be studied by scientific or other means. However, another problem of the philosopher is to explore the ambiguities of language. Politicians are expert in double-think—sometimes deliberately but often as a result of confusion. However, it is the job of the scholar to expose such attempts at double-think, however disturbing it may be for the complacency of the politician or indeed for the scholar's own particular prejudices.

NOTES

1. The references are legion. Classics are R. B. Braithwaite, *Scientific Expla-*

nation (Cambridge: Cambridge University Press, 1955); C. G. Hempel, *Aspects of Scientific Explanation* (London: Collier–Macmillan, 1965); Karl Popper, *The Logic of Scientific Discovery* (London: Hutchinson, 1959); and Bertrand Russell, *Human Knowledge: Its Scope and Limits* (London: Allen and Unwin; New York: Simon and Schuster, 1948).

2. Hempel, *Aspects of Scientific Explanation.*

3. Those who are familiar with the field will know that the opposition to empiricist explanations in the social sciences is broad. A few major references are Peter Winch, *The Idea of a Social Science and Its Relation to Philosophy* (London: Routledge and Kegan, Paul, 1958); Charles Taylor, *The Explanation of Behaviour* (London: Routledge and Kegan, Paul, 1964); and G. H. Von Wright, *Explanation and Understanding* (London: Routledge and Kegan, Paul, 1971).

4. See, for example, J. L. Austin, *How to Do Things with Words* (Oxford: Clarendon Press, 1962).

5. See William Shirer, *The Rise and Fall of the Third Reich* (New York: Simon and Schuster, 1960), pp. 117–204.

6. R. C. K. Ensor, *England 1870–1914* (Oxford: Clarendon Press, 1936).

7. M. E. Chamberlain, *Britain and India: The Intersection of Two Peoples* (Newton Abbott: David and Charles, 1976).

8. M. Hechter, *Internal Colonialism* (London: Routledge and Kegan, Paul, 1975).

9. The issue of strategic bombing is discussed in some detail in B. Paskings and M. Dockrill, *The Ethics of War* (Minneapolis: University of Minnesota Press, 1979); also see C. P. Snow, "Science and Government," in *The Two Cultures and the Scientific Revolution,* 2d ed. (Cambridge: Cambridge University Press, 1964).

10. A. J. P. Taylor, *English History 1914–1945* (Oxford: Oxford University Press, 1965); and Barbara Tuchman, *August, 1914* (London: Macmillan, 1980).

11. For a detailed discussion, see John F. McCamant, "Governance Without Blood: Social Science's Antiseptic View of Rule, or, The Neglect of Political Repression," in Michael Stohl and George A. Lopez, eds., *The State as Terrorist: The Dynamics of Governmental Violence and Repression* (Westport, CT: Greenwood Press, 1984), pp. 11–42.

12. See especially Milton and Rose Friedman, *Capitalism and Freedom* (Chicago: University of Chicago Press, 1964).

13. Its significance in the aircraft industry is made clear in Sampson Anthony, *The Arms Bazaar* (London: Coronet Books, 1978). Obviously he could report the cases of only those that got caught.

14. Imre Lakatos, "Falsification and the Methodology of Scientific Research Programmes," in Lakatos and Alan Musgrave, eds., *Criticism and the Growth of Knowledge* (Cambridge: Cambridge University Press, 1970). This is a widely cited piece. Lakatos seems to regard different research programs as inconsistent and perhaps incommensurable, whereas I simply want to indicate directions of research.

15. I discuss this issue in Michael Nicholson, *The Scientific Analysis of Social Behaviour: A Defense of Empiricism in Social Science* (London: Frances Pinter; New York: St. Martin's Press, 1983).

16. See Braithwaite, *Scientific Explanation*, who deals with the problem in detail.

17. Milton Friedman, *Essays in Positive Economics* (Chicago: University of Chicago Press, 1953).

18. Nicholson, *Scientific Analysis of Social Behaviour*.

3

The Political Origins of State Violence and Terror: A Theoretical Analysis

Ted Robert Gurr

The object of this theoretical essay is the terroristic use of coercion by the state. The purpose is to specify generally the circumstances in which political elites are likely to use terror, and to develop some analytic distinctions among types of state terrorism. The essential assumption underpinning the analysis is that state terrorism arises out of conflict between elites and non-elites: It is a particular kind of policy or strategy chosen for dealing with actual or anticipated opposition. Thus, it is not enough to explain state terrorism by reference to the characteristics of the state and its ruling elite alone. State terrorism should be seen as arising from conflict situations created by interactions among elites and their opponents. Much theorizing about the causes of rioting, revolution, and terrorism against the state has been criticized as one sided because of its single-minded concern with the grievances, ideologies, and organization of challengers and rebels.[1] A theory of state terrorism can avoid replicating the limitations and implicit bias of one-sided explanations of rebellion by treating it within the framework of conflict theory. In this perspective, a theory of state terrorism is part of the explanation of why elites use coercion as an instrument of rule.

DEFINITIONS

State terrorism as a subject of theoretical analysis is conceptually problematic because of difficulties with the definitions of "state" and "terrorism." Most definitions of the state in social scientific analysis incorporate the Weberian notion that the state is characterized by legitimacy and a monopoly of the means of coercion.[2] From this perspective, "state terrorism" is merely a pejorative label for what states do by right. Such a conception confuses the contemporary global ideology of the state, in terms of which state managers justify their claims to authority, with the objective nature of the state. The essence of the state, past and present, is a bureaucratically institutionalized pattern of authority whose rulers claim to exercise sovereign (ultimate) control over the inhabitants of a territory, and who demonstrate enduring capacity to enforce that claim.[3] The means by which rulers do so, whether through voluntary compliance based on sentiments of legitimacy or positive inducements or threat of sanctions or use of violence are variable. In this conception, the use of violence, including terrorism, is one of many policies that may be chosen to establish and maintain state authority. Throughout this analysis, we use "state" to refer to the formal–legal and institutional entity. "Regime" signifies the incumbents and policies of the moment.

Terrorism is problematic because so many and varied definitions have been offered of the concept that some scholars question the concept's analytic usefulness.[4] For our purposes, we modify Raymond D. Duvall and Michael Stohl's definition that "terrorism . . . is [coercive, life-threatening] action intended to induce sharp fear and through that agency to effect a desired outcome in a conflict situation."[5] The specification of *coercive, life-threatening* action is ours. Regimes do many coercive things to induce compliance: They threaten, arrest and jail, fine and confiscate, as well as murder. It is plausible, both analytically and psychologically, to limit the concept of state terrorism to coercion that takes or grossly endangers the lives of its targets. Thus, it includes imprisonment in conditions where many are worked or starved to death, and other denials of the means of life, as well as outright killing. "Violence" is the short-hand term used below.

The other key element in the definition concerns the intent of such actions. Violence by regimes is terroristic only if it is "instrumental," which means designed to have a wider effect on some audience. Alex P. Schmid, in his general definition of terror, distinguishes between two kinds of intention: "to immobilize the *target of terror* in order to produce disorientation and/or compliance" and "to mobilize . . . *targets of attention* (e.g., public opinion) to changes of attitude or behaviour favoring the short- or long-term interests of the users."[6] A contingent question is whether threats alone can have such effects. Duvall and Stohl's discussion is equivocal about whether threats of violence also constitute terror. From our perspective, threats have little value for terror, or social control, unless they are actualized. "State terror" implies a *patterned activity* in which instrumental violence recurs often enough that threats of similar violence, made then or later, have their intended effects on conflict outcomes. This quotation from Adolf Hitler, in power, gives substance to these abstract definitional points:

I shall spread terror through the surprising application of all means. The sudden shock of a terrible fear of death is what matters. Why should I deal otherwise with all my political opponents? These so-called atrocities save me hundreds of thousands of individual actions against the protestors and discontents. Each one of them will think twice to oppose us when he learns what is [awaiting] him in the [concentration] camp.[7]

A different conceptual problem has to do with violence on the margins of the state. Right-wing "death squads," including moonlighting soldiers and police, have become a major source of political terrorism in revolutionary conflicts in Latin America. Are their activities to be categorized as *state* terrorism? In Indonesia in 1965–1966, several hundred thousand Communists were killed following an attempted coup in a retaliatory campaign initiated by the military but carried out largely by village-level religious and nationalist groups. The military then eased President Sukarno from power, partly because of his continued support for the decimated Communist Party.[8] Was this an instance of civil war, political genocide, state terrorism, or mass vigilantism? In January 1976, Richard Turner, a white South African opponent of apartheid, was killed by a shot fired through a window of his Durban home, in the presence of two daughters. Turner, a University of Natal lecturer in political theory, was killed a few weeks before the expiration of a five-year banning order. Political activists believed he was murdered by or with the foreknowledge of security police; the case was never solved. Was this a case of state terrorism?

All these killings induced fear, one of the defining characteristics of terrorism, and the regime was known or believed to be implicated in all of them. In Indonesia, however, the military's main purpose was not to induce fear in the target group but to eliminate them: It was a purge, or to use a more contemporary term, an instance of political genocide.[9] A second test inherent in the definition of state terrorism is the existence of a *pattern* of life-threatening acts. The South African government clearly attempts to deter radical opposition to apartheid by inducing fear, relying largely on surveillance, banning, detention, and prosecution to do so. Although some political activists have died in police custody, the assassination-style killing of Dr. Turner was an isolated event. On the same night in one of Durban's black townships, a former member of the banned African National Congress who had turned state's evidence was also seriously wounded. The dissimilarity of the two men, and the fact that no further shootings occurred, suggests that a single aberrant individual was involved. Such acts contributed to a general pattern of fear in South Africa, but these two shootings probably were not designed by authorities to have that effect.[10]

A third criterion has to do with the nature of the regime's responsibility for terrorism. It would be unreasonable to restrict the concept of state terrorism to violent acts explicitly carried out under state authority:

Regimes have many reasons for concealing their involvement, not least the fear of international repercussions. The essential question is whether terrorism occurs with the explicit or implicit approval of authorities. The direct evidence on this point is often inconclusive; even the involvement of out-of-uniform military personnel is not decisive. But if terrorist acts are patterned and persistent, if they are directed at opponents of a regime, and if authorities make no substantial efforts to stop them, the acts are *prima facie* state terrorism. Moreover, their political effects are almost certainly those of explicitly authorized state terrorism: They induce fear in opponents of the regime and are, by strong inference, intended by someone—the regime or its supporters—to help defeat a regime's challengers in a conflict situation.[11]

We can return briefly to the three test cases posed above. The massacre of Indonesian Commmunists was not an instance of state terrorism, even though encouraged by the military: It was political genocide. The murder of Dr. Turner was an isolated instance of political assassination, though one that occurred in the context of a more general pattern of state terrorism directed at opponents of apartheid (see below). But the patterned violence of the right-wing death squads of Argentina in the 1970s and of contemporary El Salvador (and probably Guatemala) unquestionably constitute state terrorism. Belated efforts to prosecute high-ranking Argentine military officers for their role in disappearances, or to send bloody-handed Salvadoran officers into diplomatic exile, merely confirm the state's prior involvement.

CRITERIA FOR JUDGING STATE TERRORISM

We have not yet considered the normative dimension of state terrorism. All the analytic precision that social science can muster will not strip the term of its pejorative connotation. The use of the term implies condemnation of such policies by some external political standard, a condemnation that is arguably counter to long-established doctrines of sovereignty, by which states are free to use virtually any coercive means to maintain internal control. There is an international humanitarian standard, embodied in the U.N. 1948 Genocide Convention, which prohibits (without sanction) mass killings of religious and ethnic minorities, but it says nothing about the killing of political opponents. While one may agree with Pope John Paul that "violence is evil. Violence is unacceptable as a solution to problems"[12]—as a relative matter, it may be a lesser evil to cow political opposition through terrorism than to slaughter them en masse. It is suggested that state terrorism is a relative rather than absolute bad, a perspective that leads to several distinctions of use for both analytic and normative judgments.

The first is a "proportionality principle." Observers cannot realistically expect regimes confronted by violent opposition to meekly submit, or to limit their responses, to those prescribed in democratic theory. State terror should be judged not in the absolute but against some standard. Normatively, the standard might be that of international law (which at present condemns genocide but not state terrorism), or the domestic laws of the state in question, or the laws of culturally similar states, or some not-yet-codified conception of global human rights. By all of these standards, it is likely that *some* kinds of coercive "action intended to induce sharp fear . . . in a conflict situation" will be acceptable and some not.

From a realist perspective, one possible standard for judging policies of state terrorism is the magnitude of threat posed to a regime by its domestic opponents. If political opponents initiate a campaign of rev-olutionary violence against a regime, then by the proportionality prin-ciple, regimes are justified if they respond with whatever coercive measures seem necessary to suppress oppositional violence. The argu-ment is analogous to arguments for the "just war" in international pol-itics, by which states have the right of defense in relation to the degree of threat and level of harm done to them.[13] But internal standards of political morality may constrain the state much more in its actions against domestic opponents than against other states. The character of the chal-lenge must be judged: Does it pose such great danger that elites have no alternatives other than violent ones? If they must use violence, and do so to excess, they risk loss of legitimacy in the eyes of their own supporters. By this standard, a few visible acts of state terror may be a more efficient and less deadly response than military campaigns. But state terrorism may be judged more reprehensible by the public and thus more limited sanctions applied within the rule of law.

The proportionality principle also is hedged by international standards of morality and justice: A regime that perpetuates gross violations of human rights may be argued to have lost its sovereign right to rule by coercion, whatever its opponents do. The notion of such international standards is contentious. Terry Nardin makes a cogent argument for the evolution of such standards,[14] while Barbara Harff, among others, contends that the gross abuse of fundamental rights in one state justifies humanitarian intervention by other states.[15] Thus, the proportionality principle, that state violence is justified in proportion to oppositional violence, is constrained by both internal and international standards of political legitimacy.

Many regimes, past and present, have resorted to terror during civil and revolutionary wars, as well as in response to lesser challenges. The French used both terrorist and military tactics in their counter-insur-gency against Muslim revolutionaries in Algeria during the late 1950s. In the United States, the Federal Bureau of Investigation and police campaign against the Black Panthers in 1969–1970 was terrorist in intent and effect.[16] Such instances are distinct from preemptive uses of state terror in which a regime initiates violence to deter potential opposition. Stalin's purges in the 1930s are a case in point: A system of rule through terror was established at a time when there was very little overt or covert opposition to the regime. China's "Great Cultural Revolution," which involved the extensive use of intimidation and physical violence by the Red Guards, was also a campaign of terror, begun in this case by Mao Tse-tung and directed partly against elements in the party and bureaucracy. In the 1970s, the military governments of Argentina and Chile relied on policies of political abductions and murder that were grossly disproportionate to the tactics and threat of the Left. In all these instances, state terrorism was institutionalized for periods lasting up to a decade.

These examples suggest a distinction between *situationally specific* state terrorism and *institutionalized* state terrorism. In the former, state terrorism is used as a tactic in response to a particular kind of open challenge, but ceases (and is sometimes discredited and sanctioned) after the conflict subsides. In the latter, regimes rely on ongoing terror as an instrument of rule. The creation of state agencies that implement such policies over a long period of time is *prima facie* evidence of institutionalized state terrorism: Cases in point are the existence and activities of the Soviet KGB (before 1943 the NKVD, before 1934 the OGPU), the Shah of Iran's SAVAK, and DINA in Chile. The same effect can be achieved by the use of para-statal groups like the Red Guard, the "Secret Anticommunist Armies" of Guatemala and El Salvador, and the Argentine Anti-Communist Alliance. Examples of institutionalized state terrorism virtually by definition fail the test implied by the proportionality principle. Situation-specific state terrorism, however, may be proportional to the challenge that provokes it: French tactics against revolutionary terrorists in the Battle of Algiers arguably met the test, American terrorist tactics against posturing black militants did not.

The distinction between situational and institutionalized state terror is not an absolute one. Policies of state terror may be initiated in response to specific, violent challenges but, in the course of a protracted conflict, develop a self-sustaining momentum. Regimes that rely on state terror to combat revolutionary opponents sometimes find it useful, or functionally necessary, to continue the policy against increasingly hardened and bitter opponents. Thus, state terrorism, even more than other forms of state violence, can be a one-way street at the end of which lies a debacle like that which ended the Shah's regime.

This suggests one process by which state terrorism can originate and become institutionalized. It is one of a number of arguments to be incorporated in a more general theory of the conditions of state terrorism.

Such a theory is developed below. The conditions relevant to the occurrence and persistence of state terrorism are categorized as properties of (1) the challengers, (2) the regime and its prevailing political ideology, (3) the social structure, and (4) the international system. A distinction is made at each level between conditions that dispose elites to rely generally on policies of violence in response to challenges and those that influence their decisions to use terrorist strategies specifically. The conclusion summarizes the propositions in two causal models.

CONDITIONS OF STATE TERRORISM

The Challengers

In contemporary states, the necessary condition for state terrorism is the existence of a group, class, or party that is regarded by ruling elites as an active threat to their continued rule. Charles Tilly's term "challengers" is appropriate for such groups: They make claims that challenge the prevailing distribution of power and resources.[17] Such groups do not necessarily use violent or other unconventional means to make their claims. Their "claims" may take the form of resistance to the growing demands or changing policies of the regime. The challengers may not necessarily be mobilized for action. They may be the losers displaced by a successful revolution or coup. The extent of threat they pose may be misperceived by state managers. But without a situation of conflict posed by challengers' claims, or anticipated resistance, regimes are exceedingly unlikely to resort to terrorism. State terrorism, like oppositional terrorism, is not random: It is a response either to open opposition or to group alignments and cleavages that threaten incumbent elites. There may be historical exceptions to this generalization, such as the use of seemingly random murder by the nineteenth-century Zulu chief, Shaka, as described by E. V. Walter.[18] Terrorism by twentieth-century states, however, virtually always is politically purposeful. Indeed, it is purposeful by the definition adopted above.[19]

Few challenges provoke state terrorism. Some characteristics of challenges and challengers, however, make terrorism a more likely response than others. A general principle about state violence can be proposed, then qualified with respect to state terrorism.

A.1 The greater the political threat posed by challengers, the greater the likelihood that a regime will respond with violence. Political threat is greater to the extent that (a) the challengers' objective is to displace incumbents, (b) they are large in number, and (c) they rely on violent or seriously disruptive tactics. The first of these three determinants of political threat is most important: It is considerably more likely that regimes will use violence against rebels and revolutionaries than against challengers who have limited or "reformist" demands. Given revolutionary objectives, challengers' numbers and use of violent tactics increase the probability and magnitude of state violence. Empirical data on conflict in the 1960s are consistent with the proposition. We know that most conflict deaths are caused by regimes rather than dissidents, in part because regimes are better armed than their opponents. We also know that political protest is considerably more common than rebellion: Estimates for eighty-seven countries in the 1960s show that the typical country had five times as many man-days of participation in protest as rebellion.[20] But rebellion, and by inference the response of regimes, is far more deadly than protest: The total deaths in all reported episodes and campaigns of protest was approximately 10,000, contrasted with more than 3 million in all rebellions (including revolutions and civil wars).[21]

A2. The greater the latent support for revolutionary challengers in a population, the greater the likelihood that a regime will respond with terrorism. This is an amplification of A1. If there are many potential supporters of revolutionaries in a population, then terror may appear to be a cost-effective way of deterring them from active support. If most have already been mobilized, however—if a revolutionary party or secessionist region has fully committed itself to armed struggle—then the threatened regime will have to rely mainly on military tactics. Terrorism may be a secondary tactic in such instances of all-out internal war, or a byproduct of military campaigns, but is not likely to be the principal tactic.

A3. Challengers who rely on terrorist and guerrilla tactics are likely to be countered by state terror. The rationale for this proposition is not a simple terror-begets-terror argument. *Guerrilleros* who use strike-and-run tactics are very difficult to combat by conventional security and military means. There is ample evidence that security forces confronted by such tactics will respond with terror directed at those suspected of harboring or otherwise tacitly supporting the revolutionaries. The government of Fulgencio Batista, challenged by Fidel Castro, used terror against his urban middle-class supporters and against peasants in the army's zone of operations, because among other reasons Castro could never be maneuvered into a direct military confrontation.[22] The tactics failed in this instance, but in recent years they have worked in Brazil against urban terrorists and in Argentina against sporadic leftist guerrilla resistance (mostly urban, some rural). They have also been effective thus far in Guatemala against rural revolutionaries and their urban supporters.

A4. Regimes are more likely to use terrorism against politically marginal groups than opposition groups that have influence on or supporters among the elite. This principle, which probably applies to all uses of state violence, is based on the premise that groups that have few and weak political ties to the regime can be terrorized and killed at less political cost than others. Both examples and counter-examples can be cited. Regimes threatened by military plotters rarely use terror against them; early retirement and diplomatic exile are far more common even than executions. The French military used terror in 1957 against nationalist revolutionaries in the Battle of Algiers; by French estimates, 3,024 of 24,000 arrestees "disappeared." They did not use counter-terror against right-wing French terrorists, then operating in Algeria and later in France.[23] Police in the United States used terror against Black Panthers; more conventional and legal tactics of surveillance, arrest, and prosecution are used to restrain right-wing white extremists, such as the Ku Klux Klan, the Minutemen, and the *Posse Comitatus*.

The Algerian and American cases are instances of "zones of terror," to use Walter's phrase. The use of violence and fear is confined to a particular ethnic, political, or class group. "Outside the zone, power relations follow the rules of an ordinary system of authority."[24] In these instances, the politically marginal status of the targets of state terror was reinforced by ethnic differences. A counter-example is the Latin American creation of political zones of terror encompassing left-leaning professionals and intellectuals, people who collectively have considerable political influence. In Cuba such tactics failed because the murder of university students, among others, alienated much of Batista's middle-class support. In Argentina they seemingly worked—in the sense that there was no serious revolutionary challenge to the state in the 1970s— but the military government that sanctioned state terrorism in 1983 found it necessary to give power over to civilians, who prosecuted the former regime's terrorists.

Proposition A4 also can be tested against the experience of two of the century's most intense campaigns of state terror, in Stalin's Russia and Mao's China. In both instances, terror was directed in part against people in the upper and middle echelons of party and bureaucracy. In both instances, the policy was also later discredited and many victims were rehabilitated—in Russia, much later and posthumously. Perhaps the principle should be reshaped as guidance for policymakers: Rulers who use terror against politically influencial opponents run a substantial risk of repudiation and persecution in turn.

The State and Political Ideology

The existence of a conflict situation and the presence of challengers are necessary conditions for state terrorism, but characteristics of the state and prevailing political traditions probably are more important and immediate considerations in the calculus of terror than traits of the challengers. As above, the analysis begins with propositions about state violence in general and then shifts to the specifics of state terrorism.

B1. Weak regimes are more likely to use violence in response to challenges than strong regimes. The rationale follows from the conceptualization of regime strength and weakness: Weak regimes have limited material resources and low levels of political institutionalization by contrast with strong ones. Both conditions constrain sharply the policy options of challenged elites. Coercion is relatively cheap and within the capacity of any rulers who have a standing army. Reform, cooptation, and other non-violent strategies for dealing with challenges require re-allocable resources and political institutions capable of inducing or absorbing change. Weakness in these two senses is a relative condition: A *very* weak regime will lack even the means to fight effectively against challengers, in which case it probably will be overthrown by a successor regime that is better able to establish a coercive order. But a coercive regime, thus established, frequently lacks the political means to implement peaceful change. Hence, if it faces fresh challenges, it is likely, by both circumstance and experience, to rely primarily on violent suppression. This leads to a second general proposition about the disposition of elites to resort to violence.

B2. Elites who have secured and maintained their positions by violent means are likely to choose violent responses to future challenges. Generally, the political culture of elites strongly influences their responses to challenges, just as popular political culture shapes patterns of acceptance of or resistance to elite demands.[25] The first generation of leaders who have seized power by violence are particularly likely to be habituated to its political uses, and to perceive a threat of violent displacement in the actions, even the existence, of potential challengers. They also are likely to have the means of violent suppression ready at hand, in the form of military and special police units manned by former revolutionary fighters and zealots. This is the combination of circumstances that counts more than any other for episodes of state terrorism in post-revolutionary Russia, China, Ethiopia, Iran, and elsewhere: the habituation of revolutionary leaders to violence, and the presence of continued opposition to their policies.

Many ruling elites, not just revolutionary ones, have found violence an effective antidote to challenges. There are few states, even among European democracies, that have not made at least occasional use of violence to suppress opposition. The recurring use of violence to maintain control establishes norms that justify its future use, especially if violence seemed effective in the past. In the decision-making calculus of elites, such norms and experience have the effect of making violence an early and feasible response option rather than a last-resort option. It is also highly likely that the recurrent use of state violence gets institutional expression in the formation of specially trained units, such as secret police, anti-riot battalions, and SWAT squads. Their professional ethos centers on the use of coercion to control challenges to state authority. They may recommend violent "solutions" to opposition to their superiors, or initiate them; and their existence of itself affects rulers' calculations about the feasibility of violent means of control.

B3. Successful situational uses of state terror in polarized societies are likely to lead to institutionalized terror and to the preemptive use of terror to maintain political control. This applies the general principles, above, specifically to state terrorism. Once rulers find terror to be effective in suppressing challenges, they are likely to regard it as an acceptable tactic in future conflicts. If their society is polarized by intense and persisting conflict, the elite that has successfully used state terror once is likely to establish specialized agencies of state terror, which provide the means for its continued or "institutionalized" use. Secret police have been the archetypical agencies of state terror over the last century. Typically they are established outside the command structure of the military and civilian police and answer directly and exclusively to, the top political leadership. Their special status largely insulates them from the kinds of intra-elite political constraints and bureaucratic cross-pressures that serve as checks on abuses of power even in authoritarian regimes. Once they are established, a "law of the instrument" may prevail: It is tempting for rulers to use them to preempt potential challenges. In the extreme case, rulers can use such agencies against any undesirable groups, whether or not they pose a realistic political threat.

The Nazi Shutzstaffen (SS) exemplifies the evolution of an agency of state terror. These "guard squadrons" were formed in 1925 as a disciplined, elite kernel of the political combat leagues, the Storm Troops, whose use of violence was instrumental in the Nazis' struggle for political power. After 1932 the SS quickly acquired the characteristics of a state-within-the-state: Its sections assumed responsibility for internal security, political policing, the operation of concentration camps, the promotion of racial purity, commercial enterprises (using camp labor and confiscated Jewish assets), and military planning and occupation—all outside of effective state *or* party control. Heinrich Himmler and leaders of the SS sections helped both to define and to execute the murderous policies of the Nazi state: suppressing Communist and Social Democratic opposition, eliminating potential opponents in occupied areas, forcible resettlement of "slave" people, reprisals, and implementation of the Final Solution. The SS was an instrument used "against *all designated enemies*," so flexible that Himmler thought, at war's end, that the Allies could use the SS police powers.[26]

B4. The initial decision of a challenged elite to use state terror is usually modeled on others' successful uses of state terror. The preceding discussion accounts for the perpetuation of policies of state terrorism once they are established by a particular ruling elite. We have not yet accounted sufficiently for why some elites, not previously experienced in the practice of state terrorism, first choose such tactics. The answer does not rest entirely in the characteristics and tactics of their challengers, though there no doubt are instances in which the exigencies of a particular conflict situation have led rulers to invent terrorist tactics. The proposition is that the great majority of episodes of state terrorism in the twentieth century have been patterned either on the historical use of state terrorism in the society in question, or on the concurrent use of terrorism by other rulers—especially those of ideologically similar regimes. Analogous processes are involved in the propagation of anti-regime violence. Commonplace examples of conflict traditions are the French practice of attempting revolution by urban riot and barricades and the use of the military coup as a ritualized means of replacing leaders in many Latin countries. Evidence for contemporary demonstration effects across national boundaries is provided by studies of the contagion of terrorism and coups.[27] One would expect elites vulnerable to political challenges to be particularly well aware of the coercive strategies followed by their predecessors and to be receptive to contemporary lessons from abroad.

Russia and China provide instances of traditions of state terrorism that transcend revolutionary changes in regime. Ivan the Terrible in the 1560s instituted a reign of terror in which tens of thousands, supporters of the old Boyar nobility, died. The secret police of Czarist Russia, established in 1881 and later known as the Okhrana, employed tactics of surveillance, agents provocateur, arrest, exile, and execution against revolutionaries and other political dissidents as part of an overall strategy of counter-terror.[28] One of the early acts of the Bolshevik revolutionaries in power (on December 20, 1917, six weeks after the revolution) was to establish the Extraordinary Commission to Combat Counter-Revolution (the Cheka), later known as the OGPU, a secret police that was responsible for much subsequent revolutionary terror. Stalin's purges of 1936–1938, in which at least half a million political activists were killed, were in the same tradition, though on an unprecedented scale.[29]

The Chinese tradition of state terror can be traced from the first regime established after the Revolution of 1911. Its president, Yuan Shih-k'ai, was uneasy with the practices of Western political democracy and ordered the assassination of one of his erstwhile associates who too successfully mobilized gentry support. This act, according to John King Fairbanks, "demonstrated a principle (that the ruler is above the law) and a tactic (that opponents can best be checked by eliminating their leader) which have strangled democracy in China ever since."[30] Yuan subsequently assumed dictatorial power and, through his police, instituted a reign by terror. The nationalist Kuomintang government under Chiang Kai-shek, in power in 1927, instituted a nationwide terror to eliminate or suppress their former Communist allies. By the early 1930s, state terror was institutionalized in the Special Services, which Fairbanks characterizes as "a secret anti-Communist intelligence–terrorist organization."[31] The accession of the Chinese People's Party to power in 1949 was followed by a reign of state terror aimed at urban "counter-revolutionaries" and rural landlords, at a cost of 2 to 5 million lives.[32] Given the ideology and policies of the new regime, and the post-revolutionary Soviet example, this episode of state terror is easily explained. The terrorist campaign unleashed by Mao under the name of the "Great Cultural Revolution" in 1966–1969 was in the same tradition and bears comparison with Stalin's purges. But in the post-revolutionary Chinese pattern, it was carried out largely by peoples' organizations rather than a secret police. And though its cost in disrupted lives and social disorganization was great, relatively few of its victims died.[33]

Two familiar examples of the diffusion of policies of state terror across international boundaries can be cited. One is the replication, in Eastern European Communist regimes after 1945, of secret police agencies on Stalinist lines. The second, already cited above, has been the spreading use among conservative Latin American regimes of enforcement terror by special military units or by vigilante groups operating with the tacit approval of authorities. The practice was well established in Guatemala by the mid–1960s, where more than twenty vigilante groups opposed several leftist guerrilla groups. It is not clear that Guatemala was the initial or most influential model. More decisive was the Brazilian military's successful use of enforcement terror to suppress the agitational terror of urban revolutionaries during the late 1960s. In any case, by the end of the 1970s, such policies had been used to counter actual and threatened revolutionary (and sometimes reformist) opposition in Uruguay, Paraguay, Argentina, Chile, and El Salvador. Indicative of the level of enforcement terror relative to revolutionary terror is the estimate that in Argentina between 1976 and 1979 guerrillas killed around 700 people contrasted with some 20,000 killed by the military.[34] In the Eastern European instances, the Soviet government evidently directed the establishment of secret police agencies. In Latin America, the connection is less clear-cut. The Central Intelligence Agency-linked Office of Public Safety provided technical training in methods for controlling dissidents to many Latin American police in the 1960s and may have been a conduit for transmitting knowledge of torture techniques.[35] But in the use of death squads it is more likely that military hardliners have been emulating the successful policies of their neighbors than following North American guidelines.

B5. Democratic principles and institutions inhibit political elites from using state violence in general and terror specifically. This is a generalization based on twentieth-century experience: State violence is generally less in democratic than authoritarian regimes, and state terror has seldom been used by elites within countries with a democratic political tradition.[36] Among the few anomalies are the formerly democratic Latin American countries of Argentina, Brazil, Chile, and Uruguay, which in fact illustrate rather than challenge the generalization. In each instance, state terror was used by authoritarian military-dominated regimes after the collapse or overthrow of democratic regimes.

The disposition to use state terror is most effectively constrained if elites hold democratic values *and* are checked by democratic institutions. The relationship is not coincidental or spurious. Democratic political norms emphasize compromise in conflict and participation and responsiveness in relations between rulers and ruled, traits that are inconsistent with reliance on violence as an instrument of rule or opposition. Officials in Western democracies who use or condone violence against domestic opponents risk loss of legitimacy and office as a consequence. The handful of exceptions, such as the French and American uses of state terror against Algerian nationalists and black revolutionaries, are of limited scope in contrast to the recurring, large-scale use of state terror in authoritarian societies of Eurasia and Latin America.

Social Heterogeneity and Inequality

C1. The greater the heterogeneity and stratification in a society, the greater the likelihood that a regime will use violence as a principle means of social control. Social structure conditions the uses of violence in conflict. In ethnically and religiously diverse societies, social cohesion tends to be low; hence, challenges to the regime are more common and elites are more likely to respond violently. This is not only because of the frequency and intensity of challenges, but because compliance with regime policies is not likely to be given freely. In highly stratified societies, those with gross inequalities in wealth, power, and status across classes or strata, cohesion may be considerably greater than in heterogeneous societies because of widely shared beliefs that support systems of caste or class or party dominance. But it seems almost universally true that the ruling classes in highly stratified societies are ruthless in their use of violence to suppress threats to their domination. Underlying the frequent resort of elites to violence in heterogeneous and stratified societies is probably a lack of empathic identification between elites and non-elites. Social distance, whether based on ethnic difference or on class barriers, makes it psychologically easier to dehumanize and murder opponents.[37]

The argument is a general one, not specific to state terrorism. Most of the effects of social diversity on state terrorism are a consequence of interaction with the more immediate conditions identified above. For example, the existence of ethnic heterogeneity and sharp lines of class division increase the likelihood that challengers will use guerrilla and terrorist tactics, which situationally disposes elites to use counter-terror (A3, above). And state terror is more likely to be institutionalized in societies that are polarized along ethnic or class lines (B3, above). There is one specific structural pattern, though, that seems distinctively associated with the practice of state terror.

C2. Minority elites in highly stratified societies are likely to use terror routinely as an instrument of rule. By "minority elite" I mean an elite that is drawn from an ethnic, religious, or tribal minority in a heterogeneous society. In effect, this is a special case of C1, in which the potential for internal challenges is intrinsically high and the social distance between advantaged rulers and ethnically or religiously distinct subjects is particularly great. It is almost a certainty that elites in this situation will have to resort frequently to violence to maintain their position. The advantage of terrorism, as noted above, is its relative efficiency: It is in the short run less costly to maintain control over a restive majority by a "regime of terror"[38] than by maintaining an internal state of seige. In the long run, such policies are more problematic—but then beleaguered minority elites are much more preoccupied with the short run than the long.

The plausibility of the proposition is supported by some contemporary examples. The Afrikaaner regime of South Africa satisfies precisely the pre-conditions specified. South African society is stratified along racial lines, with the Afrikaaner minority monopolizing political power and sharing economic primacy with white Anglo–Africans. Instrumental to the maintenance of Afrikaaner control over black and white opposition are policies of internal security implemented mainly by the Bureau of State Security, which was formed from the Republican Intelligence Service in 1969 and, in 1978, renamed the Department of National Security. The tactics of terror include surveillance, bannings, detention, lengthy imprisonment, torture, and execution of political activists.[39] What is distinctively terroristic about the Afrikaaner system is not that political opposition is controlled and sanctioned per se, but the fear induced by the secret and arbitrary ways in which the regime selects activists for punishment, and the unpredictable outcomes: Some political offenders are banned (for example, subject to house arrest, typically for five years), others are detained without trial for long periods, still others are tortured and die in police custody. Between 1963, when police first received power to detain without charges, and 1983, sixty detainees are known to have died in detention, their deaths almost always reported as "suicides."[40] Those who are eventually tried may be found innocent by courts that continue to respect British legal traditions, or may be given long prison terms or sentenced to death. Death remains an uncommon outcome of political opposition in South Africa, but fear of unpredictable sanctions is pervasive.

The South Africa instance can be contrasted with conditions that prevailed in Uganda under Idi Amin, where deadly and unpredictable terror was a daily occurrence from the early 1970s to 1979. The minority basis of the regime was Islamic and tribal (Amin's Kakwa tribe and, more generally, Nubians), the "stratification" it sought to impose political and predatory: The material wants of those around Amin were satisfied by confiscation. The objects of terror, as Leo Kuper notes, incuded "almost every conceivable category of victim"—ethnic, political, religious (especially Catholics), and the educated elite, as well as randomly or whimsically chosen victims.[41] The contrast with South Africa is pronounced: In South Africa, terror has been systematized and bureaucratized, is aimed specifically at political opponents of apartheid, and is relatively non-deadly. But the general strategies and objectives are similar: In each regime, violence and, the threat of violence helped maintain a minority regime in power by inducing fear in its potential opponents.

The Global Environment

A country's position in the global network of political and economic relations can either constrain the state's use of violence against its subjects or reinforce elites' decisions to use terror. The international conditions that dispose toward or against state terrorism may be too diverse and situationally specific to warrant propositions specific to terrorism, but it is possible to identify some plausible general international influences on violence by the state.

D1. Regimes facing external threats are likely to use violence against domestic opponents. There is a widely noted tendency for internal conflict to subside in countries at war or risk of war, but it is not necessarily the result of increased social cohesion in response to external threat. In heterogeneous and politically divided societies, elites facing external enemies have strong incentives to suppress internal opposition: It weakens their capacity to meet external challenges. Moreover, in states that are militarily mobilized against external enemies, the means for suppressing internal opposition are readily available. In the United States during World War I, coercive measures were used against pacifists, as well as those suspected of pro-German sympathies, and in the aftermath of war were intensified against suspected "reds." Defense against counter-revolutionary threats from outside was similarly used as a justification for terror in the Soviet Union after 1918.

D2. Regimes involved in proxy big power conflicts are likely to use the most extreme forms of violence against challengers, including state terrorism. When internal conflicts become polarized along lines of East–West conflict, external sponsors of regimes and revolutionaries are likely to encourage their clients to use unlimited means of warfare, and to provide them with the advisors and technology to do so. In the most extreme instances, exemplified by wars in South Vietnam and Afghanistan, virtually every means of warfare short of nuclear weapons has been employed by client elites against rebels and their supporters. For armed rebels, the aim is military defeat; for their supporters, the intent is to deter through terror. In Vietnam this included assassinations of village leaders suspected of Viet-Cong sympathies—an adaptation of a classic revolutionary terrorist tactic to state purposes. In Afghanistan most rebel supporters are inaccessible except in bombing strikes, but terror in the form of arrests, executions, and mass reprisals has been widely used against townspeople of suspected loyalty. In El Salvador the U.S. government does not overtly support death squad terrorism but has been prepared to tolerate it, just as it tolerates the presence in Florida of right-wing Salvadoran exiles who are a principle source of direction and funding for such terrorism.

D3. Peripheral status in the world system increases the likelihood that regimes that rule by violence can do so with impunity. With the exception of proxy big power conflicts and military suppression of leftist challenges in Latin America, the most egregious uses of violence by rulers against subjects in the last thirty years have occurred on the periphery of the world system, in places with few political or economic ties to either the First or Second Worlds. Among the examples, some of them genocidal and all of them terroristic, are Uganda and Equatorial Guinea, Ethiopia and the Central African Republic, Burundi and Rwanda, and Kampuchea. The explanation is not merely that the perpetrators were "new leaders," little exposed to Western humanism or socialism. Many such leaders have come to power in the Third World since 1960. The distinctive international circumstance is that the practitioners of state violence in most of these cases were not significantly dependent, politically or economically, on the world system. They were not deterred by the prospect of economic sanctions, either because they were largely self-sufficient or because their trade and aid partners did not care enough to use economic pressure. Nor were their elites much concerned about hearings before the U.N. Commission on Human Rights, or condemnations by the major powers, because they had little reason to fear the international political repercussions of their policies: Their peripheral status insulated them from effective political pressure.

Underlying this argument is the assumption that international linkages are or tend to be used to deter state violence and terrorism. The major class of exceptions since World War II consists of proxy big power conflicts, in which the political interests of hegemonic powers have overridden the more general interest of most of the world community in restraining domestic uses of state violence. In part this more general interest is a principled one: Humanitarian values are widely acknowledged among the global political elite, and many national elites are in one way or another accountable to publics that are opposed to gross violations of human rights. And in part the interest is practical: Severe internal violence potentially disrupts trade and threatens to spill across international boundaries. In particular, extensive violence by weak states is an invitation to intervention, which threatens regional conflict and, in principle, challenges the principle of sovereignty, the preservation of which is perhaps the key interest that the ideologically divided political elites of the world hold in common. For whatever combination of reasons, elites who practice state terrorism can usually expect external pressures and informal sanctions to modify their policies.

CONCLUSIONS

The preceding arguments about the conditions of state terrorism are formally summarized in the causal models of figures 3.1 and 3.2. The propositions have distinguished two kinds of conditions: those that generally dispose political elites to use strategies of violence in conflict situations, and those that lead specifically to the choice of terrorism. The two sets of causal conditions are complexly inter-related. They are summarized here in two separate causal models, one of state violence (figure 3.1), the other of state terrorism (figure 3.2). The first model specifies the eight conditions that directly determine state violence (keyed alphanumerically to the propositions in the text). The main linkages among them are shown, most of them hinted at in the preceding discussion.

The second model specifies seven direct causes of state terrorism plus three indirect causes of these variables (A1, B2, and C1, which are among the conditions of state violence in figure 3.1). In effect, the model of state terrorism (figure 3.1) is nested within a larger model of the causes of state violence (figure 3.2). Each could be modeled and estimated separately, if there were data.[42] Alternatively, the relationships shown could be modeled as a "funnel of causality" in which most of the determinants of state violence would figure as more remote, indirect antecedents of policies of state terror.

Some theoretical assumptions and implications of the theory(ies) need to be drawn out. We have assumed throughout that state terror is a policy that elites choose as one of many alternative strategies in conflict situations. From a decision-making perspective, the conditions in the models are of three general sorts.

1. Some of the conditions directly affect the decision-making calculus of threatened elites. These *situational* variables include the political traits of challenges (the status and strategies of challengers, A1,2,3,4) and the elites' own political resources for countering those challenges (regime strength and police apparatus, B1,3). In the rational choice perspective, these should be the most important determinants of decisions to use state violence. They also are the kinds of conditions emphasized in Tilly's

Figure 3.1. Determinants of State Violence in Conflict Situations

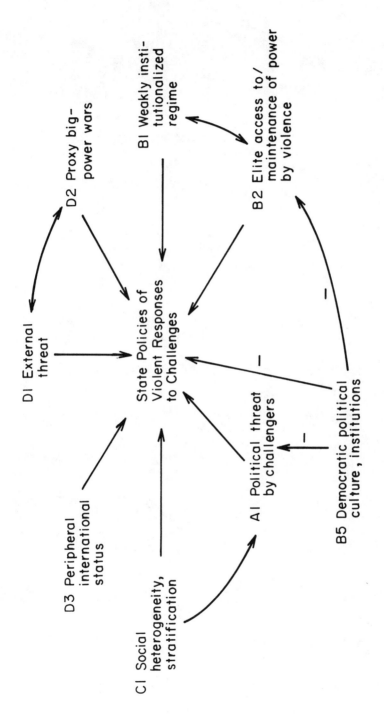

Note: All paths in figures 3.1 and 3.2 are positive unless otherwise indicated.

Figure 3.2. Determinants of State Terrorism in Conflict Situations

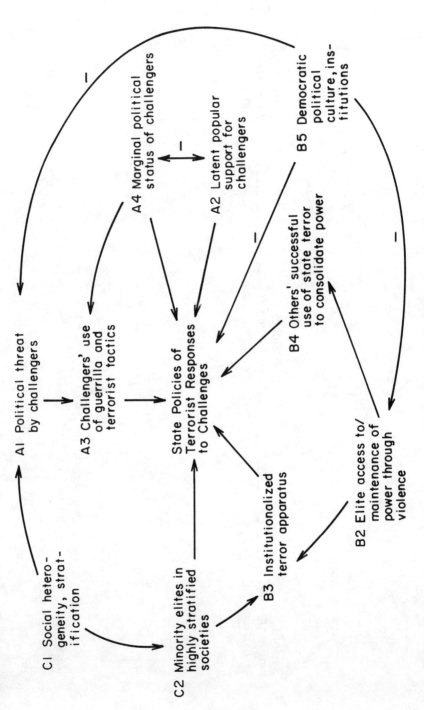

Note: The more generalized international and internal political determinants of state violence, shown in figure 3.1, interact with the direct determinants of state terror, shown here, to intensify the disposition to reliance on terrorist tactics and strategies.

resource mobilization approach to explaining why regimes repress or facilitate challengers.[43]

2. From a *structural* perspective, by contrast, the most important causal conditions should be those that define elites' relations with their opponents and determine or constrain their response options. The structural variables in our theory include the nature of social stratification and the elite's position in it (C1,2) and the state's position in the international system (D1,2,3). These are the kinds of variables whose significance for revolutionary processes and outcomes are emphasized by such theorists as Theda Skocpol and Ellen Kay Trimberger.[44]

3. Finally, the theory includes *dispositional* variables, conditions that can be expected to influence how elites regard the acceptability of strategies of violence and terrorism. Norms supporting the use of violence are shaped by elites' direct or mediated experience with violent means of power (B2,4) and are inhibited by democratic values (B5). These normative dispositions should not be forced into the procrustean bed of rational choice analysis. They are distinguished analytically here because of a conviction that there is a significant normative or evaluative component to elite decision making, one that has identifiable cultural, ideological, and experiential origins. Decisions to use violence, and terrorism, are shaped by rulers' beliefs about and experience of the acceptability of these strategies, not only by calculations about their utilities in coping with a politically threatening situation.

The two theories of state violence and terrorism can be analytically summarized and contrasted using this distinction among structural, situational, and dispositional conditions. There are eight conditions of state violence, four of which are structural traits of the international system and domestic society (D1,2,3; C1). Two of the other four are traits of the immediate political situation (A1, B1), one of which—the institutional weakness of the regime—is arguably "structural" as well. This fits well with our common-sense understanding of the politics of state violence: It seems to be used most often by the new and weak regimes of peripheral and dependent states, states whose elites have few options. There are only two dispositional variables that might offset the pressures on elites in such situations to respond violently to challenges: a commitment to democratic values (B5) and relative lack of experience with violence as an instrument of power (B2).

The resort to state terrorism, however, is more influenced by situational than structural factors. Four of the seven direct determinants of elites' decisions to use terrorism are situationally specific: the tactics of challengers (A3) and their political status and support (A2,4). Probably most important of all the immediate determinants of state terrorism is another situational factor, the availability of agencies practiced in tactics of terrorist control (B3). In contrast to these situational variables, we can identify only one structural condition, the exigencies of minority elite rule in a highly stratified society (C2), closely associated with policies of state terror. Dispositional variables, however, seem essential. Historical traditions of state terror, as in Russia and China, and the demonstration effect of successful uses of state terror elsewhere (B4), as among conservative Latin American regimes, probably encourage elites to use terror irrespective of this or other structural factors. And as is the case with state violence generally, democratic values and institutions inhibit elites from using terror (B5).

Insofar as the models are accurate, they can be used to anticipate which states, in which situations, are most likely to use violence and terrorism to counter challenges. With the exception of the properties of challenges and challengers (A1,2,3,4) and the exigencies of international conflict (D1,2), the conditions identified theoretically are readily observable and relatively slow to develop or change. It should therefore be possible to profile states' general susceptibility to using violence against domestic enemies. When conflict situations arise, through internal challenges or external threat and intervention, analysts can then make prompt, theoretically guided assessments of the situation and hence of the likelihood that elites will pursue policies of violence and terror.

Forecasting with untested models is premature, unless the forecasts are designed for the purpose of empirical testing. Three more immediate and less global kinds of research are prompted by the theoretical arguments of this chapter. One is to examine carefully, perhaps with comparative case studies, the processes by which elites become habituated to the use of terrorism as a technique of internal control, and the ways in which such policies are given institutionalized expression. This means, among other things, comparative study of the policies of post-revolutionary elites toward opposition and dissent, analysis of the structures and activities of secret police agencies, and inquiries into the connections of vigilante-style death squads to state power. A second, not necessarily less important, is to examine comparatively the means by which minority elites in stratified societies have obtained and maintained power. Such research should give substance to knowledge about two underlying structural and dispositional determinants of state violence. Third, we need to know much more about the empirical regularities between characteristics of challenges and challengers, on the one hand, and violent state responses to them, on the other. There are ample collections of coded data on violent conflicts that include information on the numbers, social bases, tactics, and other properties of the challengers and the coercive responses of authorities to their actions.[45] A number of inferences derived from propositions A1 through A4 could be tested by careful analyses of this information.

More could be said about the theoretical bases of state terrorism and the kinds of research needed to give empirical substance to conceptual analysis. It also seems feasible to put some such research to use as a means for anticipating state violence and terrorism. The first priority now is to direct serious and substantial scholarly effort to these ends. The most plausible, first empirical step is to develop systematic data on the incidence of state violence and terrorism among contempoary states and on the political circumstances in which it occurs.

NOTES

This chapter has benefited from comments by Barbara Harff and Jane-Erik Lane, as well as the editors' careful and critical reading of an earlier draft.

1. See, for example, Terry Nardin, *Violence and the State: A Critique of Empirical Theory*, Sage Professional Papers in Comparative Politics, no. 01–020 (Beverly Hills, Calif.: Sage Publications, 1971).

2. See, for example, Hans Gerth and C. Wright Mills, *From Max Weber* (Glencoe, Ill.: Free Press, 1958).

3. For conceptual discussions consistent with this definition, see Elman R. Service, *Origins of the State and Civilization: The Process of Cultural Evolution* (New York: Norton, 1975), chapter 4; and Harry Eckstein and Ted Robert Gurr, *Patterns of Authority: A Structural Basis for Political Inquiry* (New York: Wiley-Interscience, 1975), chapter 1.

4. A systematic analysis of elements in definitions of terrorism is Alex P. Schmid, *Politial Terrorism: A Research Guide to Concepts, Theories, Data Bases and Literature* (Amsterdam: North-Holland; New Brunswick, N.J.: Transaction Books, 1983), part I. Schmid concludes that there is no consensual definition but attempts to derive one.

5. Raymond D. Duvall and Michael Stohl, "Governance by Terror," in Michael Stohl, ed., *The Politics of Terrorism*, 2d ed. (New York: Marcel Dekker, 1983), p. 182. Essential elements in Schmid's definition are similar. See *Political Terrorism*, p. 111.

6. Schmid, *Political Terrorism*, p. 111, also specifies a third intent, to induce changes in "secondary *targets of demands*," by which he means terror by A against B in order to induce changes in C, with C typically being a regime that A seeks to influence. This category seems distinctive to terrorism by groups opposing those in power.

7. Herman Rauschning, *Gespraeche mit Hitler* (Vienna, 1940), p. 82, cited in Schmid, *Political Terrorism*, p. 90.

8. For summaries and analyses of these events in their political context, see Brian May, *The Indonesian Tragedy* (London: Routledge and Kegan, Paul, 1978), chapter 3; and Stephen Sloan, *A Study in Political Violence: The Indonesian Experience* (Chicago: Rand McNally, 1971), chapter 4.

9. The concept of genocide is developed by Harff elsewhere in this volume. Genocide, like state terrorism, involves life-threatening violence by an elite against some domestic group. Genocidal policies differ from state terrorism in one crucial respect, however: The intent is to *destroy* the target group by killing many (not necessarily all) of its members. See Duvall and Stohl: "Excluded from the

concept of political terrorism are actions oriented solely or primarily toward the physical harming... or elimination (e.g. assassination, genocide) of some target unit," "Governance by Terror," p. 183.

10. From articles in the Durban *Daily News* and *Natal Mercury*, and personal communications. Dr. Turner had gained notoriety for his anti-apartheid writings and activities, and for marrying and living with an Indian woman in contravention of laws prohibiting inter-racial marriage or cohabitation.

11. Stohl uses similar reasoning to identify what he calls surrogate terrorism in the international realm, in "The International Dimensions of State Terrorism," in George A. Lopez and Michael Stohl, eds., *The State as Terrorist: The Dynamics of Governmental Violence and Repression* (Westport, Conn.: Greenwood Press, 1984), pp. 43–58.

12. Speaking in Northern Ireland in 1979, as quoted in *Time*, (January 9, 1984), p. 28.

13. See Michael Walzer, *Just and Unjust Wars: A Moral Argument with Historical Illustrations* (New York: Basic Books, 1977), especially his discussion (pp. 228 ff.) of the "sliding scale" according to which the more extreme the danger, the fewer the constraints on the defenders' conduct of war (or in our case on the means chosen to defend the regime). See also Terry Nardin, *Law, Morality, and the Relations of States* (Princeton, NJ: Princeton University Press, 1983), chapter 11.

14. Nardin, *Violence and the State*, chapters 9, 10.

15. Barbara Harff, *Genocide and Human Rights: International Legal and Political Issues*, (University of Denver Monograph Series in World Affairs (Denver: University of Denver Press, 1984), especially chapter 4.

16. Duvall and Stohl, "Governance by Terror," pp. 197–198.

17. Charles Tilly, *From Mobilization to Revolution* (Reading, MA: Addison-Wesley, 1978), p. 53.

18. E. V. Walter, *Terror and Resistance: A Study of Political Violence* (New York: Oxford University Press, 1969), chapters 6, 7.

19. Not all killings by political leaders are politically purposeful. Many of the Ugandan victims of Idi Amin died to satisfy his perversions or the blood lust of his soldiers. Such killing by madmen should have a different name: genocide, or mass murder. On the Ugandan case, see Leo Kuper, *Genocide: Its Political Use in the Twentieth Century* (New Haven, Conn.: Yale University Press, 1981), pp. 167–171.

20. Based on a comparison of median values reported in Ted Robert Gurr, "Political Protest and Rebellion in the 1960s: The United States in World Perspective," in Hugh Davis Graham and Ted Robert Gurr, eds., *Violence in America: Historical and Comparative Perspectives*, 2d ed. (Beverly Hills, Calif.: Sage Publications, 1979), p. 58.

21. Ibid., p. 52.

22. A similar interpretation is Edward W. Gude, "Batista and Betancourt: Alternative Responses to Violence," in Hugh Davis Graham and Ted Robert Gurr, eds., *Violence in America: Historical and Comparative Perspectives* (Washington, D.C.: National Commission on the Causes and Prevention of Violence, 1969), chapter 20. The extent of Batista's terror is in some dispute; see Boris Goldenberg, *The Cuban Revolution and Latin America* (New York: Praeger, 1966), pp. 143–144, who suggests that the victims of terror may have numbered about 1,000

rather than the 20,000 estimated after the fact by the victorious rebels. A detailed and explicit account of rebel actions and military repression, terror, and counter-terror is Ramon L. Bonachea and Marta San Martin, *The Cuban Insurrection 1952–1959* (New Brunswick, N.J.: Transaction Books, 1974), especially chapters 8, 11.

23. On the selectivity of counter-terror measures in Algiers, see Alf Andrew Heggoy, *Insurgency and Counterinsurgency in Algeria* (Bloomington: Indiana University Press, 1972), chapter 14; on the killing of prisoners, see pp. 240–241.

24. Walter, *Terror and Resistance*, p. 6.

25. On the bases of popular attitudes about the justifiability of violence, see Ted Robert Gurr, *Why Men Rebel* (Princeton, N.J.: Princeton University Press, 1970), chapters 6, 7.

26. From Robert Lewis Koehl, *The Black Corps: The Structure and Power Struggles of the Nazi SS* (Madison: University of Wisconsin Press, 1983), quotation p. 230.

27. For a summary of research on the contagion of coups—the results of which are ambiguous—see Ekkart Zimmermann, *Political Violence, Crises and Revolutions: Theories and Research* (Cambridge, Mass.: Schenkman, 1983), pp. 269–272. On the contagion of terrorism, see Manus I. Midlarsky, Martha Crenshaw, and Fumihiko Yoshida, "Why Violence Spreads: The Contagion of International Terrorism," *International Studies Quarterly*, 24 (June 1980), pp. 262–298.

28. On the policies and domestic activities of the Czarist secret police, see Zeev Ivianski, "Provocation at the Center: A Study in the History of Counter-Terror," *Terrorism: An International Journal*, 4 (1980), pp. 53–88. On their tactics toward emigre Russian revolutionaries elsewhere in Europe, see Richard J. Johnson, "Zagranichnaia Agentura: The Tzarist Political Police in Europe," in George L. Mosse, ed., *Police Forces in History* (London: Sage Publications, 1975), pp. 17–38.

29. On Stalin's terror, see Alvin W. Gouldner, "Stalinism: A Study of Internal Colonialism," *Telos*, 34 (Winter 1977–1978), pp. 5–48; and Kuper, *Genocide*, pp. 95–99, 140–150. Aleksandr I. Solzhenitsyn, in *Gulag Archipelago*, 3 vols. (New York: Harper and Row, 1974–1978), traces Stalin's terror to its Bolshevik origins but minimizes any connection with Czarist tradition. Yet Ivianski, "Protection at the Center," p. 59, notes a striking institutional continuity: The Okhrana's extensive files on dissidents, revolutionaries, and collaborators were used by the Bolsheviks under the direction of the same official, one Zheeben, who managed the system for the Okhrana.

30. John King Fairbanks, *The United States and China*, 4th ed. (Cambridge, Mass.: Harvard University Press, 1983), p. 222.

31. Ibid., p. 252.

32. For accounts of post-revolutionary terror in China, see Maurice Meisner, *Mao's China: A History of the People's Republic* (New York: Free Press, 1977); and Jacques Guillermaz, *The Chinese Communist Party in Power, 1949–1976* (Boulder, Colo.: Westview Press, 1976).

33. Representative of academic studies of the Cultural Revolution is Byung-joon Ahn, *Chinese Politics and the Cultural Revolution: Dynamics of Policy Processes* (Seattle: University of Washington Press, 1976). Ross Terrill characterizes events and policies from Mao's perspective in *Mao, A Biography* (New York: Harper and Row, 1980), chapter 18. One of numerous journalistic accounts is Hans

Granqvist, *The Red Guard: A Report on Mao's Revolution* (New York: Praeger, 1967).

34. The Latin American material is from John W. Sloan, "Political Terrorism in Latin America," in Stohl, *Politics of Terrorism*, pp. 385–394; see also J. Kohl and J. Litt, eds., *Urban Guerrilla Warfare in Latin America* (Cambridge, MA: MIT Press, 1974).

35. On the activities and connections of the Office of Public Safety, see A. J. Langguth, *Hidden Terrors* (New York: Pantheon Books, 1978), especially chapter 4.

36. Data in Gurr, "Political Protest and Rebellion," p. 62, show that the intensity of violent conflict in First and Third World democracies during the 1960s was substantially less than in other kinds of political systems, even though the extent of conflict in democracies was greater than in autocracies.

37. See Herbert Kelman, "Violence Without Moral Restraint," *Journal of Social Issues*, 29 (1973), pp. 26–61.

38. The concept is Walter's, *Terror and Resistance*, pp. 7–8.

39. See Gordon Winter, *Inside Boss: South Africa's Secret Police* (Harmondsworth: Penguin Books, 1981).

40. On deaths in detention, see Lawyers' Committee for Civil Rights Under the Law, *Deaths in Detention and South Africa's Security Laws: Annual Report* (Washington, D.C.: Lawyer's Committee for Civil Rights Under the Law, September 1983). On torture of detainees, see Winter, *Inside Boss*, chapter 43.

41. Kuper, *Genocide*, pp. 166–167.

42. As modeled in figure 3.1, the determinants of state violence include two endogenous variables (A1 and B2) and six exogenous variables. The determinants of state terrorism in figure 3.2 include five endogenous variables and five exogenous variables. A composite model could be constructed by grafting all the linkages of figure 3.1 onto figure 3.2, with regime weakness (B1) and the three international determinants (D1,2,3) of state *violence* linked directly to state *terrorism*. This complex model (not shown here) has fifteen variables of which eight are exogenous (the most important: B1, B5, C1) and seven jointly determined (including state terrorism).

43. Tilly, *From Mobilization to Revolution*, chapter 4.

44. Theda Skocpol, *States and Social Revolutions: A Comparative Analysis of France, Russia, and China* (Cambridge, MA: Harvard University Press, 1979); and Ellen Kay Trimberger, *Revolution from Above* (New Brunswick, N.J.: Transaction Books, 1978).

45. Event "counts" are not appropriate to this purpose. More appropriate is the contextual coding of conflict events by Charles Tilly and collaborators at the University of Michigan (see Tilly, *From Mobilization to Revolution*, appendixes 1–4, on the types of data gathered); such data have been collected for France, Germany, and Italy for more than a century [see Charles Tilly, Louise Tilly, and Richard Tilly, *The Rebellious Century, 1830–1930* (Cambridge, Mass.: Harvard University Press, 1975)]. Coding of the properties of conflict events in a large cross-section of contemporary countries during the 1960s is reported in Ted Robert Gurr and Associates, *Comparative Studies of Political Conflict and Change:*

Cross National Datasets (Ann Arbor, Mich.: Inter-University Consortium for Political and Social Research, 1978). Both of these data sets include coded information on coercive responses, though not necessarily in sufficient detail to examine fully the questions posed here.

4

National Security Ideology as an Impetus to State Violence and State Terror

George A. Lopez

Governing styles that employ official violence and terror by ruling elites against segments of their own population have become all too common-place in contemporary affairs. Although it still lags behind the prevalence of the phenomenon itself, our knowledge of the frequency and diversity of circumstances associated with systematic governmental violence and terror has grown. The literature of state violence now has descriptive and explanatory dimensions, spanning theoretical and empirical social science. In postulating particular explanations for why national leaders, or their designated agents, resort to "illegal" violence and techniques of terror, this literature has steadily narrowed the frame of reference from the broad, ecological context to more detailed analysis of government strategy and elite decisions.

In an attempt to delineate a generalizable global tendency toward authoritarian rule, Richard Falk argues that the drive to centralized control has taken different institutional and decision-making forms across distinct polities. His analysis concentrates almost exclusively on the for-mer dimension. In the industrial West, Falk asserts, Trilateralism sustains the ruling elite and its structure of economic and political control. In southern developing-area capitalist systems, Brazilianization describes state rule; while Leninization constitutes the corresponding trend in the socialist developing world. For those southern states lacking a significant industrial sector, the authoritarian tendency takes the form of Praetorianization.[1]

Falk's analysis falls considerably short of generating propositions or precise indicators of the decisional criteria that will trigger a govern-ment's movement from increased centralization of economic, political, military functions to torture, disappearances, and assassination as stand-ard political practice. But he does detail the structural contours in which these actions come to be accepted as viable policy in the minds of governing elites. In some political systems, this may take the form of greater bureaucratic control of the economy. In others, it may demand the use of "emergency" powers against union leaders, university students, or political parties that resist economic development as dictated from the top downward. Still in other states, a network of secret police will be created to ensure control. Finally, in polities with a history of repression and coercive use of institutions, citizens seldom need reminders of the violent potential of the state.[2]

Within these parameters that demarcate the repressive potential of the centralized state, a number of analysts posit the decisional settings, pressures, and rules that explain government reliance on terror. Beyond the implementation of a genocide policy or the use of terror tactics in a civil war situation, George Lopez and Michael Stohl note four additional political environments in which rulers elect to use systematic state violence or terror:

1. As an extension of an oppression or repression system

2. As a method for the consolidation of power

3. As a reaction to "reformist-minded" political, social, or economic organizations and their policy demands

4. As a reaction to an insurgent challenge to the state[3]

While a quick reading might interpret these environments as points spread much too broadly on a continuum of any government's self-assessed political position, a closer examination notes that they do delineate discrete action situations facing governments. The former two indicate the selection of a strategy for increasing centralized control; the latter two, a response to challenges to government policy, and, at times government legitimacy. Thus, the resort to terror occurs as a policy choice made under particular national circumstances: either when (1) the resident ruling group engages in a drive to greater control beyond what most external observers would claim necessary for them to sustain their existing power, or when (2) the resident ruling group is faced with institutional (usually non-violent) or extra-institutional (usually violent) challenges to their power that cannot be eradicated through minimally acceptable (usually defined as legal) government force.[4]

In their attempt to develop yet a more precise calculus of the decision to employ terror, Duvall and Stohl provide further means of clarifying the dynamics of the decision by a national elite to mobilize government terror. They argue that ruling elites opt for terror when they perceive that (1) in their existing political situation, the opportunity costs of terror are low, and (2) the conditions of the wider political environment appear to permit or to encourage the use of state terror to achieve political goals.[5] Thus, the terror policy of government unfolds in circumstances far more complex than challenges to rule or desire to increase political control. Rather, such an action would appear to be a full "decision," in that it occurs as a choice within a particular setting *and* one weighed in light of other available choices and circumstances.

This sense of the purposefulness of choice on the part of elite decision makers, as set against the larger context of the existing political environment, is echoed by Ted Robert Gurr in this volume. Gurr isolates the situational, structural, and dispositional variables associated with the perception by national elites that state terror is the only viable policy response. After sketching the full dimensions of the models that link these factors, he offers a number of insightful observations regarding what scholars should and should not examine in scrutinizing how and why government elites select terror strategies. Gurr directs our attention to the "identifiable cultural, ideological, and experiential origins [of terrorism]. Decisions to use violence, and terrorism, are shaped by rulers' beliefs about and experience of the acceptability of these strategies, not only by calculations about their utilities in coping with a politically threatening situation."[6]

This chapter takes its cue directly from Gurr's assertion and integrates the research cited above in an effort to explain the decision on the part of government to employ systematic violence and state terror. I argue that the justification for and maintenance of this patterned and persistent violence by government against real and presumed adversaries rests in the discrete, identifiable, and self-reinforcing dimensions of a shared mindset of governing elites. For purposes of consistency the particular form that this chapter examines is referred to as national security ideology. Using existing discussions about and drawing examples from the implementation of national security ideology, I demonstrate how this shared mindset has served to support, if not predict, the use of terror as a preferred ruling style in a number of Latin American political systems during the last two decades.[7] The chapter proceeds with an initial analysis of national security ideology and its link to state terror. This is followed by a discussion of how each of the dimensions of the mindset— the nation, state security, and ideology—serves as a critical, but distinct, conceptual link in constructing this mindset and in generating government decisions to resort to extraordinary violence against members of its own society.

NATIONAL SECURITY IDEOLOGY: ITS SUBSTANCE AND SUPPORTERS

In the words of the Brazilian Amaral Gurgel, whom Roberto Calvo identifies as the articulator of the most widely accepted definition of the concept, national security ideology "is the guarantee given by the state to achieve or defend national goals against existing hostilities and pressures."[8] In much of South America since the 1960s, the substance of this doctrine and the governmental actions that emerged from the desire to operationalize it clearly came to be all, if not more, than Gurgel had portrayed. According to the premier U.S. analyst of these themes among Latin military leaders, Jack Child, this national security "doctrine," as he labels it, is

a perspective held by many Southern Cone military and civilian leaders under which a nation's security and survival are closely linked to modernization and development goals as defined by a small group of military and civilian technocratic leaders. It is elitist and highly centralized by nature, with a tendency to become authoritarian and anti-democratic.[9]

As I will demonstrate in the sections that follow, this national security ideology has become an amalgam of revived geo-political concepts, theories of bureaucratic centralization, axioms for economic modernization, justifications for the militarization of society, and a normative code designed to focus national attention on that elusive, but cherished, notion, the state. As such it has provided a daily operative strategy and a seemingly flawless logic of justification in which rape, torture, murder, and disappearance become accepted, and possibly necessary, actions of the state.

To explore the development of this logic of national security ideology in theory and practice begs a brief discussion of the remarkable mix of personalities and developments in the Southern Cone of Latin America since the late 1950s. Commencing with the *golpe* in Brazil in 1964, a wave of military takeovers swept South America. In the ensuing twelve years, new military regimes appeared in Argentina (1966, 1971, 1976), Bolivia (1971), Chile (1973), Ecuador (1972), Peru (1968), and Uruguay (1973). While military interdiction of civilian government was not new in most of these states (although long-standing traditions of civilian, democratic rule were coup victims in Uruguay and Chile), the officers' sense of possessing a unique mission, the depth of the desire to directly apply "new" theories of national organization and development, and their steadfastness regarding the duration of their rule were all rather unprecedented. The vision and subsequent practice of these rulers rested on the realization of national development via the application of theories of economic modernization, geo-political extension, and a national defense. As government leaders, they guided the nation boldly in these tasks, and with civilian technocratic allies they issued a call for vigilant adherence to national goals and for the control of personal political expression, and civilian politics in general.

The writings, affiliations, and actions of three particular individuals illustrate how Latin governing elites both availed themselves of the term "national security" and employed it to describe a *modus vivendi* of the new order they were about to forge.[10] In the mind of General Golbery do Couto e Silva, key adviser to Brazilian leaders of the 1960s, the national security entailed nothing short of a continental projection of power and the full activation of the economic resources this would entail.[11] To Osiris Guillermo Villegas, adviser to the Argentine government of 1966–1970, the challenge of the new society was clear: "National politics is to be understood and determined from the point of view of the National Interest and the National Security."[12] For August Pinochet Ugarte, former professor at the Chilean National War College, author of *Geopolitica*, and leader of the 1973 coup against Salvador Allende, the official ideology of the Chilean state was National Security Doctrine. In such a well-integrated scheme, he declared, national security becomes both a state objective and its guiding rationale.[13]

To demonstrate that those most noteworthy personalities who occupied the center stage of power in their respective nations held national security ideals in high esteem lends some support to the claim that this mindset played a role in organizing the new systems of state. The pervasiveness of the national security theme as a guiding concept for the management of the country, however, becomes powerfully evident upon review of the mechanisms for developing and disseminating this curious mixture of social science-derivative concepts and ideological constructs. As Philip L. Kelly notes in his discussion of General Carlos de Meira Mattos, to understand the contribution of Mattos, Couto e Silva, and those Brazilian leaders they would advise, one must recognize that these men and their ideas developed within and soon dominated *La Escuela Superior de Guerra*. From the time of its founding in 1949, this military staff school, often referred to as "the school that changed Brazil," also served as a major think tank of economic and political ideas.[14]

So too in other states, be it the more reformist-minded and economically oriented *Centro de Altos Estudios Militares* of Peru or the post-coup *Academia Superior de Seguridad Nacional* of Chile, those who came to power and established national security states over the last two decades had developed, exchanged, and refined their ideas in educational and training institutions, unencumbered by rival social theories or the more liberal assumptions of governmental goals and processes that pervaded civilian universities. They educated other officers about these doctrines and began to envision them as a solution to the particular political or economic malaise of the nation.[15] As this process further developed, and particularly after taking power, military officials would more clearly sketch the implications of national security concerns for the body politic. Occasionally, special government-sponsored publications, such as *Seguridad Nacional* in Chile, would appear to enunciate the new vision.[16]

With a wider recognition in South and then North America that this constellation of thought had become a fundamentally new conceptualization of the national agenda and had generated a new disposition toward rule on the part of the military, scholarly analysts in both halves of the hemisphere began to investigate the dimensions of this scheme. Some of these, such as Arrigada Herrera's writings, were published under sponsorship of Catholic Church groups, which were, at least at the time, reasonably free of censorship.[17] The work of Jose Comblin was one of the first to appear in English and to move beyond the detailing of the doctrine to critiques that intellectuals and the Church were raising.[18] In U.S. journals, Calvo provided full detail on Church critiques, while Stephen Gorman and Jack Child developed the critical geo-political, economic, and state security themes becoming apparent in the writings and policies of Southern Cone governments.[19] Because the work of each of these scholars informs what unfolds in the subsequent sections of this chapter, more detailed discussion of their assessments of national security ideology appropriately occurs later.

As this short discussion has indicated, national security ideology has existed as a set of action-oriented beliefs shared by South American leaders of the 1960s and 1970s as evidenced by their own writings and institutional support structures. Further, a number of scholars have thoroughly reviewed the pronouncements and theoretical expositions of these ruling elites to provide greater clarity on the contours of the ideology. But what of the relationship of national security ideology to state terror? Certainly neither the dramatic entry of the military into political affairs, nor the issuance of a new call for national pride and centralization of government provides, in and of itself, a blueprint for the irradication of thousands of individuals. And it is precisely at this point that analysis becomes more difficult and rather macro-level, when it has been attempted by the scholarly community.

Noam Chomsky and Edward Herman's widely cited study certainly discusses the connections in disposition toward terror among ruling elites and demonstrates the importance of "surrogates" in Third World states executing the ideological wars of those in the First World.[20] But other than the assertion that the local elites who serve this capacity are either coopted ideologically or simply lured by personal financial gain, there is no discerning why national leaders victimize their own people. In another often cited analysis, Michael Randle details the instrumental and structural linkages between militarism and repression.[21] Yet he is quick to back away from full-scale general claims about the particular decisions to resort to terror, preferring to note that pervasive militarism "is only one of a number of factors which influence the political, economic and social climate. What can be said is that the influence is a negative one and that it interacts with others to create or reinforce those situations in which repression occurs."[22] Similarly, discussions by Eric Garner and George Lopez that employ Randle and others as a reference point do not move us to further clarity on the decision of government elites to employ terror.[23]

The literature on terror violence cited in the introductory section, enables us to move further by employing its "findings" as guiding categories for locating a more specific decision point for the resort to terror. I summarize these categories, or conditions, for state terror as

1. The drive by the state for centralized control of political and economic processes (Falk; Lopez and Stohl)
2. The reaction by the state to reformers and challengers (Lopez and Stohl; Gurr)
3. The presence of norms and experiences to sustain terror (Gurr)
4. Low opportunity costs, high favorable supports in the political environment (Duvall and Stohl)

Using these to scrutinize national security ideology proves quite fruitful, for it reveals how the ideology provides the ruling elite with a profile of the political environment and its actors such that all four conditions associated with the onset of state terror are dramatically present. In decomposing the three distinct dimensions of this complex set of mental constructs, we see how Latin leaders of recent times have easily gravitated to terror because they have created situations, both real and imagined, in which systematic state violence of this sort has been presumed to be the only viable policy response. Although, as the discussions below will indicate, there do exist some redundancies of meaning and interpretation in the three dimensions, taken as an inter-related set of concepts, they clearly serve as the necessary and sufficient conditions for the terror choice by a government decision maker. Category 1 of the state terrorism literature appears embodied in the "national" element of national security ideology. Category 2, and under some conditions category 4, are most manifest in the concern with and interpretation of state security. In the latter two categories available from the literature, 3 and 4, we find matters exemplified most often in the ideological component of national security ideology.

The Nation

In his reflections on the nature of the state, Max Weber noted that the modern state is characterized by three particular dimensions: territoriality, legitimacy, and violence.[24] This classic analysis could have been written in the mid–1980s to describe the distinct clusters encompassing this first component of national security ideology: the development and sustenance of the nation. As these three Weberian notions have unfolded recently in Latin America, they have emerged in conjunction with an intense appeal to theoretical frameworks of the social sciences. For the territoriality dimension, geo-political theories have played a major role; for legitimacy, theories of state organization and concerns of normative political theory have been influential. The dynamic of violence has had its impetus more in indigenous factors, although it has been crucial in blending the other two concerns with the vigilance necessary to translate their implications to policy. Taken together, the three patterns of thought present a purpose and logic to the state and make imperative the centralization of control. As such, they create claims by those holding power that Louis XIV would admire: that *they*, as its rulers, embody the state. Finally, the intermingling of these ideas provides an argument for a violent response to those who challenge either this logic or its proponents. Thus, the beginning seeds of terror are sown.

Significant to the intellectual appeal of national security ideology in Latin America over the last two decades has been the extent of influence of geo-political schools of thought from both Europe and the United States. Although a full detailing of the particular theorists who have attracted the most attention is not our purpose here,[25] what is particularly curious about this contribution is that whereas discussions of geo-political theory quickly declined in importance in the areas of its origin after World War II, it not only remained, but also increased, its preeminence in Latin American military schools of thought throughout the 1950s and 1960s.[26] As the science of the relationship between geography and other areas of critical concern, geo-politics brought to national security ideology a focus on the territorial dimensions of the nation. This includes the renewed attention to borders and contested areas, a concern for exploiting national resources, an exploration of the territorial aspects of military power, and an examination of the linkage between geographic control and political control.[27]

The drive to expand, to realize previously unattainable control of resources, national areas, or political functions, took distinct forms in different states. The most striking parallels across Latin states involve the first two goals. In Brazil after 1964, the aim involved the full realization of the territorial destiny of the state, which had been analyzed as early as the 1930s by geo-political writers like Colonel Mario Travassos. Mattos, Couto e Silva, and others would amplify these ideas and translate them to a policy of expansion into the Amazon region, a continental projection of resource development for industrial growth, and a militant approach to border concerns with neighbors.[28]

Argentina, evolving its own geographic concerns under various regimes after 1966, began to develop maritime power that would both counter perceived Brazilian land expansion to its north and play a role in realizing territories under dispute, such as the Beagle Channel and the Falklands Islands.[29] In Peru, a major controversy to assert national petroleum rights and related concerns about the geographic extension of the state into lengthy territorial sea boundaries played a large role in the development of the Velasco regime. Similarly, in Chile, the Pinochet call for development of *La Patria*, the fatherland, entailed a focus on long-disputed, mineral-rich areas of the Atacama Desert and of the aforementioned Beagle Channel.[30] In the 1970s, a similar appeal to territorial and resource control was articulated by a number of Guatemalan rulers, and, as with the southern hemisphere nations, would correlate with elements of coercive national control and state terror.

The Weberian postulate of legitimacy manifests itself in the national component of the new security ideology by an appeal to organic analogies. According to its proponents, the nation, like other organisms, comprises a number of "living" systems, including territory, population, resources, and all other ingredients of the modern state. Like any organic entity, the state is only as healthy as its various systems. Health is most often defined by growth, thus tying this analogy to the territorial imperative just discussed. So, too, change and adaptation become important, with the most obvious alteration being the realization that the new state, with its new development plan or national security ideology, had become the central agent of growth and survival. As such, the heads of state compose the lifeblood of the organism, as well as its brain center, able to make necessary and intelligent decisions for the good of the state. Their ability to do so rests in both the derivation of knowledge from geo-political and economic theory and their instinctual sense as rulers to act in the interests of the state, for example, in the common good, in the health of all.

Inspired by the works of Rudolf Kjellan and other theorists of the early part of this century, Chile's Augusto Pinochet defined the nation "as an organic component, produced by a combination of a part of humanity settled on a portion of territory, both of which are united under the idea of the state. Like any existing reality, the state had a structure and a goal."[31] What has become apparent in Latin America throughout the last two decades is that the structure of the organism was the centralization of authority in the hands of those whose vision was national (as just explained) and whose goal was security (to be extrapolated below). Within this structure, rather than merely proposing options for state affairs, leaders embody the state. The state, and therefore its leaders, become reified in concepts like Pinochet's *la Patria*. Legitimacy arises less from appeal to popular participation, knowledge, and support (although mass rallies may be welcome) and more from the circular reasoning that the elements of the organism, particularly the population, nurture, for example, support politically, the entity. To fail to support the leader and the resultant system, then, is illogical in a practical sense, suicidal in an organic sense, and treason in the political sense. As contrasted with earlier forms of personalist and dictatorial ruling formats, the functions of government, patterned from the organic analogy, have become more institutionalized and regularized under national security ideology. This characteristic, known in the literature as bureaucratic–authoritarianism, further reinforces the biological image of the state and makes multi-level demands on citizens for both compliance and allegiance in ways not present in pre–1960 Latin America.[32]

This juxtaposition of geo-political and biological motifs establishes conditions for the dynamic of violence in the national component of the national security ideology. But whereas the territorial and legitimacy elements of the national component are clearly expressed in the theories and documents of the national security state, the role of violence seems conspicuously absent from both sets of material, save the "war of development" to be analyzed below. Yet, a close examination of the notions implicit in the thought patterns discussed here and of the actions taken in the name of forging the nation, in establishing the national consensus, and in ensuring national growth reveals the absolute need to resort to violence. The extensions of territory and the harnessing of resources that are in the hands of others require military ventures. The attainment of the national goals and organic growth require repression of those who might cling to alternative notions of national organization. As David Premo has argued for Guatemala, and John Sloan for Latin America more generally, elite insecurity in these processes quickly generates arbitrary violence and enforcement terror.[33] In undertaking such actions, rulers find that geo-political thought helps identify the external enemies, while the identification of the ruling elite as the personification of the state establishes the means for identifying the enemy within, namely, those who oppose the state (as embodied by its leaders).

This "national" process of consolidating vision and fusing the wills of the population, it could be argued, does not singularly predict violence of the level and type called state terror. But it does provide the major world view that authorizes, if not nesessitates, violence.[34] In light of this, the investigation then becomes: If the national component delineates the imperative for territorial growth, the identity of the rulers as the centralized state, and the impetus to violence, what other conditions translate these in a clear and direct fashion to terror violence? The answer rests in the coalescing of these national concerns with the specific dimensions of security that this imagery generates.

State Security

Every government in the modern world considers its primary obligation to be the defense of the common good, that is, the security of the state. While ruling groups of different ideological orientations and distinct historical experiences will obviously have varied definitions of the security challenge posed to their state, that the incumbent elite defends itself and, by extension, the state (most often evident in its geographic borders) from such challenges is accepted as standard behavior. If there are delineations of the security tasks of states, those concerns of greatest importance entail postulating the nature and origin of the threat, the relationship between existing security resources of the state to meet the threat and "new" efforts to be undertaken to guarantee security, and the impact of the security threat–response nexus on national life. As Barry Buzan notes in his recent treatise, security concerns always have placed a tension before governments and their populations in these areas.[35] But one particular feature of recent times has been the appeal of states to rationales of security that lie outside of the concern for the individual security of members of the social order. In fact, Buzan notes, in situations where "the state has its own purposes, then it is much more detached from, and unresponsive to, individual security needs."[36] Such has happened in the development and implementation of national security ideology and thus sets it apart from other forms of defense thinking or militarism.

As articulated and implemented by Latin American leaders during the last two decades, the security dimension of the national security ideology encompasses the perennial concerns of leaders noted above, but it has interpreted these in a manner that has accentuated this tension between state and individual security. This is because as leaders define the nature and origin of the security threat and outline the responses to it, such formulations occur within a value framework that gives priority to "national" security. This has become even more pronounced in those situations (near universal in these states) where leaders sense direct challenge to their rule. Thus, a second critical link in this mindset, which leads, almost inevitably, to the choice of the terror option by decision makers, is their assertion that national security is the ultimate institutional value and their implementation of this via a condition of internal war on challenges and challengers to regime power and program.

To fully appreciate the recent development of the security conception of Latin military elites, José Comblin argues that three fundamental assumptions must be understood. First, despite the geo-political influence on the formulators of the doctrine, the nature of the enemy against which the state must be secure is less actor and locale based and present much more in the world of ideas and social forces. That is, one central assumption of national security managers in Latin America is that Marxism (and cultural and political movements associated with it) constitutes "the incarnation of absolute evil with the will to destroy OUR nation."[37] Second, as a value, security is superior to others (for example, peace, justice, and prosperity) cherished by the nation at large because it sets the foundation from which these others will emerge. Thus, third, the only meaningful security issue is that of the survival of the state. Individual security has no meaning, either in itself or in terms of enhancing national goals and security. Under all conditions, individual security is subordinate to national security.[38]

The first assumption may be best exemplified by the speech of Augusto Pinochet delivered on the third anniversary of the anti-Allende coup, in which the general recounted the nature of the threat faced by Chile before military intervention. He wove together a number of the national and ideological themes that became closely tied to the security dimension:

Direct territorial conquest is thus replaced by the penetration of the vital centers in free countries which naively permit the access of Marxism to the control of labor unions, universities and the mass media. Even the churches, which by definition should provide the most solid protection against this avalanche, have suffered infiltration in their ranks.

The world today faces an unprecedented form of war. Communism penetrates society ideologically and at the same time, from its various centers of power, imposes upon democratic governments a line of action which favors its own advancement. The universal character of the Leninist–Marxist revolution fits in perfectly with the imperialist hegemony of the Soviet geopolitical school.

In this war, nothing can be of greater use to communism than the declaration of ideological neutrality by states which are not yet under its control.... Our country temporarily forgot these truths and experienced the bitter consequences.[39]

In an earlier section of that historic set of remarks, the Chilean leader illustrated the latter two assumptions:

Reality has laid bare the inadequacy of the concept of liberty as understood by classic liberalism and has placed us in a position of having to redefine it in its authentic significance. True liberty is not simply each individual's right to do as he pleases.... Social environment and a correct judicial order require certain restrictions on individual liberties, not only to preserve the personal freedom of others, but for the common good.... Nor are all rights of the same hierarchy. Even among natural rights, some are more fundamentally important than others. They may usually all be exercised simultaneously, but this is impossible when society becomes sick. The latter situation is precisely a symptom of political abnormality requiring an exceptional juridical regime in which the exercise of some rights is limited or can even be suspended in order to ensure the free exercise of other more important ones.[40]

While one can certainly make the case that Chile, and more so Argentina and Uruguay, were faced with pronounced economic difficulties and varying levels of political violence that was, in part, Marxist based, to suggest that this was a condition of war may seem to stretch the analogy to those outside the shared frame of reference. But today's external judgment is less the issue here than reflecting the sense of a state of war with the economic ideas of Marxism and the political violence that inevitably must (for the generals) flow from them. In recently recounting to their nation and the world at large their purpose and practices from 1976 to 1980, the Argentine military echoed these themes, which in their own case were cast against the background of growing anti-government terrorist action and political discontinuities in civilian leadership. They stated: "The nation was at war.... The nature and characteristics inherent in this form of surprising, systematic and permanent attack urged the adoption of exceptional procedures in the war being faced."[41]

Ironically, in fact, in those states where military elites assumed control amid these events, the core focus of the internal war that holds for others ascribing to the national security ideology is much obscured. The true security challenge to these leaders, as seen by a number of the theorists who informed their rule, is under-development. The state of war exists to defeat its pernicious hold on the national future. Certainly Marxism, and other economic philosophies out of tune with state-directed capitalism that will make the state secure, must be eliminated. But Marxism comprises both a symptom of the level of economic distress and a cause of political disruption in the drive to a secure modernity.

Thus, General Osiris Guillermo Villegas does not posit a tautology in asserting that "there can be no security without development, just as there can be no development without security."[42] National power, a basic ingredient of maintaining the national security, was most inadequate, in either a real or a potential sense, in the forging of Western-style economic development. For General Golbery do Couto e Silva, national security involved the maximizing of national power, which "imposes the dreadful weight of a radically destructive economy on the normal aspirations to development and welfare which are natural for all people"[43]; thus, the necessity to control individual sensibilities in economic development for security purposes.

But to view the security–economic development linkage in its fullest sense is not only to realize that power and prosperity demand that it must be an end in itself, but also to know that the nature of global competition demanded it. The war with under-development was internal, but the race for the resources and markets to achieve the victory of economic modernization was international. National leaders, as sole arbiters of foreign policy, should not be constrained by domestic forces in providing for the national security in a hostile economic world.[44] Further, with the accomplishment of full development, as evidenced by most Western, developed states, a social peace and community of harmony would result, ultimately ensuring the reality of a "nation" and reducing the need for the condition of war. Development and social harmony constitute victory in this war.[45]

With national security defined in major part as state-directed economic development and the style of the approach being a state of war, why has this situation led to state terror violence? The explanations draw us back to the three security concerns that began this section and link them to our earlier discussion of the literature of state terror. First, by defining the security issue as predominantly one of economic development and philosophy, national security ideology sets the scene for a very large number of those who disagree with either the substance of economic decisions or the style of its implementation to be labeled by the ruling elite as "enemies of the state." Under these circumstances, social science professors, union leaders, bank vice-presidents, and clergy who object to the economic policy of the state are viewed without much differentiation and are considered targets for suppression, if not outright elimination. The likelihood of their victimization increases if they have been associated with left-wing economic ideas or organizations.[46] The interpretation of the nature of the enemy may even extend to young teenagers serving as literacy workers and catechists who might be seen, even by those formulating national security ideology, as assisting in the development of the human capital necessary for economic modernization. However, the targets of (and purpose for) state terror are not always as clear as the theorists of national security ideology might predict. As Gordon Bowen has recently queried about the pattern of political murders and disappearances in Guatemala, "This oil- and mineral-rich nation desperately needs to develop its human resources through education, yet educators keep getting assassinated. Why are Guatemalans blowing their brains out? When did killing teachers become part of the defense of the Free World?"[47]

But even this analysis may be too narrow. In identifying the nature of the threat to the state and those who comprise the "enemy," we beg the issue of the character of the war to be waged. What the implementation of the security dimension of national security ideology demands is a Clausewitzian approach to the conduct of national economic and political life. In such an enterprise, the vigilance of leaders of state must be as total on the domestic front as that called for in the conduct of defense against an external aggressor. The effort, obviously total, focuses on victory, without the possibility of rest or compromise until that goal is reached. The strategy entails, as articulated by Pinochet and the Argentine military *junta* in works cited earlier, the annihilation of the enemy (under-development) and its army (those who propose alternative economic policies) and a control, as in all wars, of the political order and its liberties for the sake of the war effort. Thus, society must accept the strictures that the conditions of war impose, one of which is often terror, because the price of defeat would even be greater.[48]

Thus, the security component of national security ideology provides ruling elites with an extension of the rules of war into the national social and political order, layered with an imperative of economic development as the ultimate defense. As such, it identifies the numerous enemies for elimination, those who attempt to reform or challenge economic policy, *and* provides that they (and suspected associates) be dealt with quickly and violently. The security of the state as a higher-order value demands, and with good reason, leaders argue, that political and other rights be defined and controlled as situations of the war continue to unfold. Under these circumstances, state terror is a clearly preferred choice because it facilitates political control, economic progress, and national defense. Because the costs of failure in the effort would be so high, national leaders often have a level of support among other elites and some level of acquiescence of the larger population, which facilitate the low opportunity costs and environmental conditions noted in the state terror literature.

Ideology

To approach the ideological component of national security ideology is a dangerous undertaking. The first difficulty is assessing whether or not a discussion of the ideological dimension is itself an ideological discourse or a social science analysis (with the latter being the desideratum here). As noted by Michael Nicholson in this volume, the discussion of terror violence is sensitive, but can be, with care, dealt with in non-ideological terms. On a second level, even a solid social science discussion of the ideological dimension could claim it sufficient to note that the amalgam of national concerns and security dimensions already analyzed here coalesce to the point of providing the requisites by which most analysts consider an ideology operative. That is, these dimensions provide an identifiable pattern of abstract thought that interprets the world, is internally consistent, and calls those who hold it to particular types of actions.[49]

But our concern here is neither with the ideological "nature" of national security ideology per se nor with the self-reinforcing aspects of the doctrine, however important.[50] The key issue for this chapter, again referencing the conditions for the onset of state terror cited in the literature, is how this dimension of the set of mental constructs, as distinct from the other two, serves as an impetus to the decision to employ terror violence in the political order. Specifically, of interest here are the norms and experiences of ruling elites and their calculus that selects and then justifies the use of terror, in light of the national and security dimensions already discussed. In delineating ideology, then, I focus more on what David Rapoport in his analysis has called the "morality" of terrorism and what others argue for as the fuller sense of the term "political culture," that is, a sense of shared assumptions and actions that both explain individual behaviors and provide a picture of the wider political environment.[51] In this sense, the ideological dimension of national security ideology comprises those principles of action that guide national elites as they undertake the drive to achieve nation and security. As I will illustrate, the principles provide little criteria for understanding the use of government violence and terror as extraordinary, immoral, or optional.

This ideological dimension of national security ideology becomes manifest in two principles that repeatedly appear in the statements of those implementing national security as state policy. The first, the principle of the responsibility of the state, is closely tied to the realization of the national dimension; the second, the rules of war, is obviously crucial to the concept of security. As they unfold in the discussions of decision makers about their policy options, these two principles provide the critical conditions for what Herbert Kelman has assessed as the loss of restraints against violence. In positing the responsibility of the state, national security ideology provides the authorization for terror; in discussing the exceptional nature of the battle being a condition of war, it provides the routinization of terror that makes questioning such action relatively impossible.[52] In combination, they serve to place the use of state terror above reproach.

The responsibility of the state involves an assessment of the unique challenge facing rulers (often the military elite prior to interdiction of existing government institutions) at a particular period in time. The substance of the key elements of demonstrated challenge, the choices posed to rulers, and the unprecedented nature of both *at this time* can easily be provided by applying the criteria and categories noted above in the national and security dimensions. What the principle of the responsibility of the state adds in an essential way is the notion that *now* is the critical time and that the task is truly unprecedented. In fact, rulers faced with such extraordinary circumstances and pressures may even seek to shirk from such responsibilities, but cannot, because these are thrust upon them as the actor of last resort. Faced with such a request, the leaders accept the responsibility somewhat reluctantly, but embued with national security ideology begin to execute the call to leadership with vision and vigor.

Such sentiments have been echoed time and again by military leaders who have assumed control from civilian governments in Latin America throughout the last two decades. In postulating the rationale for armed forces action in Argentina in 1976, General Jorge Rafael Videla noted:

The country is passing through one of the most difficult periods in its history. With the country on the point of national disintegration, the intervention of the armed forces was the only possible alternative in the face of the deterioration provoked by misgovernment, corruption, and complacency.... Profoundly respectful of constitutional powers, the natural underpinning of democratic institutions, the armed forces, on repeated occasions, sent clear warnings to the government about the dangers that existed and also about the shortcomings of their senseless acts. Its voice went unheard.... In the face of this dramatic situation, the armed forces assumed control of the national government.[53]

A similar sense pervaded the posturing of the Pinochet government of its place and purpose:

It is far from agreeable for any government to assume the obligation of taking such drastic measures, especially when not personally responsible for the causes involved. But when power has been attained not through one's own will, or a personal political ambition but by a moral, historical and patriotic imperative, the exercise of authority only makes sense in the strict compliance with moral duty.[54]

What is especially curious about the Argentine situation is that in the 1983 statement released by the armed forces detailing their role in the anti-terrorist campaign that had operated since 1975, the military leaders go to great pains to note that "in that crucial historical moment, the Armed Forces were called upon by the constitutional government to fight subversion."[55] That is, the source of authorization lay outside the military. Yet, in the document itself, no mention is made of the change of agent or justification for authority after the 1976 coup. What emerges is a linear sense of responsibility to discharge the task until complete, as if changes in larger political circumstances were irrelevant.

The sanctioning of the use of terror has not developed in national security ideology by directly speaking to the issue of coercion or violence in the exercise of rule. Rather, in a very antiseptic manner, the national security elite are guaranteed the right to resort to exceptional force by the responsibility cast to them. If it were not so, proceeds the logic, then society, constitutional government, or even fate would not authorize that the reins of government be placed at their disposal for this purpose. For the Argentinian armed forces, the interpretive, if not revisionist, claim could be made that "the victory that was obtained at so high a price had the consensus of all the citizenry that understood the complex phenomenon of subversion, and stated through its leaders, the rejection of violence."[56] The complementarity of this ideological disposition with the reification of state in its rulers becomes particularly powerful in reinforcing the "right" or "authority" of rulers to employ whatever means necessary to discharge their task.

In the second principle, the operation of rules of war in the domestic arena, we find direct interaction with the security dimension discussed earlier. Certainly it would be highly unlikely to effect such a principle in the absence of security concepts that detailed a state of internal war and without the identification of who comprised the enemy. But the principle of rules of war as operationalized in national security ideology moves beyond even the boundaries of those norms and guidelines as they unfold in international legal discussions.[57] In particular, the principle posits a number of extensions of logic and interpretation of international law and of the existing situation internal to the state to weave together the sense that terror is the routine, and thus preferred, choice. It does so by extending these in arguments about the economy of force and that the unprecedented nature of the challenge to the nation was such that actions taken can be judged only as a result of experience.

In the war with under-development and the crisis of the state's future, which seems to perennially challenge the state, the national security ideology provides rulers with no alternative but engaging dissidents and challengers with the resort to force. But the use of terror as a particular form of force application is especially appealing. At one level, the economy of "kill one, frighten one thousand" operates; but so, too, does the logic also heard to justify terror bombing in conventional war or the use of the atomic bomb to conclude World War II. In the final analysis, a relative few are terrorized in order to ensure that as the battle unfolds, more and more innocents will be spared. Under a number of conditions, particularly where some domestic violence against government has unfolded (in the form of strikes, confrontations with security personnel, etc.), terror action by government may not even be considered action againt civilian innocents, but appropriate levels of force against combatants.[58]

More pronounced and clearly articulated has been the assertion that the actions of the state or their agents cannot be adequately judged because of the unprecedented nature of the era and circumstances (about which the ruling elite has been authorized to take action). The acts are thus justified because, in such extraordinary conditions, limits are unclear. Again, the report of the Argentinian armed forces provides a clear portrayal of the disposition:

The eventual deterioration of the ethical dimensions of the state and the necessity of safeguarding [*sic*] it against the risk of being ascribed to non-shared totalitarian theories as regard security, were also present in the adoption of the decisions

that materialized the frontal attack, both definitive and victorious, against subversion and terrorism. . . . The actions performed in such a way were the result
of evaluations that had to be made within the fight, with the part of passion
generated by the combat and the defense of life, in an atmosphere stained daily
by innocent blood and destruction and before a society dominated by panic. In
this almost apocalyptical framework, there were mistakes that, as it happens in
all war conflict, could sometimes surpass the limits of respect for the fundamental
human rights.[59]

Thus, the ideological dimension of the national security ideology provides the final impetus to the use of terror by national decision makers
in the manner in which it reinterprets those themes and moral principles
that might otherwise serve as appropriate restraints on continuous and
systematic harsh violence by government. While many analysts of such
terrible official action have appropriately pointed to the need for those
who call for and perpetrate such actions to "dehumanize" their targets,
the ideological dimension casts its targets in the contours of the war
situation and the authority of the state, thus failing to manifest many of
the prejudicial elements of other victimization theories.[60] In such a way,
it extends the technocratic and organic themes that distinguish the other
two dimensions and clearly rationalizes the use of terror.

CONCLUSION

This chapter has argued that the shared mindset of many Latin American military rulers of the recent era, known as national security ideology,
serves as an inter-related set of constructs that spark the resort to terror
by government. The argument has been guided by an investigation and
decomposition of the three core conditions for state terror as provided
in recent studies of this phenomenon. The results show that Latin leaders
have provided themselves with a complex and continuously reinforcing
interpretation of their nation and contemporary situation that has created, in some cases in fact and in all cases by their own assessment, each
of the requisite conditions for the occurrence of state terror as noted in
the literature of that phenomenon.

While the essence of the decision of rulers to choose terror as domestic
policy continues to be evasive, what this analysis does illustrate is that by
detailing a series of doctrines, decisions, and developments that under-
gird the ruling group that employs terror, we can come closer to understanding those necessary sufficient, and direct dimensions of rule
that precede it. In national security ideology in Latin America, we have
been able to observe just such a set of dimensions. The task of future
research will be to examine how this process in Latin America and elsewhere continues to unfold. Some beginnings can be found in the recent

work of Lester Ruiz, who examines the ideological structure of Ferdinand Marcos's rule in the Philippines and Paul Buchanan's analysis of the *Proceso* economic modernization of Argentina in the late 1970s.[61] Particularly with investigations of particular policies such as the latter, we will be able to further explain the rationale and decisions for state terror.

NOTES

1. Richard A. Falk, *A World Order Perspective on Authoritarian Regimes*, paper no. 10, World Order Models Project (New York: World Policy Institute, 1980), pp. 4–49.

2. Ibid., pp. 12–19.

3. George A. Lopez and Michael Stohl, "State Terrorism: From Robespierre to Nineteen Eighty-Four," *Chitty's Law Journal* Winter 1985/86.

4. Lopez and Stohl illustrate these with various examples (*ibid.*), as do Alexander Dallin and George A. Breslauer, *Political Terror in Communist Systems* (Stanford, Calif.: Stanford University Press, 1970).

5. Raymond D. Duvall and Michael Stohl, "Governance by Terror," in Michael Stohl, ed., *The Politics of Terrorism*, 2d ed. (New York: Marcel Dekker, 1983), especially pp. 201–212.

6. See Ted Robert Gurr, "The Political Origins of State Violence and Terror: A Theoretical Analysis," chapter 3 of this volume.

7. Although this chapter is clearly about the national security ideology in Latin America, it should be clear, as the generalizations about state terror are made using it as an illustration, that I am, by extension, interested in similar shared mindsets as they pertain to the writings and proclamations of the South African regime, the Marcos government, and the Polish regime after the imposition of martial law in December 1981. So, too, the level of externally sponsored militarization may soon create similar ideological clusters in such locales as South Korea, Ethiopia, and Honduras.

8. As quoted in Roberto Calvo, "The Church and the Doctrine of National Security," *Journal of Inter-American Studies and World Affairs* 21, no. 1 (February 1979), p. 74.

9. John Child, "Strategic Concepts of Latin America: An Update," *Inter-American Economic Affairs* (Summer 1980), p. 77.

10. There are other individual and collective portraits of the various dimensions of the national security ideology mindset. For the former, see the analysis of Philip L. Kelly, "Geopolitical Themes in the Writings of General Carlos do Meira Mattos of Brazil," *Journal of Latin American Studies* 16 (November 1984), pp. 439–461. For the latter, see "The Argentine Military Junta's Final Report on the War Against Subversion and Terrorism, 1983," *Terrorism: An International Journal* 7 (September 1984), pp. 323–339. Other helpful sources include Eric Garner, "Correlates of State Terror: Militarism, Geopolitics and National Security Ideology," *Chitty's Law Journal* (Winter 1985/86); and John F. McCamant, "Governance Without Blood: Social Science's Antiseptic View of Rule; or, The Neglect of Political Repression," in Michael Stohl and George A. Lopez, eds.,

The State As Terrorist: The Dynamics of Governmental Violence and Repression (West-port, Conn.: Greenwood Press, 1984), especially pp. 18–22.

11. General Golbery do Couto e Silva, *Geopolítica do Brasil* (Rio de Janeiro: Jose Olympio, 1967), especially pp. 165–170.

12. Osiris Guillermo Villegas, *Politicas y estrategias para ed desarrollo y la seguridad nacional* (Buenos Aires: Pleamar, 1969), p. 34.

13. Calvo, "The Church and the Doctrine of National Security," pp. 74–76.

14. Kelly, "Geopolitical Themes," pp. 442–444.

15. It is naive, of course, to suggest that debate and discussion in these schools dealt only with the conceptual dimensions of national political and economic development. For the linkage between these lines of thought, particularly as reinforced by Western liberalism and anti-communism, see Noam Chomsky and Edward S. Herman, *The Washington Connection and Third World Facism* (Boston: South End Press, 1979), especially, pp. 42–104. For the linkage between world-views and military and police technology, see Michael Klare and Cynthia Arnson, *Supplying Repression* (Washington: The Institute for Policy Studies, 1981); Arthur John Langguth, *Hidden Terrors* (New York: Pantheon, 1978); and M. Hoefnagels, ed., *Repression and Repressive Violence* (Amsterdam: Swets and Zeitlinger, 1977).

16. For a discussion of some of these publications, see Jose Comblin, "Violating the Human: Latin America and the National Security State," in Patricia Mische, ed., *Securing the Human: The Journey Toward World Law and Justice* Whole Earth Paper no. 14 (East Orange, N.J.: Global Education Associates, 1980), pp. 10–27.

17. Genaro Arrigada Herrera, "National Security Doctrine in Latin America," trans. Howard Richards, *Peace and Change: A Journal of Peace Research* 6 (Winter 1980), pp. 49–60. Arrigada's writing and that of others flourished in the Jesuit sponsored Chilean journal *Mensaje*.

18. Jose Comblin, *The Church and the National Security State* (Maryknoll, New York: Orbis Books, 1979).

19. Stephen M. Gorman, "Present Threats to Peace in South America: The Territorial Dimensions of Conflict," *Inter-American Economic Affairs* (Summer 1979), pp. 54ff; John Child, "Geopolitical Thinking in Latin America," *Latin American Research Review* 14 (Summer 1979), pp. 89–111.

20. Chomsky and Herman, *The Washington Connection*.

21. Michael Randle, "Militarism and Repression," *Alternatives* 7 (Summer 1981), pp. 67–82.

22. Ibid., p. 67.

23. Garner, "Correlates of State Terror"; and George A. Lopez, "A Scheme for the Analysis of the State as Terrorist," in Stohl and Lopez, eds., *The State as Terrorist*, pp. 59–82.

24. See Max Weber, *Theory of Social and Economic Organization* (Glencoe, Ill.: Free Press, 1964).

25. For a discussion of these theorists, see Ladis K. D. Kristof, "The Origins and Evolution of Geopolitics," *Journal of Conflict Resolution* 4 (March 1960), pp. 15–51; and James E. Dougherty and Robert L. Pfalzgraff, Jr., *Contending Theories of International Relations* (New York: Harper and Row, 1981), pp. 54–83.

26. I make this claim somewhat hesitantly, conscious of the new wave of discussion of geopolitics in a number of academic and policy-making circles.

Most contemporary analysts in this mode consider the rejuvenation to have begun with Colin A Gray, *The Geopolitics of the Nuclear Era: Heartland, Rimlands, and the Technological Revolution* (New York: Crane & Russak, 1977).

27. A thorough discussion of the bridge between European theorists and national security managers in Latin America is provided in Jose Comblin, *The Church and the National Security State*, pp. 64–78.

28. Kelly, "Geopolitical Themes," pp. 439–446.

29. Child, "Geopolitical Thinking," pp. 91–98.

30. Ibid.; Gorman, "Present Threats to Peace."

31. As quoted in Calvo, "The Church and the Doctrine of National Security," p. 75.

32. Most noteworthy among these recent analyses are Guillermo O'Donnell, *Modernization and Bureaucratic-Authoritarianism* (Berkeley: University of California Press, 1973); David Collier, ed., *The New Authoritarianism in Latin America* (Princeton: Princeton University Press, 1979); John Malloy, ed., *Authoritarianism and Corporatism in Latin America* (Pittsburgh: University of Pittsburgh Press, 1977) and Howard J. Wiarda, *Corporatism and National Development in Latin America* (Boulder, Colo.: Westview Press, 1981).

33. David L. Premo, "Political Assassination in Guatemala: A Case of Institutionalized Terror," *Journal of Inter-American Studies and World Affairs* 23 (November 1981), and John W. Sloan, "State Repression and Enforcement Terror in Latin America," in Stohl and Lopez, eds., *The State as Terrorist*, pp. 83–98.

34. On the phenomenon of authorization of acts of terror violence, see Herbert C. Kelman, "Violence Without Moral Restraints: Reflections on the Dehumanization of Victims and Victimizers," *Journal of Social Issues* 29 (December 1973), pp. 38–46.

35. Barry Buzan, *People, States and Fear* (Chapel Hill: University of North Carolina Press, 1983), especially pp. 19–24.

36. Ibid., p. 22.

37. Comblin, "Violating the Human," p. 20.

38. Ibid.

39. Speech by Augusto Pinochet Ugarte on the second anniversary of the Chilean coup. As quoted from Brian Loveman and Thomas M. Davies, eds., *The Politics of Antipolitics* (Lincoln, Nebraska: University of Nebraska Press, 1978), pp. 204–205.

40. Ibid., pp. 204–206.

41. "The Argentine Military Junta's Final Report on the War Against Subversion and Terrorism, April 1983," *Terrorism: An International Journal* 7 (September 1984), pp. 325 and 329.

42. As quoted in Calvo, "The Church and the Doctrine of National Security," p. 78.

43. As quoted in Comblin, *The Church and the National Security State*, p. 73.

44. Kelly, "Geopolitical Themes," pp. 446–461.

45. Comblin, *The Church and the National Security State*, p. 73.

46. For a thorough treatment of the nature and scope of repression and state terror victims in Latin America, see Penny Lernoux, *Cry of the People* (Maryknoll, New York: Orbis, 1979), and Ernest A. Duff and John F. McCamant, *Violence and Repression in Latin America* (New York: The Free Press, 1976).

47. Gordon L. Bowen, "Guatemala: A New Form of Totalitarianism," *Commonwealth* 140 (February 10, 1984), p. 76.

48. This logic is reflected in Herrera, "National Security Doctrine," pp. 55–57; and Comblin, "Violating the Human." Some might consider this analysis unfair to Clausewitz, who devoted his attention to external, not internal, war.

49. For the most standard definition of ideology as functioning along these lines, see Roy C. Macridis, *Contemporary Political Ideologies* (New York: Winthrop, 1980), p. 4.

50. See, for example, Comblin's *The Church and the National Security State*, pp. 70–78; and Calvo, "The Church and the Doctrine of National Security," pp. 76–77.

51. David C. Rapoport, "Introduction to Part II," in David C. Rapoport and Yonah Alexander, eds., *The Morality of Terrorism* (New York: Pergamon, 1982), pp. 127–132.

52. Kelman, "Violence Without Moral Restraints," pp. 38–44.

53. General Jorge Videla, "A Time for Fundamental Reorganization of the Nation," in Loveman and Davies, eds., *The Politics of Antipolitics*, pp. 178–179.

54. Pinochet, "A Speech," in Loveman and Davies, eds., *The Politics of Antipolitics*, p. 203.

55. "The Argentine Military," p. 331.

56. Ibid., p. 337.

57. See Herrera, "National Security Doctrine."

58. This is one of the major themes that permeates the document, "The Argentine Military Junta's Report."

59. Ibid., p. 332.

60. The most comprehensive discussion of the forging of systematic dehumanization theories is contained in Leo Kuper, *Genocide: Its Political Uses in the Twentieth Century* (New Haven, Conn.: Yale University Press, 1981), pp. 84–100.

61. See Lester Edwin J. Ruiz, "Constitutional Authoritarianism as State Terrorism: The Case of the Philippines," and Paul G. Buchanan, "State Terror as a Complement of Economic Policy: The Argentine 'Proceso', 1976–1981," in George A. Lopez and Michael Stohl, eds., *Development, Dependance and State Repression* (Westport, Conn.: Greenwood Press, 1986).

5

State Terrorism and Repression in the Third World: Parameters and Prospects

Miles Wolpin

In an era characterized by world economic crisis, accelerated global militarization catalyzed in part by superpower rivalry, and the existence of 50,000 or more nuclear warheads, it is difficult to discover grounds for optimism. Further, U.N. Human Rights declarations and the Carter Administration's halting commitment to promote respect for political human rights are not widely regarded as having radically altered a situation where numerous governments routinely execute, torture, or otherwise brutalize their critics and opponents.[1] Indeed, in a recent work, Edward Herman cites casualty data that imply that "state terrorism" alone has accounted for what appears to be several million deaths over the last two decades.[2] That this may not be an exaggeration is suggested by a more recent study by Amos Wako, a Kenyan lawyer. According to Iain Guest, "At least two million people have been summarily executed around the world in the last 15 years for their opposition to governments, according to a new report released . . . for . . . the UN Human Rights Commission." Although based on anonymous sources, "most of the information is known to have come from authoritative human rights pressure groups, such as Amnesty International and the Geneva-based International Commission of Jurists."[3]

Thus, it would seem that the following prophesy by Seymour Lipset at the close of the 1950s has come to fruition: "Given the existence of poverty-stricken masses, low levels of education, an elongated class structure, and the 'premature' triumph of the democratic Left, the prognosis for the perpetuation of political democracy in Asia and Africa is bleak."[4] If one adds to this the widely acknowledged growing socio-economic gap between North and South,[5] and the rising proportion of repressive military-dominant systems—13 percent in the 1960s to nearly 50 percent in the early 1980s—the outlook cannot be depicted as auspicious.[6] In light of the foregoing, we should give serious attention to a brilliant if highly pessimistic analysis by William Eckhardt who hypothesizes that "savagery" and "atrocities" are highly correlated with the very advance of "civilization" itself! "So far as Western Civilization was a latecomer on the civilized scene of history, we might expect it to be more atrocious than its predecessors. If this is our expectation, we shall not be disappointed."[7] Arguing that "relatively atrocious behaviors were a function of historical development rather than humana nature," Eckhardt concludes by identifying aspects of our socio-political order ("civilization") that must be modified if a holocaust is to be avoided. These include ascriptive beliefs in group superiority and external esteem needs that generate psycho-social conformity.[8] One can facilely dismiss such exhortations as utopian or even in contradiction with his rather deterministic thesis. On the other hand, our self-awareness or consciousness of this historic trend in a thermonuclear era may provide sufficient motivation to alter both the quality and the denouement of our own "civilization."

That change is indeed possible can be seen in the North when one considers not only the paucity of inter-state warfare among twentieth-century parliamentary democracies, but also the limited yet real contemporary attainments of civil rights activists, environmentalists, and feminists in the United States and the peace movements' resurgence on both sides of the Atlantic. Moreover, expansion of world food production has outstripped population growth, and we have seen a dramatic decline of famine mortalities in recent years. Beyond this there is some indication that political repression may actually have diminished rather than intensified during the late 1970s. In table 5.1, Raymond Gastil's trend data for about 150 countries are presented.[9] Even if we exclude 1973, respect for "civil liberties" and "political rights" does not appear to have deteriorated since 1977. Of course, the table obscures the fact that approximately half of the non-respessive or "free" systems are in the North, and that more than three-quarters of those in the South did suffer various degrees of repression. Yet what must be emphasized is that the proportions have remained relatively stable since the early 1970s, suggesting among other things the general ineffectiveness of Carter's human rights campaigns. Regardless of whether one accepts all of Gastil's criteria, the situation at the *global* level does not seem to have worsened appreciably.[10]

If, however, we restrict consideration to the situation in the 105 *low-income* countries that will be analyzed in this study, the 1973–1980 trend is in the direction, albeit weakly, of greater repressiveness. Again utilizing Gastil's criteria,[11] we find that while 10.5 percent of the free in 1973 were unfree in 1980, only 7 percent of the unfree had become free during that period. Similarly, although 26.3 percent of the free became

Table 5.1.
Ten-Year Record of the Survey

Survey Date	Free		Partly Free		Not Free		World Population
Jan. '73	1,029	(32.00%)	720	(21.00%)	1,583	(47.00%)	3,334
Jan. '74	1,351	(36.00%)	812	(22.00%)	1,618	(42.00%)	3,784
Jan. '75	1,366	(35.00%)	899	(23.00%)	1,602	(42.00%)	3,867
Jan. '76	803.6	(19.80%)	1,435.8	(35.30%)	1,823.4	(44.90%)	4,062.9
Jan. '77	789.9	(19.60%)	1,464	(36.40%)	1,765.9	(43.90%)	4,019.8
Jan. '78	1,454.5	(35.70%)	874.3	(21.40%)	1,753.9	(42.90%)	4,082.7
Jan. '79	1,483.2	(35.10%)	1,042.7	(24.70%)	1,700.9	(40.20%)	4,226.8
Jan. '80	1,601.3	(37.00%)	921.2	(21.30%)	1,803.6	(41.70%)	4,326.1
Jan. '81	1,613.0	(35.90%)	970.9	(21.60%)	1,911.9	(42.40%)	4,495.8
Jan. '82	1,613.9	(35.86%)	916.5	(20.14%)	2,002.7	(44.00%)	4,551.1

Source: Gastil (1982:4).
Population in millions.

partly free, only 24.5 percent of the unfree had become partly free. Relative stability, however, is reflected by the fact that 63 percent of the free countries in 1973 remained in that category for 1980, and a similar pattern held for 67.9 percent of the unfree countries.[12]

Somewhat greater precision, however, may be derived from Wolpin's classification of 102 developing countries on the basis of patterned (as opposed to exceptional) "state violence" including torture, disappearances, executions, and penal brutality against government opponents.[13] In table 5.2 we see that the proportion engaging in such practices declined from roughly two-thirds in the 1970–1975 period to about 55 percent during the 1976–1979 years. Even this probably exaggerates their incidence since the table omits countries with fewer than 300,000 persons. In any case, my more recent assessment in table 5.3 indicates that for 1980, the percentage had fallen to 37.[14] Although the 105 nations included in this analysis differ slightly, the trend was marked and underscores my conviction that, at least in this respect, some beneficial change had occurred during the "detente" era.

The primary objective of this study, however, is neither to "measure" such secular change nor to depict in detail the mechanisms of global brutality in the early 1980s. Institutional repression or more extreme violent forms are widespread, characterizing fully 91 of the 105 countries listed in table 5.3. And the situation is more grievous when we consider current trends and the number of persons affected. Thus, the 1979 population of the countries in table 5.3's "violent" category was 1.6 billion compared with slightly under 1.5 billion in the "institutional" group, while only 123 million enjoyed "minimal" repression. In short, an absolute majority of the population in the developing countries survived under regimes characterized by torture, execution, disappearances, and brutal prison treatment of those suspected of opposing the government. At the same time, close to 900 million lived under military-dominant regimes.

Since 1979, the Third World has become the vortex of intensified East–West intervention associated with what Fred Halliday calls the "Second Cold War."[15] This in conjunction with deepening mass austerity in the South due to economic stagnation,[16] high interest rates, and heavy external debt burdens for many developing countries induced me to examine a longer and more recent time frame, to wit, 1980–1984.

An indication that the situation had markedly deteriorated by 1982 is Ruth Leger Sivard's dramatic finding that

among the 114 developing countries covered in this publication, 83 countries— three out of four—are reported to have used violence against the public in the form of torture, brutality, "disappearances," and summary executions; in 48

Table 5.2.
State Violence: Torture, Executions, Disappearances, and Penal Brutality
(1970–1979)

1970 – 1975		1976 – 1979	
Yes	No	Yes	No
Albania	Algeria	Angola	Algeria
Argentina	Angola	Argentina	Benin
Bangladesh	Benin	Bangladesh	Bolivia
Bolivia	Botswana	Brazil	Botswana
Brazil	Burma	Central Africa	Burma
Bulgaria	Central Africa	Chad	Burundi
Burundi	China	Chile	Cameroon
Cameroon	Congo	China	Costa Rica
Chad	Costa Rica	Columbia	Cuba
Chile	Gabon	Congo	Dominican Rep.
Colombia	Guinea	Cyprus	Ecuador
Cuba	Guyana	El Salvador	Egypt
Cyprus	Ivory Coast	Ethiopia	Fiji
Dominican Rep.	Jamaica	Greece	Gabon
Ecuador	Kenya	Guatemala	Gambia
Egypt	Laos	Guinea	Ghana
El Salvador	Lesotho	Haiti	Guyana
Ethiopia	Madagascar	India	Honduras
Ghana	Malawi	Indonesia	Iraq
Greece	Malaysia	Iran	Ivory Coast
Guatemala	Mali	Jordan	Jamaica
Haiti	Mozambique	Malaysia	Kampuchea
Honduras	Nepal	Mexico	Kenya
India	Romania	Mozambique	Laos
Indonesia	Somalia	Nicaragua	Lebanon
Iran	Tanzania	Pakistan	Lesotho
Iraq	Thailand	Paraguay	Liberia
Jordan	Yugoslavia	Peru	Madagascar
Kampuchea	Zaire	Philippines	Malawi
Mauritania		Senegal	Mali
Mexico		Sierra Leone	Mauritania
Morocco		Singapore	Mauritius
Nicaragua		Somalia	Morocco
Niger		South Africa	Nepal
Nigeria		South Korea	Niger
Pakistan		South Yemen	Nigeria
Panama		Sudan	North Korea
Paraguay		Syria	Panama
Peru		Taiwan	Rwanda
Philippines		Tanzania	Sri Lanka
Sierra Leone		Thailand	Trinidad
South Africa		Togo	Vietnam
South Korea		Tunisia	

Table 5.2. (continued)

1970 - 1975		1976 - 1979	
Yes	No	Yes	No
South Yemen		Turkey	
Sri Lanka		Uganda	
Sudan		Upper Volta	
Syria		Uruguay	
Taiwan		Venezuela	
Togo		Yemen	
Tunisia		Zaire	
Turkey		Zambia	
Uganda		Zimbabwe	
Uruguay			
Venezuela			
Vietnam			
Yemen			
Zambia			
Zimbabwe			

Source: Wolpin (1983: Appendix F). Based upon Amnesty International (1975, 1976, 1979); U.S. Dept. of State (1979).

countries there appears to be frequent resort to these forms of violence; in an additional 35, the practice occurs but less frequently.[17]

In table 5.4, we see a reversion to the early 1970s' pattern with almost two-thirds of the countries routinely practicing violent repression. Their total population was in excess of 3.2 billion persons compared with only 282 million living under thirty-seven non-brutal regimes. It is also evident that the latter tend to be much smaller countries with an average population of 7.6 million in contrast to 47.4 million for the former.

My overriding concern here is to identify as precisely as possible other societal attributes or characteristics that are associated with greater or lesser repressive *severity*. Closely related to this is a desire to pinpoint

Table 5.3.
Repression, Military Dominance, and Development Orientation (1980)

Violent		Institutional			Minimal	
Civilian	Military	Civilian	Civilian	Military	Civilian	Military
Afghanistan (SC)*	Argentina (OD)	Albania (SS)	S. Yemen (SS)	Algeria (SC)	Botswana (OD)	Nigeria (OD)
Angola (SC)	Bangladesh (OD)	Cameroon (OD)	Sri Lanka (OD)	Benin (SC)	Cen. Afr. R. (OD)	Panama (OD)
Chad (OD)	Bolivia (OD)	China (SS)	Swaziland (OD)	Burma (SC)	Costa Rica (OD)	Portugal (OD)
Guinea (SC)	Brazil (OD)	Cuba (SS)	Tanzania (SC)	Burundi (SC)	Cyprus (OD)	
Haiti (OD)	Chile (OD)	Ecuador (OD)	Tunisia (OD)	Congo (SC)	Dominican R. (OD)	
India (OD)	Colombia (OD)	Gabon (OD)	Venezuela (OD)	Egypt (OD)	Fiji (OD)	
Iran (SC)	El Salvador (OD)	Gambia (OD)	Vietnam (SS)	Ghana (OD)	Jamaica (OD)	
Bahrain (OD)	Ethiopia (SC)	Guyana (SC)	Yugoslavia (SC)	Madagascar (SC)	Malta (OD)	
Saudi Arabia (OD)	Guatemala (OD)	Israel (OD)	Zambia (SC)	Niger (OD)	Mauritius (OD)	
S. Africa (OD)	Honduras (OD)	Ivory Coast (OD)	Zimbabwe (OD)	N. Yemen (SC)	Senegal (OD)	
Mexico (OD)	Indonesia (OD)	Jordan (OD)		Peru (OD)	Trinid.-Tobago (OD)	
Philippines (OD)	Iraq (SC)	Kampuchea (SS)		Rwanda (OD)		
Syria (SC)	Liberia (OD)	Kenya (OD)		Taiwan (OD)		
	Libya (SC)	Laos (SS)		Togo (OD)		
	Mali (SC)	Lebanon (OD)		Upper Volta (OD)		
	Mauretania (SC)	Lesotho (OD)				
	Pakistan (OD)	Malawi (OD)				
	Paraguay (OD)	Malaysia (OD)				
	Somalia (SC)	Mongolia (SS)				
	S. Korea (OD)	Morocco (OD)				
	Sudan (OD)	Mozambique (SC)				
	Thailand (OD)	Nepal (OD)				
	Turkey (OD)	Nicaragua (SC)				
	Uganda (OD)	N. Korea (SS)				
	Uruguay (OD)	Oman (OD)				
	Zaire (OD)	Sierra Leone (OD)				
		Singapore (OD)				

Sources: Amnesty International (1981, 1982); U.S. Dept. of State (1981); Gastil (1981:319–422). OD, SC, SS in parentheses refer to development orientations as determined by Wolpin's criteria (1983). OD = open door; SC = state capitalist; SS = state socialist.

Table 5.4.
Violent Repression (1980–1984)

	Frequent or Occasional State Violence			Exceptional or Non-Existent State Violence	
Country	Population (Millions)	Country	Population (Millions)	Country	Population (Millions)
Afghanistan	15.3	Libya	3.1	Algeria	20.1
Albania	2.8	Malaysia	14.7	Benin	3.7
Angola	7.4	Mauretania	7.2	Botswana	1.0
Argentina	29.2	Mexico	71.2	Burundi	4.4
Bahrain	.4	Morocco	22.2	Cameroon	9.0
Bangladesh	93.6	Mozambique	12.7	Central Afr. R.	2.4
Bolivia	5.7	Nicaragua	2.7	Costa Rica	2.6
Brazil	128.3	Pakistan	92.2	Cyprus	.7
Burma	36.2	Paraguay	3.4	Dominican Rep.	6.1
Chad	4.8	Peru	18.6	Ecuador	8.5
Chile	11.3	Philippines	51.9	Fiji	.7
China	1,044.8	Rwanda	5.5	Gambia	.6
Colombia	27.1	Saudi Arabia	9.3	Ivory Coast	8.6
Congo	1.6	Somalia	6.1	Jamaica	2.3
Cuba	9.8	South Africa	30.2	Jordan	3.3
Egypt	44.6	S. Korea	40.8	Lesotho	1.4
El Salvador	4.6	S. Yemen	2.0	Madagascar	9.1
Ethiopia	30.6	Sri Lanka	15.4	Malawi	6.4
Gabon	.9	Sudan	20.0	Mali	7.2

Ghana	12.9	Syria	9.4	Malta	.4
Guatemala	7.5	Taiwan	18.5	Mauritius	1.0
Guyana	.8	Thailand	49.7	Mongolia	1.7
Haiti	5.6	Togo	2.7	Nepal	15.8
Honduras	4.1	Tunisia	6.8	Niger	5.9
India	715.1	Turkey	48.1	Nigeria	82.4
Indonesia	157.6	Uganda	13.4	N. Korea	18.8
Iran	41.2	Uruguay	2.9	N. Yemen	5.6
Iraq	14.0	Venezuela	17.4	Oman	.9
Israel	4.0	Vietnam	55.8	Panama	2.0
Kampuchea	5.9	Yugoslavia	22.7	Portugal	9.8
Kenya	17.9	Zaire	30.4	Senegal	6.1
Laos	3.6	Zambia	6.2	Singapore	2.3
Lebanon	2.6	Zimbabwe	8.1	Sierra Leone	3.6
Liberia	2.0			Swaziland	.6
				Tanzania	19.9
				Trinidad	1.2
				Upper Volta	6.4
Total (N = 68) 3,220.4				Total (N = 37) 282.5	

Sources: Amnesty International (1983); U.S. Dept. of Commerce (1983); Thompson (1982); World Bank (1983); *New York Times* (1984); Sivard (1983).

Period subject to classification terminates March 30, 1984. Population data or estimates are for 1980, though in some cases adjoining years were used. Refers to unexceptional state resort to one or more of the following during part or all of the period: execution, torture, disappearances, brutal treatment of dissidents, or extremely harsh prison conditions.

distinctions, if any, between countries practicing brutality and countries where this is exceptional or virtually non-existent. Finally, some causal inferences will be made where appropriate.

METHODOLOGICAL APPROACH

In succeeding sections of this analysis, such societal characteristics as educational level, religious dominance and pluralism, economic development, political mobilization, social equality, development strategy, military aid and rule, along with a number of others will be treated as hypothesized correlates of repressive *severity*. Most of these relationships are postulated in the literature dealing with "democratic" aspects of political development and systematic stability by Lipset, Pye, Weber, Miliband, Paner, Huntington, Gurr, Moore, Klare, Schoultz, and Herman. Rather than summarize them here, when germane to the particular socio-cultural variables, references to or quotations from these and other scholars will be incorporated as the analysis progresses. In a number of instances, however, my own prior work was the catalyst for hypothesizing specific relationships.

The country set used in this analysis appears in table 5.3. It differs slightly from those used for the study upon which table 5.2 and several subsequent comparisons are based.[18] Because my criteria for inclusion here are 1970 population in excess of 300,000 and per capita gross national product (GNP) below $3,000, table 5.3's universe of countries differs from table 5.2's, which employed slightly different criteria. Hence, Bulgaria, Greece, and Romania are omitted, while the following have been added: Bahrain, Israel, Libya, Malta, Saudi Arabia, and Swaziland. Thus, 105 nations are analyzed in this study in contrast to the 102 included in the earlier work cited above.

The basic classification matrix employed here is a *composite* one. Rather than rely exclusively upon my own assessment, which appears in table 5.3, I compared these repressiveness rankings with Sivard's,[19] which appear in table 5.5. Because all are based upon judgment and vulnerable to error, convergence or "inter-subjective agreement" is always preferable. Furthermore, her criteria for the "highly repressive" emphasize "torture and brutality," as I do for the "violent" category. Where we differed in our classifications, I used Gastil's[20] assessment in table 5.6 to reconcile the disagreement,[21] this even though his rankings eschew special emphasis upon regime brutality or violence—what Herman refers to as "state terror."[22] Further, as mentioned in note 3, Gastil's criteria include such liberties as occupational freedom, a euphemism for capitalist endeavors. Thus, in table 5.7, I have constructed a "composite index" that is employed in the remainder of this analysis. Statistically, it correlates strongly with my rankings in table 5.3 (.92), Sivard's in table

Table 5.5.
Sivard's Military Control and Repression in the Third World (1980)

Highly Repressive		Repressive		None or Limited	
Civilian	Military Dominated	Civilian	Military Dominated	Civilian	Military Dominated
Albania (–)*	Afghanistan (3)* Taiwan (–)*	Bahrain (–)	Algeria (1)*	Angola (–)*	Nigeria (1)*
Colombia (–)	Argentina (4) Thailand (3)	Cameroon (–)	Benin (4)	Botswana (–)	Panama (2)
Guinea (–)	Bangladesh (4) Turkey (2)	China (–)	Burma (1)	Costa Rica (–)	Rwanda (1)
India (–)	Bolivia (8) Uganda (3)	Cuba (–)	Burundi (2)	Cyprus (1)	
Iran (1)	Brazil (1) Uruguay (1)	Dom. Rep. (1)	Cent. Afr. Rep. (3)	Ecuador (3)	
Malawi (–)	Chile (1) Zaire (1)	Egypt (–)	Congo (1)	Fiji (–)	
Mexico (–)	El Salvador (2)	Gambia (–)	Ghana (5)	Malta (–)	
Morocco (–)	Ethiopia (2)	Guyana (–)	Jordan (–)	Mauritius (–)	
Peru (4)	Guatemala (2)	Ivory Coast (–)	Kampuchea (1)	Mongolia (–)	
S. Africa (–)	Haiti (–)	Jamaica (–)	Liberia (1)	Nepal (–)	
	Honduras (4)	Kenya (–)	Nicaragua (1)	Nigeria (3)	
	Indonesia (1)	Laos (–)	N. Korea (1)	Oman (1)	
	Iraq (1)	Lesotho (–)	N. Yemen (3)	Portugal (1)	
	S. Korea (2)	Malaysia (–)	Sudan (1)	Senegal (–)	
	Libya (1)	Mozambique (–)	Togo (1)	Swaziland (–)	
	Madagascar (1)	Saudi Ar. (–)	Upper Volta (3)	Tanzania (–)	
	Mali (1)	Sierra Leone (2)	Vietnam (4)	Trin.-Tob. (–)	
	Mauritania (1)	Singapore (–)		Venezuela (–)	
	Pakistan (1)	S. Yemen (1)		Yugoslavia (–)	
	Paraguay (–)	Sri Lanka (–)		Zambia (–)	
	Philippines (–)			Zimbabwe (–)	
	Somalia (–)				
	Syria (3)				

Source: Sivard (1982): 17.

*Figures in parentheses refer to 1960–1982 incidence of coups.

Table 5.6.
Gastil's Military Control, Development, Orientation and Freedom (1980)

Military	Not Free** Civilian		Military	Partly Free** Civilian		Military*	Free** Civilian
Argentina (OD)	Afghanistan (SS)	Libya (OD)	Chile (OD)	Bahrain (OD)	Senegal (SC)	---	Botswana (OD)
Bolivia (OD)	Albania (SS)	Mali (SC)	El Salvador (OD)	Bangladesh (OD)	Sierra Leone (OD)		Colombia (OD)
Chad (OD)	Algeria (SC)	Mongolia (SS)	S. Korea (OD)	Brazil (OD)	Singapore (OD)		Costa Rica (OD)
Ethiopia (SC)	Angola (SS)	Mozambique (SC)	Turkey (OD)	Cyprus (OD)	S. Africa (OD)		Dom. Rep. (OD)
Guinea (SC)	Benin (SC)	N. Korea (SS)	Upper Volta (OD)	Egypt (SC)	Sudan (SC)		Ecuador (OD)
Liberia (OD)	Burma (SC)	Oman (OD)	Uruguay (SC)	Guyana (SC)	Swaziland (OD)		Fiji (OD)
Mauretania (OD)	Burundi (SC)	Rwanda (SC)		Honduras (OD)	Taiwan (OD)		Gambia (OD)
Niger (OD)	Cameroon (OU)	Saudi Ar. (OD)		Indonesia (OD)	Thailand (OD)		Ghana (OD)
N. Yemen (OD)	Cent. Afr. R. (OD)	Somalia (SC)		Iran (OD)	Tunisia (SC)		India (OD)
Pakistan (OD)	China (SS)	Syria (SC)		Ivory Coast (OD)	Uganda (OD)		Israel (SC)
	Congo (SC)	Tanzania (SC)		Kenya (OD)	Zambia (SC)		Jamaica (SC)
	Cuba (SS)	Togo (SC)		Lebanon (OD)	Zimbabwe (OD)		Malta (OD)
	Gabon (OD)	Vietnam (SS)		Lesotho (OD)			Nigeria (OD)
	Guatemala (OD)	S. Yemen (SC)		Malaysia (OD)			Peru (OD)
	Haiti (OD)	Yugoslavia (SS)		Mauritius (uD)			Portugal (SC)
	Iraq (SC)	Zaire (OD)		Mexico (OD)			Sri Lanka (OD)
	Jordan (UD)			Morocco (OD)			Trin. - Tob. (OD)
	Kampuchea (SS)			Nepal (OD)			Venezuela (OD)
	Laos (SS)			Nicaragua (SC)			
	Madagascar (SC)			Panama (OD)			
	Malawi (OD)			Paraguay (OD)			
				Philippines (OD)			

Source: Gastil (1981: 25).

*Military Dominant. See note for criteria.

**OD, SC, and SS in parentheses refer to development orientation. Gastil's "capitalist" and "capitalist–statist" are designated OD, his "communist," as SS, and the remainder as SC.

Table 5.7.
Composite Index of Global State Repression (1980)

Violent		Institutional		Minimal	
Civilian	Military	Civilian	Military	Civilian	Military
Afghanistan (SC)	Argentina (OD)	Albania (SS)	Algeria (SC)	Botswana (OD)	Nigeria (OD)
Angola (SC)	Bangladesh (OD)	Cameroon (OD)	Benin (SC)	Cent. Afr. Rep. (OD)	Panama (OD)
Bahrain (OD)	Bolivia (OD)	China (SS)	Burma (SC)	Costa Rica (OD)	Portugal (OD)
Chad (OD)	Brazil (OD)	Cuba (SS)	Burundi (SC)	Cyprus (OD)	
Guinea (SC)	Chile (OD)	Ecuador (OD)	Congo (SC)	Dominican Rep. (OD)	
Haiti (OD)	Colombia (OD)	Gabon (OD)	Egypt (OD)	Fiji (OD)	
India (OD)	El Salvador (OD)	Gambia (OD)	Ghana (OD)	Jamaica (OD)	
Iran (SC)	Ethiopia (SC)	Guyana (SC)	Madagascar (SC)	Malta (OD)	
Mexico (OD)	Guatemala (OD)	Israel (OD)	Niger (OD)	Mauritius (OD)	
Philippines (OD)	Honduras (OD)	Ivory Coast (OD)	North Yemen (SC)	Senegal (OD)	
Saudi Arabia (OD)	Indonesia (OD)	Jordan (OD)	Peru (MC)	Trin.-Tobago (OD)	
South Africa (OD)	Iraq (SC)	Kampuchea (SS)	Rwanda (OD)		
Syria (SC)	Liberia (OD)	Kenya (OD)	Taiwan (OD)		
	Libya (SC)	Laos (SS)	Togo (OD)		
	Mali (SC)	Lebanon (OD)	Upper Volta (OD)		
	Mauretania (SC)	Lesotho (OD)			
	Pakistan (OD)	Malawi (OD)			
	Paraguay (OD)	Malaysia (OD)			
	Somalia (SC)	Mongolia (SS)			
	South Korea (OD)	Morocco (OD)			
	Sudan (OD)	Mozambique (SC)			
	Thailand (OD)	Nepal (OD)			
	Turkey (OD)	Nicaragua (SC)			
	Uganda (OD)	North Korea (SS)			
	Uruguay (OD)	Oman (OD)			
	Zaire (OD)	Sierra Leone (OD)			
		Singapore (OD)			
		South Yemen (SS)			
		Sri Lanka (OD)			
		Swaziland (OD)			
		Tanzania (SC)			
		Tunisia			
		Venezuela (OD)			
		Vietnam (SS)			
		Yugoslavia (SC)			
		Zambia (SC)			
		Zimbabwe (OD)			

Sources: Amnesty International (1981, 1982); U.S. Dept. of State (1981); Gastil (1981); Sivard (1982). Military dominance and development orientation are the same as table 5.3.

5.5 (.73), though more moderately with Gastil's in table 5.6 (.45). All of these Pearson coefficients are significant at the .001 level.

Countries in both the "violent" as well as the "institutional" categories evidence high repressiveness (that is, routine use of sanctions) toward at least one significant political sector opposing the government. In some cases, of course, pre-existing sustained repression has eliminated such opposition groups. The key difference—one that I believe is highly important—between the two categories concerns the disposition toward physical *violence*—torture, executions, disappearances, and unusually harsh prison conditions. The third or "minimal" classification pertains to the absence of, exceptional, or mild resort to suppressive practices. Further, when regimes do not act vigorously against non-official "private" groups—especially those in basic sympathy with the government— the violent activities of such organizations are attributed by me to the regime. This is particularly common in Latin America and a few other countries such as Thailand and Iran.

In sections that follow, approximately sixty variables will be assessed.[23] These indicators pertain to a number of relational propositions that appear in the literature on authoritarianism or democratic stability. My focus will be upon mean differences for countries whose repressiveness in 1980 is classified as violent (or extreme), institutional (high), and minimal (low or insignificant). Although the appropriateness of statistical analysis is problematic where sampling error is irrelevant and ordinal measures of repressiveness are employed, to elucidate specific yet tentative relationships, data for each group of countries were broken down for mean values, standard deviations, significance level, and total variance accounted for (eta squared).[24] In a few instances for nominal variables such as geographical location and dominant religion, percentage distributions have been used. The complete list of variable titles and sources can be found in the Appendix.

Because two of the most salient conflicts that engender suppression of opponents in developing countries pertain to militarism and development ideology, I have subclassified the nations listed in table 5.6. The first control employed in subsequent discussion and tables is for military dominance versus civilian supremacy.[25] In addition, the countries have been differentiated according to three development strategies: (1) "open door" or "free enterprise" capitalism; (2) economic nationalism or "state capaitalism"; and (3) Marxist–Leninist or "state socialism."[26] The discussion proceeds under five broad headings or relational areas: (1) historical and geo-political attributes; (2) internal military dimensions and conflicts; (3) external military linkages; (4) foreign investment, aid, and economic indicators; and (5) socio-cultural welfare and religious dominance. When mean differences were not discerned in the breakdowns, such data generally have not been presented in my tables. A small num-

Table 5.8.
Geographical Patterns of State Repression (1980)

Region	Repressiveness*			
	Violent	Institutional	Minimal	Number
Africa	35.9%	53.8%	10.3%	39
Latin America and Caribbean	52.2	17.4	30.4	23
Asia	38.1	57.1	4.8	21
Middle East, North Africa and Mediter- ranean Area	31.8	54.5	13.6	22

Sources: Appendix; PRIO Data Bank.   *Chi-square = 12.8; p = .05; DF = 6.

ber of other findings have also been omitted to reduce the number of tables to more manageable proportions. They are, however, discussed in the text, and all data used in this study may be obtained from the International Peace Research Institute, Oslo, Norway.

HISTORICAL AND GEO-POLITICAL ATTRIBUTES

The Lipset quotation near the beginning of this work linked "poverty-stricken masses" and "elongated pyramid class structure" to a "bleak" prospect for "political democracy" in "Asia and Africa." When repressive severity is compared on the basis of four major geographical regions in table 5.8, it seems that his prediction is well founded. The lowest percentages of countries in the minimal category are in Asia (4.8) and Africa (10.3). On the other hand, in the violent category, both regions are markedly surpassed by Latin America (52.2). Thus, Herman's emphasis upon the latter in his recent analysis of state terrorism appears well justified; so do Schoultz's findings to be discussed in a subsequent section.

This may explain the significant association that I found between length of independent statehood and violent repression. While there was little difference between the institutional and minimal categories, the period since independence was on the average of considerably greater duration for the violent category. The same pattern appeared for open door regimes generally, similar development orientations under civilian rule, and in lesser measure those under military dominance. These also tended to be older states than were civilian ones.

When we turn directly to development orientations in 1980, the only unambiguous relationship for both military and civilian regimes is between minimal repression and the open door orientation. While the differences are small for the other repressive categories, table 5.9 indicates that violent repression is more strongly associated with the open

Table 5.9.
Civilian versus Military Rule, Development Orientation, and State Repression (1980)

		Repressiveness		
Civilian	Violent	Institutional	Minimal	Total
DS*	1.5	1.6	1.0	1.5
SD**	.7	.8	.0	.7
N***	14	35	12	61
ES .11 p .04				
Military				
DS	1.3	1.4	1.0	1.3
SD	.4	.5	.0	.5
N	27	14	3	44
ES .06 p .28				

Source: Appendix; PRIO Data Bank.
DS: = Difference of Squares: 1 = open door; 2 = state capitalist; 3 = state socialist;
      SD = standard deviation; ES = Eta squared; p = significance; n = number.

Table 5.10.
Development Strategy Continuity and Change (1965–1980)

1980 Development Strategy	1965-1978 Orientation	
Open Door	OD 85%	Mixed 50%
State Capitalist	SC 91	38
State Socialist	SS 100	12

Source: Appendix; PRIO Data Bank. Chi square = 94.0, p = .000, DF = 6.

door orientation—especially for military regimes. Consideration of particular development orientations over the longer 1965–1978 period reveals strong continuity coefficients but relatively weak associations with repressiveness.[27] Here the deviation is considerable only for the civilian regimes. Nevertheless, open door orientations are again most pronounced for both the minimal and to lesser degree the violent category. This provides limited support for Herman's thesis that state terror is often necessary to perpetuate dependent capitalism in the periphery.[28] Kenneth Bollen's findings that the degree of dependency correlates with repressive severity likewise is consonant.[29] But it is both inconclusive and consistent in some measure with Lipset's suggestion that "it is possible that Max Weber was right when he suggested that modern democracy in its clearest forms can only occur under the unique conditions of capitalist industrialization."[30] For Weber, however, Lipset[31] acknowledges that other "unique" conditons were also essential.[32]

Further, it appears from table 5.10 that since 1965 the open door "capitalist" systems have been least stable, while the revolutionary trend has been in the direction of state capitalism and state socialism. This may account for both the modest growth between 1973 and 1980 of Gastil's "unfree" category noted earlier as well as the small decine in violent brutality during the late 1970s.

A final correlate of repressiveness to be assessed here is the percentage of wage and salary earners who are organized in trade unions. Several scholars have approached this issue, although often tangentially. Lucien Pye stresses the importance of mass mobilization and participation for any democratic form of political development.[33] S. E. Finer associates repression and military dictatorship with a "low political culture" characterized in part by "weakly organized publics" and an absence of political consensus on regime legitimacy.[34] Lipset in turn draws upon comparative Western experience:

> In modern times, three major issues have emerged in western states. The first was the religious issue: the place of the church and/or various religions within the nation. The second has been the problem of the admission of the lower strata, particularaly the workers, to "citizenship" and the establishment of access to power through universal suffrage, and the legitimate right to bargain collectively in the economic sphere. The third has been the continued struggle over the distribution of the national income.
>
> . . .
>
> Where a number of historic cleavages intermix and create the basis for *Weltanschauung* politics, the democracy will be, not include, the concept of tolerance.[35]

To this one could add Samuel Huntington's admonition that excessive mass demands or "escalation of expectations" is likely to catalyze either revolution or repressive violence, that is, "political decay."[36]

A number of patterns are suggested by table 5.11. First, both military and violently repressive regimes have far lower percentages of organized labor than their counterparts. Although mean deviance is rather high, the very lowest percentages are found within the violent open door subclassificaton for both civilian (7.6) and military (14.8) regimes. While the association is clear, one cannot ascertain whether such regimes simply constrained organized labor's growth or decimated pre-existing organizations that allegedly "overloaded" the system by "excessive" demands. The remaining manifest pattern indicates that regardless of the severity of repression, state capitalist and especially state socialist regimes boast progressively higher percentages of organized labor. That these unions tend to be less autonomous than in *some* open door systems is widely acknowledged. The degree of difference, however, is quite problematic given pervasive union corruption, foreign manipulation,[37] and internal oligarchy (that is, Michael's law) in most, including the minimally repressive, open door low-income countries. Furthermore, trade unions

Table 5.11.

State Repression (1980) and Percentage of Wage and Salary Earners in Trade Unions (1979)

All Regimes Development Strategy M, SD, N	Violent	Institutional	Minimal	Total	ES .09, p .01
OD	12.9%	22.7%	31.4%	20.9%	
SD	13.9	24.6	23.3	21.7	
N	26	28	15	69	
SC	26.8	39.1		33.3	
	31.7	35.9		33.6	
	9	10	0	19	
SS	90.0	93		92	
	.0	4.5		4.4	
	1	8	0	9	
TOTAL	18.5	38.5	31.4	30.0	
	23.5	36.2	23.3	31.3	Total ES .48
ES .44, p .00	36	46	15	97	
Civilian					
OD	7.6	22.3	31.3	22.4	
	8.7	26.4	17.6	22.7	
	7	20	12	39	
SC	28.0	37.0		33.0	
	44.9	36.9		38.2	
	4	5	0	9	
SS	90.0	93.1		92.7	
		4.5		4.4	
	1	8	0	9	
DS TOTAL	21.2	41.7	31.3	35.2	
ES .53, p .00	34.0	38.6	17.6	34.7	
	12	33	12	57	
					Total ES .57
Military					
OD	14.8	23.6	31.9	18.9	
	15.1	20.8	46.0	20.6	
	19	8	3	30	
SC	26.0	41.2		33.6	
	22.2	39.1		31.0	
	5	5	0	10	
DS Total	17.1	30.3	31.9	22.5	
	16.9	29.0	46.0	24.1	Total ES .14
ES .07, p .10	24	13	3	40	

Source: Appendix; PRIO Data Bank.

M = mean; *SD* = standard deviation; *N* = number; ES = eta squared;
    DS = Difference of Squares; *p* = significance.

in socialist countries do assert demands and similarly represent member interests to a limited extent in the political process.

INTERNAL MILITARY DIMENSIONS AND CONFLICTS

Although a common liberal assumption is that large standing armies and high military expenditures lead to greater repressiveness, my data indicate that this proposition requires qualification. It is true that minimally repressive states have low armed forces ratios to populations. The same, however, is also true of military-dominant regimes. On the other hand, minimally repressive civilian regimes manifest the *highest rate of increase* in armed forces ratios (per thousand population) between 1967 and 1979. While the manpower burden is substantially greater for the more repressivee categories, differences between them are not significant. And for all regime classifications, mean deviance is high. Although the institutionally repressive and especially state socialist regimes exhibit the highest ratios, the latter and those in the violent civilian state capitalist category are the only ones *reducing* such burdens between 1967 and 1979. Ironically, civilians have actually increased their ratios more than military regimes, though again exhibiting considerable mean deviance. Manpower burdens in 1979 are markedly higher for the violent regimes only within the civilian and military state capitalist development approach.[38]

When we turn to financial military burdens, analogous patterns appear. Again with military expenditures as a percentage of 1979 GNP, there is a curvilinear relationship with only the low 1.8 percentage for minimal regimes being salient. Thus, while repressiveness facilitates greater financial allocations to military rather than civil purposes, there is no necessary link to brutality, which after all represents elite values and consequential policy preferences. Hence, we find such burdens are markedly higher for civilian governments and for state capitalists and especially state socialist systems. Only within the state capitalist category do we encounter the expected relationship between brutality and high MXGNP79 (see chapter appendix). In most other cases, either the differences between the violent and institutional categories are small or they exhibit a higher percentage for the latter.[39]

If we look instead at military spending as a percentage of central government expenditures (MIXCGE79; see chapter appendix), the foregoing patterns are for the most part replicated. Only within the civilian state capitalist and open door categories are the averages markedly higher for violent regimes. In overall terms, however, table 5.12 indicates that financial allocations are only slightly greater for military governments. The most significant variations pertain to development orientations. With respect to 1967–1979 budgetary percentage *changes*, relationships tend to be much less pronounced and deviance very high. Nevertheless, increases are greatest for the minimally repressive regimes and civilian governments generally! This parallels the change in armed forces ratio patterns, as does the salient *demilitarization* of the state socialist systems.[40]

When we turn to military rule itself, there is fairly strong support for the liberal assumption that such regimes on balance are more repressive than their civilian counterparts. Similar findings have been reported by Erik Nordlinger, Finer, R. D. McKinlay and A. S. Cohan, Neal Tannahill,

Table 5.12.
Military Percentage of Central Government Expenditures (1979) and State Repression (1980)

All Regimes Development Strategy M, SD, N	Violent	Repressiveness Institutional	Minimal	Total	
OD	13.2%	13.1%	7.0%	11.8%	ES .10, p .01
SD	6.4	10.5	5.4	8.3	
N	27	25	14	66	
SC	21.0	18.0		19.4	
	9.7	9.3		9.3	
	10	12	0	22	
SS		39.0		39.0	
		22.6		22.6	
	0	3	0	3	
TOTAL	15.3	16.5	7.0	14.5	
ES .27, p .000	8.0	12.8	5.4	10.6	
	37	40	14	91	Total ES .32
Civilian					
OD	14.0	12.1	5.9	10.5	
	7.8	10.3	4.6	8.8	
	7	18	11	36	
SC	22.2	16.8		19.0	
	11.7	7.6		9.2	
	4	6	0	19	
SS		39.0		39.0	
		22.6		22.6	
	0	3	0	3	
TOTAL	17.0	16.1	5.9	14.0	
	9.7	13.8	4.6	12.1	
ES .36, p .000	11	27	11	49	Total ES .42
Military					
OD	13.0	15.7	11.0	13.4	
	6.0	11.3	7.5	7.5	
	20	7	3	30	
SC	20.1	19.3		19.7	
	9.1	11.3		9.8	
	6	6	0	12	
TOTAL	14.6	17.3	11.0	15.2	
	7.3	11.0	7.5	8.6	
ES .11, p .03	26	13	3	42	Total ES .13

Source: Appendix; PRIO Data Bank. See the footnote to table 5.11 for abbreviations.

Wolpin, and Sivard among others.[41] Indeed, Sivard's more recent assessment of 114 developing countries was squarely on point: "The association between institutionalized political violence and military controlled governments is particularly strong. Of those governments most prone to use torture there are almost three times as many among the military controlled as in other Third World countries."[42] And as my table 5.13 indicates, there is a fairly strong and significant relationship

Table 5.13.
Military Rule and State Repression (1980)

All Regimes Development Strategies M, SD, N	Violent	Repressiveness Institutional	Minimal	Total	
OD	1.714	1.276	1.200	1.431	
SD	.460	.455	.414	.499	
N	28	29	15	72	
SC	1.583	1.500		1.542	
	.515	.522		.509	
	12	12	0	24	
SS	1.000	1.000		1.000	
	.000	.000		.000	
	1	8	0	9	
DS TOTAL	1.659	1.286	1.200	1.419	
ES .08, p .02	.480	.456	.414	.496	
	41	49	15	105	Total ES .22

Sources: Appendix; PRIO Data Bank.
1 = civilian; 2 = military. See the footnote to table 5.11 for abbreviations.

between military rule and brutality or violent repression. Virtually all of this is, however, accounted for by the open door regimes. On the other hand, civilian and military systems are similar with respect to institutional and minimal repressiveness; this even though twelve of our fifteen countries in the last category are civilian ruled.

Equally strong relationships appeared when Sivard's civilian versus military classification was compared with the composite index. As table 5.14 makes clear, institutionally and in particular violently repressive regimes exhibit a much greater tendency to be militarily ruled. Within the development orientations, this is also somewhat more true for the state capitalist than other regimes. Although the relationships tend to be a bit weaker for my 1965–1978 civilian versus military classification, parallel tendencies are manifested. Furthermore, we see in table 5.15 the parameters of civilian rule's decline since 1960—a trend mentioned at the outset of this study.

Not to be overlooked is the fact that violently repressive, civilian state capitalist, and military-dominant governments in 1980 were characterized by a substantially higher incidence of coups during the 1960–1982 period. Thus, Sivard records twenty prior coups for the sixty-one civilian governments compared with ninety-two for the fifty-two regimes she determined were militarily controlled or dominated.[43] Furthermore, civilian, institutionally repressive, and particularly state socialist regimes in 1980 were most victimized (in terms of average years) by foreign invasion over the two preceding decades. Table 5.16 underscores the paucity of such invasions for both military and minimally repressive civilian regimes. Similar though somewhat weaker patterns appear for years of foreign military "intervention," which at times is only technically

Table 5.14.
Sivard's Civilian versus Military Rule and State Repression (1980)

All Regimes* Development Strategies M, SD, N	Violent	Institutional	Minimal	Total	ES .19, p .001
OD	1.750	1.286	1.133	1.437	
SD	441	460	352	499	
N	28	28	15	71	
SC	1.750	1.583		1.667	
	452	515		482	
	12	12	0	24	
SS	1.000	1.375		1.333	
	000	518		500	
	1	8	0	9	
TOTAL	1.732	1.375	1.133	1.481	
ES, 04, p .10	449	489	352	502	
	41	48	15	104	Total ES .24
Civilian*					
OD	1.375	1.100	1.083	1.150	ES .06, p .20
	518	308	289	362	
	8	20	12	40	
SC	1.400	1.167		1.273	
	548	408		467	
	5	6	0	11	
SS	1.000	1.375		1.333	
	000	518		500	
	1	8	0	9	
TOTAL	1.357	1.176	1.083	1.200	
ES .03, p .38	497	387	289	403	
	14	34	12	60	Total ES .11
Military*					
OD	1.900	1.750	1.333	1.806	ES .18, p .02
	308	463	577	402	
	20	8	3	31	
SC	2.000	2.000		2.000	
	000	000		000	
	7	6	0	13	
DS Total	1.296	1.857	1.333	1.864	
ES .07, p .09	267	363	577	347	
	27	14	3	44	Total ES .23

Sources: Appendix; PRIO Data Bank.
1 = civilian; 2 = military. See the footnote to table 5.11 for abbreviations.

distinguishable from an invasion. While such intrusions may indeed catalyze repression, the patterns discussed above are both ambiguous on
this point and qualified by impressive mean deviations.

One of the surprising discoveries in table 5.17 is that despite experiencing a larger percentage of invasions and especially interventions, a
much smaller proportion of civilian governments were afflicted by internal revolutionary or civil wars. Nevertheless, their share of civilian
casualties was *more than double* that of military-dominant systems. Total
casualties were also appreciably higher. With respect to the various development orientations, open door regimes experienced fully two-thirds

Table 5.15.
The Decline of Civilian Rule (1960–1980)

1960-1967 (%) *		1980 Status
Civilian	62.2	Civilian
Military	81.8	Military
Civilian	37.8	Military
Military	18.2	Civilian
1965-1978 (%) **		
Civilian	85.7	Civilian
Military	83.8	Military
Civilian	18.6	Military
Military	10.7	Civilian
Mixed	33.3	Civilian
Mixed	66.7	Military

Source: Appendix; PRIO Data Bank.
  *Chi square = 5.9; p = .02; DF = 1; N = 85. Percentage military increased from 12.9
  to 43.4.
  **Chi square = 45.2; p = .001; DF = 2; N = 99. Percentage military increased from
  37.4 to 43.4.

of the internal wars, considerably more interventions than other development orientations, and somewhat greater casualties. The state socialist
systems, however, suffered almost as many civilian casualties despite the
smallest percentage of internal wars and interventions, although admittedly they were as highly victimized by invasions as the open door type.
Insofar as interventions were concerned, it seems that most were carried
out by North Atlantic Treaty Organization powers, with the United
States responsible for intrusions involving more than 95 percent of the
casualties.[44] Even though casualty data are based upon imprecise estimates, a reasonable inference is the high lethality of American
interventions.

EXTERNAL MILITARY LINKAGES

Eastern and Western interventions reflect the local bilateral interests
of the intervenor and more fundamentally their global rivalry within
the Third World.[45] Because of the high costs of military intervention,
more economical and less provocative alternatives have been preferred.
These facilitate overt intervention should that become necessary, and
include but are not limited to the assignment of military personnel,
officer training, and arms tranfers.[46] Foreign economic aid, which for
some Westerners is defined to include private investment, is also utilized
as a source of influence. Whether any of the foregoing are associated

Table 5.16.
Years of Foreign Invasion (1960–1982) and State Repression (1980)

All Regimes Development Strategies M, SD, N	Violent	Represiveness Institutional	Minimal	Total			
					ES	.04 p	.44
OD	.267	.750	.250	.407			
SD	.594	1.389	.500	.888			
N	15	8	4	27			
SC	2.000	.286		1.077			
	2.683	.756		2.019			
	6	7	0	13			
SS		21.000		21.000			
		32.873		32.873			
	0	4	0	4			
TOTAL	.762	4.842	.250	2.477			
ES .31 p .001	1.640	15.956	.500	10.593	Total	ES .32	
	21	19	4	44			
Civilian					ES	.05 p	.64
OD	.333	.400	.333	.364			
	.577	.548	.577	.505			
	3	5	3	11			
SC	2.500	.667		1.714			
	3.317	1.155		2.628			
	4	3	0	7			
SS		21.000		21.000			
		32.873		32.873			
	0	4	0	4			
TOTAL	1.571	7.333	.333	4.545			
	2.637	19.924	.577	14.828	Total	ES .29	
ES .29 p .04	7	12	3	22			

Source: Appendix; PRIO Data Bank.
See the footnote to table 5.11 for abbreviations.

with greater or less repressiveness is the question to which I now turn.
That some relationships of this nature should be found is suggested by
Sivard's recent analysis of 114 developing countries. With respect to such
"institutionalized political violence" as "torture, brutality, 'disappearances', and summary executions," she found that virtually "all of the
worst offenders are clients of one or the other superpower. They are
also large importers of the equipment which represents the most advanced 'repressive technology'."[47]

If we ignore the origin of foreign military personnel, several patterns
are striking. First, mean deviance is almost uniformly high. Beyond that,
however, the highest average percentages of foreign to indigenous armed
forces are in institutionally repressive, state capitalist, and particularly
state socialist regimes. Only within the civilian state capitalist group is it
substantially higher for violent as opposed to institutionally repressive
systems. Especially salient is the paucity of foreign military personnel
for minimally repressive regimes! Further, the average percentage of
civilian governments is roughly *five times* that for military-dominant systems. This last difference is largely if not wholly non-existent for coun-

Table 5.17.
Wars and Fatalities by Regime Type, Development Orientation, and Bloc Intervention (1960–1982)

Wars/Fatalities (1960-82)	Regime (1960-78)				Development Orientation (1960-78)					NAP and Warsaw Pact Interventions/Invasions				
	Military	Civilian	Mixed*	Total	OD	SC	SS	Mixed*	Total	US	Other NAP**	SU	Other Communist	Total
Exclusively Internal	50% (10)	35% (7)	15% (3)	100% (20)	77% (17)	5% (1)	- (-)	18% (4)	100% (22)	20% (4)	50% (10)	5% (1)	25% (5)	100% (20)
Intervention	27 (8)	50 (15)	23 (7)	100 (30)	82 (28)	5 (4)	- (-)	6 (2)	100 (34)	22 (2)	11 (1)	- (-)	67 (6)	100 (9)
Invasion	22 (4)	33 (6)	44 (8)	99 (18)	90 (18)	5 (1)	- (-)	5 (1)	100 (20)	21 (6)	38 (11)	3 (1)	38 (11)	100 (29)
War Total	32 (22)	41 (28)	26 (18)	99 (68)	83 (63)	8 (6)	- (-)	9 (7)	100 (76)					
Civilian Casualties*** (thousands)	31 (1939)	22 (1357)	47 (2947)	100 (6243)	52 (3289)	1 (28)	- (-)	47 (2976)	100 (6243)	45 (750)	5 (89)	5 (90)	44 (736)	99 (1665)
Total Casualties*** (thousands)	38 (4099)	17 (1861)	44 (4751)	99 (10.711)	97 (10.371)	2 (174)	- (-)	2 (166)	101 (10.711)	42 (2433)	4 (247)	2 (100)	52 (3001)	100 (5781)

Source: Sivard (1982:15); Wolpin (1983; Appendixes D, E).
  NAP = North Atlantic Pact; SU = Soviet Union.
*"Mixed" only if less than two-thirds period for specific regime type or development orientation.
**Portugal and Turkey excluded from this column; classified under regime and development orientation categories.
***Multiple column Listings.

Table 5.18.
Soviet Military Personnel (1981) as Percentage of Armed Forces and State Repression (1980)

All Regimes Development Strategies M, SD, N	Violent	Institutional	Total	
				ES .01 p .61
OD	.100%	.400%	.300%	
SD	.000	.283	.265	
N	1	2	3	
SC	16.600	18.225	17.100	
	30.630	28.102	28.697	
	9	4	13	
SS		4.900	4.900	
		5.367	5.367	
	0	4	4	
TOTAL	14.950	9.330	12.140	
	29.345	18.288	23.972	Total ES .09
ES .09 p .46	10	10	20	
Civilian				
OD	.100		.100	ES .12 p .32
	.000		.000	
SC	30.000	2.000	24.400	
	45.007	.000	40.939	
	4	1	5	
SS		4.900	4.900	
		5.367	5.367	
		4	4	
TOTAL	24.020	4.320	14.170	
ES .14 p .60	41.207	4.826	29.544	Total ES .22
	5	5	10	
Military				
OD		.400	.400	ES .06 p .50
		.283	.283	
	0	2	2	
SC	5.880	23.633	12.537	
	5.825	31.767	19.802	
	5	3	8	
TOTAL	5.880	14.340	10.110	
ES .08 p .43	5.825	25.817	18.199	Total ES .28
	5	5	10	

Source: Appendix; PRIO Data Bank.
See the footnote to table 5.11 for abbreviations.

tries with Soviet personnel. At first glance in table 5.18, it appears that the overall Soviet presence is most pronounced for violent regimes. Nevertheless, when development orientation is controlled, we see that the association is limited to four civilian state capitalist regimes, while it does not appear either for the civilian open door and state socialist systems or for any of the military-dominant regimes. In all cases, though, the relative Soviet presence is highest for the state capital variant.

This is equally true for the German Democratic Republic in the ten countries where it had personnel. Although the average percentage was

Table 5.19.
Total Communist Military Personnel (1981) as Percentage of Armed Forces and State Repression (1980)

All Regimes Development Strategies M, SD, N	Violent	Institutional	Total	
				ES .04 p .39
OD	.100%	.400%	.300%	
SD	.000	.283	.265	
N	1	2	3	
SC	21.133	23.933	22.253	
	30.599	22.667	26.843	
	9	6	15	
SS		121.320	121.320	
		214.713	214.713	
	0	5	5	
TOTAL	19.030	57.769	40.926	
	29.605	135.591	103.790	Total ES .18
ES .18 p .14	10	13	23	
Civilian				
				ES .06 p .46
OD	.100		.100	
	.000		.000	
	1	0	1	
SC	36.475	23.300	32.083	
	43.272	23.617	35.796	
	4	2	6	
SS		121.320	121.320	
		214.713	214.713	
	0	5	5	
TOTAL	29.200	93.314	66.600	
	40.853	181.975	140.569	
	5	7	12	Total ES .12
Military				
				ES .05 p .51
OD		.400	.400	
		.283	.283	
	0	2	2	
SC	8.860	24.250	15.700	
	6.673	25.884	18.420	
	5	4	9	
TOTAL	8.860	16.300	12.918	
	6.673	23.531	17.600	
	5	6	11	
ES .12 p .29				Total ES .29

Source: Appendix; PRIO Data Bank.
See the footnote to table 5.11 for abbreviations.

three times higher for military than civilian regimes, it was also consistently lower for violently as opposed to institutionally repressive systems. Cuba, whose personnel were assigned to eleven countries, manifested patterns parallel to the German Democratic Republic except that, even more than the Soviet Union, a considerably higher average percentage were in civilian than military-dominant systems. The overall pattern for Communist military personnel appears in table 5.19. The greatest relative presence is to be found in other state socialist countries, the institutionally repressive, and those following a state capitalist development

Table 5.20.
American Military Personnel (1981) as Percentage of Armed Forces and State Repression (1980)

All Regimes Development Strategies M, SD, N	Violent	Repressiveness Institutional	Minimal	Total	
OD	17.450%	1.300%	2.800%	9.500%	ES .12 p .55
SD	32.612	2.089	.000	23.540	
N	6	5	1	12	
TOTAL	17.450	1.300	2.800	9.500	
	32.612	2.089	.000	23.540	
	6	5	1	12	
Civilian					ES .31 p .25
OD	7.250	1.600		3.483	
	8.980	2.285		5.270	
	2	4		6	
TOTAL	7.250	1.600		3.483	
	8.980	2.285		5.270	
	2	4		6	
Military					ES .11 p .84
OD	22.550	.100	2.800	15.517	
	40.530	.000	.000	33.233	
	4	1	1	6	
TOTAL	22.550	.100	2.800	15.517	
	40.530	.000	.000	33.233	
	4	1	1	6	

Source: Appendix: PRIO Data Bank.
See the footnote to table 5.11 for abbreviations.

strategy. Only within the last category of civilian-dominant systems is there a higher average for the violently repressive. Few of the differences for any of the Communist countries are statistically significant, and the eta squareds in most cases are low, given the deviance and generally modest mean percentage variations.

When we turn to the American military presence in table 5.20, several contrasts are striking. First, all are in open door countries and, notwithstanding considerable deviation, far higher averages characterize the brutally repressive in both the civilian- and the military-dominant systems. Just as salient is a *fivefold* higher average in the latter than the former. Some of these patterns are absent for other North Atlantic Pact powers. While most personnel are to be found in open door systems, for civilian governments table 5.21 suggests a strong inverse relationship to repressiveness qualified only by high deviation. Further, although the average size of forces in civilian systems is thrity-eight times higher than for military regimes, among the latter Western military personnel are markedly more pronounced for violent than institutionally repressive systems.

If we look at the question of Soviet *military training*, it appears that the average impact is considerably greater for military and particularly state capitalist regimes.[48] Table 5.22 also indicates little difference between violent and institutionally repressive governments except among the ci-

Table 5.21.
Non-U.S. North Atlantic Pact Military Personnel (1981) as Percentage of Armed Forces and State Repression (1980)

All Regimes Development Strategies M, SD, N	Violent	Repressiveness Institutional	Minimal	Total	
					ES .37 p .10
OD	2.100%	18.929%	104.250%	31.382%	
SD	.141	34.706	136.825	62.744	
N	2	7	2	11	
SC	.700			.700	
	.707			.707	
	2	0	0	2	
ES .04 p .52	1.400	18.929	104.250	26.662	
TOTAL	.909	34.706	136.825	58.425	Total ES .37
	4	7	2	13	
Civilian					
OD	2.000	21.950	104.250	38.022	
	.000	36.997	136.825	68.177	ES .31 p .33
	1	6	2	9	
TOTAL	2.000	21.950	104.250	38.022	
	.000	36.997	136.825	68.177	
	1	6	2	9	
Military					
OD	2.200	.800		1.500	
	.000	.000		.990	ES .06 p .76
	1	1		2	
SC	.700			.700	
	.707			.707	
	2	0		2	
					Total ES .76
TOTAL	1.200	.800		1.100	
ES .30 p .45	1.000	.000		.841	
	3	1		4	

Source: Appendix; PRIO Data Bank. See the footnote to table 5.11 for abbreviations.

vilian category, which, however, represents but three of the fifteen recipients in question. The deviations are extraordinarily high and the mean variations relatively small. The same cannot be said for the quantitatively far more impressive American training linkages. Insofar as relative impact is concerned, it is greatest for institutionally repressive, civilian, and open door regimes. Only for military regimes of both development orientations and civilian open door governments is the average considerably higher for violent than institutionally repressive systems. Further, the deviations are large, and within the civilian and military open door categories, table 5.23 reveals that the greatest impact is upon those in the *minimally* repressive group.[49]

Arms transfers are generally stimulated by training as well as a catalyst for the latter. Hence, when we look at relative shares of imports, we can expect to find similar if weaker patterns. Reliance upon Soviet weaponry is most pronounced for the violently repressive, state capitalist, and civilian as oppposed to military regimes. The single category in table 5.24 where the institutionally repressive surpassed their brutal counterparts was the military open door regime type. When relative import shares

Table 5.22.

Soviet Trainees (1955–1979) as Percentage of Armed Forces (1979) and State Repression (1980)

All Regimes Development Strategies M, SD, N	Violent	Repressiveness Institutional	Total	
OD	2.125%		2.125%	
SD	2.271		2.271	
N	4	0	4	
SC	4.000	3.300	3.745	
	2.946	1.651	2.480	
	7	4	11	
ES .09 p .27	3.318	3.300	3.313	
TOTAL	2.766	1.651	2.459	Total ES .11
	11	4	15	
Civilian				
SC	2.667		2.667	
	1.266		1.266	
	3		3	
TOTAL	2.667		2.667	
	1.266		1.266	
	3		3	
Military				
OD	2.125		2.125	ES .002, p .88
	2.271		2.271	
	4	0	4	
SC	5.000	3.300	4.150	
	3.630	1.651	2.765	
	4	4	8	
ES .14 p .24	3.562	3.300	3.475	
TOTAL	3.197	1.651	2.695	Total ES .21
	8	4	12	

Source: Appendix; PRIO Data Bank.
See the footnote to table 5.11 for abbreviations.

for all major Eastern arms exports are examined, most of the Soviet patterns reappear, albeit in weaker form. Here, however, the averages for military regimes are moderately higher, and there is virtually no difference between violent and institutionally repressive variants.

Far less than in the Soviet case do American weapons dominate the imports of civilian- as opposed to military-ruled countries. As one might expect, table 5.25 indicates that average percentages for open door variants, with the exception of *one* civilian state capitalist recipient, tend to be higher. Further, there is little difference in the overall repressive average with the exception of a single minimal country. Worth noting is that U.S. arms transfer shares for military regimes are markedly higher for the brutally repressive countries. This was the only mean difference that was significant statistically.

The similarities are especially striking when we examine French, West German, and British arms transfers. All exhibit higher averages for the violent than the institutionally repressive group. In general, they all differ from the United States by favoring state capitalist over open door recipients, with the single exception of British arms exports to open door

Table 5.23.

American Trainees (1950–79) as Percentage of Armed Forces (1979) and State Repression (1980)

All Regimes Development Strategies M, SD, N	Violent	Repressiveness Institutional	Minimal	Total		
OD	12.483%	3.075%	13.222%	9.485%	ES .01 p .68	
SD	17.568	4.681	14.384	14.396		
N	73	16	9	48		
SC	1.400	14.540		6.875		
	1.971	31.507		20.221		
	7	5	0	12		
SS		80.175		80.175		
		105.095		105.095		
	0	4	0	4		
ES .29 p .001						
TOTAL	9.897	17.704	13.222	13.414	Total ES .31	
	16.052	48.528	14.284	32.478		
	30	25	9	64		
Civilian						
OD	6.500	3.320	11.367	6.370	ES .05 p .48	
	7.435	5.464	9.089	7.576		
	4	10	6	20		
SC	1.500	35.600		12.867		
	2.677	49.922		28.510		
	4	2	0	6		
SS		80.175		80.175		
		105.095		105.095		
	0	4	0	4		
ES .32, p .01						
TOTAL	4.000	26.569	11.367	17.510	Total ES .36	
	5.823	59.418	9.089	44.182		
	8	16	6	30		
Military						
OD	13.742	2.667	16.933	11.711	ES .09, p .22	
	18.930	3.418	24.055	17.551		
	19	6	3	28		
SC	1.267	.500		.883		
	.924	.300		.744		
	3	3	0	6		
ES .07, p .15						
TOTAL	12.041	1.944	16.933	9.800	Total ES .14	
	18.068	2.915	24.055	16.422		
	22	9	3	34		

Source: Appendix; PRIO Data Bank.
See the footnote to table 5.11 for abbreviations.

military regimes. As in the case of Americans, average arms transfers for all three are moderately higher for civilians, but again the difference is less salient than in the Soviet case. Finally, if we consider all Western major arms transfers (less the United States), there is a much higher average for military regimes, that constitute three-quarters of the recipients. Open door regimes tend to be favored, and only within the civilian category are brutally repressive regimes higher, while the reverse is the case for the much smaller number of military governments.

Aside from high deviance, few wholly uniform patterns emerge from the preceding relationships. Consistent with Herman's thesis—one shared

Table 5.24.
Soviet Arms Transfers (1973–1977) and State Repression (1980)

All Regimes Development Strategies M, SD, N	Violent	Institutional	Repressiveness Minimal	Total	
OD	$211,667	$445,000	$70,000	$283,636	ES .04, p .52
SD	436.264	562.998	.000	456.443	
N	6	4	1	11	
SC	4049,444	165,000		2350,000	
	10147.240	228.455		7674.449	
	9	7	0	16	
SS		264,000		264,000	
		150.100		150.100	
	0	5	0	5	
ES .04, p .58					
TOTAL	2514,333	265,938	70,000	1313,750	Total ES .10
	7917.910	321.845	.000	5447.682	
	15	16	1	32	
Civilian					
OD	552,500	15,000		283,750	ES .15, p .15
	774.282	7.071		544.202	
	2	2		4	
SC	10476,667	205,000		5340,833	
	17774.590	278.253		12572.093	
	3	3		6	
SS		264,000		264,000	
		150.100		150.100	
	0	5		5	
ES .10, p .52					
TOTAL	6507,000	196,500		2300,000	Total ES .28
	13699.074	192.614		7945.051	
	5	10		15	
Military					
OD	41,250	875,000	70,000	283,571	ES .02, p .84
	34.731	459.619	.000	446.269	
	4	2	1	7	
SC	1092,559	223,532		900,440	
	6	4	0	10	
ES .03, p .47					
TOTAL	518,000	381,667	70,000	443,529	Total ES .28
	912.098	467.179	.000	741.474	
	10	6	1	17	

Source: Appendix; PRIO Data Bank.
See the footnote to table 5.11 for abbreviations.

by such reformist and radical scholars as William A. Williams, Gabriel Kolko, and Harry Magdoff[50]—American military backing tends to focus upon open door regimes. For personnel stationing and training, there is a bias favoring brutal military-dominant systems. These patterns are generally in accord with those reported for the 1950s and 1960s by John S. Odell, who

found that the level of American military assistance given to a nation during the Cold War years varied with the importance of the nation to the United States as a supplier of critical raw materials, as a field for private investment and as a

Table 5.25.
American Arms Transfers (1961–1979) and State Repression (1980)

All Regimes Development Strategies M, SD, N	Repressiveness				
	Violent	Institutional	Minimal	Total	
OD	$66,032	$75,460	$100,000	$69,276	ES .004, p .57
SD	33.215	27.570	.000	31.776	
N	19	5	1	25	
SC	12,000	46,150		39,320	
	.000	43.469		40.625	
	1	4	0	5	
SS		83,067		83,067	
		13.050		13.050	
	0	3	0	3	
ES .13, p .12					
TOTAL	63,330	67,592	100,000	65,991	Total ES .19
	34.513	32.914	.000	33.484	
	20	12	1	33	
Civilian					
OD	95,400	71,833		81,260	ES .09, p .42
	6.505	33.372		27.093	
	2	3		5	
SC		100,000		100,000	
		.000		.000	
	0	1		1	
SS		83,067		83,067	Total ES .27
		13.050		13.050	
	0	3		3	
ES .08, p .77					
Military					
OD	62,576	80,900	100,000	66,280	ES .08, p .43
	33.436	26.729	.000	32.767	
	17	2	1	20	
SC	12,000	28,200		24,150	
	.000	30.018		25.814	
	1	3	0	4	
ES .21, p .02					
TOTAL	59,767	49,280	100,000	59,258	Total ES .28
	34.559	38.241	.000	35.087	
	18	5	1	24	

Source: Appendix; PRIO Data Bank.
See the footnote to table 5.11 for abbreviations.

trade partner. We found that the extent of U.S. military intervention in a Third World nation was greater the less stable the nation, but we found very little support for the hypotheses that variations in intervention could be accounted for by raw materials value or private investment amounts, either among nations or regions. Among the least-stable nations, those that provided a larger proportion of U.S. trade experienced greater intervention, and trade and intervention were also associated at the regional level. Military intervention was associated with receiving military assistance.[51]

The Soviets, on the other hand, tend to concentrate their generally more limited support upon more receptive "anti-imperialist" state capitalist regimes that challenge the dominance of Western investor interests.

Table 5.26.
Net Private Investment (1970) and State Repression (1980)

All Regimes Development Strategies M, SD, N	Violent	Represiveness Institutional	Minimal	Total	
OD	54.875	27.750	72.333	48.571	ES .01, p .66
SD	120.427	40.224	73.459	93.024	
N	24	16	9	49	
SC	27.250	91.000		48.500	
	46.018	138.304		86.888	
	8	4	0	12	
ES .001 p .99	47.969	38.800	72.333	48.557	Total ES .05
TOTAL	106.705	70.814	73.459	91.142	
	32	20	9	61	
Civilian					
OD	81.375	31.818	59.000	54.385	ES .007, p .91
	148.250	32.205	61.614	89.123	
	8	11	7	26	
SC	17.500	156.000		86.750	
	10.607	199.404		140.305	
	2	2	0	4	
ES .01, p .53	68.600	50.923	59.000	58.700	
TOTAL	133.536	79.703	61.614	94.916	
	10	13	7	30	
Military					
OD	41.625	12.400	119.000	42.000	ES .07, p .36
	106.861	56.128	121.622	98.840	
	16	5	2	23	
SC	30.500	26.000		29.375	
	53.773	26.870		46.614	
	6	2	0	8	
ES .07, p 73	38.591	16.286	119.000	38.742	Total ES .07
TOTAL	94.185	47.588	121.622	87.765	
	22	7	2	31	

Source: Appendix; PRIO Data Bank.
See the footnote to table 5.11 for abbreviations.

Their personnel and arms transfers favor civilians, while training also concentrates upon these and to a lesser degree military regimes.

FOREIGN INVESTMENT, AID, AND ECONOMIC INDICATORS

Turning to foreign investment, one is struck by the lack of any overall differences between state capitalist and open door regimes. Although the deviance is also high for the various controls, the average for civilian state capitalist regimes is markedly higher, while the reverse is true for military-dominant open door systems. Table 5.26 indicates that in general such investment is much lower for military regimes. Furthermore, while the differences between violently and institutionally repressive regimes do tend to favor the former, *especially* among military-dominant systems, it must be conceded that investment is much the highest by far among the minimally repressive. Yet, when one takes account of the fact that there were *only three* countries in the military minimal category, and the same least repressive group exhibited a *lower* investment average for the civilian systems than did the violently repressive, Herman's thesis that militarism and violent repression protect foreign investment retains considerable if qualified validity. Indeed, a more systematic statistical study recently published by Bollen found a strong relationship between the degree of politico-economic dependency and the incidence of authoritarian rule for about 100 developing countries during the 1960s and 1970s.[52] Semi-peripheral countries tended to be more repressive than core states, while the peripheral majority ranked highest on repression. Corporate investors may *prefer* minimal repression, but when reformist and/or socialist forces effectively challenge the status quo, brutal measures may be regarded as an unfortunate necessity. In short, violent repression may facilitate rather than impede private investment!

As far as per capita foreign aid (1973–1975) is concerned, observed differences were slight. Averages tended to be somewhat higher for open door and military regimes, while they were lowest by far for countries following a state socialist development strategy. Among civilian regimes, the violently repressive received less per capita aid than institutionally or minimally repressive governments. For the military, this pattern was reversed only within the open door category, while such differences evaporated for state capitalist regimes. The violently repressive open door military regimes boasted even higher averages than their violent state capitalist counterparts, while the average was twice as high for all military open door- than state capitalist-oriented systems. Thus, we can infer that prior aid did not measurably promote civilianism, leftist door development approaches, or non-brutal repression. On the contrary, these patterns are consonant with Schoultz's analysis of U.S. aid to Latin America. He concludes

that during the mid–1970's United States aid was clearly distributed disproportionately to countries with repressive governments, that this distribution represented a *pattern* and not merely one or a few isolated cases, and that human need was not responsible for the positive correlations between aid and human rights violations.[53]

As in the case of American and in lesser measure North Atlantic Pact military personnel–training relationships and direct foreign investment, the previously discussed aid patterns indicate that as Albert Szymanski contends, on a global level these Western "linkages" serve the interests of transnational corporations and disproportionately favor both brutally repressive military and open door governments.

Defenders of such "aid" would deny responsibility for these practices and regimes. Rather than functioning primarily as a support mechanism for neo-colonial and often brutal open door regimes, they allege that the aid and concomitant foreign investment will reduce mass poverty, which constitutes the primary impediment to meaningful popular participation. Indeed, Lipset has argued that "stable democracy" cannot exist without, among other things, both "legitimacy" and an "economic development complex (comprising industrialization, wealth, urbanization and education)."[54] Subsequently,

the poorer a country, and the lower the absolute standard of living of the lower classes, the greater the pressure on the upper strata to treat the lower classes as beyond the pale of human society, as vulgar, as innately inferior, as a lower caste.[55]

Others, such as Robert Heilbroner, have maintained that the elite aspiration for development itself will catalyze repressive dictatorship under such conditions.

Mild men will not ride the tigers of development. Neither will mild political or economic systems contain or impel it.
                                      . . .
In most of the underdeveloped nations the choice for the command post of development is apt to lie between a military dictatorship and a left-wing civilian dictatorship. (The difference may not be very great, since many of the younger army officers have shown strong left-wing tendencies themselves.) In any event, as Professor Mason writes, the route chosen by the revolutionary developmental elites is not apt to be that of democratic capitalism. Given the inevitable slow pace of development, the heightening of social tensions, and the inescapable rigors of the Great Ascent, the logic of events points to the formation of economic systems and political regimes which will seek to *impose* development on their peoples.
    But even the most rigorous governments can speed up development only by so much. The first great projects of social capital formation, with their brigades of labor, lend themselves easily to centralized dictatorship, and, given adequate foreign assistance, the creation of an effective industrial structure can be considerably accelerated by a ruthless concentration on strategic sectors.[56]

Approaching the "problem" from the standpoint of transcending "dependency"—itself as noted strongly correlated with authoritarianism—Bollen[57] affirms Daniel Chirot:[58]

The power of the core governments and multinational enterprises is so great that only relatively autocratic governments can control its influence. Although a strong state may limit the core's domination, it is unlikely to be tolerant of internal dissension. To keep consumption down and investment high, rule in the periphery will have to be with an iron hand.[59]

As we shall see subsequently, Lipset himself adopts a similar perspective, albeit devoid of any collectivist implications. Pye notes that "this point of view classifies democracy as a luxury which can best be afforded only after the big push for development."[60]

The data on national wealth and industrialization, like the aid and investment patterns, provide some qualifiied support for these propositions. First, the standard deviations are in most cases quite high and the mean differences rather modest. It is true that in terms of per capita GNP, the average for military regimes was less than half that for civilians. It was also markedly lower for developmentally oriented civilian state capitalist and socialist than for open door systems. Further, while intra-military repressive variations were small for the open door regimes, among those pursuing state capitalist development strategies, the violently repressive had more than double the average per capita income than their institutional counterparts. Table 5.27 also reveals that among civilian regimes, the income level was highest for the brutal category and exceedingly low among the minimally repressive! This contradicts Bollen's finding, using 1965 energy consumption per capita for a similar country set, of "the persistence of [a] positive relationship between economic development and political democracy."[61]

While some of the foregoing differences run contrary to the expected direction, in contradistinction to the above, when one turns to another developmental indicator—industrialization (MFGDP79)—there is an actual paucity of significant variations. This not only holds for the civilian–military dichotomy, but applies with equal force to the repressiveness scale, with the exception of minimally repressive military regimes whose relative manufacturing sector is somewhat larger than for the more repressive categories. As for development strategies, manufacturing is higher especially among military regimes for the open door than the state capitalist orientation, while by far the *highest* sectoral share characterizes the state socialist systems.

Such Marxist-led regimes are also far above others on the average percentage of the labor force in industry. Although this is lower for *military* state capitalist than open door regimes, the reverse is true on the civilian side. Again, there are few overall differences between military and civilian regimes. Further, while it is clear that the minimally repressive have a larger percentage of industrial workers within both civilian- and especially military-dominant systems, the violently repressive manifest higher means than the institutional within the military open door and the civilian state capitalist orientations. The reverse, however, holds for the military state capitalist and the civilian open door systems. On balance, then, it cannot be said that brutal repression is more characteristic of the poorest or least industrialized countries. There is at best a weak association that is qualified by important exceptions. Thus, the

Table 5.27.
GNP Per Capita (1979) and State Repression (1980)

All Regimes Development Strategies M, SD, N	Violent	Institutional	Minimal	Total		
OD	$ 91.036	$139.444	$25.429	$96,667	ES .01, p .65	
SD	343.226	320.851	20.030	296,644		
N	28	27	14	69		
SC	82.000	26.917		51,955		
	94.184	28.621		70,844		
	10	12	0	22		
SS	68.000	49.143		51,500		
	.000	29.396		28,020		
	1	7	0	8		
ES .01, p .72	88.128	96.348	25.429	83,081	Total ES .06	
TOTAL	292.968	250.083	20.030	250,240		
	39	46	14	99		
Civilian						
OD	239.125	183.158	22.818	148.526	ES .03, p .46	
	645.679	375.880	16.875	393,411		
	8	19	11	38		
SC	120.333	28.500		59,111		
	117.006	34.251		79,146		
	3	6	0	9		
SS	68.000	49.143		51,500		
	.000	29.396		28,020		
	1	7	0	8		
ES .02, p .64	195.167	124.844	22.818	119,782	Total ES .06	
TOTAL	521.721	295.919	16.875	330,096		
	12	32	11	55		
Military						
OD	31.800	35.625	35.000	33,097	ES .01, p .82	
	29.712	39.446	31.765	31,506		
	20	8	3	31		
SC	65.571	25.333		47,000		
	87.709	24.961		67,394		
	7	6	0	13		
ES .02, p .35	40.556	31.214	35.000	37,205	Total ES .08	
TOTAL	51.457	33.248	31.765	44,735		
	27	14	3	44		

Source: Appendix; PRIO Data Bank.
See the footnote to table 5.11 for abbreviations.

differences are insufficient and too contradictory to wholly support Barrington Moore's contention[62] or Lipset's previously cited view that the rise of an industrial bourgeoisie substantially increases the prospects for unrepressive democratic systems. On the other hand, these patterns are only partially consonant with the conclusions of such dependency theorists as Fernando H. Cardoso and Enzo Faletto as well as Peter Evans,[63] who "suggest an active industrial and commercial bourgeoisie who, rather than challenge the dependency relations, become a vital part of the system of domination."[64]

Further, if my findings concerning Heilbroner's, Lipset's, and Bollen's equation of low economic levels and repressiveness are ambiguous at best,[65] can more be said for industrial and economic *growth*? The *raison d'être* imputed by Heilbroner to authoritarianism's appeal was its presumed efficiency in stimulating economic expansion. Even Karl Marx believed that if socialism came to countries whose industrial forces of production had not been fully developed, it would be "authoritarian socialism," presumably committed to developing those forces of production.[66] Pye, on the other hand, questions the notion "that new states cannot 'afford' democracy because they must place a prior value on economic growth," doubting "the widespread belief... that efficiency in the allocation of resources and the necessary discipline in controlling current consumption in order to create the needed savings are more likely in one-party systems where there is a minimum of competitive politics." Pye counter-poses his own proposition "that at present in most situations rapid economic growth is more likely to be stimulated by a reduction in authoritarian practices and an increase in popular participation in the nation-building process."[67] Lipset, however, is less sanguine, noting that "as Weber and others have pointed out, rapid economic growth may often engender violent class and political conflict, rather than faith in the social systems."[68] Indeed, elsewhere earlier he predicted that "given the pressure for rapid industrialization and for the immediate solution of chronic problems of poverty and famine through political agencies, it is unlikely that many of the new governments of Asia and Africa will be characterized by an open party system."[69] Since the military regimes tend to be in the lowest per capita GNP countries, while only 14 percent of all 105 Third World states are minimally repressive, Lipset's prognostication is, in a broad sense, accurate. Y_t the matter is more complex as the following measures reveal.

Our first growth indicator, average 1970–1978 change in gross domestic product, provides no support for either the Pye or the Lipset–Heilbroner theses. In fact, neither development strategy nor repressiveness is associated with different average rates of growth. It is true that within the military category, prior growth had been somewhat higher for open door regimes. Yet among the latter it was also higher for the violently and minimally than the institutionally repressive.

More striking contrasts appear in table 5.28 for 1970–1979 real per capita GNP growth. Despite generally high deviations, civilian regimes had markedly higher per capita growth rates. Even greater superiority characterized the minimally repressive, especially among the civilian governments where the violent category exhibited the worst prior economic improvement. For the military-dominant systems, however, the growth rate had been worst for the institutionally repressive, with the violent in the middle yet somewhat closer to the minimal. The state socialist regimes, which we recall received by far the lowest per capita aid (1973–1975), turned in the best growth performance, very closely followed by the heavily aided open door category with the internally contraditory[70]

Table 5.28.
GNP Per Capita Real Change (1970–1979) and State Repression (1980)

All Regimes Development Strategies M, SD, N	Violent	Institutional	Minimal	Total		
OD	23.536%	25.321%	40.000%	27.543%	ES .05, p	.12
SD	28.914	30.816	40.788	32.438		
N	28	28	14	70		
SC	3.222	3.727		3.500		
	51.826	27.753		39.197		
	9	11	0	20		
SS		28.000		28.000		
		.000		.000		
	0	1	0	1		
ES .08, p .02	18.595	19.450	40.000	22.264	Total ES	.11
TOTAL	36.083	30.843	40.788	35.090		
	37	40	14	91		
Civilian						
OD	25.000	30.350	43.909	33.077	ES .07, p	.18
	34.205	28.507	44.408	34.532		
	8	20	11	39		
SC	-14.667	-4.333		-7.778		
	73.221	35.478	0.000	46.408		
	3	6	0	9		
SS		28.000		28.000		
		.000		.000		
	0	1	0	1		
ES .16, p .02	14.182	22.556	43.909	33.077	Total ES	.11
TOTAL	47.271	32.414	44.408	39.464		
	11	27	11	49		
Military						
OD	22.950	12.750	25.667	20.581	ES .02, p	.69
	27.491	34.702	23.692	28.631		
	20	8	3	31		
SC	12.167	13.400		12.727		
	43.185	11.739		31.433		
	6	5	0	11		
ES .01, p .45	20.462	13.000	25.667	18.524	Total ES	.03
TOTAL	31.126	27.359	23.692	29.206		
	26	13	3	42		

Source: Appendix; PRIO Data Bank.
See the footnote to table 5.11 for abbreviations.

state capitalist regimes a very poor third—especially the easily destabil-ized *civilian* variant.[71]

As far as the 1970–1978 growth rate of industrial production is con-cerned, table 5.29 reveals an absence of uniform patterns within the equally performing overall civilian and military categories. While in-creasing repressiveness was associated with higher industrial growth rates for the civilian regimes, the reverse was true for the military-dominant systems, where the three minimally repressive regimes were especially outstanding. In general, the open door systems performed slightly better than the state capitalists. There were few differences, however, with respect to repressiveness or civilian versus military dominance.

One final measure of economic growth—expansion of food output

Table 5.29.
Industrial Production Growth Rate (1970–1978) and State Repression (1980)

All Regimes Development Strategies M, SD, N	Repressiveness					
	Violent	Institutional	Minimal	Total		
OD	6.308%	6.435%	9.730%	7.022%	ES .04, p .28	
SD	4.937	3.714	13.767	7.181		
N	24	17	10	51		
SC	4.271	7.588		6.040		
	5.633	2.800		4.522		
	7	8	0	15		
ES .004, p .62	5.848	6.804	9.730	6.798	Total ES .05	
TOTAL	5.078	3.433	13.767	6.652		
	31	25	10	66		
Civilian						
OD	7.967	6.990	5.757	6.870	ES .06, p .45	
	2.534	2.654	5.742	3.750		
	6	10	7	23		
SC	9.050	6.533		7.540		
	7.142	1.966		4.072		
	2	3	0	5		
ES .005, p .72	8.238	6.885	5.757	6.989	Total ES .07	
TOTAL	3.482	2.443	5.742	3.739		
	8	13	7	28		
Military						
OD	5.756	5.643	19.000	7.146	ES .21, p .02	
	5.459	4.997	23.870	9.165		
	18	7	3	28		
SC	2.360	8.220		5.290		
	4.342	3.234		4.750		
	5	5	0	10		
ES .01, p .55	5.017	6.717	19.000	6.658	Total ES .03	
TOTAL	5.339	4.380	23.870	8.214		
	23	12	3	38		

Source: Appendix; PRIO Data Bank.
See the footnote to table 5.11 for abbreviations.

between 1970 and 1978—is germane to both Lipset's thesis and Moore's proposition that repression is associated with economic growth or industrialization strategies that rely upon extracting surplus from the peasantry.[72] Here the military regimes are, if anything, associated with slightly better prior expansion of food output; so, for that matter, are the violently repressive, while those in the minimal group turn in a much weaker though second-best performance. Yet on this question differences are few among civilians as contrasted to the military, where the brutal category has by far the *best* prior record of food increase! And here the same pattern holds regardless of the development strategy pursued. Among civilian development strategies, no substantial differences in performance are associated with repressive severity. On the other hand, the poorest prior performance is associated with state socialism, the best with the open door approach, with state capitalism a close second. This, of course, is an imperfect indicator of food availability and ignores the greater distributional equality within state socialist systems. The patterns nevertheless imply reservation in accepting the previously stated propositions by Lipset and Moore.

SOCIO-CULTURAL WELFARE AND RELIGIOUS DOMINANCE

Equitable distribution of welfare benefits along with their expansion through adequate economic growth are commonly viewed as alternatives to repression. Ralph Miliband, for example, argues that in advanced capitalist states non-repressive rule has been facilitated by both high productivity as well as the "mitigation" of social inequality consequential to class domination, and "the main agent of that mitigation has been the state."[73] Earlier I referred to Huntington's thesis that an "escalation of expectations" at the mass level places excessive demands upon governments in developing areas. The consequential "political decay" is manifested by repressive violence and/or insurgency.[74] Ted Robert Gurr, on the other hand, carefully avoids an elitist or counter-revolutionary bias, yet is equally concerned with minimizing insurgent and especially repressive violence. He notes:

The disposition to collective violence depends on how badly societies violate socially derived expectations about the means and ends of human action.... It is most likely to occur in societies that rely on coercion to maintain order in lieu of providing adequate patterns of value-satisfying action.

Gurr goes on to note that "one source of high governmental legitimacy [one of Lipset's pre-conditions for "stable democracy"] is its effectiveness in resolving RD [Relative Deprivation]." Minimization of relative deprivation in turn implies that "the benefits of (social, economic and/or political) progress [must] be evenly distributed."[75] Lipset articulated this point somewhat earlier with the caveat that "the need for effectiveness poses a real dilemma, because in contemporary times 'effectiveness' is apt to consist of a demand for the equitable distribution of a rapidly increasing social product."[76] A few lines later, however, Lipset premises his pessimism upon *both* inadequate growth as well as implied inequitable distribution.

In applying these considerations to the prospects for political and economic development in the "new" and/or "under-developed" states, it is important to recognize that the now economically developed, stable democracies were able to develop either in societies that for the most part possessed traditonal legitimacy or in an achievement-oriented system like the United States that also had widespread and relatively equitable distribution of land ownership for much of its early history. In addition, these societies did not have to counter a (partly artificially—

Table 5.30.
Child Mortality (1978) and State Repression (1980)

All Regimes Development Strategies M, SD, N	Violent	Institutional	Minimal	Total	
		Repressiveness			
OD	15.143	17.417	9.500	15.113	ES .06, p .08
SD	8.935	10.409	10.341	9.961	
N	28	24	10	62	
SC	25.909	21.182		23.545	
	8.654	8.364		8.651	
	11	11	0	22	
SS	2.000	11.571		10.375	
	.000	13.998		13.394	
	1	7	0	8	
ES .15, p .001 TOTAL	17.775	17.429	9.500	16.717	
	10.222	10.777	10.341	10.684	
	40	42	10	92	Total ES .21
Civilian					
OD	18.625	15.125	9.429	14.742	ES .07, p .19
	9.826	9.986	10.438	10.240	
	8	16	7	31	
SC	23.000	17.800		20.111	
	10.520	9.576		9.740	
	4	5	0	9	
SS	2.000	11.571		10.375	
	.000	13.998		13.394	
	1	7	0	8	
ES .07, p .18 TOTAL	18.692	14.714	9.429	15.021	
	10.649	10.814	10.438	10.885	
	13	28	7	48	Total ES .16
Military					
OD	13.750	22.000	9.667	15.484	ES .12, p .08
	8.410	10.308	12.423	9.828	
	20	8	3	31	
SC	27.571	24.000		25.923	
	7.786	6.753		7.262	
	7	6	0	13	
ES .22, p .001 TOTAL	17.333	22.857	9.667	18.568	
	10.187	8.708	12.423	10.263	
	27	14	3	44	Total ES .34

Source: Appendix; PRIO Data Bank.
See the footnote to table 5.11 for abbreviations.

that is, politically—stimulated) rising "level of expectation" that was beyond the capacity of the economy or polity. As it is clearly difficult to generate support in the new states on grounds of either ascription or achievement, the chances for stable democracy in any Western sense are slim. With this in mind, I shall now examine the data on whether improved mass welfare and equity are indeed associated with less repressiveness.

A good indicator of nutritional equity, sanitation, and health is child mortality. Two very sharp differences appear in table 5.30. Minimally repressive and state socialist regimes do exhibit far lower rates than their counterparts. Beyond that a moderately better showing characterized

Table 5.31.
Life Expectancy (1979) and State Repression (1980)

All Regimes Development Strategies M, SD, N	Violent	Institutional (Repressiveness)	Minimal	Total	
OD	56.393	52.931	63.933	56.569	ES .13, p .001
SD	8.066	9.841	9.422	9.865	
N	28	29	15	72	
SC	47.417	52.167		49.792	
	7.609	9.262		8.638	
	12	12	0	24	
SS	69.000	56.875		58.222	
	.000	11.295		13.399	
	1	8	0	9	
ES .09, p .01 TOTAL	54.073	53.388	63.933	55.162	
	9.081	9.880	9.422	10.088	
	41	49	15	105	Total ES .23
Civilian					
OD	53.500	53.714	64.250	56.756	ES .15, p .01
	7.728	9.981	9.117	10.341	
	8	21	12	41	
SC	49.200	56.667		53.273	
	9.628	10.424		10.326	
	5	6	0	11	
SS	69.000	56.875		58.222	
	.000	11.395		11.399	
	1	8	0	9	
ES .02, p .53 TOTAL	53.071	54.943	64.250	56.344	
	9.277	10.181	9.117	10.429	
	14	35	12	61	Total ES .21
Military					
OD	57.550	50.875	62.667	56.323	ES .13, p .06
	8.095	9.804	12.702	9.361	
	20	8	3	31	
SC	46.143	47.667		46.846	
	6.309	5.610		5.800	
	7	6	0	13	
ES .21, p .002 TOTAL	54.593	49.500	62.667	53.523	
	9.112	8.159	12.702	9.468	
	27	14	3	44	Total ES .32

Source: Appendix; PRIO Data Bank.
See the footnote to table 5.11 for abbreviations.

civilian regimes. Among state capitalist governments, somewhat higher rates distinguished violently from institutionally repressive regimes. This pattern also depicted open door *civilian* systems, although it was reversed for the military governments.

Higher life expectany at birth—another salient indicator of the quality of life at the mass level—is somewhat less strongly associated with minimal repression, state socialism, and civilianism. We see in table 5.31 that differences between violently and institutionally repressive regimes are rather modest. My impression that development strategy is more important than repressive severity is underscored by the patterns for life expectancy *change* during the 1970s (CLFEXB79; see chapter appendix).

The only difference that is consistent with both of these tables is socialist superiority. In all of these instances, their attainments would have been even greater had the war-devastated Indochinese states been excluded. The three minimally repressive countries are marginally better than the institutional group among the military regimes, yet markedly inferior to both repressive categories among the civilian regimes. Further, with respect to the latter, there is little difference between the institutional and the slightly superior brutal category. Only for both military development strategies are the violent clearly inferior despite their high per capita aid, as we saw in the preceding section.[77] Yet in overall terms the military as a group were slightly stronger than civilian regimes, and had the socialists been excluded, this difference would have been more impressive.[78]

Lipset has stressed the importance of literacy, education, and urbanization for "democracy."[79] Some support for this proposition can be found in the statistical patterns for both literacy and newspaper circulation. While differences tend to be small and vary somewhat for the two repressive groups, the minimal category and state socialist systems are impressive in their superiority. This is equally true for civilian systems on newspaper circulation, although less so in table 5.32 for literacy. As far as press freedom is concerned, it is, as we might anticipate, considerably greater for the minimally repressive, although that seems to be the only salient difference.

The previously delineated patterns for literacy and newspaper circulation are replicated in both higher educational enrollments (as a percentage of the twenty- to twenty-four-year-old group) and in the proportion of women as a percentage of university enrollment. Thus, table 5.33 demonstrates very high levels for the minimally repressive as well as the state socialist regimes and to a somewhat lesser degree for civilian systems. Within the latter category, state capitalists are superior to open door-oriented governments, although among military-dominant systems the reverse is true—a somewhat surprising finding only if one ignores their heavy per capita aid. One of the more interesting discoveries is that except among open door civilian regimes, the violently repressive are not much less urban than the institutionally repressive. In most other instances, the reverse is true, with the greatest differences to be found in the military category. In general, however, civilian governments are somewhat more urban, and this tendency is again most striking for minimally repressive and state socialist systems. Thus, here too, as with literacy and newspaper circulation, the Lipset thesis may be accepted but only with serious qualification in light of the previously identified intra-military patterns and the modest overall civilian–military differences.

Two final areas of investigation concern the treatment of minorities

Table 5.32.
Adult Literacy (1979) and State Repression (1980)

All Regimes Development Strategies M, SD, N	Violent	Institutional	Minimal	Total	
OD	56.929%	45.069%	70.933%	55.069%	ES .08, p .02
SD	27.184	24.040	25.387	27.044	
N	28	29	15	72	
SC	25.833	49.417		37.625	
	18.829	26.064		25.289	
	12	12	0	24	
SS	72.000	66.000		66.667	
	.000	28.142		26.401	
	1	8	0	9	
TOTAL	48.195	49.551	70.933	52.076	Total ES .22
ES .09, p .01	28.528	25.798	25.387	27.698	
	41	49	15	105	
Civilian					
OD	45.000	47.048	73.250	54.317	ES .15, p .01
	28.636	22.535	25.183	29.916	
	8	21	12	41	
SC	29.200	62.667		47.455	
	20.957	23.695		27.602	
	5	6	0	11	
SS	72.000	66.000		66.667	
	.000	28.142		26.401	
	1	8	0	9	
ES .04, p .28 TOTAL	41.286	54.057	73.250	54.902	Total ES .25
	26.719	24.927	25.183	27.093	
	14	35	12	61	
Military					
OD	61.700	39.875	61.667	56.065	ES .07, p .25
	25.770	28.603	29.366	27.626	
	20	8	3	31	
SC	23.429	36.167		29.308	
	18.465	22.622		20.674	
	7	6	0	13	
TOTAL	51.778	38.286	61.667	48.159	
ES .19, p .003	29.259	25.318	29.366	28.359	
	27	14	3	44	Total ES .29

Source: Appendix; PRIO Data Bank.
See the footnote to table 5.11 for abbreviations.

and religious pluralism. With respect to the former, we may note Gurr's general caveat that aspirations for "security, status, a sense of community and the right to manage their own affairs" are as important as more material satisfactions in minimizing relative deprivation.[80] He further maintains that coercion is ineffective in the long run as it is likely to inspire resistance.

We do find in table 5.34, especially within open door civilian as well as military regimes, that there is a strong linear relationship between poor treatment and repressiveness including brutality. Further, military and especially their state capitalist and violent variants are characterized by poor treatment. When we break down our data in table 5.35 to control

Table 5.33.
Higher Educational Enrollment (1976) and State Repression (1980)

All Regimes Development Strategies M, SD, N	Violent	Repressiveness Institutional	Minimal	Total	
OD	7.640%	5.579%	12.700%	7.852%	ES .10, p .03
SD	6.963	6.569	9.286	7.587	
N	25	19	10	54	
SC	5.286	5.500		5.400	
	4.271	6.908		5.629	
	7	8	0	15	
SS		9.500		9.500	
		2.121		2.121	
	0	2	0	2	
TOTAL	7.125	5.828	12.700	7.380	Total: ES .12
	6.484	6.392	9.286	7.150	
	32	29	10	71	

Civilian

	Violent	Institutional	Minimal	Total	
OD	9.000	4.429	12.857	7.577	ES .13, p .13
	9.000	6.173	9.582	8.281	
	5	14	7	26	
SC	8.500	11.000		10.000	
	4.950	9.539		7.314	
	2	3	0	5	
SS		9.500		9.500	
		2.121		2.121	
	0	2	0	2	
ES .01, p .80 TOTAL	8.857	6.000	12.857	8.061	
	7.625	6.733	9.582	7.830	Total: ES .19
	7	19	7	33	

Military

	Violent	Institutional	Minimal	Total	
OD	9.000	4.429	12.857	7.577	ES .07, p .29
	9.000	6.173	9.582	8.281	
	5	14	7	26	
SC	8.500	11.000		10.000	
	4.950	9.539		7.314	
	2	3	0	5	
SS		9.500		9.500	
		2.121		2.121	
	0	2	0	2	
ES .12, p .04 TOTAL	8.857	6.000	12.857	8.061	Total: ES .16
	7.625	6.733	9.582	7.830	
	7	19	7	33	

Source: Appendix; PRIO Data Bank.
See the footnote to table 5.11 for abbreviations.

for insurgency, it is clear that it is 50 percent more prevalent for poor as compared with fair–good treatment. Among the violently repressive, 70 percent are chracterized by insurgency, while this falls to 26.4 percent for the institutionally repressive and to 0 percent for the minimal group. Similarly, while poor treatment exists for 40 percent of the violent regimes, it distinguishes but 15.8 percent of the institutionally repressive and none of those in the minimal category. In sum, it seems that repressive brutality even more than poor treatment is associated with ethnic insurgency. Bingham G. Powell's multi-variate analysis of forty democracies including eighteen developing countries during the 1960s and

Table 5.34.
Treatment of Minorities with a Potential for Self-Determination (1980) and State Repression (1980)

All regimes Development Strategies M, SD, N	Repressiveness				
	Violent	Institutional	Minimal	Total	
OD	2.600*	1.250*	1.000*	1.931*	ES .19, p .02
SD	1.298	.452	.000	1.193	
N	15	12	2	29	
SC	2.200	2.200		2.200	
	1.095	1.304		1.135	
	5	5	0	10	
SS		2.000		2.000	
		1.414		1.414	
	0	2	0	2	
TOTAL	2.500	1.579	1.000	2.000	
	1.235	.902	.000	1.162	Total: ES .27
ES .01, p .83	20	19	2	41	
Civilian					
OD	2.500	1.375	1.000	1.692	ES .13, p .31
	1.732	.518	.000	1.109	
	4	8	1	13	
SC	1.667	1.500		1.600	
	.577	.707		.548	
	3	2	0	5	
SS		2.000		2.000	
		1.414		1.414	
	0	2	0	2	
TOTAL	2.143	1.500	1.000	1.700	
ES .01, p .90	1.345	.674	.000	.979	Total: ES .23
	7	12	1	20	
Military					
OD	2.636	1.000	1.000	2.125	ES .19, p .15
	1.206	.000	.000	1.258	
	11	4	1	16	
SC	3.000	2.667		2.800	
	1.414	1.528		1.304	
	2	3	0	5	
TOTAL	2.692	1.714	1.000	2.286	
ES .05, p .31	1.182	1.254	.000	1.271	Total: ES .34
	13	7	1	21	

Source: Appendix; PRIO Data Bank.
Minority Treatment–insurgency scale: 1 = good—no insurgency; 2 = fair–good—insurgency; 3 = poor—no insurgency; 4 = poor—insurgency. See the footnote to table 5.11 for abbreviations.

1970s revealed a "significant relationship between ethnic fragmentation and deaths by political violence." He reports that his "examination of individual riots suggests that police are more likely to use deadly force in quelling ethnically based riots."[81]

Our last two variables pertain to religion. Some years ago, David Apter posited alternative reconciliation or "secular–libertarian" versus repressive mobilizing or "sacred collectivity" models for the Third World. Within the former, religion would gradually be supplanted by science and scientific–technological institutions as the basis for democracy.[82] We have already seen that insofar as manufacturing sectoral proportions or industrial expansion are indicative of this, there is some but not particularly

Table 5.35.
Minority Treatment, Insurgency, and State Repression (1980)

Repressiveness* N, R, C, T%	1.	2.	3.	4.	TOTAL**
Violent	5	7	1	7	2.0
	25.0%	35.0%	5.0%	35.0%	
	26.3	63.6	33.3	87.5	48.8
	12.2	17.1	2.4	17.1	
Institutional	12	4	2	1	19
	63.2	21.1	10.5	5.3	
	63.2	36.4	66.7	12.5	46.3
	29.3	9.8	4.9	2.4	
Minimal	2	0	0	0	2
	100.0	.0	.0	.0	
	10.5	.0	.0	.0	
	4.9	.0	.0	.0	
TOTAL	19	11	3	8	41
	46.3	26.8	7.3	19.5	

Source: Appendix; PRIO Data Bank.
 *1 = fair–good—no insurgency; 2 = fair–good—insurgency; 3 = poor—no insurgency; 4 = poor—insurgency.
 **Chi square = 11.0, p = .09, DF = 6.

strong support for his prognostication. Admittedly, decades more may be needed since few if any of these countries can be depicted as fully industrialized. Indeed, Marx himself, like Weber, recognized that (capitalist) economic development was necessary but not a sufficient condition for the peaceful (that is, non-repressive) transition to socialism:

We are aware of the importance that must be accorded to the institutions, customs and traditions of different countries; and we do not deny that there are countries like America, England (and, if I knew your institutions better, I would add Holland) where the workers can achieve their aims by peaceful means. However true that may be, we ought also to recognise that, in most of the countries on the Continent, it is force that must be the lever of our revolutions; it is to force that it will be necessary to appeal for a time in order to establish the reign of labour.[83]

Thus, one needs to pay heed to what is often referred to as the "superstructure." Religion, of course, remains as a vital force—especially within many of the developing countries. Even within advanced capitalist states, "subcultural" including religious "cleavages" have been regarded as obstacles to stable non-repressive "democratic" government.[84] The two questions I will pose here are whether repressiveness is associated with low religious pluralism or with the dominance of particular but not other denominations.

Table 5.36 indicates that both violently repressive as well as minimally repressive regimes are less pluralistic religiously than are institutionally repressive systems. In lesser measure, this is also the case for military- as opposed to civilian-dominant systems. If Marxist–Leninism rather than traditional religions had been included for the state socialist systems, the differences in the two above-mentioned areas would have been at-

Table 5.36.
Religious Pluralism and State Repression (1980)

All Regimes Development Strategies M, SD, N	Repressiveness*				
	Violent	Institutional	Minimal	Total	
OD	1.500	2.172	1.667	1.806	ES .14, p .001
SD	.793	.928	.900	.914	
N	28	29	15	72	
SC	1.667	2.167		1.917	
	.888	.937		.929	
	12	12	0	24	
SS	3.000	2.875		2.889	
	.000	.354		.333	
	1	8	0	9	
TOTAL	1.585	2.286	1.667	1.924	Total: ES .20
ES .11, p .01	.836	.890	.900	.927	
	41	49	15	105	
Civilian					
OD	1.500	2.143	1.667	1.878	
	.756	.910	.888	.900	ES .15, p .01
	8	21	12	41	
SC	1.600	2.500		2.091	
	.894	.837		.944	
	5	6	0	11	
SS	3.000	2.875		2.889	
	.000	.354		.333	
	1	8	0	9	
ES .15, p .01 TOTAL	1.643	2.371	1.667	2.066	Total: ES .26
	.842	.843	.888	.910	
	14	35	12	61	
Military					
OD	1.500	2.250	1.667	1.710	ES .07, p .24
	.827	1.035	1.155	.938	
	20	8	3	31	
SC	1.714	1.833		1.769	
	.951	.983		.927	
	7	6	0	13	
TOTAL	1.556	2.071	1.667	1.727	
ES .001, p .85	.847	.997	1.155	.924	Total ES .09
	27	14	3	44	

Source: Appendix; PRIO Data Bank.
1 = more than 75 percent affiliated with dominant religion; 2 = more than 50 percent
      affiliated with dominant religion; 3 = less than fifty percent belonging to any
      religious denomination. See the footnote to table 5.11 for abbreviations.

tenuated. Thus, it appears that ethnic fragmentation is a better predictor
of violent repression than is religious diversity.

   More salient contrasts appear in table 5.37 when controls for particular
religions are introduced. In those countries where a majority are Hindu
or Protestant, the same proportions are minimal as violent. Weber, of
course, linked Protestantism to the rise of capitalism and cultural values
supportive of democracy. Lipset refers to a conference wherein "Ernest
Griffith [saw] a necessary connection between the Judeo–Christian heritage and attitudes which sustain democratic institutions."[85] He continues, however, by referring to a number of authors who maintain that
Roman Catholicism is antithetical to such norms. Our data fail to support
this supposition as almost one-third of the Roman Catholic countries are

Table 5.37.
Dominant Religion and State Repression (1980)

Repressiveness N, R, C, T%	1.	2.	3.	4.	5.	6.	TOTAL**
Violent	13	0	16	1	1	1	32
	40.6%	.0%	50.0%	3.1%	3.1%	3.1%	
	56.5	.0	53.3	25.0	33.3	33.3	50.0
	20.3	.0	25.0	1.6	1.6	1.6	
Institutional	3	0	13	2	2	1	21
	14.3	.0	61.9%	9.5	9.5	4.8	
	13.0	.0	43.3	50.0	66.7	33.3	32.8
	4.7	.0	20.3	3.1	3.1	1.6	
Minimal	7	1	1	1	0	1	11
	63.6	9.1	9.1	9.1	.0	9.1	
	30.4	100.0	3.3	25.0	.0	33.3	17.2
	10.9	1.6	1.6	1.6	.0	1.6	
TOTAL	23	1	30	4	3	3	64
	35.9	1.6	46.9	6.3	4.7	4.7	

Source: Appendix; PRIO Data Bank.
*1 = Roman Catholic; 2 = Orthodox; 3 = Islam; 4 = Protestant; 5 = Buddhist;
6 = Hindu.
**Chi square = 17.9, p .06, DF = 10.

minimally repressive. Although it is true that more than half are violent, many of these are in Latin America where U.S. military training impact has been most pronounced. Thus, religion may mask the effect of that variable. Future multi-variate analysis would resolve doubts about possible multi-collinearity here. The differences are more clear-cut for Muslin countries where brutality and high repression are particularly evident. With respect to Christianity, however, there are too few cases to generalize about Protestantism, and considerable doubt exists about Roman Catholicism since 30 percent of the cases do fall into the minimally repressive category although a majority are denoted as violent.

PATTERNS AND PROSPECTS

Before summarizing and where possible attempting to derive meaning from the specific patterns, it must be stressed that in varying degree they represent more than random events in a chaotic Third World. Globally there may be a dominant "world market," yet to extrapolate from this to a single "world system" is unwarranted and not particularly useful. Two rival social orders espousing antithetical development strategies are engaged in an often deadly struggle to ensure that sympathetic Third World forces remain in or accede to state power.[86] There are others, populist or "national democratic" state capitalists, who aspire for a genuinely non-aligned alternative to both open door "monopoly capitalism" as well as Marxist–Leninist state socialism. While superpower and allied competitive intervention of the other side's supporters, and militarism as well, I point to the aforementioned only as the framework or environment for Third World politico-military dynamics.[87] Obviously, imperialism, militarism, and "class interest" cannot explain *all* the repressiveness. There are endogenous antagonisms associated with religion, race, and ethnicity. Indigenous conflict over power, privilege, and prestige also are analytically and upon occasion empirically independent of the ideological framework mentioned earlier. But the effective if temporary reverses for New International Economic Order (NIEO) initiatives at a time of unprecedented Third World indebtedness and capitalist economic stagnation in a context of intensified West–East tensions helps us understand why the non-aligned movement is also in eclipse and developing countries are now experiencing a decline of residual systemic autonomy. In other words, the prospect is for greater external impact and consequential repression in Third World systems.[88]

Thus, if we have seen a modest trend since the early 1960s in the direction of state capitalism and state socialism,—the latter as we observed in previous sections offering the best socio-economic development prospects for closing the gap with advanced capitalist nations,[89]—there has also been a steady rise in the proportion of military-dominant systems. One of the most salient findings was the high incidence of violent repressiveness characterizing open door military regimes. The fact that such regimes had received the highest prior per capita aid raises doubts about the utility of economic aid in preventing brutality or repressiveness. That American training impact was strikingly high for violently repressive military governments is both more comprehensible and consistent with Herman's thesis. The weakness of organized labor in conjunction with relatively high levels of direct foreign investment for the brutal military category is also easy to reconcile within this framework.

At first glance, we face a greater challenge in explaining the associations between length of statehood, Roman Catholicism, and repressive violence. Yet, as I have argued, their high concurrence in Latin America where Washington also has long exercised predominant politico-military influence enables us to fit all of the aforementioned within the American hegemonic paradigm. Additional consistent findings on disproportionate linkages with military regimes and especially the brutal variants pertained to overseas U.S. (and in lesser measure other allied North Atlantic Pact) military personnel, training, and interventions. With respect to such interventions, the relative frequency (roughly half) and lethality (95 percent of casualties) of U.S. military involvement contributes to our understanding of both Washington's paramount imperial role as well as the gradual erosion of America's prestige since its epogee in the early 1950s.

On the other hand, we have seen that such brutality cannot be wholly reconciled with the economic determinism of such theorists as Lipset, Pye, and Huntington. Brutal countries are generally wealthier, have higher rates of increase for food production, and are as urban and industrialized as non-sanguinary repressive regimes. Nor are their economic growth rates, military manpower burdens, child mortality, or life expectancy performance markedly inferior to such non-brutal regimes.

It is true, of course, that the minimally repressive eleven civilian and three military-dominant systems fall within the open door development orientation. While they have averaged the *lowest* military manpower and budgetary allocations, this was also the case with respect to foreign military personnel. On the other hand, they were quite high on U.S. officer training impact, armed forces expansion, foreign investment, and per capita aid. Trade union organization is higher than in other open door variants, and the minimally repressive are salient in such areas as literacy, higher educational enrollments, female percentages of university enrollment, and in lesser measure life expectancy. In addition, a higher percentage of their workers are industrial workers. Thus, they do in certain but not all respects conform to Lipset's and Apter's criteria for "democratic" non-repressive systems. Their uniformly fair to good treatment of minorities is paralleled by the paucity of internal war, invasions, and interventions. What must be underscored, however, is that none of this is wholly explicable by reference to purely economic criteria—per capita GNP or manufacturing sectors—though their prior growth rates were good. As previously stated, they were characterized by high rates of increase in both armed forces manpower and financial military burdens.[90] These secular trends, despite relatively low comparative military burdens, in a context of global stagnation afflicted by renewed American militarism, bode ill for the stability of such anachronistic systems. Indeed, by mid–1984 both Nigeria and Jamaica had succumbed to military or executive coups, warranting reclassification to the institutionally repressive category.

Pessimism may also be warranted by the growing proportion of military-dominant regimes. This is particularly ominous since civilian governments tend, as we have seen, to be less brutal and repressive than their military (especially the open door) counterparts, this despite lower average per capita income and less per capita aid. Yet their GNP per capita growth rates have been superior to those of military as have their child mortality rate, educational enrollments, percentage of women in universities, treatment of minorities, relative freedom from coups, and internal war. But they have suffered the largest proportion of war casualties, foreign invasions, and in lesser measure interventions.

Such victimization has also characterized the emergent and generally non-brutal state socialist systems. By far the lowest on per capita GNP and considerably behind other variants in per capita aid and food production growth, they are nevertheless the most urban, literate, and industrialized of developing countries. Notwithstanding a paucity of internal war, they have experienced the greatest proportionate incidence of foreign invasions, interventions, and civilian casualties. If Winston Churchill's 1918 dictum was to "strangle the infant in the crib," there is no doubt that this socialist "monster" has been a prolific generator of offspring and imitators following World War II and particularly since 1960. American "failure" in a half-dozen or more countries has resulted in intensified militarization and a more belligerent stance by the United States.[91] The fear undergirding this is premised in part upon the superior Third World socio-economic performance of this rival social system,[92] along with the concomitant constriction of the number of countries in which transnational corporations enjoy total autonomy in setting the terms for their activities. Only the state socialist development strategy gives evidence of even slowly closing the socio-economic gap with the North. Not to be overlooked is the fact that despite the inevitable economic costs of structural transformation, their manufacturing sectoral shares and per capita GNP growth rates are also the highest.

On the other hand, while for understandable reasons their military burdens are also unsurpassed, it is striking that only socialist regimes—and in lesser measure civilian state capitalists—were actually reducing them. Given this demilitarization within the context of a high mobilizational and investing development orientation, we can better understand not only state socialism's superior if modest growth rates, but also their unexcelled performance on such welfare indicators as child mortality, life expectancy, literacy, newspaper circulation, urbanization, and education. More salient even is the almost complete absence of violent repressiveness with the exception of Albania and Kampuchea in the late 1970s.

The vortex of the struggle between the rival social systems centers upon open door and particularly the state capitalist regimes. The latter are characterized by the most salient state socialist military linkages with the Soviet Union and its allies, on the one hand, and similar relationships with America's allies, on the other. With respect to these radical regimes, the United States is less heavily involved insofar as training, military personnel, and arms transfers are concerned. At times in cooperation with allies (Ghana in 1966), and upon other occasions unilaterally (Chile in 1973, Nicaragua in 1984), Washington tends to rely upon its own Central Intelligence Agency-directed covert destabilization efforts. The factionalism and antagonistic capitalist versus socialist norms that characterize such radical nationalistic regimes contribute to explaining their poor economic and modest though uneven socio-cultural achievements, as well as their political instability. These parameters also go some way in helping us comprehend the brutal repression that characterizes many of them—especially the military variants. Their relative military expenditures are high as are armed forces ratios, particularly for the violently repressive.

In the final analysis, then, the secular decline in brutality was a temporary phenomenon associated with diminished polarization and tensions during the era of detente in the late 1970s. Particularly fateful was

Sivard's previously mentioned finding of a close association between superpower "client" status and repressive state violence.[93] While violent, indeed all, repression is obviously conditioned by ethnic discrimination, religion (Islam), and other cultural traditions as well as the character of situational conflicts, fears, and constraints, an appreciable quantum like war itself[94] derives from the intensity of global rivalry[95] over antithetical social orders (that is, modes of production). This interacts with and frequently intensifies domestic ethnic, class, religious, party, and personalistic conflicts that in any event would contribute to repression in many systems afflicted by immense social inequality, pervasive destitution, and a paucity of alternative elite opportunities for upward mobility. Indeed, Gunder Frank prognosticated a few years ago that global capitalist "crisis"—symbolized by stagnation and unprecedented external debt burdens—would engender even greater political repression in developing countries during the 1980s.[96]

Yet it is important to bear in mind that ecological variables—whether of an economic, social, or geographical nature—contribute only moderately to explaining repressive severity within the range assessed here. Of these it would seem that poverty in a context of great social class distance of inequality, high ethnic or religious fragmentation (pluralism), and large highly populated states are especially prone to violent repression. Given these patterns in conjunction with J. David Singer's finding that major states account disproportionately for inter-state war,[97] my policy prescription is for smaller, more ethno-religiously homogeneous states. Secessionist movements should be legitimized and encouraged.

Yet, as stressed previously, it appears that such situational variables as development orientations, religious preference, political leadership unity, and concessional dispositions along with Cold War interventionism may be more significant catalysts or inhibitors of repressive brutality now, victimizing more than 2 billion persons in close to seventy countries—roughly half of the global "community."[98] Here, policy prescription with respect to non-interventionism and alternative non-threatening national security approaches is elaborated in the work of Herbert Wulf, Earl C. Ravenal, Robert C. Johansen, and Sheldon Richman.[99] Reciprocally, future research might build upon the work of Odell, Shoultz, Herman, Bollen, Kende, and Sivard by more precisely isolating those states most "penetrated" and "dependent" in an attempt to assess their relative contribution to torture, executions, disappearances, and civilian internal war casualties.[100]

To these "costs" borne by peoples in the South must be added the less certain but potentially more devastating carnage that reinforcing "offensive" militarization in the North may visit upon both West and East. In pinpointing socio-political "conformity" and the "conviction of superiority," Eckhardt may have anticipated at the psychological level those superstructural forces that in the ultimate state terrorist "atrocity" of advancing "civilization" will stand a devastated base upon its non-existent head.

NOTES

The author is particularly grateful for research support from the Norwegian Research Council for the Sciences and the Humanities (NAVF); International Peace Research Institute, Oslo; (PRIO); Samuel Rubin Foundation; Public Concern Foundation; Inter-University Seminar on Armed Forces and Society; and the State University of New York. This is derivative of a larger project between 1980 and 1982 that could not have been undertaken without their generosity. The chapter's shortcomings, of course, are my own. They have been lessened as a consequence of helpful criticism and suggestions by George Lopez.

1. Lars Schoultz, "U.S. Foreign Policy and Human Rights Violations in Latin America: A Comparative Analysis of Foreign Aid Distributions," *Comparative Politics*, 13 (January 1981), pp. 149–170.

2. Edward Herman, *The Real Terror Network* (Boston: South End Press, 1982).

3. Iain Guest, "Report to U.N. Panel Cites 2 Million Executions," *International Herald Tribune*, (February 17, 1983), p. 3.

4. Seymour M. Lipset, "Some Social Requisites of Democracy: Economic Development and Political Legitimacy," *American Political Science Review*, 8 (March 1959), pp. 69–105; and Charles F. Cnudde and Deane E. Neubauer, eds., *Empirical Political Theory* (Chicago: Markham, 1969), p. 180.

5. Ruth Leger Sivard, *World Military and Social Expenditures: 1981* (Leesburg, VA: World Priorities, 1981), p. 20; and United Nations Secretary-General, *The Relationship Between Disarmament and Development*, Department of Political and Security Council Affairs, United Nations Centre for Disarmament, Report of the Secretary-General (New York: United Nations, 1982), p. 25.

6. Thus, among 102 low-income countries with a 1960 population in excess of 300,000 and a 1966 per capita GNP below $1,600, Miles D. Wolpin, in *Militarization, Repression and Social Welfare in the Third World* (Oslo: PRIO, 1983), found the military-dominant proportion increased from 13 percent between 1960 and 1967 to 40 percent for the 1965–1978 period. My table 5.3 employing similar criteria for a slightly different country set in 1980 reveals 43 percent, while Sivard's in table 5.14 indicates 46 percent are militarily ruled.

7. William Eckhardt, "Atrocities, Civilizations, and Savages: Ways to Avoid a Nuclear Holocaust," *Bulletin of Peace Proposals*, 13, (1982), pp. 344–345.

8. As Eckhardt notes:

The anthropological evidence would suggest that...far from being a natural instinct, human aggression seems to be a product of historical development, social discipline, and sexual frustration. Crime, punishment, slavery, and war were less prevalent among gatherers and fishers, more prevalent among hunters, even more so among farmers and herders and most of all among city dwellers.

. . .

[Similarly] the historical evidence has shown that almost all civilizations have been characterized by atrocious behaviors, including slavery and wars. . . . All civilizations were based on exploitation, but modern civilization (simply because it was a latecomer) exploited and exterminated more people more efficiently than any previous civilization. Ibid.

9. Raymond F. Gastil, "Ten Year Record of the Survey," *Freedom at Issue*, 64 (January–February 1982), p. 4.

10. Ibid., p. 7. The following excerpts delineate criteria in the two areas, which are assigned equal weight for his composite rankings.

In *political rights*, states rated (1) have a fully competitive electoral process and those elected clearly rule. Most West European democracies belong here. Relatively free states may receive a (2) because, although the electoral process works and the elected rule, there are factors which cause us to lower our rating of the effective equality of the process. These factors may include extreme economic inequality, illiteracy, or intimidating violence. They also include the weakening of effective competition that is implied by the absence of periodic shifts in rule from one group or party to another. Turning to the scale for *civil liberties*, in countries rated (1), publications are not closed because of the expression of rational political opinion, especially when the intent of the expression is to affect the legitimate political process. No major media are simply conduits for government propaganda. The courts protect the individual; persons are not imprisoned for their opinions; private rights and desires in education, occupaton, religion, residence, and so on, are generally respected; law-abiding persons do not fear for their lives because of their rational political activities.

11. Raymond F. Gastil, "The Comparative Survey of Freedom," *Freedom at Issue*, 17 (January–February 1973), and *Freedom in the World: Political Rights and Civil Liberties: 1981* (Westport, CT: Greenwood Press, 1981).

12. The chi square was 52.6, p .000 ($DF = 4$). Criteria for inclusion in this country set appear in the section that follows.

13. Wolpin, *Militarization*, appendix F.

14. My approach to the concept of repression is a conventional Western one. Thus, when there was evidence of patterned sanctioning against one or more parties or movements that had sought to alter the policies or supplant an existing government, the system was denoted as institutionally repressive. Where it also appeared that brutality (executions, torture, disappearances, very harsh prison conditions) was common rather than an exceptional occurrence, I classified the regime as "violent." If neither situation characterized the regime, it was placed in the "minimal" category. These criteria are somewhat arbitrary in that they ignore practices in certain countries (that is, Cuba or Libya) that encourage popular criticism or discussion of proposed laws and complaints against low-level officials at assemblies or in the press, etc. Although a fivefold classification could have been used to reduce this bias, it would have precluded construction of a "composite index"—explained shortly in the text—and in any case highly differentiated ranking categories are available from Gastil, *Freedom in the World*, pp. 14–17, for those who would make use of them. Further, such a degree of differentiation is not necessary for the types of relationships I propose to examine, and it is of dubious value in view of data imprecision and the frequent incremental oscillations that characterize many developing countries. It was also rejected because the inclusion of brutality—an important concern here—would have required a sixfold scale with very few countries in several of the classifications and considerable doubt about ordinal comparability.

15. Fred Halliday, *The Making of the Second Cold War* (London: Verso, 1983).

16. Andre Gunder Frank, *Crisis: In the Third World* (New York: Holmes and Meier, 1981).

17. Ruth Leger Sivard, *World Military and Social Expenditures: 1983: An Annual Report on World Priorities* (Washington, D.C.: World Priorities, 1983), p. 19.

18. Wolpin, *Militarization.*

19. Ruth Leger Sivard, *World Military and Social Expenditures: 1982* (Leesburg, VA: World Priorities), p. 17.

20. Gastil, "Comparative Survey of Freedom," p. 25.

21. If Gastil's determination tallied with either Sivard's or mine, that became the composite rank. Countries were placed in an intermediate category in a few cases only when all three of us assigned a different rank. The consequential composite index of table 5.7, however, is not appreciably different from my table 5.3 classification. Less than a half-dozen countries were affected: Albania, Madagascar, Malawi, Bahrain, and the Central African Republic.

22. Herman, *Real Terror Network.*

23. A tentative quality characterizes most statistical studies of developing nations because of data unreliability. Unavailability, fabrication, a lack of uniformity in classification, and concealment are variously discussed by Morris Janowitz, *The Military and the Political Development of New Nations* (Chicago: University of Chicago Press, 1964), p. 18; Jerry L. Weaver, "Assessing the Impact of Military Rule: Alternative Approaches," in Philippe C. Schmitter, ed., *Military Rule in Latin America: Functions, Consequences and Perspectives* (Beverly Hills, CA: Sage Publications, 1973), pp. 64–65; Stephanie Neuman, "Security, Military Expenditures and Socioeconomic Development: Reflections on Iran," *Orbis*, vol. 22 (Fall 1978), pp. 564–574; Milton Leitenberg and Nicole Ball, "The Military Expenditures of Less Developed Nations as a Proportion of Their State Budgets: A Research Note," in Asbjorn Eide and Marek Thee, eds., *Problems of Contemporary Militarism* (London: Croom Helm, 1980), pp. 286–295; Ofira Seliktar, "The Cost of Vigilance in Israel: Linking the Economic and Social Costs of Defense," *Journal of Peace Research*, 17 (1980), p. 341; Helena Tuomi and Vayrynen Raimo, *Transnational Corporations, Armament and Development: A Study of Transnational Military Production, International Transfers of Military Technology and Their Impact on Development* (Tamperi, Finland: TAPRI 1980); and Frank Blackaby and Thomas Ohlson, "Military Expenditure and the Arms Trade," *Bulletin of Peace Proposals*, 13 (1982), pp. 291–308.

24. It should also be borne in mind that statistical significance is based upon normal distributions characteristic of sampling probabilities. Here we have compared differences within the universe of countries rather than a sample. Thus, where they appear, such differences have been genuine in an empirical sense, rather than a consequence of sampling error. At most, then, failure to attain customary $p = .05$ significance reveals the degree of dispersion and the consequential "meaningfulness" of observed differences. Because funding limitations prevented the subsequent use of more sophisticated measures such as multivariate regression and longitudinal analysis, some of the observed relationships may be spurious due to multi-collinearity, that is, the association of violent repressiveness with both duration of statehood and Roman Catholicism. This has been noted in the textual discussion. All data are available from the nation data

bank of the International Peace Research Institute, Oslo, and may be subjected to further analysis.

25. If the armed forces seized civil office at least a month prior to the end of the year, the nation was classified as military dominant. The determination of repressiveness was in such cases based upon the post-coup period. Countries were classified as military dominant when one or more of the following conditions existed: (1) where the civil chief executive is either designated by the armed forces or subject to military veto; (2) when civil policies or designation of military commanders is subject to military veto; (3) where civil control over military policies or courts is marginal or non-existent; or (4) when less than a decade has passed since the armed forces have voluntarily relinquished control of civil governmental office.

26. Under monopoly capitalism or the "open door" orientation, political and bureaucratic elites generally endeavor to enhance the profitability of the private sector. Because the latter is dominated by transnational corporations [Albert Szymanski, *The Logic of Imperialism* (New York: Praeger, 1981), pp. 326–329] in most under-developed areas, so long as indigenous officials acquiesce in such relations, their domestic and even foreign policy choices tend to *depend upon* favorable reactions by such corporations and associated international financial institutions. "Dependency" has evolved historically with the growth and extension of monopoly capitalism into a world system.

"State" capitalism involves attempts to radically reduce dependency (enlarging policy alternatives) and simultaneous promotion of nationally controlled industrial development. Characteristic of such regimes are state *ownership* of or majority equity holdings in most large economic enterprises. Similarly, economic relations are diversified so that major transactions occur with Eastern state socialist systems. Other policies usually associated with state capitalist regimes are listed in Wolpin, *Militarization.*

State socialist systems may be distinguished from state capitalism in the following ways: First, the residual private sector is being *reduced* rather than tolerated as legitimate. This sector is also much smaller and generally limited to medium- and more commonly small-scale economic undertakings. Finally, *primary* elite roles are those of production mobilizers rather than bureaucratic consumers. Their socialist orientation is manifested by a futurist ethos, Spartan style of life, egalitarian Marxist ideology, and disciplined party organization.

Many societies are obviously on a *continuum.* Neither linearity of movement nor stability of position is universal. In short, state socialist systems (Yugoslavia) may "degenerate" into state capitalist regimes, while revolutionary elites who seize monopoly capitalist systems (China) can virtually telescope the state capitalist phase by moving quickly on to state socialism. Recent Chinese policy departures may indicate some "backsliding." Similarly, state capitalist regimes like Egypt and Ghana may revert in some measure toward monopoly capitalism. Reversion is, however, seldom complete. Chile is exceptional in this regard. Thus, the consonance of state capitalist production relations with the neutralization of at least some major contradictions in Third World monopoly capitalism may partially explain why the right-wing coup successor regimes (that is, Jamaica) *generally* accept enlarged state sectors—sales of a few state enterprises notwithstanding—and limit themselves to adopting a deferential stance toward new foreign investment only in as-yet-unexploited areas. Hence, the trend in monopoly capitalist systems is an ineluctable if gradual historical one toward what might be termed "creeping state capitalism." In Black Africa today, for example, eighteen of thirty states have instituted selective or comprehensive nationalizations of foreign investments. And as their technical and managerial skills improve, this will be extended to modern manufacturing (largely import assembly plants) operations, which as yet are least affected.

27. The criterion for inclusion in one of the three development orientations or strategies described in the preceding note is that such policies be dominant for at least two-thirds of the period in question. When a regime was induced to alter its approach or supplanted, it was classified as "mixed."

28. Or in the terms of Ralph Miliband, *The State in Capitalist Society* (New York: Basic Books, 1969), p. 266: "The maintenance of a social order characterized by class domination may require the dictatorship of the state, the suppression of all opposition, the abrogation of all constitutional guarantees and political freedoms. But in the countries of advanced capitalism, it generally has not.".

29. Kenneth Bollen, "World System Position, Dependency, and Democracy: The Cross-National Evidence," *American Sociological Review*, 48 (August 1983), pp. 468–479.

30. Lipset, "Some Social Requisites," p. 155.

31. Ibid., p. 154.

32. Max Weber, "Archiv fur Sozialwissenschaft und Sozialpolitik," in Weber, *Essays in Sociology* (New York: Oxford University Press, 1958), pp. 71–72. Thus, Weber stressed the occurrence of "certain" unique pre-conditions that will never repeat themselves. Let us enumerate the most important of these:

First, the overseas expansions...
Second, the uniqueness of the economic and social structure of the early capitalist epoch in Western Europe.
Third, the conquest of life by science, "the self-realization of the spirit." The rational construction of institutional life, doubtless after having destroyed innumerable "values"...
Finally, certain conceptions of ideal values, grown out of a world of definite religious ideas, have stamped the ethical peculiarity and cultural values of modern man. They have done so by working with numerous political constellations, themselves quite unique, and with the material preconditions of early capitalism. One need merely ask whether any material development or even any development of the high capitalism of today could maintain or create again these unique historical conditions of freedom and democracy in order to know the answer. No shadow of probability speaks for the fact that economic "socialization" as such must harbor in its lap either the development of inwardly "free" personalities or "altruistic" ideals.

33. Lucien Pye, *Aspects of Political Development* (Boston: Little, Brown, 1966).

34. S. E. Finer, *Comparative Government* (New York: Basic Books, 1971), pp. 537–539.

35. Lipset, "Some Social Requisites," pp. 172–173.

36. Samuel P. Huntington, *Political Order in Changing Societies* (New Haven, CT: Yale University Press, 1968).

37. Szymanski, *Logic of Imperialism*, pp. 277–283.

38. In the previously cited study by Wolpin (*Militarization*, pp. 77–78) of 102 developing countries, military-dominant systems were characterized by a higher average rate of armed forces expansion in the 1960–1977 period, though much of this occurred during the 1960s. Civilian regimes were higher on armed forces ratio increases during the twelve years from 1967 until 1979.

39. With respect to the torture classification in table 5.2, Wolpin, *Militarization*, pp. 76–77, found both those engaging in torture (1973–1975) as well as the "less free" countries had heavier financial military burdens and a higher rate of increase thereof during the 1970s.

40. In another study based upon a dichotomization of Gastil's rankings at the median, Wolpin (*Militarizaton*, p. 81)

found that more repressive systems in general had heavier *financial* military burdens and a greater increase while the more free countries were characterized by greater armed forces expansion. In general, military regimes are higher on not only repression but also exhibited heavier military financial burdens, greater armed forces expansion but a lower rise in military spending as well as slightly less welfare improvement than their civilian counterparts. U.S. training impact was also somewhat higher for both military and less free regimes (latter including many of the former) but slightly lower for those engaging in torture and related practices in 1973–1975. There was no difference on this however in 1976–1979.

41. Erik Nordlinger, "Soldiers in Mufti: The Impact of Military Rule upon Economic and Social Change in the Non-Western States," *American Political Science Review* 64 (December 1970), pp. 1131–1148; S. E. Finer, *The Man on Horseback* (Harmondsworth: Penguin Books, 1975); R. D. McKinlay and A. S. Cohen, "Performance and Instability in Military and Nonmilitary Regime Systems," *American Political Science Review* 70 (September 1976), pp. 850–864; Neal R. Tannahill, "The Performance of Military Governments in South America," *Journal of Political and Military Sociology*, 4 (Fall 1976), pp. 233–244; Wolpin, *Militarization*; and Sivard, *World Military and Social Expenditures: 1981*, p. 8.

Sivard emphasizes that "half of all the developing countries" in her survey—54—were controlled or dominated by the military, and that fully "41 have been cited for violating basic human rights to safety under the law."

42. Sivard, *World Military and Social Expenditures: 1983*, p. 19.

43. Sivard, *World Military and Social Expenditures: 1982*, p. 17.

44. Sivard, *World Military and Social Expenditures: 1981*, p. 8, records that approximately 95 percent of "the 125 or more conflicts which have occurred in the world since World War II" have been in the Third World. "In most cases foreign forces have been involved, Western powers accounting for 79 percent of the interventions, communist for 6 percent, other developing nations for the remainder." In Istvan Kende, "New Features of Armed Conflicts and Armaments in Developing Countries," *Development and Peace*, 4 (Autumn 1983), similar patterns are reported for 148 wars between 1945 and 1979.

45. Halliday, *Making of the Second Cold War*.

46. Miles D. Wolpin, *Military Aid and Counter-Revolution in the Third World* (Lexington, MA: D. C. Heath, 1973); and Szymanski, *Logic of Imperialism*, pp. 177–288.

47. Sivard, *World Military and Social Expenditures: 1983*, p. 19.

48. According to Sivard, *World Military and Social Expenditures: 1981*, p. 9, the Soviet Union trained 43,000 military personnel from developing areas between 1955 and 1979, while for the United States alone the 1950–1980 total was in excess of 411,000. "Approximately three fourths of those trained by the superpowers came from countries now under military domination."

49. For interpretative purposes in this section, I treat the four state socialist cases (Cuba, Vietnam, Laos, Kampuchea) as open door since training was of armies that remained "loyal" to Washington until their military defeat, after which they were disbanded by successful revolutionary forces. All were military dominant and violently repressive.

50. Herman, *Real Terror Network*; William A. Williams, *The Tragedy of American Diplomacy* (New York: Dell, 1962); Gabriel Kolko, *The Roots of American Foreign Policy* (Boston: Beacon Press, 1969); and Harry Magdoff, *The Age of Imperialism: The Economies of U.S. Foreign Policy* (New York: Monthly Review Press, 1969).

51. John S. Odell, "Correlates of U.S. Military Assistance and Military Intervention," in Steven J. Rosen and James R. Kurth, eds., *Testing Theories of Economic Imperialism* (Lexington, MA: D. C. Heath, 1974), p. 155.

52. Bollen, "World System Position," p. 476.

53. Schoultz, "U.S. Foreign Policy."

54. Lipset, "Some Social Requisites," p. 153.

55. Ibid., p. 164.

56. Robert Heilbroner, *The Great Ascent: The Struggle for Economic Development in Our Time* (New York: Harper and Row, 1962), p. 135.

57. Bollen, "World System Position," p. 470.

58. Daniel Chirot, *Social Changes in the Twentieth Century* (New York: Harcourt Brace Jovanovich, 1977), pp. 223–224.

59. Ibid., pp. 80–81.

60. Pye, *Aspects of Political Development*, p. 72.

61. Bollen, "World System Position," p. 477.

62. Barrington Moore, Jr., *The Social Origins of Dictatorship and Democracy*, (Boston: Beacon Press, 1966).

63. Fernando H. Cardoso and Enzo Faletto, *Dependency and Development in Latin America* (Berkeley: University of California Press, 1979); and Peter Evans, *Dependent Development* (Princeton, NJ: Princeton University Press, 1979).

64. Bollen, "World System Position," p. 470.

65. Heilbroner, *Great Ascent*; Lipset, "Some Social Requisites"; and Bollen, "World System Position."

66. Shlomo Avimen, *Social and Political Thought of Karl Marx* (New York: Cambridge University Press, 1971).

67. Pye, *Aspects of Political Development*, pp. 72–73.

68. Seymour M. Lipset, *The First New Nation: The United States in Historical and Comparative Perspective* (New York: Basic Books, 1963), p. 246.

69. Lipset, "Some Social Requisites," p. 181.

70. Miles D. Wolpin, *Militarism and Social Revolution in the Third World* (Totowa, NJ: Alanheld, Osmun, 1981).

71. Had I excluded the three Indochinese states—Vietnam, Kampuchea,

and Laos—which suffered the havoc of war during the decade, the state socialist average would have been even higher yet. The same is true for Cuba, whose economy was severely damaged by the U.S. embargo. According to a Banco Nacional de Cuba study, it has cost that nation's economy in excess of $9 billion. See Colin McSeveny, "Lack of Foreign Currency Forcing Cuba to Seek Debt Re-Scheduling," *International Herald Tribune*, (February 28, 1983), p. 7.

72. Moore, *Social Origins*.

73. Miliband, *State in Capitalist Society*, p. 266.

74. Elsewhere ("Some Social Requisites," p. 169) Lipset posed the same challenge:

Many of the newly independent nations of Asia and Africa face the problem of winning the loyalties of the masses to democratic states which can do little to fulfill the utopian objectives set by nationalist movements during the period of colonialism, and the transitional struggle to independence.

75. Ted Robert Gurr, *Why Men Rebel* (Princeton, NJ: Princeton University Press, 1970), pp. 317–352.

76. Lipset, *First New Nation*, pp. 246–247.

77. Wolpin, *Militarization*. Wolpin's analysis of relationships between U.S. training impact (1950–1976 as a percentage of 1977 armed forces) indicates that it is negatively related to physical welfare (1976–1978) for military (r - .48) and open door (r - .–45) regimes during the 1965–1978 period. This was also true (r - .–56) for "less free" countries (that is, respect for political rights and civil liberties) in 1973. For all countries, the correlation coefficient was y-.44 (p - .01), while those in the "open door" category exhibited the highest mean values for U.S. training impact regardless of whether they were civilian or military. In general, however, such impact was greater for military than civilian regimes. And while countries in the early 1970s that were not characterized by torture, political executions, and disappearances scored slightly lower on U.S. training impact, by 1976–1979 the difference had evaporated.

78. In the previously cited study (Wolpin, *Militarization*, pp. 77–81), which included a large number of physical welfare variables for 102 developing countries, the following were among the more salient findings: (1) military-dominant systems tended to be inferior on welfare improvement during the 1970s, although the differences were often small and frequently lacked statistical significance; (2) the "less free" (Gastil, 1973, 1982) were superior on these variables, and the differences tended to be greater than for the civilian–military dichotomy; (3) this despite the fact that the less free were lower on per capita income, industrialization, and prior economic growth. In seeking to reconcile these patterns, it was stressed that (1) the less free also received higher per capita aid, and this in turn was correlated with superior welfare change; and (2) the less free category also included state socialist systems, which by far were the best performers.

79. Seymour M. Lipset, *Political Man: The Social Basis of Politics* (New York: Doubleday, 1960), pp. 154, 157–165.

80. Gurr, *Why Men Rebel*, pp. 358–359.

81. Bingham G. Powell, *Contemporary Democracies: Participation, Stability and Violence* (Cambridge, MA: Harvard University Press, 1982), pp. 46–47.

82. David Apter, *The Politics of Modernization* (Chicago: University of Chicago Press, 1965).

83. Karl Marx, "Speech at Amsterdam," from *Selected Works*, vol. 18, (Moscow, 1935).

84. Arend Lijphart, "Typologies of Democratic Systems," *Comparative Political Studies*, 1 (April 1968), pp. 14–17.

85. Lipset, "Some Social Requisites," pp. 52, 190.

86. Halliday, *Making of the Second Cold War.*

87. Indeed, Kende, "New Features," found that the intensity of this East–West conflict was highly correlated with the frequency of Third World—largely internal—wars in the 1946–1979 period. Foreign involvement—most often Western and particularly American—was a salient parameter of these wars.

88. One can also point to the demise of the Organization of Oil-Exporting Countries, reservations by the United States and other major powers to the new regime for oceanic seabed exploitation, Arab weakness and disunity during and since the invasion of Lebanon, similar Latin American indifference to Nicaragua's fate, the paucity of Front Line material aid to Angola or Mozambique, their recent compromise with South Africa, and the sharp divisions within the Organization of African Unity over Chad and the Western Sahara.

89. Szymanski, *Logic of Imperialism*; Wolpin, *Militarism* and *Militarization.*

90. Powell, in *Contemporary Democracies*, stresses the relevance of such variables as the quality of political leadership and unity.

91. Michael T. Klare and Cynthia Arnson, *Supplying Repression: U.S. Support for Authoritarian Regimes Abroad* (Washington, D.C.: Institute for Policy Studies, 1981); Halliday, *Making of the Second Cold War*; and Kende, "New Features."

92. Szymanski, *Logic of Imperialism*; Wolpin, *Militarism*; and Erwin Marquit, *The Socialist Countries* (Minneapolis: Marxist Educational Press, 1983).

93. Sivard, *World Military and Social Expenditures: 1983*, p. 19.

94. Kende, "New Features" and Sivard *World Military and Social Expenditures: 1983.*

95. Halliday, *Making of the Second Cold War.*

96. Frank, *Crisis*, p. 2.

97. J. David Singer, "Accounting for International War: The State of the Discipline," *Journal of Peace Research*, (1981), pp. 1–18.

98. As mentioned in the methodological section, this investigation is intended to be suggestive, tentative, and in a sense heuristic. For more precise determination of the relative impact of each "variable," as well as the exclusion of all possibilities of multi-collinearity, the data can be subjected to multi-variate analysis.

99. Herbert Wulf, "Dependent Militarism in the Periphery and Possible Alternative Concepts," in Stephanie C. Newman and Robert E. Horkavy, eds., *Arms Transfers in the Modern World* (New York: Praeger, 1979); Earl C. Ravenal, *Strategy Disengagement and World Peace* (Washington, D.C.: CATO Institute, 1979); Earl C. Ravenal, "Doing Nothing," *Foreign Policy*, 39 (Summer 1984), pp. 28–39; Robert C. Johansen, *Toward an Alternative Security System: Moving Beyond the Balance of Power in the Search for World Security* (New York: World Policy Institute,

1983); and Sheldon Richman, "The Culture of Intervention," *Inquiry*, (March–April 1984), pp. 12–13.
100. Odell, "Correlates"; Schoultz, "U.S. Foreign Policy"; Herman, *The Real Terror Network*; Bollen, "World System Position"; Kende, "New Features"; and Sivard *World Military and Social Expenditures: 1983*.

APPENDIX: VARIABLE TITLES AND SOURCES

PRIONU: PRIO Nation Code. Nation Identification Numbers. Source: International Peace Research Institute, Radhusgt. 4, Oslo 1, Norway.

WOLPIN: W/A 1 (One). Indicated Countries Included in Data. Source: Miles Wolpin, SUNY, Potsdam, NY.

AFRT1079: W: Armed Forces per Thousand: 1979. Source: USACDA (1982).

AFSIZE79: W: Armed Forces Size: 1979. Source: Sivard (1982).

AIDTOT75: W: Per Capita Average Foreign Aid Total: 1973–1975. Source: Kurian (1979).

AIET6179: W: Arms Imports/East as Percentage of Total: 1961–1979. Source: Sivard (1981).

AIUS6179: W: Arms Imports/U.S. as Percentage of Total: 1961–1979. Source: Sivard (1981).

AIWT6179: W: Arms Imports/West (Excl. U.S.) as Percentage of Total: 1961–1979. Source: Sivard (1981).

CAFR6779: W: Percentage Change in Armed Forces per Thousand: 1967–1979. Source: USACDA (1978, 1982).

CFOODP78: W: Change in Food Production: 1977–1978 Average (1969–1971 = 100). Source: UN (1978).

CGDPA78: W: Gross Domestic Product Average Annual Growth Rate: 1970–1978. Source: World Bank (1980:112–113).

CGPC7079: W: GNP Per Capita Real Change: 1970–1979. Source: World Bank (1982).

CHILDM78: W: Child Death Rate (1–4 Years): 1978. Source: World Bank (1980:150–151).

CINDPD78: W: Industrial Production Growth Rate: 1970–1978. Source: World Bank (1980:112–113).

CIVMIL67: W: Civilian (1) vs. Military (2) Rule: 1960–1967. Minimum Period 5 Years. Source: Wolpin (1981).

CIVMIL79: W: Civilian (1) vs. Military (2) Rule: 1980. Sources: Gastil (1981); U.S. Dept. of State, (1981).

CLFEXB79: W: Life Expectancy Change: 1970–1978. Sources: World Bank (1982); Sivard (1981).

CMCG6779: W: Change in Military Expenditures as a Percentage of Central Government Expenditures: 1967–1979. Sources: USACDA (1978, 1982).

CMFPRD78: W: Manufacturing Production Growth Rate: 1970–1978. Source: World Bank (1980:112–113).

CMLSIV80: W: Sivard's Index of Civilian (1) vs. Military (2) Rule: 1980. Source: Sivard (1982).

COUP6080: W: Sivard's Calculation of Coups: 1960–1982. Source: Sivard (1982).

CVML6578: W: Civilian (1) vs. Military (2) Rule: 1965–1978. Minimum Period 9 Years (Mixed = 3). Source: Wolpin (1981).

DEVSTR80: W: Development Strategy, 1980: Open Door (1); State Capitalist (2); State Socialist (3). Sources: Gastil (1981); U.S. (1981); Banks and Overstreet (1980); *Statesman's Yearbook* (1982).

DOMREL80: W: Dominant Religion Where Majority Are: Roman Catholic (1); Orthodox (2); Islam (3); Protestant (4); Buddhist (5); Hindu (6). Sources: *Statesman's Yearbook* (1982); *Countries* (1978).

DVST6578: W: Development Strategy, 1965–1978: Open Door (1); State Capitalist (2); State Socialist (3); Mixed (4). Minimum Period 9 Years. Source: Wolpin (1981).

FMAMER82: W: Foreign Military Personnel, 1982: American as Percentage of 1979 Armed Forces. Source: Sivard (1982).

FMCOM82: W: Foreign Military Personnel, 1982: All Communist as Percentage of 1979 Armed Forces. Source: Sivard (1982).

FMCUBA82: W: Foreign Military Personnel, 1982. Cuban as Percentage of 1979 Armed Forces. Source: Sivard (1982).

FMGDR82: W: Foreign Military Personnel, 1982: GDR as Percentage of 1979 Armed Forces. Source: Sivard (1982).

FMNOAL82: W: Foreign Military Personnel, 1982: Non-aligned Military Personnel as Percentage of 1979 Armed Forces. Source: Sivard (1982).

FMONAT82: W: Foreign Military Personnel, 1982: NATO (Excluding U.S.) as Percentage of 1979 Armed Forces. Source: Sivard (1982).

FMSAIS82: W: Foreign Military Personnel, 1982: South African and Israeli as Percentage of 1979 Armed Forces. Source: Sivard (1982).

FMTOTL82: W: Foreign Military Personnel, 1982: Total as Percentage of 1979 Armed Forces. Source: Sivard (1982).

FMUSNT82: W: Foreign Military Personnel, 1982: All NATO as Percentage of 1979 Armed Forces. Source: Sivard (1982).

FMUSSR82: W: Foreign Military Personnel, 1982: Soviet as Percentage of 1979 Armed Forces. Source: Sivard (1982).

FRARTR77: W: French Arms Transfers ($ Millions, Current): 1973–1977. Source: USACDA (1979).

FRGART77: W: Federal Republic of Germany Arms Transfers ($ Millions, Current): 1973–1977. Source: USACDA (1979).

GEOGHY80: W: Geographic Region: Africa (1); Latin America and Caribbean (2); Asia (3); Middle East and Mediterranean (4). Source: *Statesman's Yearbook* (1982).

GNPPER79: W: Gross National Product per Capita: 1979. Source: Sivard (1982).

HIEDEN76: W: Higher Education Enrollment as a Percentage of 20–24 Age Cohort. Source: World Bank (1980).

INDEP80: W: Duration of Independent Statehood: Post–1955 (1); 1900–1955 (2); Pre–1900 (3). Source: *Statesman's Yearbook* (1982).

INDLAB78: W: Industrial Percentage of the Labor Force: 1978. Source: World Bank (1980:146–147).

INTR6082: W: Years of Internal War: 1960–1982. Source: Sivard (1982:15).

INTV6082: W: Years of Foreign Military Intervention: 1960–1982. Source: Sivard (1982:15).

INVD6082: W: Years of Foreign Military Invasion: 1960–1982. Source: Sivard (1982:15).

LIFEXB78: W:Life Expectancy at Birth: 1978. Source: World Bank (1980:150–151).

LITRCY79: W:Adult Literacy Rate: 1979. Source: Sivard (1982).

MFGDP78: W: Manufacturing as Percentage of Gross Domestic Product: 1978. Source: World Bank (1980:114–115).

MINOR80: W: Treatment of Minorities, 1980: Fair/Good—No Insurgency (1); Fair/Good—Insurgency (2); Poor—No Insurgency (3); Poor—Insurgency (4). Source: Gastil (1981).

MIXCGE79: W: Military Expenditures as Percentage of Central Government Expenditures: 1979. Source: USACDA (1982).

MXGNP79: W: Military Expenditures as Percentage GNP: 1979. Source: Sivard (1982).

NDPINV70: W: Net Direct Private Investment ($ Millions, Current): 1970. Source: World Bank (1980:136–137).

NEWSPR70: W: Daily General Interest Newspaper Circulation per 1,000 Inhabitants: 1970. Source: UNESCO (1976).

ORGLAB79: W: Wage and Salary Earners Percentage in Unions: 1979. Source: CIA (1979).

POPLTN70: W: Population in Millions: 1970. Source: USACDA (1972).

POPLTN79: W: Population in Thousands: 1979. Source: CIA (1979).

RELDOM80: W: Dominance of Largest Religion, 1980: More than 75% (1); Between 50 and 75% (2); Less than 50% (3). Sources: *Statesman's Yearbook* (1982); *Countries* (1978).

REPCOM80: W: Repression Composite Index, 1980: Violent (1); Institutional (2); Minimal (3). Sources: REPWOL80; REPSIV80; REPGAS80.

REPG7380: W: Repression Scale Gastil, 1973: Unfree (1); Partly Free (2); Free (3). Source: Gastil (1973).

REPGAS80: W: Repression Scale Gastil, 1980: Unfree (1); Partly Free (2); Free (3). Source: Gastil (1981).

REPSIV80: W: Repression Scale Sivard, 1980: High (1); Moderate (2); None/Limited Evidence (3). Source: Sivard (1982).

REPWOL80: W: Repression Scale Wolpin, 1980: Violent (1); Institutional (2); Minimal (3). Sources: Amnesty International (1981); U.S. Dept. of State (1981); Gastil (1981).

SUARTR77: W: Soviet Arms Transfers ($ Millions, Current): 1973–1977. Source: USACDA (1979).

SUTGAA79: W: Soviet Military Trainees (1955–1979) as Percentage of 1979 Armed Forces. Source: Sivard (1982).

UKARTR77: W: United Kingdom Arms Transfers ($ Millions, Current): 1973–1977. Source: USACDA (1979).

URBANP76: W: Urban Percentage of Population: 1976. Source: Sivard (1982).

USTGAF79: W: U.S. MAP Trainees (1950–1979) as Percentage of 1979 Armed Forces. Sources: Klare and Arnson (1981); Sivard (1982).

WOUNIV79: W: Women as Percentage of University Enrollment: 1979. Source: Sivard (1982).

6

Genocide as State Terrorism

Barbara Harff

This chapter examines genocide as a particular form of state terror. Genocide is here defined as mass murder, pre-meditated by some power-wielding group linked with state power, directed against any target group within the state however defined.

There are problems in treating genocide as an aspect of state terrorism. For example, the Holocaust is treated by some scholars as the ultimate instance of the more general concept of genocide, whereas others treat the Holocaust as specific to the Nazi state, and genocide as a different general phenomenon.[1] The goal here is to investigate the reasons why and the circumstances in which different states engage in genocide. Though it appears that certain types of regimes, such as fascist ones, are more likely to practice state terrorism than others, not all fascist states engage in genocide. Despite ideological and temporal similarities, fascist Germany architected massive genocide while fascist Italy did not. When comparing cases of genocide, one must recognize that autocratic leadership seems to provide the type of political climate conducive to repression and genocide. But genocide is not a form of repression, because the latter seeks to intimidate; rather, genocide is pre-meditated large-scale murder by those in control. Repression does not constitute a necessary condition for genocide to occur, nor is genocide a continuation of severe repression through other means, but a phenomenon of a different kind.

The Holocaust was overwhelming in the numbers of dead, the total dehumanization of the killers, and the helplessness of the victims. The fact that bureaucrats meticulously planned and regulated systematic murder throughout occupied Europe added a distinct dimension to the Holocaust. However, this instance of genocide will not be considered in detail here. Why? There certainly exists an enormous literature on the

Holocaust, but few scholars use comparative methods systematically to explain this instance of genocide as part of a recurring phenomenon (exceptions are Helen Fein's *Accounting for Genocide* and Leo Kuper's *Genocide*). Genocide studies suffer from parochial and sectarian divisions because too many scholars reserve the right to consider their particular genocide unique.[2] In light of the great variety of past acts of genocide, an emphasis on case studies inhibits the development of general theories that could explain continuities in the processes of genocides as they unfold throughout history. Many people have shared the fate of annihilation, and recent mass slaughters attest to the fact that nobody is safe from genocide. The psychologically satisfying notion that the readiness to commit genocide was peculiar to Nazi Germany simply does not stand up in light of the evidence. A few recent examples include the Bengalis in Bangladesh (1971), Southern Sudanese by the Northern Sudanese (1955–1970), Tibetans by Communist Chinese (1959), Kurds by Iraqis (1960s to 1975). The Jewish Holocaust, though not used here as one of the cases, is employed as the yardstick, the ultimate criterion for assessing the scope, methods, targets, and victims of the genocides of Burundi (1972), Cambodia (1975–1979), East Timor (1975), and the genocide against the Armenians in the Ottoman Empire. Comparison of such cases may assist social scientists who hope to explain why elites may opt for genocide rather than repression, and to anticipate their likely victims.

THEORETICAL FRAMEWORK

Why do nation-states engage in genocide? Is there any evidence to suggest that something in the international environment, such as polarity, lack of international morality, lack of sanctions, etc., promotes the re-occurrence of genocide? Given that the Holocaust occurred during wartime and the dormancy of the League of Nations, this seems a possible avenue for further research. Given that historical genocide occurred when international organization was non-existent, for example, the persecutions of Jews from the Crusades until the eighteenth century, this direction becomes even more attractive. It is easy to blame the re-occurence of genocides on the lack of effective international control, which may encourage regimes to engage in genocidal policies. Presently the U.N. Charter does not recommend or authorize either unilateral or collective intervention for humanitarian purposes. The protection of human rights through the use of force stands in direct opposition to non-intervention and to the legal restraints on the unilateral use of force. The weightiest argument against the use of force in such circumstances is the principle of sovereignty, a cornerstone of general international law. This principle asserts that nothing should threaten the territorial integrity and political independents of a state. Thus, the United Nations is unable to protect victims from genocidal violence.[3]

It is equally possible, in the twentieth century, for genocide to be a conscious choice of policymakers, one option among others to repress opposition groups, as the Holocaust demonstrates. Thus, genocide is not an aberration or chance occurrence, one that needs to be dealt with only on an individual basis. I argue that genocide is sometimes politics as usual, but that it occurs only under certain conditions in the international environment and under a specifiable array of factors within a given society. Some scholars, for example, Israel W. Charny,[4] argue that *all* men are potential genociders, while Irving Louis Horowitz finds tendencies toward genocide in all states.[5] Does it follow, then, that all people and all states are also *likely* to become genociders? No, only under extraordinary circumstances and when provoked can people be motivated to become genociders. In the following propositions, I postulate that genocides occur under similar circumstances and under a given array of internal conditions. Specifically, national upheaval sets the pre-conditions for the pursuit of genocidal policies against national minorities and powerless majorities. National upheaval is defined as an abrupt change in the political community caused, for example, by the formation of a state through violent conflict, when national boundaries are reformed, or after a war is lost. Thus, in neo-colonial regimes, prior tribal rivalries may become exacerbated because only one tribe is vested with authority in the new state, making other tribes rebellious opposition groups. Genocidal tribal warfare in both Burundi and Rwanda are two clear examples.

For states having lost a war, battered national pride, often associated with lost territories or partition, may lead to genocide against ethnic or religious minorities perceived as alien or having "dangerous" foreign connections. Battered national pride often generates an exaggerated emphasis on national identity in which blame is projected on "others" for the loss of national dignity. This scapegoat syndrome may have fueled the resentment felt by the Germans after World War I against religious and ethnic minorities, leading eventually to the Holocaust.

Post-revolutionary regimes test the power of competing groups and redefine authority in favor of the winning faction. The new ideologue sometimes fights former comrades, and often, depending on the strength of convictions, views reactionaries in all others not directly involved in the revolutionary struggle. Kampuchea under Pol Pot is an extreme case in point: Under his leadership, some 2 million people were slaughtered or died from a conscious program of starvation. His vision of Communist society had no place for the educated, city dwellers, or wealthy peasants, much less supporters of the previous regime.

The concept of national upheaval does not refer merely to simple regime change, but includes territorially redefined states (that is, those that lost territory or were partitioned), new states (post-colonial, secessionist), and states with new regimes (that is, post-revolutionary and post-coup regimes, post-monarchical regimes, and fascist successors to democratic regimes). The emphasis here is seemingly on structural change, but structural change alone constitutes only a necessary but not sufficient condition. A second crucial factor conducive to the development of genocide is the existence of sharp internal cleavages prior to the upheaval. Was there a history of struggle between competing groups? If so, the intensification of struggle is likelier than in times of national stability. Yet another important factor is the strength of group identification within competing groups. The stronger the identification, the more likely that extreme measures will be taken to suppress the weaker group(s). Polarization is intensified by strength of religious identification and different values, traditions, and ideology. There are numerous examples from past horrors in which group polarization provided the background to genocide: Gentiles versus Jews, Muslims versus Hindus, Fascists versus Communists, Germans versus Gypsies, Muslims versus Catholics, to name a few.

In addition, the concept of national upheaval establishes a link to the international environment. Often structural changes are externally induced, through a lost war, by decolonization, when conflict in neighboring countries spills over, because of subversion by foreign intruders, or as a result of direct intervention by a foreign power. Also, the lack of external constraints, such as the lack of international sanctions or foreign interventions against past genocides, encourages policymakers to perceive genocidal policies as an option—the most extreme option. A further international dimension of genocide involves its consequence for regional stabilization or destabilization. Genocidal elites may extend their policies outside their borders, as did Nazi Germany in killing European Jews, Gypsies, and Poles. Finally, the occurrence of genocide invites intervention, as in Vietnam's intervention in Kampuchea.

In light of the claim that upheaval alone does not make genocide, is genocide possible in a homogeneous society? It is possible that one murderous conqueror or national leader—a Genghis Khan or Tamurlaine—may institute a reign of terror culminating in genocide. Today, the possibility of genocide in a homogeneous society depends on creating an enemy within. Often groups are targeted as victims by reference to their political and/or social affiliations (for example, Kampuchea under Pol Pot).

The following well-documented cases, the Armenian genocide of 1915, the genocide in East Timor in 1975, the Bahutu genocide of 1972, and the Kampuchean mass slaughter of 1975–1979, test the plausibility of my argument. A brief historical background of each case will be given, followed by a description of the genocidal events. The analysis will focus on identifying the genocider, the victims, and the circumstances leading to the slaughter.

GENOCIDES IN THE TWENTIETH CENTURY

Genocide I defined above as mass murder, pre-meditated by some power-wielding group linked with state power, directed against any target group within the state however defined. More elaborately, the Convention on the Prevention and Punishment of the Crime of Genocide delimits genocide in Article 2 as follows:

In the present Convention, genocide means any of the following acts committed with intent to destroy, in whole or in part, a national ethnic, racial, or religious group, as such:

A)   killing members of the group;

B)   causing bodily or mental harm to members of the group;

C)   deliberately inflicting on the group conditions of life calculated to bring about its physical destruction in whole or in part;

D)   imposing measures intended to prevent birth within the group;

E)   forcibly transferring children of the group to another group.[6]

The official U.N. definition has spurred intense interest and disagreement about the subject of genocide. Horowitz characterizes genocide as a "structural and systematic destruction of innocent people by a state bureaucratic apparatus."[7] My definition differs insofar as it broadens the scope of the victims and perpetrators. Thus, any group linked with state power may become the perpetrators (for example, death squads in Latin America), and any group may be targeted for annihilation. The Holocaust is treated here as the ultimate instance of genocide, in contrast to those scholarly treatments of the Holocaust as a unique event defying comparison. Though the formal definition of genocide appears, at first glance, to cover all its aspects, it is lacking, because one of the worst genocides of the twentieth century in sheer numbers of dead, the Kampuchean mass slaughter, cannot be properly called genocide because it lacks an identifiable target group of victims. Thus, from a formal/legal perspective based on the Genocide Convention in 1946, the slaughter of an estimated 2 to 3 million people does not qualify as a genocide, and as such does not warrant the ever-so-fragile protection of the Convention.[8]

In Kampuchea one cannot readily identify target groups because the victims had only their humanity in common: The slaughter included members from all groups of Khmer society. Thus, murder in the name of a new political order ought to be included. In retrospect, the many political opponents who vanished under the Nazis in concentration camps are an example of a similar set of victims. However, people killed in the process of fighting regimes are not included in my defintion. Rebels knowingly engage in activities that may result in death, while genocidal victims are not engaged in any pursuit that may identify them as political opponents. It is their innocence that is criminalized by the perpetrator, who selects his victims. Lastly, genocide tends to be recognized as such only after hundreds or thousands of people are dead. This sometimes leads to the false conclusion that genocide refers only to events resulting in the death of many. My definition specifies only the victims and per- petrators, it does not count the victims. Helen Fein's definition of gen- ocide suffices for my purpose to identify victims and give some rationale to the motives of the perpetrators. Fein suggests that genocide

must be first appreciated as rational, premeditated action by its perpetrators, before one relates its causes and preconditions theoretically or empirically to collective violence generally.... Genocide is a rational function of the myth cho- sen by a ruling elite which serves as a "political formula" to legitimate the ex- istence of the state as the vehicle for the destiny of the dominant group, a circle based on underlying likeness (mechanical solidarity) from which the victim is excluded by definition. Such a formula assumes (or creates) a myth exalting the unique origins of the dominant group and reifying the idea of the people so that the "real" nature of the group cannot be judged by the performance of its members.[9]

In other writings, such as those of Hannah Arendt,[10] this phenomenon is referred to as "tribalism." However, the "unique" people formula does not accurately characterize the mass slaughter in Kampuchea, where the victims represented all parts of the society. The dominant group in Kampuchea defined itself politically and its victims had no distinguishing cultural, ethnic, religious, or other characteristics in common other than being considered opponents of the murderous regime. In my conception it was genocide nevertheless.

Genocide in Burundi

In 1884 Rwanda and Burundi became a part of German East Africa. After World War I both territories became a League of Nations mandate administered by Belgium, which continued to act as trustee under the United Nations. Independence came to the countries on July 1, 1962, after three years of extended rebellions against Belgian and tribal au- thorities. The two countries with a common history, traditions, and peo- ple were thus permanently divided.

The people of Rwanda and Burundi number about 7 million. Most numerous are the Hutus who make up about 85 percent of the population, followed by the Tutsis (14 percent) and the Twa Pygmies (1 percent). The latter are a "primitive" people thought to be the original inhabitants of the region, who were supplanted by the Hutus, an agricultural people. About 400 years ago, the Tutsis, of Hamitic stock, reached the area from Ethiopa. The Tutsis were warriors and cattleherders. The passivity of the Hutus allowed for the total domination over time of a majority by a minority. For all practical purposes, the Hutus were reduced to the status of serfs. Feudal domination under a Tutsi king lasted to the 1960s, when the Congo rebellions spilled over to Rwanda and Burundi.

The year 1959 witnessed the beginnings of tribal liberation for the Hutus who made up the majority in Rwanda, where tribal domination by the Tutsi had been absolute. After three years of violence in Rwanda, the Tutsi government was totally defeated and many Tutsis were dead through arson, decapitation, and shootings, while approximately 140,000 fled to other countries.[11] Violence and death came again to Rwanda after an aborted coup by Tutsis, resulting in reprisals by the ruling Hutu government. Rene Lemarchand notes: "Between December, 1963 and January, 1964, at least 10,000 Tutsis died under the blows of the Hutus."[12]

In Burundi, where the population was similarly distributed, Tutsi domination was somewhat limited by inter-marriage and some representation of Hutus in government matters. From the time of independence, governments emerged and were toppled in quick succession. Political rivalries seemed to outweigh tribal/ethnic rivalries. However, the king was a Tutsi and the balance of power was in favor of the Tutsis. An aborted coup by the Hutus in 1965 and savage attacks on Tutsi families in the countryside, resulting in hundreds of deaths, were followed by reprisals by the Tutsis with estimates by the International Red Cross ranging from 2,500 to 5,000 Hutu fatalities. An attempted coup by the Hutus in 1969 resulted in some twenty-three executions of prominent Hutu citizens.[13]

A third attempt by the Hutus to rid themselves of an unwanted minority government on April 29, 1972, led to *the* genocide of Hutus, though obviously prior massacres could equally qualify. The *New York Times* in April and June 1973 described the Burundian genocide as "one of the worst tribal massacres on record." Specific records tell of the extent of the slaughter, which had an estimated 200,000 victims. This included 8 of 18 Hutu doctors, "60 of 130 teacher training students; 120 of 350 university students; 170 of 400 technical school students; 2,000 of 10,000 secondary school children; 40 percent of 700 grammar school children."[14] The massacres continued well into 1973 and sporadically thereafter.

Genocide in East Timor

From a population of about 600,000 Timorese, close to 100,000 vanished during the genocide following the invasion by Indonesian forces in December 1975. Just weeks earlier, the former Portuguese colony had unilaterally declared its independence. The Portuguese, who first held all of Timor, arrived there during the late sixteenth century, but had to relinquish some of their holdings to the Dutch, who arrived in the early seventeenth century. The treaties of 1859 and 1893 settled the border between Dutch and Portuguese Timor. The latter comprised most of the eastern half of the island. Dutch Timor became Indonesian territory when Indonesia gained independence from the Netherlands in 1949. Portuguese Timor was to gain independence from Portugal in 1978, but preempted that step in 1975.

The people of Timor are of Malay and Papuan stock, predominantly Christian with some Muslim minorities present. Past rivalries were confined largely to inter-party rivalries among APODETI, a pro-Indonesian party that favored union with Indonesia and enjoyed about 5 percent of the popular vote; UDT, which called for some future alliance with Portugal, counting 10 percent of the people as their supporters; and FRETILIN, enjoying 60 percent of the popular vote, which was staunchly anti-colonial and anti-Indonesian and thought to be infiltrated by Communists. This supposed infiltration was the justification used by the Indonesian government to intercede and invade East Timor. A small-scale civil war between UDT and FRETILIN forces, which took the lives of around 2,000 Timorese, preceded the invasion. FRETILIN guerillas withdrew into the mountainous interior and reportedly are still involved in active resistance. Indonesia claims sovereignty over East Timor. East Timor's population has been decimated through outright slaughter, malnutrition, and the destruction of Timorese agriculture and infra-structure. Noam Chomsky and Edward S. Herman describe the Indonesian takeover as "an annihilation of simple mountain people."[15]

The Armenian Genocide

Armenia is a region that includes parts of northeastern Turkey, parts of Iranian Azerbaijan, and the Armenian Soviet Socialist Republic. An ancient people, believed to have settled in the area about 800 B.C., they had gained independence as a nation as early as 600 B.C. Armenia is considered the earliest Christian state (third century) and has remained prey to its powerful neighbors, the Arabs, Persians, Huna, Byzantines, and in modern times Russians and Turks. By the sixteenth century, Armenia was conquered by the Ottoman Turks and remained under

Turkish rule, though parts of eastern Armenia came under Russian rule in 1828. Remnants of Armenians remained in Iran.

Under the dominant Muslim culture, Armenians were treated similarly to other religious minorities. They were given local autonomy in civil and religious matters, which was guaranteed by Islamic law. However, their political status, as well as the status of other minorities, such as Jews, remained politically inferior until 1911. For example, under Ottoman rule, Armenians were not allowed to bear arms.[16] In addition, Ottoman sultans frequently resettled "Kurds in Armenian regions to serve as governing agents."[17] Kurds seemingly were considered a closer kin group to the Ottoman rulers, probably because they were Muslims. Exploited by their Kurdish chieftains, "Armenians constituted a minority" in their own lands—"from 27 to 39%."[18]

The late nineteenth century witnessed the emergence of Armenian nationalism, partly as a result of weakening Ottoman influence elsewhere. To keep Armenians under control, Sultan Abdu-I-Hamid II instituted a systematic plan to exterminate Armenians. Kurdish tribesmen "committed massacres against the Armenians resembling the pogroms the Black Hundreds in Russia committed against Jews during the same period. . . . Between 1895 and 1908 (when the Sultan's despotism ended), 100,000 to 300,000 Armenians were estimated to have been killed."[19] Between 1908 and 1913, the party of the "Young Turks" elicited and gained the support of national minorities by pressing for a restoration of the 1876 Constitution, which granted equal rights and justice under the law to all subjects. In 1913, when the leader of the Young Turks, Enver Pasha, gained virtual dictatorial powers through a *coup d'état*, appeasing national minorities was no longer the policy of their movement. To the contrary, the Young Turks called for "Turkification" based on racial origin and demanded the minorities to disband and cease to exist as an independent group, but elicited little enthusiasm from such minorities as Maronite and Greek Christians and Armenians.

The last and most deadly genocide began when the Young Turks, armed with pan-Islamic revivalism and extreme nationalism, slaughtered or deported an estimated 1.8 million Armenians in 1915.[20] This estimate represents about two-thirds of the total number of Armenians in the Ottoman empire. Ironically, American nationalists first sought the support of the Young Turks, who were perceived as the instrument to lead Turkey into the twentieth century. However, the myth of Pan-Islamism came to an abrupt end when during World War I the Arabs sided with Britain against Turkey and the Central powers. New Turkish nationalism, instigated by the decay of what was a formidable empire until World War I, turned against other minorities who sought self-determination. Armenians were the last large minority group in the former Ottoman empire, which witnessed the secession of almost all its former

European possessions, with the exception of a small area across from Istanbul. Seemingly Armenian nationalism, combined with their Christianity, had little chance in a time of fledgling Turkish nationalism. Postwar defense concentrated on establishing the guilt of the victims, accusing them of conspiring with Russia, provoking reprisals through attacks on Turks, and collaborating with other Christian powers. Most remaining Armenians emigrated after World War I. Today a small number of Armenians, numbering less than 1 percent of the population, remain in Turkey, living predominantly in Istanbul.

Genocide in Kampuchea

Cambodia's history begins in the first century, when the Funan empire was established in the region. With the rise of the Khmer empire in the sixth century, Cambodia became the leading power in Southeast Asia. From the fifteenth century, the country became prey to its stronger neighbors, especially Siam (Thailand) and Annam (central Vietnam), losing part of its territory to them. In 1863 Cambodia became a French protectorate, after the king appealed to the French for help, and in 1887 the country became part of Indo-China. During World War II the Japanese gained control over the region. In 1947 Cambodia was established as a constitutional monarchy under the leadership of Prince Norodom Sihanouk. In the course of the war in Vietnam between the French and Vietnam nationalists and Communists, an invasion of Vietminh troops into Cambodia led to an armistice and complete independence in December 1954.

During the ensuing decade, Cambodia steered a course of neutrality, trying to prevent infiltration by Communist insurgents. Increasing economic difficulties led to the deposal of Sihanouk in 1970 and the establishment of the Khmer Republic under Lon Nol. During the course of the year, the war in Vietnam spilled over into the Khmer Republic, involving American and North and South Vietnamese forces, as well as pro- and anti-Republican Khmer forces. The subsequent withdrawal of American and North Vietnamese forces from Cambodian soil left the country in turmoil. Republican forces supplied by the United States and the United National Front (including the Communist Khmer Rouge) supported by North Vietnam and China fought each other in a civil war. With the capture of the capital of Phnom Penh in April 1975, the Khmer Rouge Communists emerged as the winner. From 1975 until its overthrow by the Vietnamese in January 1979, Pol Pot instituted one of the bloodiest regimes known in the twentieth century. Foreigners were expelled and the country systematically cut off from external contacts.

In a country ravaged by civil war, its economic infra-structure destroyed, and its agricultural productivity at an all-time low, the new rulers engaged immediately in a vigorous agricultural program. In the process, most townspeople were driven out in mass migration to the countryside, and "the whole country was turned into an agricultural work site.... Exhaustion, from the extremely arduous work, malnutrition from minimal diets, starvation and disease took a heavy toll of lives."[21] Though the forcible evacuation of all major towns resulted in the death of thousands of people, the main carnage was directed against all those who were associated with the former regime. This included "former military officers, senior officials, policemen, intelligence officers, country officials, and military police.... Minor officials, non-commissioned officers, soldiers ... were also executed.... "Intellectuals" such as doctors, engineers, professors, teachers and students, have also been summarily executed, especially since 1977."[22] In addition, the slaughter extended to people who were deemed anti-regime, often based on minor infractions (such as talking to each other at work). Whole extended families vanished in the extermination program, in the process of eradicating the "old" society.[23] The estimates range from 2 to 3 million dead of a population estimated at 7 million at the beginning of the genocide. For a time the United States and the Soviet Union seemed united in the condemnation of the atrocities, and in January 1979 the Soviets charged Kampuchea with genocide in the U.N. Security Council.

COMPARATIVE ANALYSIS AND EVALUATION

The theoretical argument specifies three general conditions of genocide that I argue have functional equivalants across different cultures. The question here is whether each of the cases summarized manifests these three conditions.

The genocides in Burundi, East Timor, and Kampuchea and against the Armenians in the Ottoman empire were preceded in all cases by major structural upheavals. Such fundamental changes in the political structure, combined with a history of ethnically or religiously polarized conflict within a given country and lack of constraints in the international environment, sometimes result in genocidal policies by those in power against powerless minorities or majorities.

Burundi shows a pattern not atypical of colonial regimes, in which independence is followed by a bitter struggle between competing tribal interests. The introduction of Western values, combined with other African nations' drive for self-determination, stimualted national consciousness among both Tutsis and Hutus. Tribal separation existed for 400 years in which the Hutus were condemned to serfdom by the powerful warrior Tutsis. This feudal pattern was interrupted when Western-educated Hutus challenged the legitimacy of the system.[24] A seemingly minor incident unleashed the simmering conflict between the two tribes, one that ended in numerous bloodbaths, and one that has the potential of erupting again, because Burundi is still governed by the Tutsi minority.

Burundi appears a straightforward case in which two tribes fought for control within a given state. Independence exacerbated the simmering ethnic conflict, only briefly postponed through rebellions directed against Belgian authorities (1959–1962). Burundi's Tutsis continue to control the majority Hutus, if necessary through genocidal policies. Hutu identity is more precarious than Tutsi identity. The former warriors enjoyed the status of protector for the passive Hutus. In traditional society, status thus "came from ability" for the Tutsi, whereas a Hutu's status was determined "by lineage and position."[25] Hence, the show of force by Tutsis in Burundi, this time directed against the former protectee, may still be seen as a sign of that "ability." In Rwanda the Tutsis lost against the majority of Hutus, and many fled to neighboring Burundi. The example set by the brother country (Rwanda) thus may induce further rebellion by the Hutus in Burundi, resulting in even further bloodshed.

The Burundi case appears to fit the theoretical argument that national upheaval and prior internal struggle combined with lack of external constraints are conducive to genocide. But this does not answer the question of why this or other regimes engaged in genocide rather than using less draconian measures. Though this question cannot be answered here, it opens a whole array of other questions, which I will touch upon in the conclusions. However brief, a thought in that direction may help to clarify what should be considered in future research. Is it possible that if Rwanda and Burundi had been partitioned between Tutsi and Hutu, genocide would not have occurred? Given the 400 years of domination by the Tutsis over the Hutus, would such a division have encouraged the Tutsis to conquer the Hutu state, or would they have been satisfied to live among themselves? Is it not the goal today of many nations to live alone, rather than share "their" state with other nationalities? Or is it possible for different tribal people/nationalities to live in harmony, given a more equal distribution of power among competing groups, as the example of Switzerland suggests? The situation today seems to indicate the opposite. In a world where each tiny nation seeks its own territory, integration seems ever less acceptable to national minorities.

The East Timorese are ethically quite similar to the peoples who make up the Indonesian republic. The main ethnic stocks are the Javanese and Sundanese (in Java), Balinese (Bali), Madurese, Aceh, Bataks, Minankabaus (Sumatra), Sasaks (Lomok), Menadonese and Buginese (Sulawesi), Dayaks (Kalimantan), Irianese (Irian Jaya), and Ambonese (Moluccas)—many of them potentially separatist. This polyglot of ethnic groups can roughly be divided into Malays and Papuan, with some groups representing a mixture of both. In addition, there are minorities of Indian, Pakistani, Chinese,and Arabs in Indonesia. The overwhelming majority of Indonesians are Muslims, though some are animists or Christian. Christians are a majority in East Timor, which may be one contributing factor to the development of self-identity among the Timorese. In addition, religion was most likely a factor among those who favored union with Indonesia and thus voted for APODETI, a party that held 5 percent of the popular vote. It was surely not the factor that led to the civil war preceding the invasion by Indonesia and genocide, because APODETI also received votes from appreciably large numbers of Christians. Clearly there was no neat division among parties along religious lines. The more important issue was whether or not parties favored union with Indonesia or not. The Timorese Popular Democratic Association (APODETI) did and so did the Timorese Democratic Association (UDT), though the latter initially called for self-government under Portuguese leadership and later changed course. The only party calling for self-rule and denouncing colonialism and neo-colonialism was the Revolutionary Front of Independent East Timor (FRETILIN). FRETILIN enjoyed the greatest popular support, and large numbers of former UDT supporters joined the party after UDT declared their support for a union with Indonesia.[26] In August 1975 UDT forces attempted to seize power but were very quickly (by late August) subdued by FRETILIN forces. Independence of Timor was officially declared in November 1975. Indonesia immediately initiated a blockade against Timor and invaded the country in December 1975 with the help of UDT and APODETI forces. The result was devastating: looting, torture, and outright slaughter, with nearly 10 percent of the population killed.

Obviously the great majority of Timorese did not favor union with Indonesia; those few who did fought alongside the invading Indonesians. Apparently the coming of independence from Portugal did bring into full conflict the political divisions already in existence. Indonesia, with its ethnic and religious mix of people and cultures, seemed to be the logical ally for Timorese aligned with UDT and APODETI. FRETILIN followers obviously saw no advantage in becoming part of an existing entity, which would exchange colonial rule for governance by Indonesia.

East Timor is not an exceptional case of regional revolt in Indonesia; many of Indonesia's islands have separate histories. Indonesia's history of great native empires include the seventh-century Buddhist kingdom of Sri Vijaya on Sumatra and the thirteenth-century Hindu kingdom of Majapahit on Java. With the arrival of Arab traders and Islam in the fifteenth century, Indonesia degenerated into many small and weak states, which became easy prey to European imperialism. Timor was occupied by Portugal from the sixteenth century onward and as such probably developed an identity different from that of Java or Bali, which were

occupied by the Dutch. The question remains of how much of the colonial culture rubbed off on the local population. However, there is little
doubt that the colonial political and/or economic patterns leave a formidable imprint.

One form of indigenous revolt in the twentieth century was against
colonial masters and occupiers, like the Japanese during World War II.
Other movements, however, called for greater autonomy from the new
Indonesian state. Sumatra, the Moluccas, and West Irian all have or have
had groups of insurgents favoring independence. Indonesia's harsh policies in quelling internal revolts are well documented, the most infamous
example being the slaughter in late 1965 of Communists, 80,000 to
500,000 in estimated number, because of their supposed responsibility
for an attempted coup. In Timor FRETILIN was perceived as leftist by
the Indonesian government, which was not interested either in a "Cuba"
at their doorstep or in an independent island that would encourage other
autonomy movements to re-emerge.[27] Thus, to deter others, Indonesia
invaded Timor under the pretense of preserving democracy.[28]

Those are some general similarities between the Timorese and Burundi genocides. In both cases, major upheavals preceded the slaughter:
Burundi's quest for independence from colonial/neo-colonial rule was
successful, that of Timor was not. Though genocide in Burundi was
perpetrated by one tribe against the other from within a given territory,
there also are parallels with Timor. Both genocides were executed by
those in power: In Timor national political minorities supported Indonesian brutality, while Tutsis supported Tutsis in Rwanda and Burundi. Though open conflict between the Tutsis and Hutus broke out
during the twentieth century, it came as no surprise to those aware of
tribal animosities between the two prior to independence. Inter-party
political rivalries are a newer phenomenon, and in specific cases it may
be that these rivalries are representative of greater existing divisions,
that is, along cultural, class, or religious lines. The genocidal measures
taken by the Indonesian government seemingly sought to deter others
from following a similar path to FRETILIN in East Timor, a policy the
Indonesian military had used once before, in response to the aborted
coup in 1965.

Foreign concern was largely negligible. The Organization of African
Unity effectively endorsed President Micombero's genocidal policies by
sending a delegation to Burundi in 1972, which declared its solidarity
with the murderous regime. There was some activity in the United Nations, but largely one of diplomatic/privte approaches, providing some
measure of humanitarian relief. In East Timor U.N. action resolved
itself in calling for the withdrawal of Indonesian troops from East Timor,
which Indonesia ignored. Little or no pressure came from Western nations in contrast to the condemnations of the Kampuchea regime.

Armenians were caught in the post-World War I attempt of Turkish nationalists to rid themselves of the centuries-old rule of local autocrats, in addition to adjusting to the new realities resulting from a lost war. Armenians were the only large minority group left in what was once the Ottoman empire, different in culture and religion. Throughout their history, they were at the mercy of numerous conquerors, shifting between independence and occupation. Turkish rule since the sixteenth century left its imprint. Successful as merchants, they were nevertheless discriminated against along with other infidels.

The Armenian quest for self-determination became more organized during the late nineteenth century. Organized rebellions, leading to severe repressions under the Ottomans, eventually resulted in massacres against Armenians between 1894 and 1896.[29] However, the genocide of 1915 not only outweighed in sheer number of dead the genocidal policies implemented by Sultan Abdi-I-Hamid II, but elicited few excuses from the government then in power. To the contrary, Enver Pasha, leader of the Young Turks revolution of 1908, took full responsibility for the deportation orders that led to the massacres.[30]

A number of factors may have led to the Armenian genocide by the Young Turks. The Armenians may have simply served as scapegoats in the new movement's effort to gain people's support, showing their strength after the unfit rule of the former Sultans. For the sake of unity, the new Turkish nationalism had to exclude all national minorities. To make way for the new Turkey's emphasis on secularism, the Young Turks had to break with the old Islamic tradition that allowed for some internal autonomy of *dhimmis*. Armenians may have provoked reprisals because of perceived foreign support for their cause.[31] Since Armenians were often merchants and as such controlled some aspects of the local economy, envy by Turkish peasants may have been a contributing factor leading to the excesses. Finally, Kurdish and Armenian rivalries also are sometimes named in the chain of events leading to the genocide.

The most fundamental explanation is the age-old division and separate cultural development of Christians versus Muslims. Sometimes described as a "mercantile race," Armenians "controlled 60% of the imports, 40% of the exports, and at least 80% of the commerce in the interior."[32] Thus, economic jealousy may have added to the rift. Adding fuel to the spark that started the murderous activities was the cry for holy war against foreign intervenors and foreign elements within, in great contrast to the modernization program later instituted by one of the Young Turks, Mustafa Kemal (known as Ataturk).

No doubt the defeat of the Ottoman empire and the Treaty of Sevres (1920), which granted autonomy to Armenia (later renegotiated at Lausanne in 1923), made it easier for the subsequent government under Ataturk to identify Armenians as the internal enemy, a group that had collaborated with the Russians during the war. How real that enemy was is hard to answer. The better question to ask is, What parts of the Ottoman empire would have satisfied Armenian national aspirations? After all, the old Armenia is just an extension of the Anatolian highlands, which forms an integral part of the Ottoman empire. It is possible that here we deal with two competing national interests fighting for the same land, however unequal in power, resources, and population (and thus similar to the Israel/Palestinian conflict). The Armenian genocide shows that deep cleavages combined with a history of sporadic violence between nationalities may in times of political upheaval lead, indeed, to genocide.

The Kampuchean genocide is one of the worst genocides of the twentieth century, not just in sheer numbers of dead but also in terms of the indiscriminate killing of innocent people. The Kampuchean mass slaughter shows the dilemma posed by the official Genocide Convention, which does not cover the events here because an identifiable target group is lacking. Thus, the criminal state cannot be held responsible under the Genocide Convention, because the killings were outside of the realm of what constitutes genocide. However, the Genocide Convention, which is so pointedly reserved for large-scale pre-meditated murder by states, ought to include Kampuchean-style mass slaughters, if only to give such killings their proper name and as such the world attention they deserve— resulting, it is hoped, in worldwide condemnation. One rationale for the exclusion is the identification of the victim as a political opponent. Political opponents, the argument goes, may include rebellious and subversive elements, against whom drastic actions may have to be taken. In addition, political groups as such have fluctuating membership, or may already be covered under the provisions of the Genocide Convention because they are composed of a single ethnic, national, racial, or religious group.[33] This author argues the necessity of including "political opponents" in the definition of genocide, because the only other category available to describe the victims of the Kampuchean slaughter is—people. People of all persuasions, wealthy, poor, influential or not, intellectuals and peasants, were among the victims of Pol Pot. His "new order" called for a return to an agricultural society, in which all people potentially unable to perform the task (townspeople with industrial skills, educators, businesspeople) were designated as expendable. Struggle may be necessary to induce radical changes, which may eventually better the lot of most people. However, the imposition of ideologies on unwilling subjects through mass slaughter is nothing but a terrorist act by a predator state.

In terms of the theoretical argument, Kampuchea is an example of a post-revolutionary system that went through a total restructuring of government and society. Though historical struggle within the country was directed against colonial authorities, the struggle that led to the takeover of the Khmer Rouge was between political groups. These included Sihanouk's independent, nationalist forces, Lon Nol's pro-American, pro-capitalist forces, and Pol Pot's Communist forces. However, the victims included members of all three groups, and purges of party cadres were the order of the day.[34] Here again, the major upheavals caused through a revolutionary takeover, combined with extreme political divisions, led to genocidal policies targeted at unwanted present and future opposition groups. In the case of Kampuchea, it included men, women, and children, an estimated one-third of the population.

The Kampuchean genocide shows the necessity of rethinking what we mean by genocide. Here I am referring to the inclusion of political groups in the Genocide Convention. The assumption that internal cleavages leading to conflict are confined to racial, ethnic, or religious divisions is faulty. Underlying this assumption is the rationale that genocide is less likely in a homogeneous society, or is confined to racist, fascist states. In light of the evidence in Kampuchea and East Timor, where the victims were defined largely as members of a political group and the society was homogeneous, this was obviously not so. Even the Burundi and Armenian genocides could be interpreted as calculated though pathological means of policymakers to eliminate opposition in their drive to consolidate their power. The difficulty in the Armenian and Burundi cases lies in the fact that the victims were also members of a different ethnic group. Thus, the divisions between ethnic, racial, religious, and political victims are sometimes fuzzy or overlapping. However, in those cases where political identifications are the only common denominator, they should surely warrant the title of genocide. There has to be a recognized system of guarantees that extends the right to live to all groups, including political ones.

The Armenian case is the classic case of genocide, strongly resembling the Holocaust and especially important because it gives us many clues as to the possible causes of genocide. In the Holocaust, the Jews, Gypsies, and mentally handicapped were officially defined as expendable; thus, the victims become legitimate targets. This process is facilitated through bureaucratic and legal measures. The Armenians were fair game, owing to official deportation orders, for the widespread massacres that occurred during their journeys to their final destinations in the Syrian desert or similar desolate areas. A similar argument can be made for all other cases of genocide. The first step to victimization is the approval and sanctioning of categories of people defined as fair game by the established elite.[35] Burundi, Kampuchea, and East Timor show that pattern, whereby the genocidal targets were declared to be all those opposing the ruling regime.

In other respects, the Armenian and Kampuchean genocides resemble the Timorese and Burundi cases. Whereas in Burundi and East Timor major upheavals were caused largely by the quest for independence from colonial rule, the Armenians fought for liberation from Ottoman domination (though East Timor was equally a secessionist movement bent at overthrowing the domination of Indonesia), and Kampuchea demonstrates that major upheavals caused by revolutions may also lead to genocide. Note that the importance lies not in what causes a major restructuring of the political culture, but that certain events may lead to major upheavals in a given state/nation, such as revolutions, coups, and/ or introduction of extreme ideologies. However, for reasons of identifying potential genocidal regimes, the development of types of societies linked with genocide is a desirable task for future research.

In all these cases, genocidal policies were directed against political groups, though the Burundi and Armenian cases offer the additional identifier of a different ethnicity in the former and a different religion and ethnicity in the latter. Whereas political rivalries are often the expression of class differences, they are also sometimes representative of divisions along cultural and religious lines. A recent example is Lebanon, where massacres have taken place in the turmoil produced by the civil war.

The reason why elites chose genocidal policies over repressive tactics is an unsolved puzzle. Herbert C. Kelman argues that certain victims simply stand in the way of the execution of larger policy objectives.[36] Here we may remind ourselves of American activities in Vietnam. Others argue that throughout history some fell victims to the march toward civilization, as the genocide against Tasmanian Aborigines testifies. A likely but not exclusive explanation is that certain groups provoke hostile responses, because they are perceived as a threat by the dominant group. Thus, the greater the perceived threat to the interest of the dominant group, the likelier violence is justified against the provocateur. In terms of the theoretical argument, such threats against the dominant interest may be perceived as being externally induced. Popular Nazi propaganda saw the Jewish threat as part of an international conspiracy against Christian civilizations. Similar Turkish propaganda accused Armenians of siding with the Russian enemy and conspiring against the legitimate Turkish government. Irredentist movements elsewhere help to boost the claims of the perpetrators, the Armenian and Burundi cases providing examples. Analogously, American support for the Lon Nol regime in Cambodia encouraged the subsequent slaughter of pro-American/anti-Pol Pot elements of the population.

Let me briefly comment on the relation of the four cases here to the Holocaust. Where the Holocaust set the stage for an outburst of anti-Semitism, the Armenian case proceeded along similar lines. The Young Turks' emphasis on Turkification, which was based on a mystical racial Turanian heritage and on the common bond of Islam, set the stage for anti-Christian outrages against the Armenians. Other similarities are in the relative status of Jews and Armenians in Nazi Germany and the Ottoman Empire. Perceived as the mercantile race in both countries, both groups were targets of economic jealousy, though with little justification since many Armenians and Jews were anything but wealthy. However, both groups produced more educated people relative to the dominant group, which probably created envy among the lower strata of society. Though the mechanized murder of Nazi victims was perfected during the Holocaust, the effective elimination through widespread systematic massacres had its forerunner in the Armenian genocide. Though Burundi, Kampuchea, and Timor lacked calculated, efficient, and institutionalized means to destroy millions of victims, given time the slaughters may have been perfected. Seemingly the longer the time span allowed for the uninterrupted implementation of genocidal policies, the more likely is the total annihilation of the target group. Systematic efforts to understand the reasons for the Armenian genocide could have helped in retrospect to anticipate the Holocaust.

CONCLUSIONS: A RESEARCH AGENDA FOR FUTURE GENOCIDES

Genocide is the most extreme policy option available to policymakers bent on state terror, and is likely to be used to eradicate troublesome opposition groups. It tends to be most likely in times of violent national upheaval, that is, after a coup or revolution, following a lost war, or when new states come into existence through open conflict. A first step toward anticipating genocide is to identify potential genocidal elites and their prospective victims. It might then be possible to dissuade the perpetrators before they begin. Saul H. Mendlovitz insists that in the name of "humane goverance" there "must be sensitivity to processes in which the unit is cohesive unto itself or more or less autonomous with regard to decision-making, yet provides an opportunity for review, appeal and even intervention by an authority applying universal standards."[37] In other words, potentially murderous elites should know that others are watching, which is a first but not necessarily sufficient condition to deter them.[38] The world is capable of producing another Holocaust, as is witnessed by Kampuchea and the rebirth of Adolf Hitler in Idi Amin. As such, much can be gained if future research helps identify those leaders, and polities, that are likely to engage in genocide. We should be concerned with the development of a collective conscience, by which it is recognized that genocide affects all men and that today's victims may become tomorrow's genociders.

There is need to test further the general proposition that a major upheaval in a national/political entity combined with a history of prior struggle along lines of national/political cleavages and the lack of constraints in the international environment set the stage for genocide. This may be done by looking at other cases of genocide throughout history. To further comparative inquiry, researchers should

1. Examine changes on the systemic level. Focus on genocides that took place prior to the development of the modern nation–state system. Identify the links between genociders and formal/institutionalized authority. Ask whether or not the scope and intensity of genocide are greater the stronger the links are between the genociders and some recognized/institutionalized authority.

2. Consider international/regional linkages among genociders and among victims, for example, alliances, irredentist claims, tribal/ethnic/ religious connections. It could be argued that the stronger the international linkages/support for the target group, the less likely it is that genocidal policies will be successfully executed. The parallel hypothesis is that the stronger the linkages/support for the genociders, the more likely it is that genocidal policies will be successfully executed.

3. Assess the changes resulting from major upheaval internally. Disaggregate groups and classify them according to ethnic, class, religious, and political affiliation. Employ multiple indicators to assess the relative political strengths/influence of the various groups, for example, levels of education, wealth, control over trade between groups. Are some kinds of groups more likely to become victims/genociders than others?

4. Compare dissimilar cases. Genocide occurs in one country after major upheavals combined with a history of prior struggle along lines of ethnic/religious/political cleavages given the lack of international constraints, yet not in another with similar characteristics. What accounts for the difference? Can we argue that there are lawless societies that undergo sporadic episodes of genocide? Is cruelty more acceptable to one society than another, and how is societal cruelty related to individual cruelty and vice versa?

5. Develop indicators that test the proposition that the greater the political/economic cleavages are between groups, the more likely they lead to recurring genocidal activities against certain groups, such as scapegoating.

6. Design research that examines the relationship between certain ethnic characteristics and the propensity of a group to be targeted as a genocidal victim, such as by comparing the fate of similar groups elsewhere.

7. Assess the effects of other internal and external conditions on the prospects of genocidal behavior. For example, is genocide a more likely phenomenon during times of worldwide depressions—in other words, is genocide a cyclical phenomenon? During times of economic prosperity, the likelihood of genocide is diminished; in contrast, genocide is more likely to occur in times of economic hardship. The argument has been

made that the rise and fall of anti-Semitism, often a cause for massacres and pogroms, are directly related to cycles of economic prosperity; in other words, Jews enjoyed greater freedoms and tolerance during times of economic well-being.

8. Examine the effects that past genocidal behavior has on internal stability, for example, on the two Germanys after the Holocaust. Compare "survivors' " attitudes with attitudes of members of the genocider group. Test whether or not collective guilt/fear leads to subsequent hawkish/dovish international behavior.

Finally, research on genocide should have a policy thrust emerging from empirical findings on genocide. A concentration on preventive or sanctioning devices that would enable the international community to control/deter potential genociders might be the goal of such work. Though the utility of economic sanctions has received some attention from scholars, more work is needed.[39] If economic sanctions are to provide more than political satisfaction, goals must be clearly defined among the states imposing sanctions. The greater the desired modification, the more compliance is necessary among the sanctioning states. But most important is an evaluation of what kind of sanctions are most effective. As such, one possibility is to develop an economic profile of the targeted state. This will help policymakers decide which kinds of economic pressures, that is, monetary versus trade versus aid, will yield the desired results in different economies. It should be possible to design sanctions that can be introduced in response to the first evidence of genocide.

Needless to say, no single study can take into consideration all of the above recommendations. These suggestions should lead to the accumulation of evidence that will provide us with much-needed information, which may help answer the questions, Under which circumstances are genocides likely to occur? What can be done?

NOTES

1. Irving Louis Horowitz, *Taking Lives: Genocide and State Power* (New Brunswick, N.J.: Transaction Books, 1980).

2. For a sampling of the voluminous literature on the Holocaust, see Yehuda Bauer, *The Holocaust in Historical Perspective* (Seattle: University of Washington Press, 1978); Lucy Dawidowicz, *The War Against the Jews, 1933–1945* (New York: Holt, Rinehart and Winston, 1975); and Raul Hilberg, *The Destruction of the European Jews* (Chicago: Quadrangle, 1967).

3. For an extended discussion, see Barbara Harff, *Genocide and Human Rights: International Legal and Political Issues*, Monograph Series in World Affairs (Denver: University of Denver Press, 1984).

4. Israel W. Charny, *How Can We Commit the Unthinkable? Genocide: The Human Cancer* (Boulder, Colo.: Westview Press, 1982).

5. Horowitz, *Taking Lives*.

6. Convention on the Prevention and Punishment of the Crime of Genocide/

Declaration by the General Assembly of the United Nations, Resolution 96, dated December 11, 1946, Article 2.

7. *Ibid.*

8. Francois Ponchaud, *Cambodia Year Zero* (Harmondsworth: Penguin Books, 1978), p. 14.

9. Helen Fein, "A Formula for Genocide: Comparison of the Turkish Genocide (1915) and the German Holocaust (1939–1945)," *Comparative Studies in Sociology* 1 (1978), pp. 273–274, quoting Gaetano Mosca, *The Ruling Class* (translated by H. Kahan and revised by Arthur Livingston) (New York: McGraw-Hill, 1939).

10. Hannah Arendt, *The Origins of Totalitarianism* (New York: Harcourt, Brace and World, 1966).

11. Norman Wingert, *No Place to Stop Killing* (Chicago: Moody Press, 1974).

12. Rene Lemarchand, *Rwanda and Burundi* (New York: Praeger, 1970), p. 216.

13. Wingert, *No Place to Stop Killing*, quoting *Africa Report* (November 1970), p. 3.

14. Wingert, *No Place to Stop Killing*, p. 70.

15. Noam Chomsky and Edward S. Herman, *The Washington Connection and Third World Fascism* (Boston: South End Press, 1979), p. 143. The discussion of East Timor draws in part upon an unpublished paper by Christian C. Mattioli, "Invasion and Genocide in East Timor," Department of Political Science, Northwestern University, 1983.

16. A. O. Sarkissian, *Martyrdom and Rebirth* (published by the Armenian Church of America; New York: Lydian Press, 1965).

17. Fein, "Formula for Genocide," quoting H. Boyajian, *Armenia: The Case for a Forgotten Genocide* (Westwood, N.J.: Educational Book Crafters, 1972).

18. Fein, "Formula for Genocide."

19. *Ibid.*, quoting Boyajian, *Armenia*, and quoting Abraham Hartunian, *Neither to Laugh nor to Weep* (Boston: Beacon Press, 1968).

20. Viscount Bryce, *The Treatment of Armenians in the Ottoman Empire 1915–1916* (prepared by Arnold Toynbee; London: HMSO, 1916).

21. Leo Kuper, *Genocide: Its Political Uses in the Twentieth Century* (New Haven, CT: Yale University Press, 1981).

22. Analysis 4/1335, dated January 30, 1979 (prepared by U.N. Sub-Commission on Prevention of Discrimination and Protection of Minorities), quoted in Kuper, *Genocide*, p. 156.

23. This researcher collected accounts of atrocities during interviews in the Holding Center (a refugee camp) of Phanat Nikkon near the Thai/Kampuchean border in December 1981. The atrocity accounts were monstrous—people "hacked to death, cut open alive, buried alive, brothers ordered to kill the other, and clubbed to death." One survivor I interviewed was a young man left for dead by the Khmer Rouge. His head showed a large indentation, the result of being clubbed with the butt of a rifle, which left him retarded. He is now cared for by the only survivor of the family, his aged grandmother.

24. Wingert, *No Place to Stop Killing*, quoting the Bahutu Manifesto of 1957 in Rwanda, p. 270.

25. Wingert, *No Place to Stop Killing*, p. 23.

26. Jill Joliffe, *East Timor: Nationalism and Colonialism* (Australia: University of Queensland Press, 1978).

27. For an extended discussion, see Chomsky and Herman, *Washington Connection.*

28. Justus M. van der Kroef, *Patterns of Conflict in Eastern Indonesia* (London: Eastern Press, 1977); and Brian May, *The Indonesian Tragedy* (London: Routledge and Kegan Paul, 1978).

29. Fein, "Formula for Genocide," p. 277.

30. Henry Morgenthau, Sr., *Ambassador Morgenthau's Story* (Garden City, NY: Doubleday, 1918).

31. For an extended discussion, see Richard G. Hovannisian, *Armenia on the Road to Independence* (Berkeley, University of California Press, 1967); and Hovannisian, *The Republic of Armenia* (Berkeley: University of California Press, 1971).

32. Kuper, *Genocide*, quoting Johannes Lepsius, *Armenia and Europe* (Hodder & Stoughton, 1897); *Le rapport secret de Johannes Lepsius ... sur les massacres d'Armenie* (Paris: Payot, 1918); *Deutschland und Armenien, 1914–1918* Sammlung Diplomatischer Aktenstuecke (Potsdam, 1919).

33. For an extended discussion, see an unpublished paper by Lawrence J. LeBlanc, "Genocide and Political Groups," Department of Political Science, Marquette University, 1983.

34. For an extended discussion, see Kuper, *Genocide*; and Ponchaud, *Cambodia Year Zero.*

35. Herbert C. Kelman, "Violence Without Moral Restraint: Reflections on the Dehumanization of Victims and Victimizers," *Journal of the Social Issues*, 29 (1973), pp. 21–62.

36. Ibid.

37. Saul H.Mendlovitz, "The Struggle for a Just World Order: An Agenda of Inquiry and Praxis for the 1980's," *World Order Models Project Working Paper 20*, (New York: Institute for World Order, 1982).

38. Raymond D. Duvall and Michael Stohl, "Governance by Terror," in Michael Stohl, ed., *The Politics of Terrorism*, 2d ed. (New York: Marcel Dekker, 1983), pp. 179–219.

39. Recent work on economic sanctions are Shaheen Ayubi et al., *Economic Sanctions in U.S. Foreign Policy* (Philadelphia: Foreign Policy Research Institute, 1982); and Miroslav Nincic and Peter Wallensteen, eds., *Dilemmas of Economic Coercion: Sanctions in World Politics* (New York: Praeger, 1983).

7

Terrorism, Counter-Terrorism, and the Democratic Society

Grant Wardlaw

Liberal democracies face peculiar difficulties in coping with political terrorism. Some of the essential characteristics of a democratic society make it appear to be more vulnerable to terrorism than other forms of society. Such factors as adherence to the rule of law, lack of restrictions on residence, place of employment and travel, uncensored news media, freedom of speech, assembly, and other civil rights, right to a jury trial in open court with appeal to higher judicial authority, and a democratically elected representative government conspire to restrain the harsh, repressive reaction to terrorism that makes possible its virtual elimination from society.

Statistics on terrorism seem to confirm the existence of a threat to democratic states. The highest proportion of acts of international terrorism in the period 1973–1982 occurred in Western Europe (36.8 percent of all incidents), while almost none occurred in the Soviet Union/ Eastern Europe (1.3 percent).[1] But, of course, statistics can be extremely misleading. Apart from the inherently inaccurate nature of terrorism statistics, deriving from both definitional problems and the political or ideological biases of collection agencies, raw figures give no indication of the degree of threat to the societies on whose territory the attacks take place.[2] There are a number of sound reasons for Western Europe being the centre of international terrorism.[3] There are large contingents of ethnic Palestinians, Armenians, and Croatians, for example, which provide a base upon which to develop a logistical infra-structure to support terrorist actions relating to struggles in the home countries. The primarily targetted nations (Israel, Turkey, and Yugoslavia, respectively) are geographically near Western Europe. Western Europe itself is geographically compact, with excellent transportation systems. There is a concentration of attractive targets and a pervasive media coverage that ensures maximum exposure for any terrorist spectacular. All these characteristics make Western Europe a magnet for international terrorist attacks. But while these assaults are sometimes deadly and often destructive, they are not, in the main, directed against the policies of the state on whose territory they are mounted. Often, the "incident state" is little more than the battleground upon which combat over issues concerning other nations is conducted.

If the vital interests of the incident state are not threatened by acts of international terrorism, it is difficult to see how one can argue that the state is so fundamentally at risk that basic changes have to be made to society in order to counter the threat! But this is precisely the line that security authorities in many democracies have advanced in response to the growing incidence of international terrorism. The major problem for such advocates is that the high incidence of acts of international terrorism (for example, in Western Europe) bears no necessary relation to the degree of threat confronting governments on whose territory the acts take place. One cannot rely on incidence statistics alone (even if accurate) to determine the degree of threat to the state.

Arguably, there are only two forms of terrorism that are really threats to democratic societies. The first is terrorism conducted by a state on another state's territory in pursuit of its own foreign policy or defence interests. Counter-measures against such state terrorism need largely to be outward looking and would not usually involve changes to the internal characteristics of the target state. The second threat comes from terrorism that fundamentally questions the legitimacy of the state *and* is actually or potentially able to mobilize a significant portion of the population into support of the aims of the terrorist group. In the contemporary world, it would seem that only terrorism associated with secessionist or irredentist movements fulfil these conditions. Some analysts go so far as to say that claim to a well-defined territory is "the single most important element determining the success or failure of terrorist actions or movements."[4] By this view, movements such as the Basque Homeland and Freedom (ETA) terrorists or the Irish Republican Army (IRA) might be viewed as real threats in Spain and Northern Ireland, but the Japanese Red Army and similar groups with essentially millenarian motives would not constitute a basic threat to any state. But the IRA might not be considered the same sort of threat in mainland Britain as it is in Northern Ireland because it does not challenge the legitimacy of the state on the mainland. At issue is the legitimacy of Britain to govern the province of Ulster. The distinction between the two types of legitimacy is central to a determination of the degree of threat posed by the IRA in each context.

The presumption that terrorism can, and in some countries does, pose a real threat to the fabric of democratic states is fundamental to the introduction of special anti-terrorist legislation and other security measures in a number of liberal democracies. The difficulty for democratic

states is that attempts to limit the freedom of action of terrorists necessarily impact adversely on a wider group of people, interfering with
the liberties enjoyed by many citizens, including, particularly and significantly, non-violent opponents and critics of the state.[5] To erode civil
liberties in this way undermines, at least in the view of a section of the
population, the legitimacy of the government and can provide evidence
for those advocates of violence who maintain that the seeming liberality
of democratic regimes is but a facade that hides an essentially repressive
system. As official repression becomes harsher and state-imposed controls become tighter, the diminishing personal freedom available to citizens may well impel even those who advocate non-violent changes in
society to support those who see recourse to violence as the only path
to change open to them. Thus, while some turn to civil disobedience
and terrorism as a matter of tactical choice,[6] others may do so largely
in anger and frustration at official acts of repression or social control,
which are seen by them as disproportionate responses to posited threats.[7]

In a sense, then, terrorism may be a threat, may weaken democracy.
But democracy may not be inherently threatened. It may merely become
"the structural victim of terrorism."[8] The cycle has now become common.
A terrorist attack prompts the enactment, enforcement, or strengthening
of anti-terrorist or emergency legislation, usually with little debate and
often with even less parliamentary opposition. The legislation suspends
constitutional safeguards and increases the power of state agencies, leading almost inevitably to an increasingly arbitrary exercise of that power.
This in turn stimulates an acceleration of terrorist activity under the
added impetus of overturning an undemocratic and harsh regime. If
the primary response to terrorism is a concentration on increased state
power and security measures, the danger is very real that democratic
societies will be converted into "garrison states or a new feudalism in
which security firms usurp public police power, often widening rather
than limiting the scope of lawless operations."[9] In short, in trying to
combat terrorism, a democratic state is always in danger of handing the
terrorists a major victory by allowing themselves to be provoked into
repression.

That this is a primary aim of much terrorism is widely appreciated.[10]
But even liberal treatments of terrorism that acknowledge the danger
suggest responses to terrorism that, at the very least, are on the slippery
slope to anti-democratic practice. Thus, Paul Wilkinson, in an otherwise
sensible set of proposals for responding to terrorism in democratic states,
slips in some suggestions that should be vigorously resisted.[11] Arguing
that universities are often the recruiting base for terrorist organizations,
he suggests that the authorities "should have close liaison with academic
authorities known to be sympathetic to the task of protecting free societies in order to elicit their cooperation in avoiding recruiting to uni-

versity staff people who are likely to act as terrorist agents and propagandists."[12] Clearly, such a course of action would have serious implications for academic independence, freedom of speech, and individual liberties. How will "sympathetic" academic authorities be identified? Presumably a salient qualification will be "acceptable" political views and lack of criticism of the government or security forces. How will these authorities identify people with suspect motivations, particularly when what is being identified is *likelihood* of support for terrorist activities? While the proposal seems quite reasonable at one level, if taken to its logical conclusion, a new form of McCarthyism, this time with terrorists as the target, could be set in train. Such a travesty makes a mockery of democracy. A democracy must be able to tolerate the expression of diverse views, and the universities exist, in part, to nurture this diversity and provide an atmosphere in which they may be expressed and criticized. If people of "suspect" views aid terrorists, by all means let them be *prosecuted* for their *acts*, but individuals must not be *persecuted* for their *views*.

One thing that all commentators seem to be able to agree on is that democracy may be under as much threat from the response to terrorism as from terrorism itself. Sometimes this acknowledgement is rather hollow, however. Thus, Neil Livingstone, having first noted the difficulty a democratic state has in charting "a course between the rival, and equally undesirable, antipodes of overreacting and underreacting to terrorism," then goes on to claim that "terrorism is war without limits, and unless the state can respond accordingly, measure for measure, it will be at a considerable disadvantage when confronted with an enemy which is not restrained by the same rules that it is."[13] The "democratic" state envisaged by Livingstone has no intention of being so disadvantaged. Presumably writing of terrorism as it is thought most likely to affect democratic states (and not, for example, of a large-scale insurrection), Livingstone cites approvingly the deployment of state-sponsored "hit" squads (modelled on the deadly, if not always accurately targetted, campaign waged by Israel's Mossad intelligence agency against Palestinian terrorists), relocation and resettlement of populations into protected areas, checks on freedom of movement ("citizens innocent of crimes should have little to fear from such methods; generally they will be only slightly inconvenienced"),[14] curfews, cordons, employment of troops, and reprisal raids. The total emphasis of these and Livingstone's other suggestions is on military-oriented harsh measures. Examples of techniques used in counter-insurgency operations in peasant societies are juxtaposed with those more common in combatting urban terrorism, and no distinction is drawn between them. Neither is their appropriateness questioned. The use of torture as an interrogation measure is rather apologetically described as "a sign of frustration and an admission of the insecurity that accompanies a lack of clearly defined strategy or

proper range of options for combatting the enemy,"[15] but is not condemned. Neither is the use of government-sanctioned vigilante groups
(such as the South and Central American death squads), which are merely
described and evaluated in the following terms: "Death squads contributed significantly to the defeat of terrorism in the nations of Uruguay
and Guatemala."[16] The final impression left is that, in reality, any method
at all is justified in the fight against terrorism.

Those who propose the sort of hard anti-terrorist methods extolled
by Livingstone often seem unwilling to concede that any reasonable
person could object to such tactics. Such behaviour is to be expected
from extreme hardliners, but even academics considered to be liberal
manage to dismiss any criticism of security measures as coming only
from "terrorist sympathisers." Thus, Wilkinson, discussing the advantages and disadvantages of special powers such as detention without trial
and proscription of terrorist organizations, begins his argument by say-
ing: "Much nonsense is uttered equating the use of Special Powers with
the abandonment of political democracy. Of course, the terrorists' political propaganda eagerly seizes upon any crude and confused emo-
tionalism about basic rights being 'trampled on' and uses it to foster its
myth of repression."[17] There is no doubt that propaganda victories are
as important for terrorists as are their tactical successes, and that a major
aim of terrorist propaganda is to make a government's actions *seem* repressive. But we must not lose sight of the fact that anti-terrorist measures *can* be unduly harsh, unjustified by the actual threat posed, or even
instituted for ideological reasons divorced from terrorism but using the
threat of terrorism to disguise the real motives of the authorities. Obviously those who criticize the anti-terrorist measures have many motivations, not all of which are what their proponents pretend them to be.

However, by implying that anyone who criticizes, for example, the
provisions of emergency powers legislation, or questions the need for
its introduction, is by that act supporting the terrorists is to seriously
undermine one of the cornerstones of democracy. Surely the hallmark
of democracy is the right to openly and honestly question official policy,
especially when that policy will result in limitations on commonly accepted freedoms or rights. It is as legitimate to question the motives of
states as it is to question those of terrorists. It is not enough to point to
the short-lived nature of controversial anti-terrorist methods in contemporary democracies as evidence of the common sense of *governments*.
For example, Martha Crenshaw claims that "fears of the transformation
of Western democracies into garrison states...seem exaggerated."[18]
However, the examples, she cites of harsh measures or abuses of human
rights that avoided incorporation into the continuing security practices
of the states concerned (ill treatment of captured terrorist suspects in
Germany and Great Britain and the imposition of the wide powers con-

ferred by the Canadian War Measures Act in response to terrorism in Quebec in 1970) were all those in which the practices ceased as a result of responsible criticism of what the authorities viewed as legitimate measures. They serve, indeed, to remind us of the central role that free speech has to play in the maintenance of democracy.

Horowitz claims that "the consequences of terrorism have little to do with the rise and fall of societies and a great deal to do with the limits each society imposes on the civil liberties of its citizens in order to secure its survival."[19] In order to preserve democracy, it may be necessary to accept that at least some forms and levels of terrorism are permanent and inevitable features of contemporary society, in much the same way as other forms of deviance (such as prostitution, gambling, and drug taking) are ineradicable features of developed, mobile, and liberal societies. If this is so, the appropriate response to terrorism can be arrived at only by viewing it in perspective and not elevating it to a central role as an issue upon whose resolution democracy will stand or fall. Crenshaw provides this sense of perspective when she says that "a focus on terrorism should not blind policy-makers to other political, social, and economic problems. However compelling the search for a solution may seem, it must be placed in perspective. Terrorism is not the most important problem modern governments face."[20]

It follows that in order to arrive at a realistic perspective on terrorism, the most important task facing policymakers is to identify what, if any, forms of terrorism pose particular threats or what levels of each type of terrorism must be reached before a genuine threat to democracy exists. It is the accurate (and honest) assessment of threat, however, that is the central stumbling block to coping with terrorism in a democratic society.

Yehezekel Dror sees terrorism as part of a mosaic of challenges to the capacity to govern that face democratic governments everywhere.[21] Environmental issues, ethnic politics, unemployment, nuclear confrontation, and similar problems all cause some section of the community to become disaffected and to question the legitimacy of the state. Under such conditions, terrorism can emerge as a divisive and damaging influence. There are a number of ways this damage may occur. In weak democracies, Dror argues that if democratic institutions cannot cope with decaying internal security generally, terrorism may serve as a convenient "enemy," ostensibly justifying the change toward a non-democratic regime. In robust democracies, on the other hand, terrorism may also have deleterious effects by distorting policy agendas, causing panic decisions, and devoting an excessive amount of resources and senior policymakers' thought to it.

The greatest potential damage, however, comes from the breakdown of the monopoly that governments have traditionally exercised over violence and the elimination of inhibitions against the use of violence as a political tool. As Dror writes:

Contemporary democracies are characterized by increasing levels of political tension, disconsensus, single-interest groups, true-belief movements, extra-parliamentary militant action, and other tendencies that intensify conflict. Under such conditions, the thresholds between acceptable means of public pressure and illegitimate violence tend to erode. Combined with weakened government authority and legitimation, on one hand, and ethnic tensions and economic depressions on the other, the potential for escalating violence grows.[22]

The problems posed by terrorism are therefore multi-factorial in origin, and any attempts to view terrorism in isolation and to attack it without consideration of the complex context within which it arises are doomed to failure. The result of focusing exclusively on terrorism as an *act* will usually be to ignore the real causes and to place limits on democracy that may be very difficult to remove. The institutionalization of excessive anti-terrorist measures in contemporary South and Central American polities should serve as a warning to all liberal democracies of the difficulties inherent in dismantling a state coercive apparatus. Luigi Bonante has suggested that the institutionalization of repressive anti-terrorism measures results in societies that are "blocked," that is, incapable of advancing but at the same time immune to disintegration.[23] A situation prevails in which the government, even if it wishes to, feels unable to answer its citizens' requests for change lest it be perceived as acceding to terrorist pressure and being weak and open to manipulation. At the same time, it is unlikely that the repressive mechanisms of the state will disintegrate of their own accord because of the large-scale political and bureaucratic effort that went into their development. As a number of analysts have noted, the gradual reform of terror systems from within is highly unlikely.[24] Consequently, the establishment of a state repressive apparatus as a response to terrorism in a democracy must be viewed with alarm, even if justified by the state as only a short-term measure. We must be alert to the fact that

rush measures to deal with an emergency usually have no "self-destruct" mechanism built in. Consequently, these accretions of power are nearly always difficult to reverse. Police manpower is usually provided by career appointments so that, even when no longer needed in an emergency sense, its use is still necessary to keep the exanded service fully employed, technical equipment has to be kept in repair and updated, vested interests are created in any new extension of the bureaucracy, and these are now being multiplied.... Laws are always easier to make than to repeal.[25]

The fear that "emergency" powers may come to be seen as unexceptional with the passage of time and pass into the "normal" repressive armamentarium of the state, to be used not against terrorists but against ordinary criminals or dissidents generally, is currently being expressed in Great Britain with regard to the Prevention of Terrorism Act. In November 1974, some eight days after bombings of pubs in Birmingham in which a number of people were killed or injured, the British Parliament passed into law the Prevention of Terrorism (Temporary Provisions) Act 1974. The Act contained a number of features, including greatly expanded police powers, which attracted criticism from civil liberties groups but not from parliamentarians, on the whole, who passed the legislation in a flurry of morally outraged rhetoric. The major provisions of the Act were to proscribe the IRA and make display of support for it illegal; give the secretary of state the power to exclude from Great Britain, Northern Ireland, or the United Kingdom as a whole persons suspected of connection with terrorism; give the police power to arrest suspected terrorists and detain them for forty-eight hours, with the possibility of extension for up to a further five days if authorized by the secretary of state; empower police to detain suspected terrorists at a port or airport for up to seven days, with the possibility of further authorized extension; and give the police power to carry out security checks on travellers entering or leaving Great Britain. The inclusion of the words "Temporary Provisions" in the title of the Act and the fact that Parliament had to specifically renew it every twelve months were seen by the government as underlining the extraordinary and, it was hoped, short-term nature of the powers conferred.

In 1976 the 1974 Act was replaced by the Prevention of Terrorism (Temporary Provisions) Act 1976, which was only slightly different from its predecessor. Additional offences of contributing or soliciting contributions toward acts of terrorism and withholding information relating to acts of terrorism or persons committing them were created. The National Council for Civil Liberties criticized the Acts on a number of grounds, including that the proscription provisions offend against the principle that people should be punished for their actions and not their beliefs or their associations with others; that the definition of "terrorism" ("the use of violence for political ends") is so broad that it could encompass many non-terrorist situations; that the period between arrest and charge is not controlled; that people could be excluded without being charged and without the right to know the evidence against them; that normal due process protections are abandoned; that the onus of proof is reversed; and that the danger in abolishing traditional safeguards as an emergency measure is that the new procedures may come to be accepted as the norm.[26]

In view of such criticism of the Acts, in 1978 the British government commissioned Lord Shackleton to review their operation. His report accepted the necessity for the powers and recommended that the Act should continue in much the same form.[27] This recommendation was in spite of the mounting evidence that "because it is not subject to critical scrutiny it is being used for purposes outside of its intended ambit, notably to collect low-grade intelligence and to intimidate those whose political views, although not illegal, are not approved of by the authorities."[28] With the passing of each annual renewal debate in Parliament, however, came also the increasing realization that "temporary" measures were becoming accepted as part of an ongoing process, and a growing number of voices expressed their disquiet about the operation of the Act. In response to opposition dissent during the renewal debate in March 1982, the government commissioned Lord Jellicoe to undertake a further review of the Act. Jellicoe was asked to assess the operation of the Act with particular regard to its effectiveness and its impact on individual liberties, but his terms of reference specifically restrained him from questioning the actual necessity for the legislation.

In general terms Jellicoe felt that the legislation is an effective weapon against terrorism, but concluded that it should remain in force only while effective, only if the general law cannot be used to achieve its aims, if the inroads into civil liberties are not excessive, and if the possibility of abuse is minimized by the provision of effective safeguards.[29] While this appears reasonable and level headed, the thrust of Jellicoe's actual recommendations is to make the whole Act more part of the "normal" processes of the criminal law. For example, he recommends that the phrase "Temporary Provisions" be removed from the Act's title and that, while still requiring annual renewal, the Act have a maximum life of five years. He suggests that further legislation should require a new bill preceded by a *private* review of the Act's operation. He suggests that the focus of the Act should shift from Irish terrorism to international terrorism. Within the area of arrest and interrogation, Jellicoe opposes the abolition of the power of extended detention and recommends the extension of the power of arrest for use against suspected international terrorists of any group, cause, or nationality. He seeks to provide for civil liberties concerns by way of greater personal involvement by the secretary of state, the application of the Judges Rules (the code relating to the treatment of persons in ordinary police custody), the absolute right of access to a solicitor after forty-eight hours of detention, and some minor points such as improved training and the handing of a notice of rights to any person detained for one hour. The report leaves the exclusion provisions of the Act largely intact, especially the provision that it is the home secretary, and not the courts, that has the final decision-making power.

Jellicoe's report has been severely criticized by Joe Sim and Philip A.

Thomas who argue that it "makes the 'temporary', 'draconian', and extraordinary powers available under the Act more permanent, more ordinary and more central to the administration and practice of criminal
justice in Britain."[30] One of Jellicoe's stated objectives was to bring the
Act into line with normal police powers, practices, and procedures. But
the benchmark against which he measures the Act's powers are the
powers contained in the controversial Police and Criminal Evidence Bill,
which itself greatly extends police powers and has been subject to cogent
criticism.[31] Jellicoe's recommended safeguards to protect civil liberties
are also castigated as hollow symbolism. Sim and Thomas point out that
the suggested application of the Judges Rules to persons detained under
the Act ignores the widespreaad criticism of the failure of the Rules to
provide adequate protection to suspects even in ordinary police custody.
While Jellicoe's intellectual honesty in recommending the removal of the
words "Temporary Provisions" from the title to the new Act is recognized, Sim and Thomas claim that "the move towards accepting the
permanence of such legislation is encouraged by a descriptive title which
in turn promotes the recognition of the long term inevitability of anti-
terrorist laws."[32] They argue further that the danger is that "during the
life of this legislation the process of normalisation may move the burden
of responsibility from those seeking to extend anti-terrorist law on to
those who seek to repeal it. Arguments to retain 'emergency' legislation
are different and more onerous than those to retain 'normal' legislation."[33]
    The concern expressed by critics of the Shackleton and Jellicoe reports
seems justified in view of the way the Acts have been applied in practice.
There has been no proper evaluation that has shown the Acts to be
effective. But the statistics issued by the Home Office concerning de-
tentions and charges under the Acts indicate that they have been used
largely to gather intelligence and intimidate those involved in legitimate
political activities. Over the entire period of operation of the Acts, less
than 2 percent of persons detained were charged. Further, the National
Council for Civil Liberties claims that "all the people detained under the
Act and subsequently charged with criminal offences would have been
arrested and questioned without using the detention powers of the Act
itself. . . . [It is] efficient and speedy police work, not emergency powers,
which result in suspects being brought to trial."[34]
    Quite clearly, Britain has not become an undemocratic society because
of the existence of the Prevention of Terrorism Act. But seen in the
context of other existing or pending legislation that strengthens police
powers and provides only cosmetic concessions to civil liberties concerns,
it can be seen as part of a package that increases the emphasis on law
and order, on state control, and on incorporating into normal practice
powers that have hitherto been seen as exceptional. The acceptance of
Lord Jellicoe's recommendations and their inclusion into the Prevention

of Terrorism Bill introduced into the House of Commons in late 1983 are clear evidence of this trend. The lesson for those concerned with preserving true democracy and not allowing an unnecessary slide into an authoritarian society is clear. If governments consider anti-terrorist legislation necessary, they must be forced by public opinion to provide adequate evidence that the threat is real and that existing powers are insufficient. Any legislation introduced must have a finite life; and if the government wishes to re-introduce it, there should be a requirement to demonstrate its effectiveness in meeting its objectives. Finally, since all anti-terrorist legislation necessarily involves restrictions on civil liberties and can be used for purposes or against groups other than those for which it was ostensibly designed, the legislation should include some adequate mechanism for ongoing monitoring of its operations.

If developments on the British mainland have attracted criticism, the imposition of various anti-terrorist measures in Northern Ireland has stimulated even more concern. Arguing from the obvious fact that terrorism poses a much greater threat in Northern Ireland than in mainland Britain, the British authorities have introduced a number of laws that suspend many of the usual protections of British law. The increasing level of terrorist violence in the 1960s led the government to introduce internment in 1971. Under the authority of the Stormont Special Powers Act 1922, British soldiers arrested 342 suspects on August 1, 1971, and a further 648 by November of that year. Over half were released within a few weeks or months, fuelling accusations that many people were unjustly suspected of terrorist activities on the basis of false, inaccurate, or outdated information. Internment remained in force for several years [under a 1972 Order in Council after the British assumption of direct rule, and later under the Northern Ireland (Emergency Provisions) Act 1973], but was abandoned in late 1975 when the British government concluded that the resentment it engendered among the Catholic population outweighed any advantages the practice may have had. Significantly, there was no dramatic upturn in terrorism following the release of a mass of "terrorists."

Probably the most contentious aspect of the internment period centered on interrogation methods used on those detained,[35] which were judged by the European Court of Human Rights to constitute inhumane and degrading treatment, but not torture. In response to concern over the practices, the government set up an inquiry that recommended a number of changes in practice to provide some measures of protection for human rights and to prohibit some interrogation methods.[36] The thrust of these developments was to persuade the British government to modify the legal system to be used to keep terrorists out of circulation. Following the recommendations of the Diplock report,[37] the Emergency Provisions (Northern Ireland) Act 1973 was passed, which provided for the Royal Ulster Constabulary to have much widened powers of arrest and interrogation, suspended jury trials for terrorist suspects, and radically altered the law to allow confessions that would otherwise be excluded under common law. All of these developments have been subject to severe criticism in ensuing years on the grounds that they make more inroads into civil liberties than are warranted by the situation and that the elasticity of the rules allows them to be applied to situations that are not clearly of a terrorist nature.

Dermot Walsh examined arrest and interrogation practices and procedures under the emergency legislation in Northern Ireland.[38] He found that of a total of 4,069 persons arrested by the police and army under the emergency legislation in the first ten months of 1980, a mere 428 (or less than 11 percent) were actually charged with a scheduled offence. In other words, 89 percent were released without charge. This compares with between 10 and 20 percent released without charge in England and Wales after questioning under normal police powers.[39] In attempting to discover the reason for this discrepancy, Walsh interviewed a sample of those detained. His findings indicated that the reason was that the police and the army used their powers of arrest and detention to collect intelligence and to check on involvement in terrorist activity without having any real suspicion of individual complicity other than residence in a particular area or membership in particular families. Thus, "despite the fact that all the suspects were arrested on suspicion of involvement in terrorism etc. and that the majority were detained in carefully pre-planned operations, as many as 72% claimed that they were not questioned about their involvement in specific incidents."[40]

Walsh also examined the adequacy of the safeguards for accused in police custody recommended by the Bennett committee.[41] In general, he concluded that while significant improvements had occurred, these could be attributed to public concern over the practices condemned by civil rights groups rather than to the new procedures administered by the police themselves. Rights such as access to solicitors, providing suspects with a sheet of their rights, and not subjecting suspects to verbal abuse were still frequently not enforced. Walsh argues convincingly that burdening the police with the primary responsibility for enforcing safeguards seriously reduces the possibility of their ever becoming a reality. If the safeguards fail to work properly in practice, there will inevitably develop a greater imbalance between police powers and individual liberties than should be tolerated in a democracy.

Another controversial power now available in Northern Ireland is the creation of so-called "Diplock courts," which can try scheduled offences without a jury when the director of public prosecution finds that a fair trial could not be held in the normal manner because of biased or intimidated jurors. In addition, for some offences (such as unlawful possession of arms or explosives), the onus of proof has been reversed so that the accused has to satisfy the court of his or her innocence. Finally, the rules for admission of evidence have been relaxed, permitting the admissibility of statements by the accused "unless the accused was subjected to torture or to inhumane or degrading treatment in order to induce him to make a statement.[42]

These departures from British legal practice have been criticized from a number of quarters. For example, the offences listed in the schedule to Act that allow a Diplock court to be held include murder, serious offences against the person, robbery, arson, firearms and explosives offences, aggravated burglary, and intimidation. As Anthony Jennings has pointed out: "The criterion, therefore, in deciding if a case is heard by a "Diplock court," is not the terrorist connections of the accused, but the type of offence committed. This means that in a system designed to deal with terrorists, "ordinary criminals" can be denied trial by jury."[43] Jennings cites as evidence that this is, in fact, happening. A BBC "Panorama" program (October 24, 1983) claimed that 40 percent of cases in Diplock courts had no political "overtones."

Other authors have criticized the changes to court procedure on the grounds that they constitute a powerful symbolic political weapon against terrorism, with implications for respect for the judicial process and for discussion of legitimate differences of opinion over the causes of and cures for terrorism in Northern Ireland. Thus, Birthe Jorgensen argues:

In a society made ungovernable by conflict, selecting such a symbol of consensus as a court of law whose rules are expected to reflect a consensus decision as to relevancy and justice, can only further mark the fissure between dominant and subordinate groups. These courts ensure that the conflict in Northern Ireland is framed so as to deflect attention from the larger political questions while stifling the political questions pertinent to those brought before them."[44]

In the Northern Ireland context, it is vital that the law be seen as democratic and fair by the Catholic minority, and not as a repressive security tool. But the changes in legal powers and procedures, together with a growing controversy over the conviction of persons accused of terrorism on the basis of uncorroborated evidence of "converted terrorists" (commonly known as "supergrasses"), make it difficult for the minority to view the law other than as a means of state self-protection, not of justice. The facts that supergrasses are often granted immunity from prosecution for their own offences, are provided with new identities, and are paid substantial rewards make it easy to believe that their evidence is tainted and unreliable. This view is reinforced by descriptions of proceedings in actual cases[45] and by claims such as those made on the BBC's "Panorama" program that the acquittal rate in Diplock courts was 33 percent compared with 50 percent in Northern Ireland's jury courts.[46]

Again, the lesson is clear. If emergency measures are necessary, the government must take legislative and administrative action to ensure that deprivation of rights or legal protections is balanced by meaningful oversight and review mechanisms, that the security forces are not permitted to use the powers to deal with any group other than terrorists, and that the powers have a finite life and can be renewed only after a full public inquiry into the continuing necessity for emergency legislation, an evaluation of the efficacy of the powers in actually reducing terrorism, and due consideration of whether the inroads made into civil liberties are a reasonable price to pay for whatever successes the legislation has permitted.

The fact that anti-terrorist legislation that entails major reversals of normal legal forms or protections has been passed or introduced in democracies facing markedly different levels of terrorist threat illustrates that governments have given insufficient attention to distinguishing between different types of terrorist threat.[47] Clearly, governments perceive terrorism as a monolithic entity that is a real threat to the state. The question is, Why is this so, when careful analysis of specific terrorist campaigns shows the threat to be grossly exaggerated? Indeed, Andrew Mack, in one of the most balanced discussions of a number of terrorist campaigns, claims that "terrorist groups are, by their very nature, and that of the strategies they pursue, incapable of posing *any* threat to democratic states."[48] (He might have more accurately added that any threat posed comes from the nature of the response to terrorism, which can, indeed, extinguish democracy). Mack argues convincingly that while revolutionary terrorism can be effective under certain circumstances, the necessary conditions do not exist in democratic societies. It is largely the exploitation of the terrorist image by the media and the perceptions that flow from sensationalist coverage of terrorist spectaculars that are responsible for the widespread belief that terrorism poses a significant challenge to the survival of democracy. In many ways, our perceptions of terrorism and reactions to it fall within the category of a "moral panic,"[49] in which there is a major discrepancy between the perceived threat and the reality.

The consequence of the disjunction between perception and reality is to elevate terrorism to undeserved prominence on policy agendas and to grossly inflate the importance of terrorist groups. Indeed, as Philip Cerny observes: "The potential power of these groups seems to lie not in their threat to overthrow society by force of arms *per se*, but in their ability to symbolise the fragility and vulnerability of the social order and to force that order to subvert itself by eroding the liberal and democratic values upon which its own legitimacy is based."[50]

In spite of the fact that the terrorist threat has been grossly exaggerated, however, there remains the reality that governments must take some action to protect life and property against such violence and to avoid giving the appearance of being so weak that there will be an escalation of terrorism aimed at securing minor tactical successes against governments. How should democratic governments approach the problem of terrorism? The answers are less than satisfying, and therein lies the major problem for governments, which, naturally, like to appear (and whose public demands them to be) in control of the situation. The first principle is to assess the threat accurately and take measured responses accordingly. This, of course, is easier to suggest than to carry out, but governments could certainly assist the process of accurate threat assessment by avoiding being the willing accomplices of the media in generating and maintaining the hysteria that surrounds the issue of terrorism. We must realize that in liberal democratic societies "not all interests will ever be satisfied and that in view of the opportunities modern conditions provide for an individual or a small group prepared to take disproportionate personal risks, political violence is likely to be a more or less normal feature of modern political life."[51] As writers such as J. Bowyer Bell recognize,[52] governments must both respond positively to real and legitimate grievances and learn to be moderate and judicious in their response to violence. Further, the public needs to be apprised of the real threats posed by terrorism in an effort to inhibit reactions of outrage and indignation that pressure governments into counter-productive responses.[53] Althouth it is unlikely that they will do so, it would also be helpful for governments in capitalist societies to realize that there *do* exist "structural contradictions of a kind which governments *cannot* solve and without whose solution some interests are *permanently* unsatisfied and are, in consequence, more or less permanent bases of potentially violent resistance."[54] A realistic appraisal of this violence shows, however, that such violence poses no fundamental challenges to democracy other than the threat of governmental over-reaction. The best defence against that eventuality is a vigorous defence of the rights to personal freedom and to free speech.

NOTES

I am grateful to Peter Grabosky for his critical reading of the draft of this chapter.

1. U.S. Department of State, *Patterns of International Terrorism: 1982* (Washington, D.C.: GPO, 1984).

2. Grant Wardlaw, *Political Terrorism, Theory, Tactics, and Counter-Measures* (Cambridge: Cambridge University Press, 1982).

3. Dennis Pluchinsky, "Political Terrorism in Western Europe: Some Themes and Variations," in Yonah Alexander and Kenneth A. Myers, eds., *Terrorism and Europe* (London: Croom Helm, 1982), pp. 40–78.

4. Irving Louis Horowitz, "The Routinization of Terrorism and Its Unan-

ticipated Consequences," in Martha Crenshaw, ed., *Terrorism, Legitimacy, and Power. The Consequences of Political Violence* (Middletown, Conn.: Wesleyan University Press, 1983), p. 42.

5. Chris Rootes, "Living with Terrorism," *Social Alternatives*, 1 (June 7, 1980), pp. 46–49.

6. Paul Walton, "The Case of the Weathermen: Social Reaction and Radical Commitment," in Ian Taylor and Laurie Taylor, eds., *Politics and Deviance* (Harmondsworth: Penguin Books, 1973), pp. 157–181.

7. Nigel Young, *An Infantile Disorder? The Crisis and Decline of the New Left* (London: Routledge, 1978).

8. Horowitz, "Routinization of Terrorism," p. 49.

9. Ibid., p. 51.

10. Carlos Marighela, *For the Liberation of Brazil* (Harmondsworth: Penguin, 1971).

11. Paul Wilkinson, "Proposals for Government and International Responses to Terrorism," in Paul Wilkinson, ed., *British Perspectives on Terrorism* (London: Allen & Unwin, 1981).

12. Ibid., p. 168.

13. Neil Livingstone, "States in Opposition: The War Against Terrorism," *Conflict*, 3 (February 3, 1981), p. 83.

14. Ibid., p. 99.

15. Ibid., p. 101.

16. Ibid., p. 102.

17. Wilkinson, p. 173.

18. Martha Crenshaw, "Introduction: Reflections on the Effects of Terrorism," in Crenshaw, *Terrorism, Legitimacy, and Power*, p. 14.

19. Horowitz, "Routinization of Terrorism," p. 50.

20. Crenshaw, "Introduction," p. 146.

21. Yehezekel Dror, "Terrorism as a Challenge to the Democratic Capacity to Govern," in Crenshaw, *Terrorism, Legitimacy, and Power*.

22. Ibid., p. 73.

23. Luigi Bonante, "Some Unanticipated Consequences of Terrorism," *Journal of Peace Research* 16, no. 3 (1979), pp. 197–211.

24. George A. Lopez and Michael Stohl, "State Terrorism: From Robespierre to Nineteen Eighty-Four," *Chitty's Law Journal* (Winter 1985/86).

25. W. Clifford, "Terrorism and Overkill," *Terrorism: An International Journal*, 5 (1981), pp. 284–285.

26. Patricia Hewitt, *The Abuse of Power, Civil Liberties in the United Kingdom* (Oxford: Martin Robertson, 1982); Catherine Scorer, *The Prevention of Terrorism Acts 1974 and 1976. A Report on the Operation of the Law* (London: National Council for Civil Liberties, 1976); and Catherine Scorer and Patricia Hewitt, *The Prevention of Terrorism Act: The Case for Repeal* (London: National Council for Civil Liberties, 1981).

27. Lord Shackleton, *Review of the Operation of the Prevention of Terrorism (Temporary Provisions) Acts 1974 and 1976*, Cmnd. 7324 (London: Her Majesty's Stationery Office, 1978).

28. Wardlaw, *Political Terrorism*, p. 129.

29. Lord Jellicoe, *Review of the Operation of the Prevention of Terrorism (Temporary*

Provisions) Act 1976, Cmnd. 8803 (London: Her Majesty's Stationery Office, 1983).

30. Joe Sim and Philip A. Thomas, "The Prevention of Terrorism Act: Normalizing the Politics of Repression," *Journal of Law and Society* 10, (1983), p. 72.

31. John Baldwin and Roger Leng, "Police, Power and the Citizen," *The Howard Journal*, 23 (1984), pp. 88–89; and Lee Bridges and Tony Bunyan, "Britain's New Urban Policing Strategy—The Police and Criminal Evidence Bill in Context," *Journal of Law and Society* 10, no. 1 (1983), pp. 85–107.

32. Sim and Thomas, "Prevention of Terrorism Act," p. 76.

33. *Ibid.*

34. Scorer and Hewitt, *Prevention of Terrorism Act*, p. 39.

35. Peter Taylor, *Beating the Terrorists? Interrogation in Omagh, Gough, and Castlereagh* (Harmondsworth: Penguin Books, 1980).

36. Judge H. G. Bennett, *Report on the Committee of Inquiry into Police Interrogation Procedures in Northern Ireland*, Cmnd. 7497 (London: Her Majesty's Stationery Office, 1979).

37. Lord Diplock, *Report of the Commission to Consider Legal Procedures to Deal with Terrorist Activities in Northern Ireland*, Cmnd. 5185 (London: Her Majesty's Stationery Office, 1972).

38. Dermot P. J. Walsh, "Arrest and Interrogation: Northern Ireland, 1981," *Journal of Law and Society*, vol. 9, no. 1 (1982), pp. 37–62.

39. Sir Cyril Phillips, *Report of the Royal Commission on Criminal Procedure*, Cmnd. 8092 (London: Her Majesty's Stationery Office, 1981).

40. Walsh, "Arrest and Interrogation," p. 49.

41. Bennett, *Report of the Committee of Inquiry*.

42. Northern Ireland (Emergency Provisions) Act 1978, 58(2).

43. Anthony Jennings, "Supergrasses and the Northern Ireland Legal System," *New Law Journal* 133, no. 6131 (November 25, 1983), p. 1043.

44. Birthe Jorgensen, "Defending the Terrorists: Queen's Counsel Before the Courts of Northern Ireland," *Journal of Law and Society* 9, no. 1 (1982), p. 123.

45. Sean Damer, "The Lawmongers," *New Socialist* 16 (March–April 1984), p. 25.

46. Cited in Jennings, "Supergrasses," p. 1044.

47. For example, the Federal Republic of Germany. See Thomas Blanke, "Berufsverbote and Political Repression in the Federal Republic of Germany," *International Journal of the Sociology of Law* 9 (1981), pp. 397–406; and Martin Oppenheimer, "The Criminalization of Political Dissent in the Federal Republic of Germany," *Contemporary Crises* 2, no. 1 (1978), pp. 97–103. For Sweden, see Gorin Elwin, "Swedish Anti-Terrorist Legislation," *Contemporary Crises* 1, no. 3 (1977), pp. 289–302. For the United States of America, see Kitty Calavita, " 'Law and Order' and the Anti-Terrorist Act of 1983," *Crime and Social Justice* 20 (1984), pp. 138–143.

48. Andrew Mack, "The Utility of Terrorism," *Australian and New Zealand Journal of Criminology* 14 (1981), p. 199.

49. Stuart Hall, Chas Chritcher, Tony Jefferson, John Clarke, and Brian Roberts, *Policing the Crisis, Mugging, the State, and Law and Order* (London: Macmillan, 1978).

50. Philip Cerney, "France: Non-Terrorism and the Politics of Repressive

Tolerance," in Juliet Lodge, ed., *Terrorism: A Challenge to the State* (Oxford: Martin Robertson, 1981), p. 92.

51. Rootes, "Living with Terrorism," p. 48.

52. J. Bowyer Bell, *A Time of Terror: How Democratic Societies Respond to Revolutionary Violence* (New York: Basic Books, 1978).

53. Rootes, "Living with Terrorism."

54. Ibid., p. 48.

8

The Superpowers and International Terrorism

Michael Stohl

INTRODUCTION: THE CONTEXT OF STATE TERRORISM

This chapter is part of a continuing effort to address the role of terrorism as an instrument of state policy.[1] It provides a context within which a state's choice of a terror strategy may be understood. This analysis of state terrorism in international affairs begins with propositions at the systemic level that simply (and, it is hoped, accurately) characterize the post-World War II world as it applies to and shapes U.S. and U.S.S.R. behavior. The propositions are followed by a brief analysis of the behavioral developments of the post-war period and the strategies that lay beneath superpower behavior. An expected utility approach to the choice of terrorist strategies and a brief introduction to the range of choices in international affairs follow. The heart of the chapter is an examination of superpower use of coercive diplomacy, clandestine operations, and surrogate terrorism.

Systemic Propositions and Assumptions

1. "Two superpowers, each incomparably stronger than any other power or possible combination of other powers, oppose each other."[2]
2. "In a world in which two states united in their mutual antagonism far overshadow any other, the incentives to a calculated response stand out most clearly, and the sanctions against irresponsible behavior clearly achieve their greatest force."[3]
3. "The periphery of the balance of power now coincides with the confines of the earth."[4]

In short, our basic assumptions regarding the international system recognize that there are two politico-military superpowers and that the two superpowers understand that it is foolish to resolve their differences by actually facing one another directly in a superpower war, but they compete for power and influence on a world scale regardless of the risks this entails.

We recognize this distribution of power and its consequences as the core of our concept of a bipolar system. There are recognizable consequences for interaction patterns of states within a bipolar system. A first consequence, we have already noted, is that the two poles tend to define problems vis-à-vis one another, and these problems are seen to overshadow all other aspects of the system. A second consequence is to define the remainder of the system in terms of what it means to the two poles and the continuation of the bipolar system.

Certain patterns of behavior tend to flow from a bipolar system with nuclear weapons. Since the two polar states seek to preserve themselves, and as a consequence the system, they seek to avoid superpower war. They must therefore, in addition to maintaining or increasing their own military potentials if they are to continue to attempt to secure advantages vis-à-vis one another, do so by a combination of the following policies:

1. Increasing the number of states that support them
2. Decreasing the number of states that support their opponent
3. Increasing the number of trouble spots that their opponent will have to confront
4. Decreasing the number of trouble spots that they themselves will have to confront

Following these prescriptions does not alter the fundamental structure of the system—at least in the short run—but failure to do so might alter the structure in the not-so-long run.

Kenneth Waltz suggests that the bipolar world and technological and other changes that have occurred in the post-war period were assumed to inhibit the use of force in the international arena notwithstanding that

seldom, if ever has force been more variously, more persistently, and more widely applied; and seldom has it been more consciously applied as an instrument of national policy. Since World War II we have seen the political organization and pervasion of power, not the cancellation of force by nuclear stalemate.[5]

Force has been widely used. Scholars, and quite often the superpowers themselves, examining the record have congratulated the superpowers on their controlled use of force and their understanding of the new "rules of the game,"[6] which have been introduced to prevent or at the least make more unlikely the direct confrontation of the superpowers over most issues in international politics. In the peripheries, the superpowers sought to seek the advantages the system would lead us to expect. We should note that the label "Superpower" obscures the fact that for many years the Soviet Union simply did not have the capacity to do more than verbally encourage periphery struggles and perhaps send a few advisers. The historical domination of the West of the colonial and recently former colonial areas placed the U.S. role in the position of defender. The "new rules of the game" and the use of force were arrived at after a number of years of tacit bargaining and accommodation.

Spheres of Influence

In a bipolar world we expect certain patterns of behavior to develop vis-à-vis relations with the poles. In what were traditionally referred to as great powers spheres of influence it was assumed that great powers have "positions of local preponderance" and other great powers "avoid collisions or friction between them" in these areas.[7]

Through a process of thrust and reaction, the two superpowers may be seen to have established an accommodation of behavior within their own clearly defined spheres of influence. As T. Franck and W. Weisband skillfully demonstrate, by 1968 the Brezhnev and Johnson doctrines faithfully mirrored one another, and these verbal rationalizations of interventionary behavior, while drawing ritual verbal opposition, did not bring forceful responses on the part of the other superpower.

The analysis of Soviet and American verbal behavior in this study reveals that both we and they have committed ourselves very explicitly to an international system in which two superpowers exercise a kind of eminent domain, each within its own geographical region.[8]

While American presidents promised no more Cubas, the Soviet leadership sought to prevent further Yugoslavias. If the superpowers could control the system, there would be no more Fidel Castros and no more Titos as symbols of opposition within the core areas of the sphere of influence.

Wars of National Liberation and Counter-Insurgency

We now generally recognize that a major source of the split between the Soviet Union and the People's Republic of China, which we date from the late 1950s, lay in the approach that was to be taken vis-à-vis the United States. Nikita Khrushchev favored what was perceived by the Chinese as a clearly conservative (that is, revisionist) line. He argued that nuclear weapons recognized no class interests and therefore the Soviet Union and the United States needed to reach a rapprochement so as to avoid an "unthinkable nuclear war." His January 1961 speech, in which he called for Soviet support for "wars of nation liberation," was read, at least in the United States, as an indication of the expansionist nature of the Soviet threat. In China the same speech was interpreted as evidence of the non-revolutionary character of the Soviet regime. It is now better understood as further evidence that Khrushchev was interested in minimizing the direct threats of nuclear confrontation with the West while maintaining the forms of Communist support for revolutionary challenges to the capitalist West—a message thus intended as much for consumption within the Communist world as in the West.[9]

The contemporaneous U.S. assessment was, in John F. Kennedy's words, that "we are opposed around the world by a monolithic and ruthless conspiracy that relies primarily on covert means for expanding its sphere of influence."[10] The conclusion was reached that to oppose such an enemy the United States had to continue to engage in covert activities and to develop the capacity to, in the words of the military doctrine of the time, "respond flexibly" to any eventuality. In fact, of course, the United States had been groping for such a strategy since the end of the Second World War, but the Kennedy years saw the policy become part of doctrine as the "New Frontier" sought to "rationalize" the American use of force worldwide. In the beginning, this was applied in Southeast Asia, Latin America, and the Congo. Later, flexible response grew out of all proportion to engulf the United States in the quagmire of Vietnam. At the end of the 1960s, a perceived lesson of the Vietnam experience was translated into the Nixon doctrine. As enunciated on the island of Guam on July 25, 1969, the president suggested that nations in the peripheral world now would have to defend themselves with U.S. material support and encouragement, but primarily with their own troops. Throughout the period, however, the underlying assumption of the need to react against the threat of Soviet expansion and the assumption that peripheral difficulties were to be defined as superpower problems remained the operative principle. While the United States engaged in numerous operations to destabilize foreign governments, these were seen as restorative not revolutionary. In short, these actions were perceived as attempts to return the system to an earlier status quo, to reverse the revolutionary challenges that had created new governments that threatened the neo-colonial Third World system (for example, Guatemala, Iran, Indonesia, Cuba).

These structural conditions and the behavioral manifestations that have developed during the post-war period provide the framework within which we may discuss a state's decision to employ strategies and tactics of terrorism. To understand how states might choose a terrorist strategy, we turn to some previous work on such choices within domestic affairs.

Expected Utility: A Cost–Benefit Approach to State Terrorism

Raymond Duvall and Michael Stohl argue that an expectancy X value theory or expected utility model is useful for understanding a government's choice of terrorism as a strategy and tactic in domestic affairs.[11] It may also be usefully applied to behavior in international affairs. In short, we argue this utility theory may be expressed as:

$$U_i = P_i (B - C_i),$$

where:

U_i is expected utility from engaging in action i,
B is the benefit gotten from the desired state of affairs,
P_i is the believed probability with which action i will bring about the desired state of affairs,
and C_i is the believed probable costs from engaging in action i.

We argued, therefore, that states might choose terrorism both when they perceived themselves powerless—the sense that other means of governance were unavailable or less useful—and when they were in a situation of confident strength—when the costs were low and the probability of success believed high in relation to other means.

Further, we argued that two kinds of cost can be distinguished: response costs and production costs. Response costs are those that might be imposed by the target group and/or sympathetic or offended bystanders. The bystanders in the foreign policy realm may include domestic and foreign interests, while the target in international as in domestic affairs may be wider than the attacking party may have planned or expected.

Production costs are the costs of taking the action regardless of the reactions of others. In addition to the economic costs—paying the participants, buying the weapons and the like—there is the psychological cost of acting in a manner that we normally characterize as unacceptable civilized behavior.

Discussing this problem in regard to domestic policy, Duvall and Stohl argued that the psychological costs that an actor can expect to experience from perpetrating violence on an incidental instrumental victim involve two factors operating in conjunction.[12] First is the extent to which human life is valued (or conversely the strength of internalized prohibitions against violence in general). Second is the extent to which the victim can be or has been dehumanized in the mind of the violent actor. Where moral/normative prohibitions are weak and especially where victims can be viewed in other than human terms, the self-imposed costs of terrorist action are apt to be low.

Further, we argued that the extent to which victims and potential victims can be dehumanized is affected by two important variables. The first is the perceptual social distance between the government and the victim population. The second is the extent to which action is routinely and bureaucratically authorized, so that responsibility for the consequences of action is personally avoidable by all persons in the decisional chain. Thus, self-imposed costs for terrorist action are apt to be lower for governments, especially in a conflict situation with believed "inferior" peoples and/or with a highly bureaucratized coercive machinery.

In the international realm, these two important variables are often maximized. Inhibitions are lowered, making it easier for governments to choose to employ terrorist strategies. In terms of the focus of this chapter the two superpowers operating within a bipolar system have also provided an overarching framework in which other nations and their peoples are defined as less important than the continuation and maintenance of the international system itself. It is no longer necessary to perceive such peoples as racially or culturally inferior. Rather these peoples may be dismissed, as they are considered less important than the survival of the free world, socialist states, or the international system as a whole.

The foregoing provides the context within which an analysis of state terrorist behavior in the international realm transpires. I will argue that the United States and the Soviet Union both engage in what by convention we normally refer to as a coercive diplomacy in the international realm.

While both superpowers engage in coercive diplomacy of the non-terrorist as well as the terrorist variety, it is the contention of this chapter that the United States does so more frequently and in a wider sphere. This is not to argue that the United States is guilty of greater moral deficiency. On the contrary, if such a consideration were at issue, I would argue the imbalance lies in the opposite direction. Relative moral deficiency is not at issue here; behavior and opportunities for behavior, however, are. In terms of global reach, the United States has many more flexible and active fingers and toes on its outstretched limbs than does the Soviet Union.

While we may expect superpowers, or in earlier epochs great powers, to react in certain predictable patterns of concern as they respond to threats to their perceived sphere of influence and to their perceptions of the international balance of power, we should remember that today's superpowers are, despite (1) their overwhelming preponderance of power vis-à-vis the other states in the system and (2) the debates in the United

States over the military readiness and relative strengths of the two, quite different states with very different capabilities and global interests. While the Soviet Union may be described as a global power, it does not have the same global power and interests as the United States. It does not have the economic inter-connectedness and therefore the economic and political leverage that the United States does. Its client states are fewer in number and far less important to its own perceptions of welfare and economic security, and this may be expected to influence heavily its behavior and choice of coercive targets.

Forms of State Terrorism in International Relations

In a previous work, I identified three broad forms of state terrorist behavior in the international sphere.[13] The terrorism component within each of these categories was defined as the purposeful act or threat of violence to create fear and/or compliant behavior in a victim and/or audience of the act or threat. Terrorism as a form of *coercive diplomacy* constitutes the first. Here the aim is to make non-compliance with a particular demand, in the words of Thomas Schelling, "terrible beyond endurance."[14] While the threat is openly communicated by the actions of the state, it may be implicit and quite often is non-verbal. Coercive diplomacy is overt behavior. The parties to the conflict are fully aware of the nature of the threat.

Covert behavior categorizes the second form of state terrorism. The clandestine services of the national state are responsible for these actions. Government agents operating across national boundaries may choose either national elites or the foreign society itself as the target. In this type of state terrorism, states may thus attempt to directly intimidate government officials through campaigns of bombing, attacks, and assassinations and by sponsoring and participating in attempted *coups d'état*. Alternatively, national states participate in the destabilization of other societies with the purpose of creating chaos and the conditions for the collapse of governments, the weakening of the national state, and changes in leadership. The threats to the regime and the society are obvious, but there is an attempt at deniability nonetheless. It is the pattern of such behavior and the threat of such a pattern being initiated that constitute the terroristic aspects of this type of action.

The third form of state terrorism involves assistance to another state or insurgent organization that makes possible or "improves" the capability of that actor to practice terrorism both at home and abroad. This form we label *surrogate* terrorism, as the obvious effect and intent of the assistance provided are the improvement of the assisted actor's ability either to carry out terrorist actions to maintain a regime's rule or to create chaos and/or the eventual overthrow of an identified enemy state regime.

We shall briefly examine each of these forms of terrorism for the United States and the Soviet Union with an eye to (1) describing their behaviors and (2) detecting similarities and differences in their modes of behavior in each of the three types of terrorism. We argue that the probabilities of choosing surrogate, covert, or overt coercive strategies depend on the differences for each case in the production and response costs of terror. Those costs and also the benefits will vary depending further on whether the target state lies in the U.S. or U.S.S.R. sphere of influence or the periphery, and whether they are friends or foes of either of the two superpowers.

COERCIVE DIPLOMACY

The defining characteristic of coercive diplomacy as distinct from both diplomacy and traditional military activity is that the force of coercive diplomacy is used "in an exemplary, demonstrative manner, in discrete and controlled increments, to induce the opponent to revise his calculations and agree to a mutually acceptable termination of the conflict."[15] We may speak of terrorism as a subset of coercive diplomacy when violence or its threatened use is present. Not all coercive diplomacy employs violence. For example, one may employ economic sanctions in an allowedly coercive manner as did the members of the United Nations with respect to South Africa without employing violent tactics. We will confine our analysis to the violence of coercive diplomacy whose central task was described by Alexander George as "how to create in the opponent the expectation of unacceptable costs of sufficient magnitude to erode his motivation to continue what he is doing."[16]

The willingness of the superpowers to employ force and to threaten its use in the post-war period provides a context within which to understand their employment of terrorism as a strategy. Barry Blechman and Stephen Kaplan provide parallel studies of the American and Soviet use of force in this period.[17]

Kaplan's analysis of Soviet behavior illustrates a number of different purposes and tactics for coercive diplomacy available to strong nations. There were 158 separate incidents in which the use of U.S.S.R. armed forces or the threat of such was employed. Important patterns regarding each of these types of Soviet activities emerge.

Kaplan argues that the Soviet Union pursued coercive diplomacy for expansionary purposes only once after 1951. This occurred when a "show of force" in 1975 in the form of a missile test in the Barents Sea was intended for the consumption of the Norwegian government. On the other hand, the use of armed force to maintain fraternal Communist regimes remains an important instrument of Soviet diplomacy. The Soviet Union threatened intervention, placed ground forces in nearby positions, activated units, repositioned military units, and participated in the active suppression of outbreaks against Eastern European regimes throughout the last three decades. It has intervened with military force in East Germany (1953), Hungary (1956), and Czechoslovakia (1968) to protect "orthodoxy" in Eastern Europe. In the case of Poland in 1980–1981, it was clear to all Poles that U.S.S.R. troop maneuvers and other diplomatic consultations with Eastern Europe units were orchestrated to indicate the necessity for limiting threats to orthodoxy in Poland.

The Soviet Union also used coercive diplomacy to "intimidate neighbors or react to perceive threats presented by neighbors." This pattern shifted from the early post-war period when the concern was more clearly the intimidation of neighbors for Soviet Union-perceived security needs to the more recent past when the issue has been the manipulation of threats to gain diplomatic advantage or reduce possible threats to that country. This use of the threat of armed force within the Eastern European sphere of influence is, of course, a conventional behavior pattern for a great power. Nonetheless, this "convention" involves the threat of the use of force for coercive bargaining purposes. It is meant to intimidate not simply the government whose behavior is being challenged at any one point in time, but also the other fraternal governments and their populations. It should therefore properly be labeled as a terrorist subset of coercive diplomacy.

Soviet use of coercive diplomacy in the Third World appears very different from American usage. Kaplan records only one small action in the Third World after autumn 1962 in which the Soviet Union threatened military force. This involved the deployment of two warships near the coast of Ghana in 1967 after two Soviet trawlers had been seized. This is not to say that the Soviet Union has not been active politically in the Third World. Rather, it is simply to state that the Soviets appear to place little reliance on the threat of violence in their diplomacy in the Third World. This represents an approach quite different from that of the United States.

The United States has also not been adverse to the use of force as a political instrument in the post-World War II era. Blechman and Kaplan identify 215 incidents in which force was employed.[18] The United States employed its armed forces as a political instrument to maintain friendly regimes, to provide third party support in conflicts, to assist allies in conflict, and to encourage parties to terminate their use of force. These U.S. actions, ranging in intensity and danger from threats directed to demonstrate support for the pro-Western governments of Greece and Italy in the early post-war period to the Christmas bombings of North Vietnam in 1972 and the *Mayaguez* operation in 1975, illustrate the commonplace nature of great powers "using armed forces to pursue objectives abroad without going to war."[19]

The United States has been far more active in the Third World than the Soviet Union. This has been so in part because the U.S. sphere of influence includes a portion of the Third World (Latin America and the Caribbean), but also because the United States, perceiving itself as the status quo power, often defines changes in government in the Third World as threats to the status quo. The United States has sought to restore or to protect regimes that were clearly pro-Western. As this has been an area of much change and instability, the opportunities for intervention have been much greater.

These two studies demonstrate once again that the range of actions open to a modern state, particularly a superpower with unlimited geographical range, is extraordinary. We may see further evidence of this range of activities and also illustrate the process of coercive diplomacy and the threat of violence by briefly examining the two superpowers' latest coercive operations—Nicaragua and Poland.

Our purpose here is not to provide a definitive analysis of either interaction. Rather at this time we wish merely to report on the instruments and tactics employed as the two superpowers attempted to meet their objectives without recourse to war. In confronting Nicaragua the Reagan Administration appears to have had a number of objectives: (1) to end Nicaraguan support to the FDR and FMLN in El Salvador, (2) to distance the regime from Cuba and the Soviet Union, (3) to protect capitalist enterprise still existent, and (4) as time passed to aid and abet the overthrow of the Sandinista regime itself. Familiar economic instruments of coercive diplomacy were employed against the regime: suspension of aid, blocking of loans in the InterAmerican Development Bank, disruption of export trade, and concentrated diplomatic attack on the Sandinistas in international forums and in public statements emanating from the White House and the Department of State. But an examination of the *New York Times* for the period also reveals the following tactics from the Blechman and Kaplan list of coercive force options that have been employed: providing a U.S. presence, patrol/reconnaissance/surveillance, movement of a target's military forces or equipment, and interposition. In addition, the Administration also assisted in the mining of Nicaraguan harbors, as well as being intimately involved in covert operations against the Sandinistas, as we will discuss below.

In Poland, the Soviet Union was faced with a situation it found unacceptable, another challenge to "orthodoxy" in Eastern Europe. The rise of Solidarity and the apparent inability of the Polish Communist Party and Polish government to easily manage the situation led to a crisis in which the question of protecting the integrity of fraternal Communist regimes was once again raised by the Kremlin. The Brezhnev doctrine and the past interventions in East Germany, Poland, Hungary, and Czechoslovakia provide the context within which activities relating to the goals of re-establishing clear control and the elimination of challenges to the orthodox status quo may best be understood.

Soviet behavior in this instance was clearly linked to the activities of the Polish authorities. While numerous observers speculated on whether or not the Soviet Union would actually invade and if the cost/benefit equation would favor such intervention given the threat of facing Polish troops on the battlefield defending their homeland, the Soviets employed the traditional instruments for threats of the use of violence: mobilization, troop maneuvers, joint exercises, warnings of Soviet intervention if the situation was not controlled, naval maneuvers by Warsaw Pact forces, landing operations on the Polish coast, border exercises, and alerts. These instruments were accompanied by the standard non-violent instruments of coercive diplomacy: statements of concern for the internal situation in Poland, assurances that the Polish regime would deal effectively with counter-revolutionary elements, and joint communiques by Warsaw Pact allies regarding their solidarity. These threats were clearly linked to the willingness of Polish authorities to use their own coercive strategies and instruments. When the military, after its takeover of the government apparatus, demonstrated anew its willingness to use force, the threat of Soviet and Warsaw Pact intervention receded until, with the imposition of martial law, the threats came to an end and were replaced by statements concerning the validity of the Brezhnev doctrine.

One may argue that the coercive strategies adopted in these two cases illustrate the virtues of such a strategy, "achieving one's objectives economically, with little bloodshed, for fewer psychological and political costs, and often with much less risk of escalation."[20] Saving lives is indeed a virtue. This virtue, however, does not alter the fact that the strategy is based on terror and the power to destroy if "proper" responses are not engendered by the threats and/or the relatively low levels of violence employed. Coercive strategies that rely on the threat of violence are therefore state terror policies, regardless of whether or not they save lives or if we approve of them.[21]

CLANDESTINE OPERATIONS

Whereas the terror of coercive diplomacy is obvious to all observers, even if many shrink from labeling the behavior as such, the terror of the clandestine apparatus of the state in international relations is often quite difficult to discern. Knowledge of these instances of international governmental terrorism is dependent on investigators bringing them to light, and this process of illumination often occurs quite long after the fact. This type of terror in international relations is usually not aimed directly at producing compliance but rather fear and chaos. It is hoped that as a result of increased fear and chaos, governments at some later point will be in a weaker bargaining position or will be more willing to make concessions, given the costs that have become apparent. It is the threat of this type of behavior *in general* that serves to keep elites fearful of outside interference and produces public statements by Third World leaders regarding American interference that to the American public often, particularly before the Pike committee report was made public in 1976,[22] are dismissed as the ravings of unstable, paranoid, or ideological opponents who seek merely to embarrass, or blame their internal difficulties on, the United States.

The reaction by the U.S. media and public to the claims of Fidel Castro and Mu'ammar Qadhafi that the Central Intelligence Agency (CIA) had attempted to assassinate them are excellent cases in point. We have, at present, no direct knowledge in the case of Qadhafi, but by now the attempts on Castro throughout the last two decades are well known.[23]

The clandestine services of the United States have had much experience in the last few decades in this type of behavior. The organization most often responsible for such behavior is the CIA. Victor Marchetti and John Marks suggest that "the crudest and most direct form of covert action is called 'special operation'. . . . By definition, special operations are violent and brutal."[24] A partial listing of well-known CIA special operations indicates the range of such activities. In Guatemala (1954), Indonesia (1958), Iran (1953), and the Bay of Pigs, Cuba (1961), the United States trained, equipped, and provided tactical assistance to groups attempting to overthrow established governments.

Between 1970 and 1973, the United States worked on a number of levels to overthrow the elected government of Salvador Allende in Chile. In addition to non-terroristic strategies such as bribery after the election campaign, the United States embarked on a program to create economic and political chaos in Chile. The CIA was implicated in the assassination of Rene Schneider, the commander-in-chief of the Chilean army, who was selected as a target because he refused to sanction plans to prevent Allende from taking office.

The United States government attempted to foment a coup, it discussed coup plans with the Chileans later convicted of Schneider's abduction, it advocated his removal as a step toward overturning the results of a free election, it offered payment of $50,000 for Schneider's kidnapping and it supplied the weapons for this strategy.[25]

After the failure to prevent Allende from taking office, efforts shifted to obtaining his removal. At least 7 million dollars was authorized by the United States for CIA use in the destabilization of Chilean society. This included financing and assisting opposition groups and right-wing terrorist para-military groups such as *Patria y Libertad* (Fatherland and Liberty). Finally, in September 1973, the Allende government was overthrown in a brutal and violent military coup in which the United States was intimately involved. President Gerald Ford stated, "I think this was in the best interests of the people of Chile and certainly in our best interests."[26] The message for the populations of Latin American nations and particularly the Left opposition was clear: The United States would not permit the continuation of a socialist government, even if it came to power in a democratic election and continued to uphold the basic democratic structure of that society.

In the last few years, major U.S. efforts at destabilization of an increasingly less than covert nature have taken place as part of the strategy of destabilizing and overthrowing the Sandinista regime in Nicaragua. The so-called "secret war" attracted so much attention that the House of Representatives voted on December 8, 1982, to halt covert activities abroad by the CIA for the purpose of overthrowing the government of Nicaragua or provoking a military exchange between Nicaragua and Honduras.

But Nicaragua, while the best known, is not the only nation in which U.S. agents have operated in the last years. Leslie Gelb reports that the CIA is secretly aiding Iranian exiles.[27] The *Washington Post* reports that the CIA is conducting a covert operation affecting Angola, presumably involving support for Jonas Savimbi and his UNITA forces.[28] It has been charged by the Soviets, and Administration officials have allowed the impression to be created, that the United States is engaged in assisting the Afghanis against the Soviet occupation.[29]

It thus appears that the Soviet Union has been far less able or perhaps less willing to intervene in the Third World on the scale that the United States has in the last few decades. This is apparently the case for both overt and covert interventions. While much is made in the West of the strength of the Soviet KGB and the threat that the Soviet Union poses in the Third World, in much of the Third World the Soviet presence appears to be relatively benign. They have far less leverage than the Western powers and far less infra-structure within which to conduct covert operations. A. Rubinstein argues that in Third World policy in general the Soviet Union appears opportunistic and responsive to local initiatives and conditions. Unlike the United States, "the Soviets have not been well placed to meddle effectively in leadership quarrels and have wisely concentrated on maintaining good government-to-government relations, reinforcing convergent policy goals and providing such assistance as is necessary to keep a client in power."[30] This is not to argue that the Soviet Union does not involve itself in "liberation struggles." They quite often are, and have assisted groups (for example, the MPLA in Angola) they believe will be pre-disposed to them after achieving power. But assistance to such groups involves the use of a third type of state terror activity, surrogate terrorism, and should be distinguished from covert terror activities of direct intervention.

INTERNATIONAL TERRORISM AND TRANSNATIONAL TERRORISM—LINKAGES AND THE SUPERPOWERS' ROLE

The Soviet Union

In his first news conference as President Ronald Reagan's newly appointed secretary of state, Alexander Haig responded to a question (and a follow-up question) concerning strategic interests in Latin America by charging that the Soviet Union was "involved in conscious policies, in programs if you will, which foster, support, and expand this activity [international terrorism]." Mr. Haig indicated that the Soviet role included training, funding, and equipping international terrorists.[31] He was supported in this position by key members of the Reagan Administration such as National Security Adviser Richard Allen[32] and Secretary of Defense Casper Weinberger.[33]

Haig's charges focused public attention on an issue that had found increasing attention in the second half of the 1970s: the role of states in the apparently increasing activities of terrorists who operate both within and across state boundaries. Questions had been raised as to how such organizations could operate so capably, and suspicions grew that to do so, they needed organizational infra-structure and state support. The obvious candidate for the role of state supporter was the Soviet Union. The conclusion was reached because the Soviets would receive the greatest benefits from a "program" that encouraged the destabilization of the West. In place of evidence for suspicions raised, the question of *cui bono* (who benefits) was substituted. If direct Soviet involvement could not be found because of the highly secretive and closed nature of Soviet behavior, it was argued that one should assume Soviet backing because of the benefits that would accrue to them and focus on surrogates and intermediaries with the tentacles of the plot leading back to the Soviet Union. Much of this searching was not conducted by scholars, but by journalists, and that work contributed by scholars was not placed within an international relations framework that might have proved useful in framing the issues.

In 1977 Ovid Demaris, a freelance reporter, published *Brothers in Blood: The International Terrorist Network*, in which he argued that terrorist groups had established worldwide liaisons. Through such a network of liaisons, terrorists could obtain whatever was necessary for their operations, including the possibility of nuclear weaponry. Demaris argued:

Although there is no single terrorist conspiracy responsible for acts of terrorism on a worldwide basis, there is a loose network of relationships between various groups that, for lack of a better term, has been called Terror International. . . . They are joined mainly by an anti-imperialist, anti-establishment bias and a determination to replace the few democratic societies left in the world with totalitarian governments.[34]

Also in 1977 the CBS television program "60 Minutes" broadcast a story about "Terror International," an organization that reputedly organized and controlled terrorists and terrorism worldwide. The story claimed that it was simply a matter of time before Terror International turned its attention to the United States. The CIA and Federal Bureau of Investigation (FBI) were unwilling to confirm the existence of such an organization.

In 1979 Robert Kupperman and Darrell Trent argued:

There is evidence of increasing cooperation among national and international terrorist organizations in the form of common financial and technical support. . . . For example Palestinian terrorist camps in Lebanon, Syria, Libya (and until 1970, Jordan) have trained revolutionaries from Western Europe, Africa, Latin America, Asia and North America in terrorist techniques.[35]

Further, they asserted:

There is also evidence available of other alliances: the close association between the IRA and the Breton and Basque separatists, the exchange of training and arms support among the Eritreans, Al Fatah, the PFLP, Syria's Sai qa and the Arab countries, and similar exchanges among groups in Argentine, Uruguay, Peru, Venezuela and Nicaragua.[36]

In 1980 L. R. Beres wrote: "Terrorists have always formed alignments with sympathetic states . . . but they are now also beginning to cement patterns of alliance and partnership with each other. The result of such behavior patterns is a terrorist adaptation of Trotsky's theory of "permanent revolution."[37]

The argument was advanced with most effect in 1981, when Claire Sterling published *The Terror Network: The Secret War of International Terrorism*. In this work Sterling attempts to build a case that there is an international terrorist network within whose center one finds a Palestinian connection and a Russian patron, and that the prime beneficiary of the terrorism is the Soviet Union. She argues that the evidence has been out there for a long time but Western governments have refused to condemn the Soviet Union for their role.[38]

During the Reagan Administration, the situation has been reversed. The publication of the Sterling work coincided with the condemnation of the Soviet Union by Secretary of State Haig "for training, funding and equipping international terrorists."[39] The Administration was unable to convince any of its own intelligence agencies to support its view of the Soviet role, nor has it been able to produce any evidence for the existence of such a network.[40] In fact, in October 1981, what should have been interpreted as a highly embarrassing report appeared in the *New York Times* authored by Leslie Gelb (formerly codirector of the Pentagon Papers project). It began: "Early Reagan Administration charges that the Soviet Union was directly helping terrorists were essentially based on information provided a decade ago by a Czechoslovak defector. ...One official said, "There is no substantial new evidence."[41]

The Reagan Administration also embroiled itself in a bureaucratic battle to redefine terrorism. Publication of the 1981 CIA report on international terrorism in 1980 was delayed while various government departments debated the inclusion or exclusion of "threats" as well as actual acts of politically motivated violence.

The magic result, a state department official told reporters, would be to double— from 3336 to 7000—the previously reported "incidents" of world terrorism from 1968 through 1979. The number killed or murdered, of course, would remain the same—about 800—since this bookkeeping sleight-of-hand merely makes the same situation look twice as bad as it did before.[42]

U.S. officials now portray the terrorism problem as the "most serious threat to human rights around the world." The Soviet Union is considered the major proponent and source of this terrorism and thus concurrently the source of the greatest threat to human rights as well as military security. This approach will not provide much new insight on the actual problem of state terrorism and state support for terrorist activities, because it is short on substance and neglects the major requirements in the study of terrorism, for example, an analysis, rather than an assumption, of the historical and political sources of the terrorism within a conflict situation. But the Administration will pursue this approach because it is ideologically comfortable and the alternative would force it to confront the roots of terrorism in societies and situations it does not wish to examine.

There are two major thrusts in an inter-connected argument concerning the role of the Soviet Union in international terrorism. The first concern the question of cooperation and possibly organizational coordination among terrorists, and the second Soviet involvement and possibly organizational control.

Despite the assurance with which Sterling, Haig, Beres, Demaris, and others speak, there has been little evidence publicly available of Soviet control and of an actual organizational infra-structure. Few dispute the existence of working relations among some terrorist groups, resulting in relatively low-level cooperation regarding safe houses, travel documents, weapons information, and the like. The cooperative network does not appear any more sophisticated than the "ordinary" criminal network that exists for the purchase of visas, weapons, and silence throughout the world. That groups cooperate at this level should come as no surprise to anyone familiar with organized criminal or insurgent terrorist behavior. It is a long leap to assert that this cooperation implies any coordinated effort or long-term policy agreement regarding revolutionary upheaval around the world. It is a leap, nonetheless, that in the current American political climate many will willingly make, particularly if they can connect the Soviet Union to the network.

Indeed, some, such as U.S. Senator Jeremiah Denton of Alabama, for obvious political purposes, have gone so far as to suggest that American citizens do not find the link-up with the Soviet Union because the Soviet Union manipulates a gullible American press! The Soviet Union has had such success in their "disinformation" program to convince Western news readers that they have had no part in international terrorism that it is now difficult to find Americans willing to believe the Soviet role. Some go much further. Robert Moss, formerly of the *Economist*, is quoted approvingly by Charles Horner "for his identification 'of a conspiracy of silence' about the evidence of Soviet involvement in terrorism which operates in order to preserve the appearance of detente."[43] This conspiracy includes the news media and government officials.

On the other hand, Sterling simply cannot find an explanation. She, in despair, suggests: "No single motive could explain the iron restraint shown by Italy, West Germany, and all other threatened Western governments in the face of inexorably accumulating evidence."[44]

The fact that the intelligence services have not been able to provide the evidence the analysts all *assume* is there does not seem to provide a simple direct answer. But we should look further into the charges. Sterling, for instance, does not simply suggest, as did Secretary of State Haig, that the Russians are behind it *all*. Rather, she argues that no matter what the original motive and organization of the terrorist movements in the Western world, the Soviet Union, through the Palestinians with the KGB as agent, has infiltrated and gained a key role in the various terrorist movements in the Western world.

Direct control of the terrorist groups was never the Soviet intention. All are indigenous to their countries. All began as offshoots of relatively non-violent movements that expressed particular political, economic, religious or ethnic grievances.[45]

. . .

The heart of the Russian's strategy is to provide the terrorist network with the goods and services necessary to undermine the industrialized democracies of the west.[46]

While Sterling argues that "the case rests on evidence that everyone can see, long since exposed to the light of day,"[47] Grant Wardlaw asserts that "nobody has yet provided unequivocal evidence that supports a simple-minded Soviet-culprit theory of terrorist control and neither are there any serious analyses of Soviet strategic objectives and the manner in which these ends would be served by support for terrorism."[48] Much of this argument against the Soviet Union rests on the assumption that the Soviet Union as an anti-status quo power favors anarchy and disruption within the world system. Thus, the Soviet Union will assist those opposed to the Western states system and particular states, the status quo, because it is to their long-term advantage. Friedlander (citing Edward Marks, coordinator for anti-terrorist activities of U.S. Department of State) refers to this as the fishing-in-troubled-waters thesis.[49] The simple-minded approach to this argument is most clearly presented by Sterling: "In effect, the Soviet Union had simply laid a loaded gun on the table leaving others to get on with it. Why would the Russians do that? Well, why not?"[50] A more sophisticated answer to the question why is given by Edward Luttwak:

It was only when it became clear that the Soviet Union was ineluctably losing the support of the trade unions and left-wing mass movements of the West that the Soviet leaders began to accept terrorists as useful allies; with the Leninist programme of revolution by the working classes finally exposed as totally unrealistic.[51]

In other words, Luttwak argues that Soviet leaders reversed the long-standing Leninist antipathy to terrorism, an antipathy based on the belief that mass movements would not be built upon terrorist campaigns when these mass movements were also deemed to be failures.[52] While this is not evidence for the position, it does at least have the virtue of providing an explanation for the possibilities of doctrinal shift.

Ray Cline and Yonah Alexander, in the latest salvo in what has become, with the continuing lack of new evidence, a mainly polemical battle, assert without seeming to worry if it makes a difference if the Soviet Union "benefits" or directs terrorist activity:

In the 1970s terrorism, whether backed directly or indirectly by the Soviet Union or *independently initiated*, appeared to have become an indispensable tactical and strategic tool in the Soviet struggles for power and influence within and among nations. In relying on this instrument, Moscow seems to aim in the 1980s at achieving strategic ends in circumstances where the use of conventional armed forces is deemed inappropriate, ineffective, too risky or too difficult.[53]

Likewise, they argue:

It is obvious from the PLO documents [captured in Beirut, Lebanon, by the Israelis in 1982, a selection of which is translated and reproduced in Cline and Alexander (1984)] that there exists a carefully developed international terrorist infrastructure that serves Moscow's foreign policy objectives of destabilizing non-communist governments.[54]

When all the charges and evidence are carefully reviewed, what can we conclude with confidence concerning Soviet involvement with Palestinian terrorists? The Soviets have trained, funded, and equipped some Palestinians for what they would describe as guerrilla warfare. Some Palestinians are Marxists and have developed links with other Marxist and non-Marxist political organizations, governments, and also terrorist organizations including most member states of the United Nations and all of the states in the Arab League. Radical Arab states that have purchased arms from the Soviet Union have made some of these arms available to Palestinians. (Conservative Arab states that have purchased arms from the United States and other Western states have also made arms available to the Palestinians.)

We can and should thus make the argument that the Soviet Union, by training Palestinian guerrillas and others in military techniques, weapons use, and tactics at bases within the Soviet Union and the Middle East, must bear a share of the responsibility for the practices for which that training is employed. But in the Palestinian case, the same argument about responsibility may be directed at others with very different motives and with concomitant anti-Soviet aims:

Let us be clear about what we do not know. We do not know the extent, if any, to which the Soviets direct any terrorist organization. Moscow seems to have had great influence over the popular front for the Liberation of Palestine (PFLP) but less over other factors within the Palestine Liberation Organization (PLO). Most of the money for many terrorist groups probably comes, not from the Soviet Union, but from wealthy Arab nations and from criminal activities.[55]

In the current ideological climate, such skepticism and raising of questions regarding Soviet involvement have not been well received:

Apologists for Soviet foreign policy, on the other hand, are skeptical about direct and indirect Soviet control of terrorist groups. While admitting that Moscow approves of and gives some assistance to what it considers legitimate "liberation movements," or struggles of people for their independence, proponents of this view argue that the dynamics of modern terrorism are so uncontrollable as to make the Soviet leaders ambivalent about the usefulness of this form of warfare.[56]

The United States

Within the United States and within the literature of terrorism, there has been far less interest in the U.S. role in aiding, abetting, and funding international terrorism. While, of course, there is a critical literature concerned with the role of the CIA and its covert operations, that literature is generally concerned with the activities of Americans in clandestine operations and not with the connection among "terrorist" organizations. In part this is obviously the result of the current distribution of power within the world. The United States as the premier status quo power simply does not have as many opportunities in choices to make in this area as the Soviet Union. The United States supports more regimes and governments, the Soviet Union more opponents and insurgents.

However, we should not conclude that the United States has had no cooperative arrangements with terrorists, nor involvement. CIA covert operations in Nicaragua, Angola, Iran, and Afghanistan obviously involve the United States with insurgents who would be labeled terrorist if they were opposing regimes friendly to the U.S. There is an additional group of terrorist organizations (so identified by the FBI) with whom the United States has links. These groups are Cuban, and much of the network descends from the ill-fated 1961 Bay of Pigs invasion.

According to the FBI, the most dangerous terrorist group operating within the United States in the 1970s was OMEGA 7, the clandestine operations arm of the Union City branch of the Cuban Nationalist Movement. In the CIA ITERATE transnational terrorism data base for 1969–1979, Cuban exile groups are given responsibility for eighty-nine separate terrorist incidents within the United States and the Caribbean area. Many of the actions involved attacks on Cuban and U.S.S.R. diplomatic personnel in the United States.

One clear international linkage provided by these Cuban organizations concerns their role in the assassination of Orlando Letelier, the exiled former foreign minister of the Allende regime. DINA, the Pinochet secret police in Chile, recruited OMEGA 7 members for help in the assassination. While there is no evidence, and we are not suggesting that the CIA was directly involved in the assassination of Letelier, organizations with which the CIA was intimately involved were. The linkage but not the responsibility for the particular action is clear. An organization that the CIA found useful for other purposes had become involved without CIA help in the assassination of a former ambassador a few miles from CIA headquarters.

Warren Hinkle and William Turner argue:

Cuban exile terrorism began with assassinations and bombings in the United States, picked up tempo during the 1970s and by the end of the decade had spun a murderous web linking Cuban exiles with elements of the American CIA, the Chilean gestapo known as DINA, the Venezuelan secret police, the Korean CIA and European paramilitary fascist groups.[57]

Further, they assert that the CIA financed covert forays against Cuba between 1964 and 1975 through the Castle Bank and Trust Ltd., a CIA bank established in the Bahamas for such purposes.

More recently, U.S. links with terrorists in Nicaragua have also involved connections with the Argentinians. Training centers were established by Nicaraguan groups within the United States, and a blind eye was turned toward them.[58] Camps were also run by Panamanian and Cuban exiles for the purpose of overthrowing their governments.[59]

In short, in addition to what Edward Herman describes as the "real terror network," among the organizational linkages and structural conditions that foster cooperative government linkages promoting state terrorism, the United States does appear to have established links with insurgent terrorist organizations. Both the literature on these links and the network of linkages themselves appear far smaller than those attributed to the Soviet Union. This relative lack of size may result from the reverse of the structural condition that we noted earlier: The United States supports relatively more governments, the Soviet Union relatively more insurgents and "wars of national liberation." We should therefore expect different levels of superpower involvement in the activities designed to support their respective clients related to the numbers of actual opportunities to become involved.

SURROGATE TERRORISM

Within the structures of dominance that exist in the international system, powerful states do not simply exert military force and threats to control all aspects of both the internal and the external relations of subordinate states. Above I have discussed the intervention of relatively powerful states in the affairs of the less powerful. Powerful states also aid the less powerful states in their domestic and international affairs, and these less powerful states in turn assist the powerful to pursue their objectives. The superpowers sell, grant, and otherwise provide favorable terms by which their coalition partners, allies, client states (and at times neutrals and even adversaries) obtain equipment enabling their regimes to *continue* and/or expand practices of repression and terrorism. I argue that in such cases the superpowers are practicing a form of surrogate terrorism. When the superpowers train the personnel that conduct the terror operations and consult with and advise (for "reasons of state") the security services of "friendly" states in their use of terrorism, this tool is a form of surrogate terrorism.

States as Domestic Surrogates

The U.S. army runs a school of the Americas at the Atlantic entrance to the Panama Canal. Begun in 1946, the school has had more than 46,000 graduates who have returned to their nation's military forces. The current commandant, bristling at the suggestion that he commands what has been called a "school for *juntas*," argued that human rights training was now included in the school "even if it was just a question of teaching non-commissioned officers that it was more valuable in intelligence to keep prisoners alive than to kill them."[60]

In 1974 Congress banned U.S. assistance to the police and internal security agencies of foreign governments. Before the ban more than 7,000 high-ranking police, intelligence, and internal security officers were trained at the International Police Academy in Washington, D.C. The professionalization of Latin American police forces was the object of the International Police Academy and the International Police Services Inc., the latter a CIA-sponsored organization that also had students from Asia and Africa.[61] Graduates of the Academy often returned home to practice their trade with exemplary zeal.

While official Academy policy was against torture, etc., many students became proficient at interrogation while enrolled. Knowledge of the establishment of the *Esquadrao da Morte* (Death Squad) in Brazil did not immediately reduce American assistance to Brazilian security efforts. Similar efforts in other nations were accepted for long periods without sanction by the United States. The defeat of Communism and instability was considered a greater benefit than the costs of "due process" violations and state-sponsored and -supported terror practices. Death squads have appeared in at least ten Latin American states whose military and police were supported and trained by the United States. In March 1984 the head of El Salvador's Treasury Police, one of the most notorious and brutal of the country's security forces, was accused of being a major figure in the organization of that nation's death squads and a paid operative of the CIA. While he denied both accusations, the CIA dug the ground out from below him, claiming there was nothing wrong with their paying such foreign nationals because of the useful services they perform for the agency and the United States.[62]

It is interesting to note that the Kissinger Commission on Central America recommendations include a proposal to lift the ban on U.S. aid to national police forces. The Commission argues that the ban "dates back to a previous period when it was believed that such aid was sometimes helping groups guilty of serious human rights abuses."[63] The "Realpolitik" orientation of the Commission's chair leads back once again to the cost/benefit calculations that led originally to the congressional reaction against Mr. Kissinger's dismissal of human rights concerns.[64]

States are also quite willing to help provide other states with the tools of the terror trade. Steve Wright, and Michael Klare and Cynthia Aronson make clear that the new technologies of repression are widely available and widely distributed.[65] The United States has been an active provider of the instruments of terrorism and repression to Third World client states to employ on their populations and also in quite a number of cases to train the security services of these societies in the proper employment of these instruments. (It is also a lucrative trade and assists the U.S. corporations to market their wares.)

Other Western governments similarly assist their national corporations in this regard, and the Soviet Union has sought needed hard currency by supplying small (and large) arms to willing purchasers. When in November 1979 the Carter Administration informed the Shah of Iran that they would continue to back the Peacock Throne and sent tear gas, police batons, protective vests, and other riot control equipment, it was clear that even a president reviled by his conservative critics for being "soft" and placing human rights above security was not going to deny the instruments of repression (which were used for terror purposes as well) to an ally in need. This followed, of course, upon the heels of Carter's post-Black Friday (September 8, 1979) phone call to the Shah in which he reiterated U.S. support and hopes for continued liberalization following the imposition of martial law and the gunning down of somewhere between 700 and 2,000 people.[66] In the end, the Shah's use of terror fell short. Once the population en masse had indicated they were not afraid to continue to die in order to rid themselves of the Shah, the threat of death that the security forces could present no longer was politically meaningful. On the other hand, the reaction of many American policymakers and particularly those of the new Administration is important in this regard. The presumption appears to be that the Shah's regime fell in the end because the Carter Administration was unwilling to provide *enough* military hardware and possibly the actual employment of American troops to prevent the overthrow. The U.S. use of surrogate terror thus apparently also fell short of providing the "proper ending." But it was not for lack of trying and most importantly not because policymakers assumed that such strategies were illegitimate.

The United States under successive administrations assisted the Shah and the governments of El Salvador, Guatemala, Nicaragua under Anastasio Somoza, and numerous other repressive client states because they concluded it was easier and less costly to do so than to "do the job themselves." In other words, these governments provided a mechanism by which the United States believed its national interest would be served. Likewise, the Soviet Union continues to train and support its own surrogates in Afghanistan (where its original surrogate government was not up to the task), in Ethiopia, and, of course, in Eastern Europe and, some would argue, in Cuba.

States as International Surrogates

In a bipolar world within which the polar powers have nuclear weapons, it has become obvious to most observers (the views of the current occupants of the White House and Department of Defense notwithstanding) that it is impractical and undesirable to become involved in major wars, that the infinite cost of a nuclear holocaust outweighs the possible benefits of eliminating the opposing superpowers. In the post-Hiroshima world, to engage in war is to risk *all*. A conventional war may easily slide into a nuclear holocaust if both sides have access to weapons. The U.S. experience in Vietnam, the Soviets' experience in Afghanistan, and the recent ongoing Iranian/Iraqi war (think of the possible consequences had not Israel destroyed the reactor at Osiraq) should also have demonstrated that protracted, "low-level" war may be equally unattractive as an instrument of national policy.

Some military experts (ignoring much of the reality of the existence of what has been discussed above) have therefore recently argued that terrorism *may* become accepted as part of a nation's military strategy. Brian Jenkins worries that nations might employ groups as surrogates for engaging in warfare with other nations.[67] These surrogates (both state and non-state actors) might be employed (1) to provoke international incidents, (2) to create alarm in an adversary, (3) to destroy morale, (4) to cause the diversion of an enemy's resources into security budgets, (5) to effect specific forms of sabotage, or (6) to provoke repressive and reactive strategies and, it is hoped, the revolutionary overthrow of targeted regimes (what we may designate the Marighela strategy as applied by state rather than insurgent actors).

We recognize that terrorism has become simpler for insurgents because of advances in transport, communications, weapons, technology, and access to the media. We should also recognize that the vast resources of the state allow it to make far greater use of these developments than may individuals and insurgent groups.

Beginning with the Nixon doctrine and extending into the Carter Administration, there was much discussion of the development and employment of the forces of regional power centers to avoid direct U.S. military action in the Third World. Currently the United States appears to be building up the Honduran army to serve a surrogate role in the Central American region.

The Soviet Union likewise, it may be argued, appears to employ state surrogates, particularly in Africa. While the reasons for Cuban involvement in Africa may be directly related to the policy prescriptions of Fidel

Castro rather than Soviet leaders,[68] there does appear to have developed a system whereby the Soviet Union and East Germany provide most of the technicians and advisers and the Cubans most of the foreign troops. These activities have been located entirely within nations friendly to these powers and as of yet they have not participated in overt military activities against other regimes. Their disposition in this manner, however, combined with U.S. support rather than direct participation in Africa reduces the likelihood that clashes in Angola, for example, will escalate so as to involve the superpowers in a direct confrontation. We should expect more rather than less of this pattern in the future. Here as elsewhere in the consideration of terrorism as a strategy, cost/benefit analysis leads superpowers to choose a terror strategy rather than a straightforward traditional policy or direct military force.

CONCLUSIONS

The preceding pages argue that strategies and tactics of terrorism have become important foreign policy instruments of the modern state. As in the domestic realm, the practice of terror, when identified as such, brings almost universal condemnation. But as in the domestic realm, when it is the state that is the perpetrator of the terrorist act, few even pause to label the action as such. States and proponents of their actions shrink from labeling what they themselves do as terror, preferring more "neutral" designations such as coercive diplomacy, nuclear deterrence, and assistance to a friendly state in its pursuit of internal security. Differences in the behavioral patterns of the superpowers may be seen as resulting from the constraints and opportunities presented them as the defenders of the current international system. While both need the survival of the system, and by implication the survival of their major adversary, they both seek advantages within that system. The current system finds the United States with more governments than the Soviet Union to aid and abet, while the Soviet Union is involved with a greater number of insurgent organizations and "wars of national liberation." The behavioral patterns may thus be dissimilar, but this does not translate to a necessary difference in motivations or scruples. Both superpowers employ terrorism when they calculate that response and production costs are lower than probable benefits.

NOTES

1. Michael Stohl, "International Network of Terrorism," *Journal of Peace Research* 20, no. 1 (1983), pp. 87–94; Michael Stohl, "International Dimensions of State Terrorism," in M. Stohl and George Lopez, eds., *The State as Terrorist: The Dynamics of Governmental Violence and Repression* (Westport, CT: Greenwood Press, 1984), pp. 43–58; Michael Stohl, "National Interests and State Terrorism,"

Political Science 36, no. 1 (July 1984), pp. 37–52; and Raymond Duvall and Michael Stohl, "Governance by Terror," in M. Stohl, ed., *The Politics of Terrorism* (New York: Marcel Dekker, 1983), pp. 179–219.

2. Hans Morgenthau, *Politics Among Nations*, 5th rev. ed. (New York: Alfred A. Knopf, 1978), p. 351.

3. Kenneth Waltz, *Theory of International Politics* (Boston: Addison-Wesley, 1979), p. 173.

4. Morgenthau, *Politics Among Nations*, p. 359.

5. Waltz, *Theory of International Politics*, p. 188.

6. Raymond Cohen, *International Politics: The Rules of the Game* (New York: Longman, 1981).

7. Hedley Bull, *The Anarchical Society* (New York: Columbia University Press, 1977).

8. T. Franck and W. Weisband, *World Politics* (New York: Oxford University Press, 1972), p. 9.

9. Franz Schurman, *The Logic of World Power* (New York: Pantheon, 1974), pp. 314–327; and Adam Ulam, *Expansion and Coexistence* (New York: Praeger, 1974), p. 635.

10. Quoted in John Lewis Gaddis, *Strategies of Containment* (New York: Oxford University Press, 1982), p. 208.

11. Duvall and Stohl, "Governance by Terror," p. 202.

12. Ibid., p. 209.

13. Stohl, "International Dimensions."

14. Thomas Schelling, "Thinking About Nuclear Terrorism," *International Security* 6 (1982), p. 15.

15. Alexander George, "The Development of Doctrine and Strategy," in A. George, D. Hall, and W. R. Simons, eds., *The Limits of Coercive Diplomacy* (Boston: Little, Brown, 1971), p. 18.

16. Ibid., p. 26.

17. Barry Blechman and Stephen Kaplan, *Force Without War* (Washington, D.C.: Brooklings Institution, 1978) and Stephen Kaplan, *The Diplomacy of Power* (Washington, D.C.: Brooklings Institution, 1981).

18. Ibid., p. 48.

19. Kaplan, *The Diplomacy of Power*, p. 2.

20. George, "The Development of Doctrine and Strategy," p. 19.

21. Thomas Schelling, *Arms and Influence* (New Haven, Conn.: Yale University Press, 1966), pp. 16–17.

22. Morton Halperin, Jerry Berman, Robert Borosage, and Christine Marwich, *The Lawless State* (New York: Penguin, 1976).

23. For the most comprehensive coverage of this, see Warren Hinkle and William Turner, *The Fish is Red* (New York: Harper and Row, 1981).

24. Victor Machetti and John Marks, *The CIA and the Cult of Intelligence* (New York: Dell Publishers, 1974), p. 108.

25. Robert C. Johansen, *The National Interest and the Human Interest* (Princeton, N.J.: Princeton University Press, 1980), p. 210. For fuller details of the role of the U.S. government in the fall of Allende, see James Petras and Morris Morley, *The United States and Chile: Imperialism and the Overthrow of the Allende Government*

(New York: Monthly Review Press, 1975) and Tad Szulc, *The Illusion of Power* (New York: Viking, 1978).

26. Halperin et al., *Lawless State*, p. 28.

27. *New York Times*, (March 7, 1983), p. 1.

28. *Washington Post*, (October 4, 1983).

29. Weinberg, *New York Times*, (October 2, 1983).

30. A. Rubinstein, *Soviet Foreign Policy Since World War II* (Cambridge: MA.: Winthrop, 1981), pp. 214–235.

31. Alexander Haig, "News Conference," *Current Policy No. 258* (Washington, D.C.: U.S. Department of State, January 28, 1981), p. 5.

32. Judith Miller, "Soviet Aid Disputed in Terrorism Study," *New York Times*, (March 29, 1981), p. 4.

33. "CIA Report on Soviet Disputed by Weinberger," *New York Times*, (March 30, 1981).

34. Ovid Demaris, *Brothers in Blood: The International Terrorist Network* (New York: 1977), p. 183.

35. Robert Kupperman and Darrell Trent, *Terrorism: Threat, Reality, Response* (Stanford, Calif.: Hoover Institution Press, 1979), p. 22.

36. Ibid., p. 31.

37. L. R. Beres, *Apocalypse* (Chicago: University of Chicago Press, 1980), pp. 112–113.

38. For a more full review of Sterling and her evidence, see Stohl, "International Network of Terrorism."

39. Haig, "News Conference," p. 5.

40. Robert Pear, "F.B.I. Chief Sees No Evidence Soviet Aids Terrorism in U.S.," *New York Times*, (April 27, 1981), p. 8; Judith Miller, "Soviet Aid Disputed" *New York Times* (April 27, 1981), p. 4; Philip Taubman, "U.S. Tries to Back Up Haig on Terrorism," *New York Times*, (May 3, 1981), p. 1.

41. Leslie Gelb, "Soviet Terror Ties Called Outdated," *New York Times*, (October 18, 1981).

42. Tom Wicker, "The Great Terrorist Hunt," *New York Times*, (April 28, 1981).

43. Charles Horner, "The Facts About Terrorism," *Commentary* 69, no. 6 (June 1980), p. 40.

44. Sterling, *Terror Network*, p. 291.

45. Claire Sterling, "Terrorism, Tracing the International Network," *New York Times Magazine*, (March 1, 1981), p. 16.

46. Ibid., p. 54.

47. Sterling, *Terror Network*, p. 292.

48. Grant Wardlaw, *Political Terrorism* (New York: Cambridge University Press, 1982), p. 56.

49. Robert A. Friedlander, "A Riddle Inside a Mystery Wrapped in an Enigma: Terrorism and the Soviet Connection," a paper for the International Association of Chiefs of Police, 1983.

50. Sterling, *Terror Network*, p. 293.

51. Edward Luttwak, *The Grand Strategy of the Soviet Union* (New York: St. Martin's Press, 1983), p. 64.

52. F. Terekhov, "International Terrorism and the Struggle Against It," *Novoye Vremya*, (March 15, 1974), pp. 20–22.

53. Ray Cline and Yonah Alexander, *Terrorism: The Soviet Connection* (New York: Crane and Russak, 1984), p. 6, emphasis added.

54. Ibid., p 55.

55. Wilson, "Thinking About Terrorism," p. 36.

56. Cline and Alexander, *Terrorism*, p. 5, emphasis added.

57. Hinkle and Turner, *The Fish Is Red*, p. 317.

58. *New York Times*, (March 17, 1981), p. 14.

59. *New York Times*, (December 24, 1981), p. 14.

60. Paul Ellman, "Training Democrats and Dictators," *The Guardian*, (1983).

61. A. J. Langguth, *Hidden Terrors* (New York: Pantheon, 1978), p. 124.

62. *New York Times*, (March 23, 1984), p. 7.

63. Nicholas Goldberg, "Don't Aid Central American Police," *New York Times*, (February 23, 1984).

64. Michael Stohl, David Carleton, and Steven Johnson, "Human Rights and U.S. Foreign Assistance from Nixon to Carter," *Journal of Peace Research*, 21, no. 3 (1984), pp. 215–226.

65. Steve Wright, "New Police Technologies," *Journal of Peace Research* 15, no. 4 (1978), pp. 305–322; and Michael Klare and Cynthia Aronson, *Supplying Repression* (Washington, D.C.: Institute for Policy Studies, 1981).

66. Barry Rubin, *Paved with Good Intentions* (New York: Penguin Books, 1981), p. 214.

67. Brian Jenkins, "International Terrorism: A New Mode of Conflict," California Seminar on Arms Control and Foreign Policy research paper no. 48, Santa Monica, Calif., 1975.

68. For an excellent analysis, see Carla Robbins, *The Cuban Threat* (New York: McGraw-Hill, 1983).

9

The Implausible Dream: International Law, State Violence, and State Terrorism

Robert A. Friedlander

From both a popular and a political perspective, international law either has come under attack or is widely assumed to be inherently suspect. International legalists themselves have expressed numerous doubts or reservations about the current role and efficacy of the international legal system.[1] It is no secret, of course, that many journalists, social scientists, and political commentators hold to a view that international law is what the lawyers say it is, but appeals by governments to claims of right under the international legal process when they suffer some real or imagined injury are inexorable and probably inevitable.[2]

From its earliest beginnings, the primary function of public international law had been to establish and maintain a minimum standard of world public order. Until recently, the accepted name for international public law (as opposed to private) was the law of nations. Until the post-Charter decades, states were considered to be the only subjects of international law, and national sovereignties determined not only the content of international law, but the extent to which they would be bound.[3] This meant, literally, that nation–states were supreme within their own territories, and that sovereign entities were exempt from outside interference by any other sovereign authority.[4] Thus, a government could do whatever it liked to its own subjects.

Long before international law finally came to grips with this centuries-old challenge, the two seminal English political theorists of the Age of Reason—Thomas Hobbes and John Locke—reached diametrically opposed conclusions of lasting historical significance over the limits and purpose of state power. Both recognized, in different ways, the probable abuse of sovereign authority and the consequent harm that could befall a subject population. But whereas Hobbes emphasized legitimacy and security, Locke posited a consensual social contract and a right to revolution rooted in the principles of natural law.[5] External violence became inextricably intertwined with the rise of the nation–state. Internal violence provided a necessary concomitant to the theory of absolutism and the growth of centralized governmental administration.

Modern (as opposed to contemporary) history has by tradition had its origins attributed to the outbreak of the French Revolution. One of the most pervasive, and unfortunate, legacies of that important historical era was the lethal admixture of popular sovereignty and state violence. Ideology and terror formed the wellsprings of the revolutionary process, with the color of legality supplied by revolutionary tribunals. Terror from above became institutionalized as it would again become in the totalitarian regimes of the twentieth century. "It is less a question today of revolutionizing," the Committee of Public Safety wrote to the representative on mission in the Calvados Department, "than of building up the Revolutionary Government."[6]

Not until another century had passed did international law finally seek to deal with state oppression of peoples in occupied territories, at the two Hague Peace Conferences of 1899 and 1907. These assemblages resulted in the first international codification of the laws of war. One could also argue, however, that the motivation of the participating governments was far from altruistic, and that the Hague Conventions regulating the use of armed force were really an anticipation of the forthcoming global maelstrom, though no one really expected the military confrontations to last very long or to be waged on a worldwide scale.[7] A half-century earlier, Francis Lieber, who was an adviser to the Union army during the American Civil War, drew up a code on the laws of war, which the U.S. army then published under the title *General Order 100: Instructions for the Government of Armies of the United States in the Field.* The Lieber Code, as it came to be called, functioned as a precatory guide rather than a mandatory set of regulations. Nonetheless, it remained the official U.S. army position on military conduct in armed conflict until the turn of the nineteenth century, and indirectly influenced the Hague Conventions of 1899 and 1907.[8]

According to political theorist Hannah Arendt, "Terror as an institutional device, consciously employed to accelerate the momentum of the revolution, was unknown prior to the Russian revolution."[9] Sociologist E. V. Walter, in his classic study of the subject, refers to a regime of terror, wherein those who already dominate the institutions of power also utilize governmental violence in order to destroy, to control, or to punish.[10] The twentieth century has spawned a depressing number of totalitarian and authoritarian regimes that have often harbored genocidal tendencies. The bloodiest examples in an extraordinarily bloody century were Adolf Hitler's Germany and Stalinist Russia, which practiced genocide and humanicide on a scale unprecedented in all of human

history. Taking these barbaric regimes as her paradigms, Arendt concluded that "terror is the essence of totalitarian domination."[11] State
violence has historically provided an effective means of social control.
But "without terror, the costs of total enforcement are prohibitive."[12]

It was no accident that the reaction to totalitarian barbarism and the
Nazi Holocaust resulted in the development of international norms,
some of which were incorporated into the U.N. Charter, which then
provided the foundation for the international protection of human rights.
From the Nuremberg and Tokyo war crimes trials to the Universal
Declaration of Human Rights, the Genocide Convention, the International Covenants, and the European Court of Human Rights, concern
by the international community with the welfare of the individual has
become, in theory, part of public international law.[13] The experience of
the Second World War led to a general determination that state violence
could be remedied only by legal means, and the remedies involved would
have to be of an international legal nature.[14]

A complicating legal factor in the development of international human
rights theory is the role of Article 2(7) of the U.N. Charter. This is a
throwback to the principles of customary international law as they evolved
during the pre-Charter centuries, and flatly declares that "nothing contained in the present Charter shall authorise the United Nations to intervene in matters which are essentially within the domestic jurisdiction
of any state." Since almost every U.N. convention, declaration, and resolution lacks any enforcement mechanism whatsoever, and carries no
legal obligation per se,[15] human rights norms must be viewed as precatory rather than mandatory. One respected legal scholar has challenged the common wisdom of the majority of his colleagues on the
efficacy of human rights norms, arguing that there is an "inevitable
mixture of the scientist and the propagandist in the scholar's role" as
human rights analyst.[16] His controversial conclusion is that human rights
advocacy has distorted serious international legal study, and that its
proponents have attempted "to use international law to subvert or destroy the very states that give that law meaning." In other words, human
rights legalists not only "ignore political reality," but they distort the
modalities of the international legal system.[17]

The U.S. government has also confused (and sometimes confounded)
the contemporary view of state terrorism. Disregarding the lessons and
the legacy of the French Revolution and the horrors of the Holocaust
era, the State Department now defines governmental terrorism as the
support of third party terrorist groups and *not* as the oppression of one's
own innocent nationals.[18] An ancillary definition, referring in part to
the terror bombings of the American, French, and Israeli forces in Lebanon, refers to "states which are directly involved in carrying out international terrorist acts." This includes "states which find it in their

interest to provide arms, training, and logistical support to terrorist organizations."[19] The Reagan Administration approach to this global challenge has been mere angry rhetoric, dating from its very first week in office, but little else.[20]

Then what, if anything, can be done, and who is to do it? The answer must of necessity be found in the operative norms and procedures of international law. Dag Hammarskjöld, the most visible and the most influential secretary-general of the United Nations, not only called for the codification of international law, but also pursued the alluring vision of an international common law.[21] For those who argue that this is an implausible dream, the antithesis to the rule of law is a condition (perhaps the prevailing one) of power politics, defined by its most distinguished legal analyst as "a system of international relations in which groups consider themselves as ultimate ends."[22] Lord Acton's famous dictum on the corruption of personal power[23] is paralleled by an equally corrupting, unbridled growth of state control: "Unlimited power of the sovereign easily leads to abuses of governmental authority, and the less controlled the sovereign, the greater the likelihood of such abuse."[24]

The leading critics of the role of law—let alone the rule of law—in international relations have not come forward with a truly viable alternative.[25] Hammarskjöld's vision may be an imperfect one, but neither is the world a perfect place. Some sort of minimum world order, taking into account the rights, dignity, and worth of the individual, is both desirable and necessary. The remaining choice is one of lawlessness, violence, and bloodshed.

ORIGINS OF INTERNATIONAL LAW: THEORY

Traditional international law is said to have begun, in practice, with the Peace of Westphalia in 1648, which concluded the Thirty Years' War.[26] But theory preceded practice, and the concept of an international law actually began with the great classical writers—Vitoria, Ayala, Gentili, Suárez, Grotius, and Puffendorf. These illustrious pathfinders defined and refined the principles and ideas that eventually came to be recognized as international law. They were a mixture of the secular and the religious in their backgrounds and beliefs. What all had in common was a deep desire to universalize through spirit and substance a developing law of nations.

Francisco de Vitoria, a Dominican friar, was appointed Professor of Sacred Theology at the University of Salamanca in 1526. Author of at least a half-dozen works, Vitoria was the first prominent classical legal theorist of international law and the first Early Modern European scholar to stress the idea of a law of nations, which he declared was taken "from the common consensus of all peoples and nations" and was the product of positive rather than natural law.[27] Vitoria anticipated Hobbes in the view that a sovereign was absolute in his domestic authority, and that the laws of a tyrant were binding no matter how extensive the tyranny. "Unless obedience is rendered to the tyrant," Vitoria cautioned, "the State must perish."[28] This political justification for the Age of Absolutism also helped to establish the principle that internal matters were not of external concern in international law.

Balthazar Ayala was involved in the laws of war as a practitioner, rather than a theorist, in his capacity of judge advocate general to the Spanish army of Phillip II, occupying the Netherlands under the command of the Prince of Parma during the late sixteenth century. In fact, Ayala dedicated his pioneering study to the Prince on October 31, 1581, and it was published the following year. As subsequent commentators were to do after him (and as Thomas Aquinas had done before him), Ayala postulated the theory of the just war and eschewed "all lust of conquest."[29] Ayala did not allow, however, for any encroachment on the sovereignty of either states or monarchs.[30] Their independence was taken for granted, and there was to be no outside restraint upon their freedom of action. Nonetheless, he urged that states in time of war not act rashly or cruelly against their enemies, and that intentional murder of innocents (that is, women and children) be absolutely impermissible. Hostage taking, he added, was allowable only in wartime, and then it had to be done for just cause.[31] He also dealt with the rights and obligations of diplomatic practice, enunciating the classic principle that "ambassadors were safe and inviolable among all peoples." This he ascribed to "the law of nations."[32] In a phrase carrying modern implications, Ayala warned that "this law of ambassadors, like the other laws of war, holds only in the case of enemies (*hostes*) and not in the case of robbers and rebels"[33] and— one may add—terrorists.

The first "English" theorist of international law was an Italian legal scholar and former jurist who found asylum in England from the terrors of the Italian Inquisition. He eventually joined the faculty of Merton College, Oxford, and in June 1587 Alberico Gentili became Regius Professor of Roman Law and Jurisprudence. In 1585 he published his first major work, *De Legationibus* which he dedicated to Sir Philip Sidney. As with Ayala before him, to whom Gentili acknowledged a debt, the latter asserted the inviolability of envoys on mission and the rights and immunities of ambassadors, who are ministers of peace.[34]

Gentili's most significant study, *De Iure Belli*, first appeared in three parts between 1588 and 1589 (coinciding with the infamous Spanish Armada), and then were re-issued together in Prussia in 1598. He recalled that the great Roman law codifier, Justinian, made reference to the law of nations,[35] and for his part Gentili often cited a similar law of nations throughout his treatise.[36] He was of two minds about tyrants and the exercise of sovereign power. On the one hand, he admitted, "It is sometimes expedient and just to overthrow monarchies."[37] But, on the other, he argued that "it would not be just for subjects to make war upon their sovereign" on account of religious differences. Moreover, he insisted that both people and sovereign are mutually bound to one another as a general norm. If a sovereign betrays his people, however, he thus "slays them," and lays himself open to some sort of retribution.[38] It should be remembered that Gentili published this study during a critical time in the reign of Elizabeth I, when the Tudor crown was open to external challenges of legitimacy and several threats of outside attack upon the monarchy itself. It has even been claimed that this treatise may have inspired Grotius with the idea of developing his own commentaries.[39]

In 1612 a Jesuit theologian and legal philosopher, Francisco Suárez, argued against an absolutist view of sovereign independence in a tract entitled *De Legibus*. Suárez stressed the universality of international society and emphasized "mutual assistance, association, and intercourse."[40] The *jus gentium*, according to Suárez, applied between individual states but was not common to all sovereignties, and therefore differed from the operation of natural law.[41] His writings not only helped to establish the parameters of classical international legal theory, but also unintentionally demonstrated the continuing divergence between theory and practice in public international law, since his views were in part the antithesis of the prevailing political reality. Less than a decade after the publication of this important study, Europe fell victim to the outbreak of the Thirty Years' War.

Despite the aforementioned contributions of early classical legal theorists, history and tradition have awarded the title of the founding father of public international law to Hugo de Groot, better known by the Latin version of his name, Grotius. Lawyer, historian, diplomat, politician, and theologian, Grotius produced his seminal study, *On the Law of War and Peace* (*De Jure Belli ac Pacis*),[42] as the first phase of the Thirty Years' War was drawing to a close in 1625. His landmark treatise was written in exile from his native Holland at Paris, and following a few years' residence in Hamburg from 1631 to 1634, Grotius returned to Paris as ambassador from Sweden. There he remained until the year of his death in 1645.

As one might expect given the temper of his times, Grotius emphasized the law of war as a controlling element in the law of nations. War, he maintained, "is undertaken in order to secure peace, and there is no controversy which may not give rise to war." Nonetheless, "war itself will finally conduct us to peace as its ultimate goal."[43] Grotius defined international public law as that body of law "concerned with the mutual relations among states or rulers of states . . . having its origin in custom and tacit agreements."[44] There exists a common law among states valid for both peace and war.[45] In an observation that still has validity for our own contemporary world, Grotius attributed the "obligatory force" of international law to "the will of all nations, or of many nations." Custom, he noted, is the prime source for international law.[46]

The celebrated French political analyst, Raymond Aron, skeptical over the role and efficacy of international law, points out that traditional European international law never took, as a basic principle, the outlawry of conflict. Although it developed a series of limitations and restrictions upon the conduct of combatants, international law actually legalized war as a means of state policy.[47] Like his predecessors, Grotius was concerned with the notion of the just war and who was entitled to engage in lawful conflict.[48] His general principle was that "war ought not to be undertaken except for the enforcement of rights. . . ."[49]There were, of course, exceptions and qualifications, one of which being the right to make war against usurping, aggrandizing, or illegitimate sovereigns.[50] Grotius also carried on the work of his precursors in setting out diplomatic rights and privileges.[51] One aspect of classical public law that has undergone a severe change is Grotius's advocacy of the use of assassination against one's external enemies.[52] Government-supported terrorist assassins have become all too familiar in the Terror Decade of the 1970s and the Dangerous Decade of the 1980s.

Although Grotius's influence upon the development of public international law was extraordinary, his relevance to the course and consequences of the Thirty Years' War was virtually non-existent.[53] Religion had been replaced by politics as the prime motivation of conflict, and legal theory was subordinated then, as now, to the prevailing practice of *raison d'état*. Even his first major disciple, Samual Puffendorf, contradicted and disagreed with his distinguished predecessor more than he accepted and expanded the Grotian worldview.[54]

Puffendorf's first major treatise, published in 1660, was a jurisprudential study, concerned primarily with natural law and the nature of sovereignty, with only an incidental reference to the law of nations relating to ambassadors and legates.[55] As with his contemporary Thomas Hobbes, Puffendorf's views strongly supported the notion of unrestricted sovereign authority. A monarch's subjects had no redress against a tyrant, who was responsible only to divine judgment. It is impermissible, Puffendorf flatly declared, for a people to challenge the actions of a lawful prince.[56] Puffendorf's theory of sovereignty, like that of Hobbes and Locke, was based upon the social contract. His Hobbesian view emphasized that when the people chose to grant authority to the sovereign, they likewise assumed for themselves "the obligation to obey."[57]

The original edition of Puffendorf's most important work was published in 1672, and then considerably revised and expanded by a second edition, which appeared in 1688, the year of Britain's Glorious

Revolution which installed William and Mary as joint occupants on the English throne.[58] In this tome, also, the law of nature took precedence over the law of nations. Once again Puffendorf argued that the lawful commands of the sovereign were not to be resisted.[59] He did recognize, however, that the nature of states and the composition of regimes do change, and monarchies can be transformed into aristocracies or even democracies. Whatever the form of governance, he asserts the modern view that, absent the destruction of a polity, succession states should honor treaties and conventions made prior to their establishment.[60]

If an entire people perishes, however, its sovereign status is also destroyed.[61] Puffendorf refrains from embracing the good faith approach to interstate agreements in time of war, claiming that "the peculiar treatment of peace is faith."[62] In this he goes against the philosophy of the other classical writers, who had already propagated the principle of *pacta sunt servanda*. Although he took a limited view of the lawful causes of just wars (reducing them essentially to offensive and defensive),[63] Puffendorf nevertheless followed Grotius's lead in supporting the use of hired assassins for a just cause against a hostile enemy.[64] Puffendorf's influence upon the natural law school of legal philosophy has been considerable, despite the criticism of a prominent nineteenth-century legal scholar that the former "left the science of international law in the same state in which he found it, so far as it respects any positive improvement in its principles."[65]

For some reason, history has not been appreciative of Puffendorf's contemporary, Johann Wolfgang Textor, a maternal ancestor of Johann Wolfgang von Goethe, professor (Altorf and Heidelberg), jurist, and counselor of the city of Frankfurt-am-Main. Textor's main contribution to international law, the *Synopsis Juris Gentium* (*Synopsis of the Law of Nations*) was published in 1680, but lacked the influence and the recognition accorded to Puffendorf's work. Textor emphasized the Roman background of international law, claiming that there were no grounds "for distinguishing between the Grotian definition of the Law of Nations and that of the Roman lawyers."[66] Textor was a forerunner of the modern position of proportional self-defense, advocating a use of force in proportion to the threat of harm or injury suffered.[67] In fact, on a number of issues and principles, Textor more than Puffendorf foreshadowed modern international legal norms. He listed merely two requisites for waging a just war: "(1) A serious grievance, suffered by the party making the war; (2) a refusal of redress by the other side." And Textor went on to warn, "He, then, who is not really hurt, or only moderately, has no just cause of war."[68] Textor also disapproved of political murder or assassination, determining these acts as "repugnant to the probity and the healthy usage of nations."[69]

Perhaps the most significant legal commentator for the development of modern international law (and that includes Grotius) was Emmerich de Vattel, minor *philosophe* during the eighteenth-century Enlightenment, minor Saxon diplomat, and finally privy councilor to the cabinet of Saxony's monarch, Augustus III. Vattel's *magnum opus*, first published in 1758, begins by echoing the earlier worldview of Suárez that all states are equal in law, free and independent of one another, and have need of cooperation and mutual assistance. However, a state's primary obligation is to itself rather than the international community, although it must not destroy the rights of others. "From this equality it necessarily follows that what is lawful or unlawful for one Nation is equally lawful or unlawful for every other Nation." There is, in other words, "a perfect equality of rights among independent Nations."[70]

Vattel, expanding upon the earlier work of Grotius, put forward the modern view that treaties and custom provide the basic sources for public international law.[71] Following the lead of Textor, and writing in a century of global conflict, Vattel emphasized a nation's inherent right to self-defense, which he termed "self-preservation." The primary duty of a nation–state, he insisted, was that of self-preservation. "The right of self-preservation carries with it the right to [do] whatever is necessary for that purpose.... A Nation or State has the right to whatever can assist it in warding off a threatening danger, or in keeping at a distance things that might bring about its ruin."[72] Such a philosophy in our own contemporary world underlies recent conflicts like the Russian invasion of Afghanistan, the Israeli invasion of Lebanon, the Anglo–Argentine mini-war, and the U.S.–Nicaraguan confrontation. Vattel also encouraged the controversial and inherently dangerous theory of anticipatory self-defense, as well as the much-debated doctrines of reprisal, retaliation, and intervention.[73]

He succinctly summed up the position of traditional pre-Charter international law (pre-human rights) on the independence of states by declaring that each state "has the right to govern itself as it thinks proper," and that no one polity has a right to interfere in the governance of another, except in self-defense.[74] The legacy of this approach can be found in Article 2(7) of the U.N. Charter, which has served to inhibit the application of the international protection of human rights on a truly extensive and meaningful basis.[75] Though Vattel, too, dealt with the just causes of war,[76] he sought to formalize its character, which he legitimated only "as a remedy against injustice." A declaration of war was a necessity on the part of the contending parties, for that not only identified the nature of the conflict, but allowed for a final effort at negotiation without any bloodletting.[77]

Vattel's greatest importance lay in his distinctive treatment of civil war and internal strife; what we now call insurrection and rebellion he termed sedition and insurrection. There are times, Vattel admitted, when "a denial of justice on the part of the sovereign...can excuse the violence of a people whose patience is exhausted, and can even justify it, if the evils are intolerable and the oppression great and manifest."[78] In this important subject area, Vattel broke with his predecessors and adopted a position that forecasted the modern view. Custom, he declared, makes an internal war a civil war, and suspends the ordinary bonds of society, creating "two separate bodies politic, two distinct Nations." In this event, the established laws of war must also apply to internal conflict.[79] This is the underlying rationale of the two 1977 Protocols Additional for the Geneva Conventions.

More than any of the early classic theorists, Vattel stressed the importance of peace as the normal condition of humankind and the obligation of states to cultivate peace. A violation of peace without just cause affects the health and safety of all nations and is against the law of nature. He even hinted at the need for a balance-of-power approach to curb an excessive and dangerous enemy.[80] Vattel also encouraged the right of asylum for political crimes, but drew the line at "poisoners, assassins, or incendiaries" (that is, terrorists), for whom he advocated a universal jurisdiction on the part of apprehending states as with pirates and piracy. His extradite-or-prosecute attitude[81] reinforced Grotius's and is at the heart of the three present-day conventions dealing with interference with air transport, as well as several anti-terrorist regional pacts. For international legal theory, Vattel provided a watershed point of departure analogous to that of the French Revolution and its influence upon the origins of modern political theory.

ORIGINS OF INTERNATIONAL LAW: STATE VIOLENCE AND THE BALANCE OF POWER

A well-regarded mid-twentieth-century French diplomatic historian has observed that customary state practice in times of both peace and war actually brought forth a system of international juridical principles that antedated the celebrated writings of the classical international legal scholars.[82] By the late fifteenth century, the Italian Renaissance city–states were exchanging ambassadors, and Venetian diplomats soon acquired a reputation for skillful negotiation and political analysis. Permanent embassies had begun to be established by the early sixteenth century (although ambassadors generally did not come from high aristocratic rank and were more passive observers than they were active policy executors). Consultants and consuls also made their appearance during this same period.[83]

The so-called Peace of Westphalia, consisting primarily of the Treaties of Münster and Osnabrück (October 1648), was produced by the first general European Congress composed of diplomats, princes, and monarchs.[84] A second smaller conference met at Nuremberg the very next year for a follow-up implementation of the earlier agreements.[85] Two of the major powers, Spain and England, were not contracting parties, although the former signed its own prior peace treaty with the Netherlands at Münster in January 1648.[86] Sovereignty and independence were the basic elements of the settlement, but it was the dynastic principle rather than a nationalistic spirit that prevailed.

Except for a few dissenters, legal commentators have long held that classical or traditional international law originated with the Peace of Westphalia.[87] One reason for this questionable view is that politics replaced religion as the basis of the peace settlement: Henceforth, war should be fought for political rather than religious objectives. Secularism's triumph at Münster and Osnabrück meant that there would be equality between several faiths (Catholicism and Protestantism) among the different states, principalities, and free cities, but not equality of political power and sovereign authority.[88] The Treaty of Münster required that:

all parties in this Transaction shall be oblig'd to defend and protect all and every Article of this Peace against any one, without distinction of Religion; and if it happens any point shall be violated, the Offended shall before all things exhort the Offender not to come to any Hostility, submitting the Cause to a friendly Composition, or the ordinary Proceedings of Justice.[89]

If those differences could not be resolved within three years' time, then the offended or injured party had the right to call upon the other signatories to come to its assistance "with Counsel and Force to repel the Inquiry . . . and the Contravener shall be regarded as an Infringer of the Peace." No imperial state was to be permitted to pursue its claims of right by force of arms.[90]

These provisions have led some commentators to make rather extravagant claims for the Peace of Westphalia as the precursor of the nineteenth-century Concert of Europe and the twentieth-century world peace-keeping organizations.[91] One highly regarded contemporary American scholar goes so far as to claim that the Westphalian settlement "was accompanied by the vision of an order generated by the highest principles of reason and charity."[92] A prestigious nineteenth-century American analyst believed that "it in effect recognized the principle of the right of popular resistance to intolerable oppression on the part of rulers."[93] Both of these assertions are wide of the mark, for Westphalia represented more than anything else the emergence of the balance-of-power theory in European international relations. That did not go so

far, however, as to give the major European powers the right of intervention to enforce treaty agreements (as later developed under the Concert system).[94] In a number of ways, the Peace of Westphalia did represent
a new departure for the development of public international law in
Western history,[95] but its importance for legal theory and application
lies more in symbolic meaning than in actual result.

Whatever the Münster signatories really had in mind, even if they
truly intended that accord to be a restraint upon state violence, the harsh
reality was one of inter-state conflict and power politics. The apogee of
seventeenth-century absolutism was characterized by dynastic ambition
and territorial conquest, while the succeeding eighteenth-century international scene became one of state building and imperial expansion.
Small wonder that a sympathetic interpreter of the Peace of Westphalia
reluctantly admits, "In the period immediately following the Peace, of
the objective validity of international law there may be some doubt."[96]
France, the foremost European power under the reign of Louis XIV
during the last half of the seventeenth century, was also the foremost
violator of the European equilibrium ostensibly represented by the Peace
of Westphalia. "I am the state," boasted Louis,[97] and his grand design
stretched from the Low Countries to the Spanish Peninsula.

Louis could not separate his concept of *gloire* from the dynastic principle, and he temporarily exhausted the resources of his nation in numerous attempts to expand the political boundaries of France. War for
Louis provided the means to attain the greater territorial ends. He not
only embraced conflict, but one historian has even claimed that making
war was part of his very essence.[98] According to Archbishop Fenelon,
tutor to the Duke of Burgundy, Louis XIV's greed desolated Europe by
the expenditure of blood, the sacking of provinces, and the burning of
towns and villages.[99] These wars had another, still more significant effect.
The coalitions of states that formed to challenge Louis XIV, and to
confront the armies of the French Revolution and Napoleon in the
succeeding century, adhered to the doctrine of the balance of power
first developed at Westphalia: namely, that no one polity should become
more powerful than the remaining community of states, and that any
attempt by one power to disrupt the prevailing equilibrium would be
forcibly opposed by those who were most threatened.[100]

The Peace of Utrecht in 1713, a combination of five agreements,[101]
differed from that of Westphalia in emphasizing partition in place of
the balance of power. Nevertheless, from Utrecht until the outbreak of
the French Revolution in 1789, despite the growth of England's empire
(offset by the loss of the American colonies) and the aggressive state
building by Frederick the Great, the general equilibrium was not fundamentally disrupted.[102] In fact, the idea of a community of nation–
states persisted until the ideological stirrings of Revolutionary France.

For most of this period, Europe was, however, involved in an almost endless series of territorial conflicts on the Continent and literally around the globe.

Although the balance of power continued to operate in one form or another, "there was no mechanism for maintaining it."[103] A French commentator of the post-World War I era caustically observed that the eighteenth century saw little progress for international law in the development of state practice.[104] Overseas competition for empire aided in diffusing the problem of state violence, and the rules of international conduct were more concerned with the high seas than with land warfare. Article 35 of the Treaty of Commerce and Navigation between France and Great Britain, signed at Utrecht in 1713, specifically required the signatories to apprehend and punish pirates and freebooters.[105] Terrorism on the high seas was at last outlawed by formal agreement between Europe's most prominent military and naval powers.

STATE VIOLENCE AND THE BEGINNINGS OF STATE TERRORISM

Terrorism in its modern politico-ideological context originated with the Jacobin dictatorship during the radical phase of the French Revolution (1793–1794). The Reign of Terror not only formally introduced the concept of state terrorism, but also represented a major watershed in the history of inter-state violence. In its Jacobin context, the Terror referred solely to state or governmental terrorism, which can be defined as any organized form of violent repression directed by governments against their citizens or subjects.

The Jacobin leadership utilized terror (in the form of rapid trials and public executions) as an instrument of political discipline and social control.[106] Maximilien de Robespierre, the commanding figure of the Terror, ominously declared that the Jacobin revolutionary regime employed "the despotism of liberty against tyranny."[107] The Reign of Terror was therefore a state-directed activity, motivated by a heady brew of ideology and politics, laced with a messianic religious fervor.[108] It also adopted the forms of law and legal procedure, if not the substance. The machinery of the Terror included the Committee of Public Safety, the Committee of General Security, the Revolutionary Tribunal of Paris, provincial revolutionary tribunals, and the enormously powerful representatives on mission who were literally proconsuls in their own regional departments. At first, legal proceedings:

were recognizably those of a court of law, with the accused having the right to obtain counsel, to give evidence, to cross-examine. As time went on and men had fewer doubts as to the adequacy of the inner light, the proceedings became mere public pillorying of the already condemned. Death was the only sentence.[109]

In the words of Jacobin journalist and ex-lawyer Camille Desmoulins, "There are no suspect peoples, there are only those accused of crimes fixed by law."[110] But Desmoulins, himself a victim of the Terror's blade, missed the point. France, internally, had become a lawless state with a government out of control and a people either unwilling or unable to stem the terrorist tide (which finally occurred when the dwindling number of Robespierre's enemies finally banded together against him). Terror, to invert a Marxian phrase, had been used by the incumbent Jacobin regime to achieve a negative freedom. Its twin legacies of intimidation and retribution would provide frightening examples for the technological twentieth century. Thomas Carlyle's famed condemnation of the Revolution run amuck still rings true—a "New Golden Era going down in leaden dross and sulphurous black of the Everlasting Darkness."[111]

The Treaties of Paris and the Congress of Vienna (1814–1815) once again restored the European equilibrium and revived the notion of a community of nations. Inter-state violence, though not legally proscribed, was placed under the control of a new alliance structure. As unprecedented as was the forced exile of Napoleon to the island of Elba by the newly formed Quadruple Alliance (England, Austria, Prussia, and Russia), all the more so was the outlawing of Bonaparte by the great powers during the Hundred Days and his imprisonment on the island of St. Helena. This made Napoleon, in effect, the first modern war criminal, and set a precedent for the twentieth-century war crimes trials, or attempted trials, of the leaders of defeated states.

The Vienna Settlement did not put back the historical clock, as many historians have maintained,[112] but it did rewind the political mechanism in favor of a new international order where "change could be brought about through a sense of obligation, instead of an assertion of power."[113] Displaced sovereigns and disrupted sovereignties were granted some sort of legal recognition with certain minor exceptions. The so-called principle of "legitimacy and compensation" was actually a legalistic formula invented solely to justify the return of the French and Spanish Bourbon monarchs to their lost thrones.

In truth, modern international law began with the Final Act of the Congress of Vienna, signed in June 1815.[114] A host of international rules and provisions were decided upon,[115] and a new alliance system emerged (which soon included France), often called the Concert of Europe. According to the terms of the Quadruple Alliance, done at Paris five months later, the signatories would meet periodically "for the purpose of consulting upon their common interest and for the consideration of measures most salutary for the maintenance of the peace of Europe."[116]

Attempts by the Russian tsar to form a Holy Alliance in favor of Christian principles and of intervention against revolutionary movements resulted in a document signed at the end of September 1815 by Austria, Prussia, and Russia (with the English Regent sending a letter of approval); but aside from causing confusion with the European Concert in the public mind, it meant very little.

One present-day legal scholar implies that Vienna really stood for the emergence of a great power system, and this arrangement continued for almost half a century.[117] But there was no legal obligation on the part of any signatory to act in concert with its treaty partners, or even to act at all. A number of congresses were actually held in 1818, 1820, 1821, and 1822, but outside intervention apart from Spain and Greece did not occur, European revolutions did not stop, and inter-state violence did not cease, though it continued to be waged on behalf of the balance of power for well over a generation.[118] Great Britain's position during much of this time was the by-now-traditional one "that internal affairs were not a matter of international adjudication" or outside interference.[119] There are, however, exceptions to every rule, and Greece provided that opportunity.

HUMANITARIAN INTERVENTION AS AN INTERNATIONAL REMEDY

For most of the nineteenth century, international law was largely irrelevant unless it served a national interest or great power objective. The principal legal contributions were the guarantee of Belgian neutrality, the neutralization of the Turkish Straits, creation of the International Red Cross, norms governing internal conflicts (influenced by the American Civil War), and the emergence of the increasingly controversial doctrine of humanitarian intervention.

The Greeks had risen against their Ottoman overlords in 1821, and by 1823 the Turks were taking terrible reprisals against Greek populations in Thessaly, Macedonia, and Asia Minor. One of the unexpected consequences in the early nineteenth-century Age of Romanticism was the combination of political liberalism with cultural Philhellenism on the Continent and particularly in England. Uhland and Müller in the Germanies, Hugo and Chateaubriand in France, and Shelley and especially Byron in England helped to stimulate popular passion for the Greek cause. "We are all Greeks," Shelley intoned.[120] But it was Lord Byron who made the Greek cause his own, and in so doing led the Concert to become involved in the first instance of humanitarian intervention in international law.

When the Egyptians intervened on behalf of the Ottoman sultan, the Russian tsar, Nicholas I, and the Duke of Wellington, who had been sent by the British government as an emissary to Russia, came to the joint conclusion that the Egyptian military forces were being used to exterminate the Greek people. France was brought into the quarrel the following year (1827) by the Treaty of London; and when the Turkish sultan refused mediation, his fleet was destroyed by an Anglo–French squadron. Russia went to war against Turkey six months later, and the issue was not finally resolved until the London Protocol of February 1830, which declared Greece to be an independent kingdom under the protection of England, France, and Russia. Not only was Greek liberation extremely popular with the Western European peoples, but it may even have served as a partial inspiration for the liberal uprisings of 1830.[121]

Not until the *Caroline* controversy of the mid-nineteenth century were the legal parameters of humanitarian intervention actually spelled out, and even then these limitations were avoided as much in the breach as they were observed in practice. The *Caroline* was an American light steamer utilized to supply recruits, weapons, and matériel to 1,000 U.S. citizens decamped as a military expedition on Canadian territory. A small British commando force seized the *Caroline*, set it ablaze, and dumped it over Niagara Falls. Two Americans were killed and twelve were injured. In a famous communication dealing with the case, Secretary of State Daniel Webster defined for the British Foreign Secretary, Lord Ashburton, the act of necessity and the nature of self-help. The threat presented, Webster declared, must be "instant, overwhelming, and leaving no choice of means, and no moment for deliberation."[122] As with self-defense in Anglo–American law, the type of intervention should be proportional to the degree of harm, and there must be a close relationship between the wrongful act or acts and the retaliatory measures taken. A twentieth-century corollary has added the requirement that there should be no permanent injury to the political independence or the territorial integrity of the offending state.[123]

No greater disparity between newly emergent theory and long-standing practice can be found than in the origins of the Crimean War. Humanitarian intervention in its nineteenth-century form occurred when one state intervened against another in order to protect a victimized population. The Crimean War had its roots in a dispute as to who would control the holy shrines in Jerusalem, under Turkish suzerainty—Roman Catholics or Greek Orthodox. Gradually the Catholic faction made itself predominant and fighting broke out between the two groups. The Russians then demanded what effectively would have been a protectorate over the 12 million Christian subjects of the Turkish sultan. The Turks, under the promptings of the British ambassador, persuaded the sultan to declare war on Russia in October 1854; and when the latter refused to withdraw from what is now Rumanian territory, Britain and France went to war with Russia in March 1854. Russian intervention, ostensibly on behalf of her coreligionists, had been transformed into a generalized conflict over expansion of borders and control of the Straits.[124]

The Peace of Paris (1856) provided for such important limitations upon state power as the internationalization of waterways, the demilitarization of the Black Sea, and a formal recognition of neutrality rights and obligations on the high seas.[125] The humanitarian aspects of the original dispute had become incidental at best.[126] In a highly praised work, several Yale scholars list the following examples of further humanitarian intervention: the intervention in 1860–1861 by the five European great powers on behalf of persecuted Christians in Syria; a further intervention in 1866–1868 on the side of oppressed Christians in Crete; the Russian conflict with the Ottoman Empire in 1877–1878 over Bosnia, Herzegovina, and Bulgaria; great power intervention between 1903 and 1908 against Turkish atrocities in Macedonia; and "humanitarian intercession" (purely diplomatic and not very strong at that) by the United States with respect to the slaughter of the Armenians between 1904 and 1916.[127] Quite unexpectedly, the authors omit the two most classic examples of humanitarian intervention—the Spanish–American War of 1898 and the multi-national rescue force sent to Peking to rescue the besieged European colony during the Boxer Rebellion of 1900.[128]

Both the legal bases and historical precedents for humanitarian intervention were considerably expanded by U.S. concern over the plight of Cuba prior to the outbreak of the Spanish–American War and by the multi-national Western rescue mission sent to Peking during the Boxer Rebellion. These two incidents and their resolution clearly revealed the main differences between self-help, on the one hand, in carrying out the *Caroline* principles, and third party intervention, on the other, where political independence and territorial integrity have been rarely respected. This bifurcated approach has continued in our own contemporary era, where the style of humanitarian intervention is most often determined by the motive for its occurrence. It should also be noted that the nature of humanitarian intervention, dating from its earliest beginnings, was more often than not multi-lateral in character.

In the post-Charter decades, the three most cited examples of this increasingly controversial principle have been the Congo U.S. hostage rescue operation, the Bangladesh war for independence, and the famed Entebbe commando raid.[129] With respect to the first Congo crisis (1960–1961), the Belgians attributed their military role to humanitarian intervention, whereas the U.N. Emergency Force, in the eyes of Secretary-General Dag Hammarskjöld, operated according to the dictates of "preventive diplomacy" and "executive action." The United States assisted the Belgians with the explanation that its support was "humanitarian" rather than military.[130]

Although India maintained that its military aid to Bangladesh was humanitarian in nature, the real motive was to fragment the territory of its chief enemy, Pakistan. The Indian army enabled Bangladesh to achieve independence, which was the goal not only of the rebel leaders but also of the Indian government.[131] The Entebbe raid of early July 1976 was probably one of the three most dramatic events of the Terror Decade of the 1970s (the other two being the Munich Olympics massacre and the kidnap–murder of Aldo Moro). The majority of commentators considered the Entebbe rescue to be "justified as a humanitarian intervention permitted under contemporary international law."[132] There were also critics, however, who argued that humanitarian intervention as exemplified by Entebbe or similar situations was in basic contradiction of post-Charter international law.[133]

For Americans, the most conspicuous and most debated act of humanitarian intervention was the abortive Iranian hostage rescue mission that took place in late April 1980. Nowhere in the arguments of the supporters and defenders of the Carter Administration can one find a reference to humanitarian intervention. The main motivations of the U.S. government were expediency and necessity.[134] The fact that the rescue attempt occurred during the deliberations of the International Court of Justice showed the desperate condition that the American president had allowed himself to fall prey to. The Court's decision shied away from making any determination on the legality of the rescue attempt, although there were several vigorous dissents. At the same time the opinion criticized the United States for taking this action in a context that could only undermine respect for the international judicial process.[135]

Controversy continues over whether humanitarian intervention is legally permissible under the provisions of the U.N. Charter.[136] An early twentieth-century definition of the then-leading American commentator is much too broad for current usage: "intervention for humanity [and] for the purpose of vindicating the law of nations against outrage."[137] What can be said is that the doctrine is a general exception to existing norms, is to be invoked only as a last resort, and must conform to the rules of proportionality. In this sense, it functions as a useful limitation upon harmful acts of state violence and state terrorism.

ATTEMPTS TO CONTROL INTERNATIONAL VIOLENCE, STATE TERRORISM, AND THE ONSET OF GLOBAL WARS

In the two decades following the Crimean War, inter-state conflicts involving the majority of the European powers were as much unifying as they were disintegrating factors.[138] With the restructuring of the alliance system after the Franco–Prussian War of 1870–1871, a new concept of the balance of power came into being. Thanks to Otto von Bismarck and his legacy, the balance of power came to signify the preservation of a precarious equilibrium between two competing alliance structures. The almost inevitable result was a growing arms race, forcible acquisition of colonial possessions, and a proliferation of war plans and mobilization timetables. Might, once again as in the past, came to determine whose rights were valid and whose were not.

Although it has been little noted and less remembered, Tsar Alexander II in 1881 issued a summons for an international conference to deal with the problem of political terrorism (a phenomenon that would result in the Tsar's murder the very next year). Although his call for this conference was undoubtedly self-serving, it did set a precedent for the later successful, and similarly self-serving, request by Nicholas II for a disarmament conference in 1898. The First Hague Conference of 1899 did not arrive at any solution with respect to the disarmament question, and thereby acted as an intended spur to the armaments race. It did manage to establish a Permanent Court of Arbitration, located at the Hague (in actuality an arbitration panel), which is, technically, still in existence. It also set up a commission to begin formulation of the laws of war.

Historians have been rather callous in their assessments of the 1899 Conference, but the German kaiser's reaction was downright caustic: "I consented to all this nonsense only in order that the Tsar be not discredited before Europe. In practice, however, I shall rely on and call upon only God and my sharp sword!"[139] The Second Hague Peace Conference of 1907 was concerned primarily with the laws of war. Numerous agreements were reached and several significant conventions were adopted by forty-four state delegations, and the regulations arrived at provided the legal foundation for the development of the law of armed conflict in the twentieth century.

The two Hague Peace Conferences of 1899 and 1907 were ostensibly attempts to control state violence through arbitration, conciliation, and formalized regulations governing the conduct of states parties during time of war. This became particularly important for the major European powers since they were in the process of re-aligning themselves politically and militarily in preparation for a general European conflict. Another way of viewing the Hague Conferences and their results is that those pacts agreed upon were a clear sign that the European balance was already beginning to shift out of control, and that the countries represented assumed that conflict was inevitable. Ironically, the alliance system that was originally designed by Bismarck to be a constraint upon state violence ultimately turned into an instrument of conflict promotion.[140]

An act of state-supported terrorism set in motion the immediate events leading to the outbreak of the First World War, but the triumphant Allies were to ignore the implications of the Austrian archduke's assassination and focus instead upon war guilt and war criminality. A notorious Serbian terrorist organization called the "Black Hand" was utilized by the Serbian government as an operative instrument of foreign policy. State terrorism not only meant persecution of innocent citizens by an oppressive regime, as was the case in the French Revolution, but now it also stood for government-sponsored terror violence by means of individuals and groups.[141] Terror violence as surrogate warfare had suddenly come of age. The older type of state terrorism was well represented by the notorious Armenian massacres during the years 1915–1916, and the numbers were truly genocidal.[142] Present-day Armenian perpetrators of terror violence are attempting to punish Turkey and the West for those sins and massacres of the past.[143]

Article 231 of the Treaty of Versailles, the infamous war guilt clause, placed upon Germany and her allies the responsibility for a war of aggression.[144] But Articles 227 to 229 were equally important for the future context of war criminality. Article 227 created a special tribunal to try the German kaiser "for a supreme offence against international morality and the sanctity of treaties."[145] Fortunately for the Emperor (and international law), Wilhelm II had fled to the Netherlands, and despite the plea contained in that Article, the Dutch refused to surrender him. Articles 228 and 229 empowered the Allies to create military tribunals to try individuals accused of "having committed acts of violation of the laws of war and customs of war" or "criminal acts against the nationals of one of the Allied and Associated Powers."[146] The Leipzig war crimes trials, however limited in their scope and result,[147] provided the basis for the Nuremberg and Tokyo Tribunals at the end of the Second World War. One prominent French legal scholar could not control a flush of optimism occurring in the aftermath of the war to end wars: "The authors of the Treaty of Versailles ... have instituted a penal sanction; they have foreseen a superior jurisdiction to States."[148]

The League of Nations was intended by its creators to be the executor of the Versailles Treaty and to enforce an effective limitation upon the spread of international violence. It was first and foremost a peace-keeping organization, and was designed not only as a control mechanism but also as a preventative instrumentality.[149] Sadly, the League failed to live up to its promise or potential. Neither the Locarno Pact (1925) nor the Kellogg–Briand Pact (1928) proved to be an effective restraint on interstate violence, and both agreements actually undermined the authority of the League. The failure of the League proved to be not endemic but external. Its authority and, ultimately, its existence were negated by its member states acting exclusively in their own interests. Before the interwar period had lapsed, a new imbalance of power had developed, resting upon the twin pillars of military triumph and diplomatic defeat.

The dismemberment of four empires during or after the First World

War, the restructuring of the map of Europe, and the resultant growth of sizable minorities in the Central and Eastern European states posed a possible threat of state violence or state terrorism in the classic sense. In an attempt to prevent oppression of these minorities by incumbent regimes, the treaty drafters in Paris attempted to insert minority clauses and protections for populations subject to potential harm. The so-called minority treaties contained identical language when referring to the guarantees of the League of Nations.[150] Unfortunately, for the peoples involved and for the world, these first attempts to establish an international protection of human rights either were stillborn or fell victim to the collapse of democracy in the 1920s and the 1930s. Adolf Hitler used claims of self-determination to destroy and dismember many of the post-World War I settlement states, replacing them with an even harsher tyranny of unprecedented proportions.

The word "totalitarianism" entered the political vocabulary of the twentieth century in association with Nazi barbarism and Stalinist despotism. "Lawlessness is the essence of non-tyrannical government and lawlessness is the essence of tyranny."[151] State terrorism during the 1930s became synonymous with Soviet Russia and Nazi Germany, and the Occupation years from 1940 to 1945 in both Europe and East Asia were classic examples of state violence and state terror in their most deadly form. Genocide was transformed from a term of art into an international crime of almost unthinkable magnitude.[152]

Although internal state repression was not a matter of international law between the two world wars, state-sponsored individual and group terrorism was another matter. The dual murders of Yugoslavian King Alexander I and French Foreign Minister Louis Barthou by Croatian terrorists (trained in fascist Italy) at Marseilles in 1934, and the assassination of Austrian Premier Englebert Dollfuss by Nazi thugs that same year, led to an extensive League of Nations debate and eventually a Conference on Terrorism held in Geneva in 1937.[153] Not surprisingly, given the atmosphere of the times, the Conference brought forth two stillborn Conventions on the Prevention and Punishment of Terrorism (which dealt solely with elements of individual and group terrorism) and on the estalishment of an International Criminal Court.[154] Between them they secured only one ratification (India), and their significance was at best symbolic. From the standpoint of international law, they have had only minor precedential value.[155]

WAR CRIMES, GENOCIDE, AND HUMAN WRONGS: FROM NUREMBERG TO TEHERAN

The inability of the League of Nations, or the Anglo–French alliance, to deal with state violence in the 1930s led one disillusioned American legal analyst to concede, after the Munich Conference, that "the rights of states in the community of nations, as the rights of individuals in a national community, may have to be sacrificed to preserve the greater interest of the community as a whole."[156] This surrender to power politics, if adopted and pursued by the Western democratic powers, would have destroyed the very foundations of public international law as they had evolved from the time of the classical European writers and the Peace of Westphalia. Instead, the Second World War intervened, and its successful outcome (for those seeking to restore the balance of power) brought forth a new phase of the international legal system—which may properly be called contemporary international law.

One year before the Second World War came to an end, the Allies created a U.N. War Crimes Commission with the specific purpose of establishing a U.N. War Crimes Court, which would be granted jurisdiction to try German civilians and soldiers for acts of war criminality. The resulting Nuremberg and Tokyo Military Tribunals provided both a moral and a legal basis for a major departure from traditional international law—the international protection of human rights. Nuremberg and Tokyo not only led to reformulations of the laws of war as codified in the Geneva Conventions of 1949,[157] but transferred the focus of public international law to center on individuals as well as upon states. Although the charge of "crimes against humanity" was not considered in the Final Judgment, the underlying philosophy and general concept carried over to the Genocide Convention and the Universal Declaration of Human Rights (1948).[158]

The Genocide Convention, approved by the U.N. General Assembly on December 9, 1948, was the offspring of the Holocaust horrors and the Nuremberg war crimes trial. Originally the inspiration of Professor Raphael Lemkin, it was formed into an international convention following a U.N. General Assembly Resolution on the Crime of Genocide, adopted on December 11, 1946.[159] It is significant that the drafters of the Genocide Convention drew back from the attribution of state responsibility in the matter of genocidal acts.[160] Although eighty-six states are parties to the Convention (the United States has yet to ratify), no charges have ever been filed against any individual or group, and no trials have ever been held. Sadly, still flourishing in its practice, the convention is at best a proscriptive principle of international law rather than a mandatory prohibition or a peremptory norm. The impact of the Convention on the practice of state terrorism has been just about nil.

The Universal Declaration of Human Rights was adopted by consensus on December 10, 1948. It was first proposed by Panama, Mexico, and Cuba at the 1945 preparatory conference of the United Nations in San Francisco, then put forward by the Human Rights Commission in a forty-eight-article draft document, and proselytized with ceaseless energy by

Eleanor Roosevelt. Charles Malik, then rapporteur of the Human Rights Commission and president of the Economic and Social Council, explained before the Declaration's passage that the basic issue was "whether the State is subject to higher law ... or whether it is a sufficient law unto itself."[161] The Declaration can be construed as an international guarantee against state terror and repression. But despite the stirring language and noble sentiments, the Universal Declaration is merely an advisory guideline and not a mandatory list of protected rights. Its status today is best summed up by the 1984 president of the U.N. General Assembly:

The condition of the individual in today's world is indeed a grim one; arbitrary and summary executions, enforced and involuntary disappearances, atrocities in armed conflicts or emergency situations, death from hunger and starvation, torture, gross violations of human rights, protracted and widespread political imprisonment, racial and religious intolerance, absence of democracy and respect for the popular will—all these inflict a heavy toll on human lives and human souls.[162]

After long debate and sharp disagreement, the U.N. International Law Commission drew up a list of Nuremberg Principles and presented them to the General Assembly in 1950, but the coming of the Korean War and deep divisions within the world community prevented these Principles from obtaining any further consideration.[163] Nuremberg had become an embarrassing memory. The attempt of the democratic industrial nations at the Bonn Economic Summit (1978) and its follow-up at Ottawa (1981) to penalize state-supported hijacking and the granting of safe havens to terrorists by sympathetic governments have received much publicity but have meant very little. The Bonn Declaration has proved to be long on rhetoric and weak on performance.[164]

The U.N. Convention Against the Taking of Hostages, approved without recorded vote on December 17, 1979, was in reality a response to the pressures exerted by the Western democracies on the U.N. General Assembly in the early stages of the Iranian hostage seizure. The Convention still has not entered into force, and its prospects are not of the best. Attacks upon diplomats, consulates, and embassies continue inexorably, and the world community merely admonishes but does not act. As a protection against state-sponsored hostage-taking activities, the Hostage Convention has not proven to be effective.[165]

The Interim and Final Judgments of the International Court of Justice in the Iranian case serve as an unhappy reminder that the rule of law and the rule of reason are often ignored in the international arena, and that the global village is still barely civilized. The Court's withdrawal of its rulings in May 1981, upon the request of the United States, leaves the significance of the decisions very much in doubt.[166] The message to potential terrorist regimes is clear: Might may not make right, but it can bring about compromise and capitulation by victim governments.

CONCLUSION: THE RULE OF LAW VERSUS THE ROAD TO CHAOS?

In the eyes of its critics and often its supporters, the international legal system "has no mechanism for enforcing its laws; democracies, therefore, have to be able to practice realpolitik as well as uphold principle."[167] This is a callous view and ultimately a dangerous one. Although the strength of international law is as much a matter of will as it is a matter of substance, the latter can sometimes exert a positive influence upon the former. One can well argue that little progress has been made against inter-state violence and state terrorism since the promulgation of the U.N. Charter four decades ago.[168] Restraints have been neither successful nor persuasive. Yet, the quest goes on, and the lure of a better world continues to beckon.

The United Nations, on a variety of fronts (however sincere the attempt by the state members involved), has developed, by way of the International Law Commission, a Draft Code of State Responsibility; is attempting to redefine the status of diplomatic couriers and diplomatic bags; and has revived consideration of the Draft Code of Offences Against the Peace and Security of Mankind.[169] The European Convention on Human Rights and the European Commission of Human Rights already have demonstrated the possibilities and the effectiveness of a well-developed regional system.[170] A great deal of attention has been paid to the Irish case (*Ireland v. United Kingdom*) decided by the European Court of Human Rights Commission in December 1977, which held Great Britain accountable for submitting Irish suspects to torture and inhuman and degrading treatment prior to 1973.[171] The status and condition of the Maze prisoners under the Thatcher government apparently were not affected by this decision.

Two American cases give an indication of the potentialities for the reach of the rule of law in a domestic jurisdiction with an international application. *Letelier v. Republic of Chile*, decided in March 1980,[172] held that a victim or a victim's personal representatives could sue in federal court for money damages and could be entitled to collect compensation from a foreign government responsible for either personal injury or death as a result of acts of political violence carried out in this country by the offending government. The court concluded it was immaterial that outrageous tortious acts originated in a foreign jurisdiction, if actions of foreign agents brought about injury or harm in the United States. *Filartiga v. Pena-Irala* (1980) represents the most controversial contemporary holding in American domestic law with respect to state terrorism and human rights.[173] In a sweeping opinion, much of which arguably is dictum, Judge Irving R. Kaufman in an appellate decision of the Second Circuit held that relatives of a torture victim residing in the United States could sue the alleged torturer who was visiting the United States. The torturer, like the pirate, declared Judge Kaufman, is *"hostis humani generis,* an enemy of all mankind." That is true not only for international law but American law as well.[174] Kaufman knew exactly what he was doing in fashioning this decision.[175] Whether it represents a major step forward for human rights or is merely an anomaly in American jurisprudence remains to be seen. But in the mind of Judge Kaufman, without dreaming the dream of future fulfillment, there can be no progress in present life.

From its earliest theories and most rudimentary practice, international law has symbolized the hopes, the desires, and the aspirations of humankind. It has been both a goal-setting mechanism and a means of conflict resolution. This has been particularly true in areas of inter-state violence and the systematic violence of the state. Much like other areas of international law, idealism has often predominated over realism; yet in an age when tyranny has registered many triumphs, nobility of purpose is not a small achievement. The danger for those committed to the rule of law in a world of power politics is that reality becomes illusion, and commitment gives way to self-deception.

As this chapter has illustrated, the commitment to the rule of law, evidenced by jurists, scholars, and often court decisions and state action, as it aims to constrain state violence and state terror, has not been lacking. But concentrated state action against violence and preemptive behavior sparked by law lags considerably behind the commitments. So it has always been. So it will continue to be, unless the nations of the world choose humanity over humanicide. Thus far, the historical record does not give cause for optimism.

NOTES

1. For a rather sophisticated if somewhat cautious approach by an international legal academic, see especially G. J. H. van Hoof, *Rethinking the Sources of International Law* (Deventer, the Netherlands: Kluwer, 1983), pp. 13–28.

2. The Turkish Cyprus invasion, the Arab oil boycott, the Iranian hostage crisis, the Falklands Islands conflict, the U.S.–Nicaraguan confrontation, and the Iran–Iraqi War are but a few examples of disputes where both sides appealed to international law as a means of self-justification.

3. H. Lauterpacht, *The Function of Law in the International Community* (Oxford: Oxford University Press, 1933), pp. 3–4; and L. Oppenheim (H. Lauterpacht, ed.), *International Law: A Treatise,* vol. 1, 8th ed. (London: Longmans, Green, 1961), pp. 5–6, 19–20, 636–639.

4. Charles G. Fenwick, *International Law,* 4th ed. (New York: Appleton-Century-Crofts, 1965), pp. 297–298.

5. The classic treatment by Sabine is still a useful introduction. See George A. Sabine, *A History of Political Theory,* 3d ed. (New York: Holt, Rinehart and Winston, 1961), pp. 455–456, 461–473, 523–526, 531–540.

6. Quoted in André Decouflé, *Sociologie des révolutions*, 2d ed. (Paris: Presses Universitaires de France, 1970), p. 99. See the observation of Hannah Arendt that "Robespierre's rule of terror was indeed nothing else but the attempt to organize the whole French people into a single gigantic party machinery." Hannah Arendt, *On Revolution* (New York: Viking Press, 1974), p. 250.

7. See Robert A. Friedlander, "Who Put Out the Lamps? Thoughts on International Law and the Coming of World War I," *Duquesne Law Review* 20, no. 4 (Summer 1982), pp. 573–575, 582–583.

8. Frank Freidel, "Francis Lieber," in Warren F. Kuehl, ed., *Biographical Dictionary of Internationalists* (Westport, Conn.: Greenwood Press, 1983), p. 435.

9. Arendt, *On Revolution*, p. 95.

10. E. V. Walter, *Terror and Resistance: A Study of Political Violence* (New York: Oxford University Press, 1972), pp. 7–8, 15.

11. Hannah Arendt, *The Origins of Totalitarianism*, new ed. (New York: Harcourt Brace Jovanovich, 1973), p. 464.

12. Alexander Dallin and George W. Breslauer, *Political Terror in Communist Systems* (Stanford, Calif.: Stanford University Press, 1970), p. 102.

13. Moses Moskowitz, *International Concern with Human Rights* (Leiden: Sijthoff; Dobbs Ferry, N.Y.: Oceana Publications, 1974), p. 160.

14. John P. Humphrey, *Human Rights and the United Nations: A Great Adventure* (Dobbs Ferry, N.Y.: Transnational, 1984), pp. 10–15.

15. Louis B. Sohn, "Protection of Human Rights Through International Legislation," in Karel Vasak, ed., *Problemes de protection internationale de droits des hommes* (Paris: Editions A. Pedone, 1969), observes that during its first 25 years "the United Nations adopted more than a dozen of special conventions relating to specific human rights problems" (p. 326).

16. J. Shand Watson, "Legal Theory, Efficacy and Validity in the Development of Human Rights Norms in International Law," *University of Illinois Law Forum* 3 (1979), p. 637.

17. Ibid., pp. 640–641. An entire symposium was devoted to a critical reply, but the tone and substance of many of the contributors enhance rather than detract from Watson's position. See "Symposium on the Future of Human Rights in the World Legal Order," *Hofstra Law Review* 9, no. 3 (Winter 1981), pp. 433–447.

18. Presentation by Ambassador Edward Marks, Deputy Director, Office for Combatting Terrorism, U.S. Department of State, Pipestem, W.V., October 23, 1982.

19. *Department of State Bulletin*, 82 (August 1982), p. 5.

20. See, for example, the remarks of Walter Laqueur, "Reagan and the Russians," *Commentary* 73 (January 1982), pp. 19–21.

21. See Emery Kalen, ed., *Hammarskjöld: The Political Man* (New York: Funk and Wagnalls, 1968), pp. 6, 9–10, 73, 125, 135–138.

22. Georg Schwarzenberger, *Power Politics: A Study of World Society*, 3d ed. (London: Stevens and Sons Limited, 1964), p. 14.

23. "Power tends to corrupt. Absolute power tends to corrupt absolutely." Lord Acton.

24. Schwarzenberger, *Power Politics*, p. 89.

25. For a discussion of the Anglo–American critics and their influences, see

Robert A. Friedlander, "Power Politics and the Rule of Law: Pre-Charter Origins and Post-Charter Views," *Yearbook and World Affairs* 38 (1984), pp. 43–58.

26. Leo Gross, "The Peace of Westphalia, 1648–1948," *American Journal of International Law* 42, no. 1 (1948), pp. 20–41, reprinted in Gross, *Essays on International Law and Organization*, vol. 1 (The Hague: Transnational; Boston: Martinus Nijhoff, 1984), pp.3–21.

27. Francisco de Vitoria, *De Jure Gentium et Naturali* (translated by Francis Crane Macken), in James Brown Scott, ed., *The Spanish Origins of International Law: Francisco de Vitoria and His Law of Nations* (Oxford: Oxford University Press; London: Humphrey Milford, 1934), pp. cxi-cxii.

28. Francisco de Vitoria, *Relectio de Potestate Civili* (translated by Gwladys L. Williams), in Scott, *Spanish Origins*, pp. xc-xci. On the contributions of Vitoria, see also Henry Wheaton, *History of the Law of Nations in Europe and America: From the Earliest Times to the Treaty of Washington, 1842* (Albany: Gould, Banks, 1845), pp. 35–43.

29. Balthazar Ayala, *De Jure et Officiis Bellicis et Discipline Militari* (translated by John Pawley Bate), vol. II (Washington, D.C.: The Carnegie Institution, 1912), p. 95; see also Wheaton, *History of the Law*, pp. 33–34. For a widely praised recent commentary, see Michael Walzer, *Just and Unjust Wars: A Moral Argument with Historical Illustrations* (New York: Basic Books, 1977).

30. Ayala, *De Jure*, p. 140.

31. Ibid., pp. 33, 105.

32. Ibid., p. 88.

33. Ibid., p. 90.

34. Alberico Gentili, *De Legationibus* (translated by Gordon J. Laing), (New York: Oxford University Press, 1924). See the summary analysis in Wheaton, *History of the Law*, pp. 51–54.

35. Alberico Gentili, *De Iure Belli* (translated by John C. Rolfe), (Oxford: Oxford University Press; London: Humphrey Milford, 1933), p. 4.

36. Ibid., pp. 4, 10–11, 332, 364, to mention only a few examples.

37. Ibid., pp. 52, 337.

38. Ibid., pp. 49, 114–116.

39. Wheaton, *History of the Law*, p. 51.

40. Cornelius F. Murphy, Jr., "The Grotian Vision of World Order," *American Journal of International Law* 76, no. 3 (July 1982), pp. 479–480. Murphy's date for the publication of *De Legibus* is in error.

41. Gerhard von Glahn, *Law Among Nations: An Introduction to Public International Law*, 2d ed. (New York: Macmillan, 1970), pp. 38–39. There was, in other words, no universal civil law and no universal sovereign authority. See Murphy, "Grotian Vision," pp. 496–497.

42. See Hugo Grotius, *De Jure Belli ac Pacis* (translated by Francis W. Kelsey et al.), (Oxford: Clarendon Press; London: Humphrey Milford, 1925).

43. Ibid., p. 33.

44. Ibid., p. 9. Suárez also stressed the importance of custom as a controlling factor in international law. See James Brown Scott, *Law, the State, and the International Community*, vol. 2, rep. ed. (Westport, Conn.: Greenwood Press, 1970), pp. 249–250.

45. Grotius, *De Jure*, p. 20.

46. Ibid., p. 44.

47. Raymond Aron, *Peace and War: A Theory of International Relations* (translated by Richard Howard and Annette Baker Fox), (New York: Frederick A. Praeger, 1967), p. 111.

48. See Grotius, *De Jure*, pp. 164–165, 169–185.

49. Ibid., p. 18.

50. Ibid., pp. 156–163.

51. Ibid., pp. 438–449. For an extensive and detailed analysis of Grotius's concept of war and peace, see Peter Haggenmacher, *Grotius et la doctrine de la guerre juste* (Paris: Presses Universitaire de France, 1983), pp. 448–629.

52. Grotius, *De Jure*, pp. 653–656. But Grotius also denounces the doctrine of tyrannicide.

53. Prior to the three hundredth anniversary of his birth, there were approximately fifty editions of his landmark treatise printed in nearly a dozen different languages.

54. See the comments of Murphy, "Grotian Vision," pp. 482–483.

55. Samuel Puffendorf, *Elementorum Jurisprudentiae Universalis* (translated by William Abbott Oldfather), (Oxford: The Clarendon Press; London: Humphrey Milford, 1931), pp. 166–167.

56. Ibid., pp. 288–289, 292–293, 295.

57. Ibid., p. 295.

58. Samuel Puffendorf, *De Jure Naturae et Gentium*, 2d ed. (translated by C. H. Oldfather and W. A. Oldfather), (Oxford: Clarendon Press; London: Humphrey Milford, 1934).

59. Ibid., p. 1,103.

60. Ibid., p. 1,360.

61. Ibid., p. 1,367.

62. Ibid., p. 1,316.

63. Ibid., pp. 1,294–1,297.

64. Ibid., pp. 1,308–1,309.

65. Wheaton, *History of the Law*, p. 98.

66. Johann W. Textor (translator of the 1758 edition by John Pawley Bate), *Synopsis Juris Gentium* (Washington, D.C.: Carnegie Institution, 1916), p. 3.

67. Ibid., pp. 38–39.

68. Ibid., p. 167.

69. Ibid., pp. 186–187.

70. Emmerich de Vattel, *The Law of Nations or the Principles of Natural Law Applied to the Conduct and to the Affairs of Nations and Sovereigns* (translated by Charles G. Fenwick), (Washington, D.C.: Carnegie Institution, 1916), pp. 6–7, 126. For the application of Vattel's theories in a current context, see Alfred Verdross and Heribert Franz Koeck, "Natural Law: The Tradition of Universal Reason and Authority," in R. St. J. Macdonald and Douglas M. Johnston, eds., *The Structure and Process of International Law: Essays in Legal Philosophy Doctrine and Theory* (The Hague: Martinus Nihjoff, 1983), pp. 37–39.

71. Vattel, *Law of Nations*, p. 127.

72. Ibid., p. 141.

73. Ibid., p. 130.

74. Ibid., p. 131.
75. See *supra*, notes 16 and 17.
76. Vattel, *Law of Nations*, pp. 257–258.
77. Ibid., pp. 254–256.
78. Ibid., p. 336.
79. Ibid., p. 338.
80. Ibid., pp. 343–345.
81. Ibid., pp. 92–93.
82. Gaston Zeller, *Les temps modernes*, vol. I: *De Cristophe Colombe à Cromwell* (Paris: Librairie Hachette, 1953), p. 3.
83. Ibid., pp. 4, 9–13.
84. See Clive Parry, ed., *The Consolidated Treaty Series, 1648–1649*, vol. 1 (Dobbs Ferry, N.Y.: Oceana Publications, 1969), pp. 198–269, 319–356.
85. Zeller, *Les temps modernes*, I, p. 265. See the Convention signed between France and the German Imperial states at Nuremberg, September 24, 1649, in Parry, *Consolidated Treaties Series*, 1, pp. 463–468 (Latin original).
86. See, Parry, *Consolidated Treaties*, pp. 3–118, for both the Latin version and the French translation.
87. See, for example, Gross, "Peace of Westphalia," pp. 24–30; and George-Frederic de Martens, "Discours préliminaire sur les différents recueils de traités publiés jusqu'à ce jour," in Parry, *Consolidated Treaties Series*, I, p. xxi, first published in 1802.
88. Gross, "Peace of Westphalia," p. 40, holds that "equality of states" was one of the legacies of the Peace of Westphalia.
89. Parry, *Consolidated Treaties Series*, 1, Article CXXIII, p. 354.
90. Ibid., Article CXXIV, p. 354.
91. For a *contra* view, see Zeller, *Les temps modernes*, I, p. 264.
92. Murphy, "Grotian Vision," p. 497.
93. Wheaton, *History of the Law*, p. 70.
94. Gross, "Peace of Westphalia," pp. 24–28.
95. See Wheaton, *History of the Law*, pp. 70–77.
96. Gross, "Peace of Westphalia," p. 38. See the observation of H. de Louter, *Le droit international public positif*, vol. 1 (Oxford: Oxford University Press, 1920), p. 105: "This treaty is, however, still more significant for its tenor than by the importance of its contractors."
97. President Francois Mitterrand declared in similar fashion during November 1983 that "The masterpiece of the strategy of deterrence in France is the chief of state, it is me; everything depends upon his determination." *Le Monde*, (November 18, 1983).
98. Gaston Zeller, *Les temps modernes*, vol. II: *De Louis XIV à 1789* (Paris: Librairie Hachette, 1955), p. 9.
99. Ibid., p. 50.
100. See Wheaton, *History of the Law*, pp. 80–83; and Arthur Hassall, *The Balance of Power, 1715–1789*, 5th ed. (London: Rivingtons, 1950), pp. 1–3.
101. See Clive Parry, ed., *The Consolidated Treaty Series, 1713–1714*, vol. 28 (Dobbs Ferry, N.Y.: Oceana Publications, 1969), pp. 1–188.
102. Hassall, *Balance of Power*, pp. 1–3, 7–9.

103. Penfield Roberts, *The Quest for Security, 1715–1740* (New York: Harper and Brothers, 1947), p. 33.

104. Louter, *Le droit international*, p. 106.

105. Parry, *Consolidated Treaties Series*, 28, p. 21. Only the French version is given.

106. See the still provocative analysis of Crane Brinton, *A Decade of Revolution, 1789–1799* (New York: Harper and Brothers, 1934), pp. 139–140, 158–163.

107. Quoted in ibid., p. 161.

108. Ibid., pp. 108–109, 123.

109. Ibid., p. 126.

110. Quoted (in French original) by J. L. Talmon, *The Origins of Totalitarian Democracy* (New York: Frederick A. Praeger, 1960), p. 97.

111. Thomas Carlyle, *The French Revolution*, vol. III, chapter 8, reprinted by Alan Shelston, ed., *Thomas Carlyle: Selected Writings* (Harmondsworth: Penguin Books, 1980), p. 148.

112. See, for example, A. J. Grant and Harold Temperley, *Europe in the Nineteenth and Twentieth Centuries, 1789–1950*, 6th ed. (London: Longmans, Green, 1956), p. 132.

113. Henry A. Kissinger, *A World Restored: Metternich, Castlereagh, and the Problems of Peace, 1812–22* (Boston: Houghton Mifflin, 1957), p. 172.

114. See Clive Parry, ed., *The Consolidated Treaty Series, 1815*, vol. 64 (Dobbs Ferry, N.Y.: Oceana Publications, 1969), pp. 453–493. Only the French text is provided. Several prior agreements such as the Arrangement for the Free Navigation of Rivers (March 1815) can be included as parts of the overall settlement. See pp. 13–26.

115. For a short summary of these, see Friedlander, "Who Put Out the Lamps? p. 571.

116. Quoted by Frederick B. Artz, *Reaction and Revolution, 1814–1832* (New York: Harper and Brothers, 1934), p. 117. France was admitted to the Quintuple Alliance at the Congress at Aix-la-Chapelle in 1818, although the members of the Quadruple Alliance secretly renewed its terms (pp. 160–161).

117. R. P. Anand, "The Influence of History on the Literature of International Law," in Macdonald and Johnston, *Structure and Process*, p. 350.

118. R. J. Vincent, *Nonintervention and International Order* (Princeton, N.J.: Princeton University Press, 1974), p. 83.

119. See Artz, *Reaction and Revolution*, pp. 184, 207–208, 252–255.

120. Paul G. Trueblood, *Lord Byron* (New York: Twayne Publishers, 1969), pp. 120–134.

121. Artz, *Reaction and Revolution*, pp. 256–262.

122. Robert A. Friedlander, "Retaliation as an Anti-Terrorist Weapon: The Israeli Lebanon Incursion and International Law," *Israel Yearbook on Human Rights* 8 (1978), p. 64.

123. See Robert A. Friedlander, "The *Mayaguez* in Retrospect: Humanitarian Intervention or Showing the Flag?" *Saint Louis University Law Journal*, 22 (1979), p. 604; Myres McDougal, Harold D. Lasswell, and Lung-Chu Chen, *Human Rights and the World Public Order: The Basic Policies of an International Law of Human Dignity* (New Haven, Conn.: Yale University Press, 1980), pp. 239–242; and

Ellery C. Stowell, "Humanitarian Intervention," *American Journal of International Law* 33, no. 4 (October 1939), pp. 733–736.

124. See Barbara Jelavich, *A Century of Russian Foreign Policy, 1814–1914* (Philadelphia: J. B. Lippincott, 1964), pp. 113–122.

125. See Clive Parry, ed., *The Consolidated Treaty Series, 1855–1856*, vol. 114 (Dobbs Ferry, N.Y.: Oceana Publications, 1969), pp. 410–425 (French texts).

126. See Clause IX of the Treaty of Peace, couched in very ambiguous language. *Ibid.*, p. 414.

127. McDougal et al., *Human Rights*, pp. 240–241.

128. Julius W. Pratt, *A History of United States Foreign Policy*, 2d ed. (Englewood Cliffs, N.J.: Prentice-Hall, 1965), pp. 212–215, 242–243; and Richard W. Leopold, *The Growth of American Foreign Policy: A History* (New York: Alfred A. Knopf, 1962), pp. 167–179, 215–216.

129. See McDougal, et al., *Human Rights*, pp. 242–246.

130. *Ibid.*, pp. 242–243; Georges Abi-Saab, *The United Nations Operation in the Congo* (Oxford: Oxford University Press, 1978), pp. 1–3, 21–24.

131. Astri Suhrke and Lela Garner Noble, "Spread or Containment: The Ethnic Factor," in Astri Suhrke and Lela Garner Noble, eds., *Ethnic Conflict in International Relations* (New York: Praeger, 1977), pp. 231–232.

132. McDougal et al., *Human Rights*, p. 245.

133. See, for example, the legal analysis of John F. Murphy, "State Self-Help and Problems of Public International Law," in Alona E. Evans and John F. Murphy, eds., *Legal Aspects of International Terrorism* (Lexington, Mass.: D.C. Heath, 1978), pp. 554–562. It is also important to note that the West German commando exercise at Mogadishu in October 1977 does not qualify, since the Somalian government was not involved and had given permission to the West Germans to carry out their rescue operation.

134. See, Zbigniew Brzezinski, *Power and Principle: Memoirs of the National Security Adviser, 1977–1981* (New York: Farrar, Straus and Giroux, 1983), pp. 486–500; and Cyrus Vance, *Hard Choices: Critical Years in America's Foreign Policy* (New York: Simon and Schuster, 1983), pp. 408–413.

135. See the detailed and stimulating analysis of Ted L. Stein, "Contempt, Crisis, and the Court: The World Court and the Hostage Rescue Attempt," *American Journal of International Law* 76, no. 3 (July 1982), pp. 499–504.

136. See Richard B. Lillich, ed., *Humanitarian Intervention and the United Nations* (Charlottesville: University of Virginia Press, 1973). Friedlander, "The *Mayaguez*," p. 610, lists a number of critics, the most recent of whom are John F. Murphy, *The United Nations and the Control of International Violence: A Legal and Political Analysis* (Totowa, N.J.: Allanheld, Osmun, 1982), pp. 179–199; and Francis Boyle, "International Law in Times of Crisis: From the Entebbe Raid to the Hostage Convention," *Northwestern University Law Review* 75, no. 5 (December 1980), pp. 771–856.

137. Ellery C. Stowell, *Intervention in International Law* (Washington, D.C.: John Byrne, 1921), p. 51.

138. One should not overlook the American and Mexican civil wars.

139. Quoted by Koppel S. Pinson, *Modern Germany: Its History and Civilization* (New York: Macmillan, 1957), p. 309.

140. See the analysis in Friedlander, "Who Put Out the Lamps?" pp. 572–575.

141. Ibid., pp. 580–581.

142. Leo Kuper, *Genocide: Its Political Use in the Twentieth Century* (New Haven, Conn.: Yale University Press, 1981), pp. 105–115.

143. Andrew Corsum, "Armenian Terrorism: A Profile," *Department of State Bulletin* 82, no. 2065 (August 1982), pp. 31–36.

144. Clive Parry, ed., *The Consolidated Treaty Series, 1919* (Dobbs Ferry, N.Y.: Oceana Publications, 1981), p. 286.

145. Ibid., p. 285.

146. Ibid., pp. 285–286.

147. The original list of 901 war criminals was eventually reduced to 45; only 13 were convicted, several escaped, and most did not even serve out their sentences (which ranged from six months to four years). The jurisdiction exercised was domestic rather than international. Remiguisz Bierzanek, "War Crimes: History and Definition," in M. Cherif Bassiouni and Ved P. Nanda, eds., *A Treatise on International Criminal Law*, vol. I: *Crimes and Punishment* (Springfield, Ill.: Charles C Thomas, 1973), pp. 562–569.

148. H. Donnedieu de Vabres, *Introduction à l'étude du droit penal international: Essai d'histoire et de critique sur la compétence criminelle* (Paris: La Société du Recueil Sirey, 1922), p. 461. Professor Donnedieu served as the French Judge on the Nuremberg Tribunal.

149. See the succinct analysis of Leopold, *Growth of American Foreign Policy*, pp. 374–378.

150. See Louis B. Sohn and Thomas Buergenthal, eds., *International Protection of Human Rights* (Indianapolis: Bobbs-Merrill, 1973), pp. 213–251.

151. Arendt, *Origins of Totalitarianism*, p. 464.

152. The literature on the Holocaust and Stalin eras is immense, and the evidence is overwhelming. See, for example, Lucy S. Dawidowicz, *The War Against the Jews, 1933–1945* (New York: Holt, Rinehart and Winston, 1975); Nora Levin, *The Holocaust: The Destruction of European Jewry, 1933–1945* (New York: Schocken Books, 1975); Robert Conquest, *The Great Terror: Stalin's Purge of the Thirties* (New York: Macmillan, 1968); Joel Carmichael, *Stalin's Masterpiece: The Show Trials and Purges of the Thirties—The Consolidation of the Bolshevik Dictatorship* (New York: St. Martin's Press, 1976); and Richard L. Lael, *The Yamashita Precedent: War Crimes and Command Responsibility* (Wilmington, Del.: Scholarly Resources, 1982).

153. See Allen Roberts, *The Turning Point: The Assassination of Louis Barthou and King Alexander I of Yugoslavia* (New York: St. Martin's Press, 1970); Bennett Kovrig, "Mediation by Obfuscation: The Resolution of the Marseille Crisis, October 1934 to May 1935," *The Historical Journal* 19, no. 1 (1976), pp. 191–221; and Frank P. Walters, *A History of the League of Nations*, vol. 2 (London: Oxford University Press, 1952), pp. 509–650.

154. A. Sottile, *Le terrorisme internationale* (Paris: Recueil Sirey, 1939).

155. Robert A. Friedlander, *Terror–Violence: Aspects of Social Control* (New York: Oceana Publications, 1983), pp. 88–89.

156. Quincy Wright, "The Munich Settlement and International Law," *American Journal of International Law* 33, no. 1 (January 1939), p. 31.

157. An exceptionally detailed and able analysis of aspects relating to all four

conventions, but emphasizing the status of prisoners of war, can be found in Howard S. Levie, *Prisoners of War in Armed Conflict* (Newport, R.I.: Naval War College, 1977); see also the Geneva Convention Relative to the Protection of Civilian Persons in Time of War, T.I.A.S. No. 3365, 75 U.N.T.S. 287, entered into force February 2, 1956.

158. M. Cherif Bassiouni, "International Law and the Holocaust," *California Western International Law Journal* 9, no. 2 (Spring 1979), pp. 209, 212–215, 229–231; McDougal et al., *Human Rights*, pp. 354–355.

159. United Nations Sub-Commission on Prevention of Discrimination and Protection of Minorities, *Study of the Question of the Prevention and Punishment of the Crime of Genocide*, U.N. Doc. E/CH.4/Sub. 2/416, July 4, 1978, pp. 1–10.

160. Fritz Munch, "State Responsibilty in International Law," in Bassiouni and Nanda, *A Treatise*, p. 148.

161. See "Recollections of 1948," *UN Chronicle* 21, no. 2 (February 1984), pp. ii-iii. The Declaration is presented complete with annotations on pp. ix-xx.

162. Ibid., p. xx.

163. Report of the International Law Commission, 5 U.N. GAOR, Supp. (no. 12), U.N. Doc. A/136, 1950.

164. See *Department of State Bulletin*, 82 (August 1982), p. 5; and Robert A. Friedlander, "Terrorism and International Law; Recent Developments," *Rutgers Law Journal* 13, no. 3 (Spring 1982), pp. 495–499.

165. Friedlander, "Terrorism and International Law," pp. 505–507.

166. Ibid., p. 507–508.

167. Morton Kondracke, "Beyond the Melting Pot," *The New Republic*, (July 9, 1984), p. 31.

168. One estimate claims that more than 300 major or minor conflicts have occurred throughout the world since 1945. *The War Atlas*, cited in *The Blade* (Toledo), (July 17, 1983).

169. See Stephen C. McCaffrey, "The Thirty-Fifth Session of the International Law Commission," *American Journal of International Law* 78, no. 2 (April 1984), pp. 457–460, 467–475.

170. See the detailed commentaries provided in A. H. Robertson, ed., *Human Rights in National and International Law* (Manchester: Manchester University Press; Dobbs Ferry, N.Y.: Oceana Publications, 1970).

171. Michael O'Boyle, "Torture and Emergency Powers Under the European Convention on Human Rights: Ireland v. the United Kingdom," *American Journal of International Law* 71, no. 4 (October 1977), pp. 674–706; and Richard B. Lillich and Frank C. Newman, eds., *International Human Rights: Problems of Law and Policy* (Boston: Little, Brown, 1979), pp. 589–614.

172. *Letelier v. Republic of Chile*, 488 F. Supp. 665 (1980).

173. *Filartiga v. Pena-Irala*, 630 F. 2d 876 (1980).

174. Ibid., p. 890.

175. Irving R. Kaufman, "A Legal Remedy for International Torture," *New York Times Magazine*, (November 9, 1980), p. 52.

Bibliographic Note

In the bibliographic essay to our first volume, *The State As Terrorist: The Dynamics of Governmental Violence and Repression* (Greenwood Press, 1984), we detailed the literature on authoritarianism and genocide and included some comments on data sources useful to social science investigation of state violence and terror. Readers of this volume ought to consult this earlier work for citations in those areas. Here we note those works most prominent in the study of state violence and repression, with some particular attention devoted to the burgeoning literature on human rights. We caution the reader that this note is not designed to be a comprehensive view of the field but reflects our assessment of the most useful sources currently available; in addition, the contributors to this volume have also referenced a myriad of materials necessary for serious scholarship in this area, many of which do not appear in this note.

We find a number of recent works insightful in their treatment of the problem of state violence, repression and terror. Robert Justin Goldstein has produced two first-rate historical analyses of repression in his *Political Repression in Modern America: 1870 to the Present* (Schenkman, 1978) and *Political Repression in Nineteenth Century Europe* (Barnes and Noble, 1983). Terry Nardin's *Violence and the State* (Sage, 1971) and Ernest A. Duff and John F. McCamant's *Violence and Repression in Latin America* (Free Press, 1976) may still provide, respectively, the best theoretical and empirical beginning points for inquiry into this topic. David Pion-Berlin has produced an award winning doctoral dissertation on repression in his *Ideas as Predictors: A Comparative Study of Coercion in Peru and Argentina* (University of Denver, 1984).

The literature on political terrorism generally considered has grown almost exponentially since *The State As Terrorist* with but a few sources examining the problem of state terror or related issues of state terror response to insurgent terror. Useful works include an impressive reference source by Alex P. Schmid, *Political Terrorism: A Research Guide to Concepts, Theories, Data Bases and Literature* (Transaction Books, 1984), which contains a section on state terrorism. Henry H. Han has compiled a large volume entitled *Terrorism, Political Violence and*

World Order (University Press of America, 1984), which warrents consideration, as does Martha Crenshaw (ed.), *Terrorism, Legitimacy and Power* (Wesleyan University Press, 1983), and Grant Wardlaw, *Political Terrorism: Theory, Tactics, and Counter-measures* (Cambridge University Press, 1982).

Those interested in genocide and other particular forms of massive state violence should consult Amnesty International (AI), *Political Killings By Government* (AI, 1983) and *Torture in the Eighties* (AI, 1984). New scholarly treatments are provided in Jack N. Porter (ed.), *Genocide and Human Rights* (University Press of America, 1982) and Barbara Harff, *Genocide and Human Rights: International Legal and Political Issues* (University of Denver Monograph Series in World Affairs, 1984).

Those studies of state violence as human rights abuses that have taken an investigative route particularly helpful to social science include Ronald Dworkin, *Taking Rights Seriously* (Harvard University Press, 1977), Jorge Dominguez et al. (eds.), *Global Human Rights: Public Policies, Comparative Measures and NGO Strategies* (Westview Press, 1981), Peter Schwab and Adamantia Pollis (eds.), *Towards A Human Rights Framework* (Praeger, 1982), and especially the recent work of Jack Donnelly, *The Concept of Human Rights* (St. Martin's, 1985).

Regional studies include Jack L. Nelson and Vera M. Green (eds.), *International Human Rights: Contemporary Issues* (Human Rights Publishing Group, 1980), Claude E. Welch, Jr., and Ronald I. Meltzer (eds.), *Human Rights and Development in Africa* (Albany State University Press, 1984), Rhoda Howard, *Human Rights in Commonwealth Africa* (Rowman and Allanheld, 1986), Lars Schoultz, *Human Rights and United States Foreign Policy Toward Latin America* (Princeton University Press, 1982), and for the Soviet perspective, F. M. Burlatsky et al., *The Rights of the Individual in Socialist Society* (Progress Publishers [Moscow], 1982).

Either for reasons of lack of quality manuscripts or editorial policy, international relations journals, especially those noted for empirical research, publish relatively few articles on topics of internal state violence, repression, and state terror. The one exception is the *Journal of Peace Research*. Most journal studies in this area can be found in *Human Rights Quarterly* and the *Human Rights Law Journal. Chitty's* and the *Rutgers Law Journal* have published both special issues and occasional articles on these themes.

Index

Afghanistan, 61
Afrikaaner regime, 59
Albania, 150
Algiers, Battle of, 50, 53
Allende, Salvador, 218–219, 258–259
Americas Watch, 22
Amin, Idi, 10, 30, 60
Amnesty International, 1, 3, 11, 97
Apter, David, 144
Arendt, Hannah, 170, 236
Argentina, 11, 50, 57, 58, 76, 78, 85
Argentine Anti-Communist Alliance, 50
Armenians: genocide of, 166, 168, 172–175; genocide of compared with other genocides, 176–183
arms transfers, 125–130
Atacama Desert, 81
Ayala, Balthazar, 238–239

Bachrach, P., 12
Bahutu, 168
Bangladesh: genocide in, 166–168; genocide in compared to other genocides, 176–183
Baratz, M. S., 12
Barents Sea missile test, 214
Basque Homeland and Freedom, 190
Batista, Fulgencio, 52
Beagle Channel, 81

Bell, J. Boyer, 203
Bennett Committee, 200
Berman, M., 15
Black Panthers, 53
Blalock, Hubert, 16–17
Blechman, Barry, 214–216
Boer War, 32
Bolivia, 76–78
Bollen, Kenneth, 112, 131–134, 151
Bolsheviks, 56
Bonante, Luigi, 195
Bowen, Gordon, 86
Brazil, 52, 58, 76, 78–80
Breslauer, George, 4
Brezhnev (Leonid) doctrine, 209–216
British Prevention of Terrorism Acts (1974, 1976), 196–199
bureaucratic-authoritarianism, 81–82
Burundi: genocide in, 61, 166–167, 170–171; genocide in compared to other genocides, 176–183; Organization of African Unity (OAU) and, 177–178
Buzan, Barry, 83

Calvo, Robert C., 75, 78
Cambodia (Kampuchea): genocide in, 166, 174; genocide in compared to other genocides, 176–183
Canadian War Measures Act (1970), 193–194

Cardoso, Fernando H., 134
Caroline Incident, 250
Castro, Fidel, 52, 218
Central African Republic, 61
Central Intelligence Agency, 150,
    218–219
Centro de Altos Estudios Militares,
    80
Cerny, Phillip, 202
challengers, 51–52
Charny, Israel W., 167
Chiang Kai-shek, 56
Child, Jack, 76–78
Chile, 50, 57, 58, 76, 78, 84, 85, 150,
    218, 258–259
Chilean National War College, 77, 80
Chinese People's Party, 57
Chomsky, Noam, 78, 172
Churchill, Winston, 149
CIA, 218–219
coercive diplomacy, 212–217
Cohen, A. S., 115
colonial (defined), 30
Comblin, Jose, 78, 83
Congress of Vienna, 248
Couto e Silva, General Golbery, 77,
    80, 85
Crenshaw, Martha, 193–194
Crimean War, 250–251
Cuba, 53
Cultural Revolution (China), 50, 57

Dallin, Alexander, 4
DINA, 50
Diplock Court, 200–201
Diplock Report, 199–200
Dror, Yehezekel, 194–195
Duarte, Jose Napoleon, 8
Duvall, Raymond, 2, 4, 46, 74, 79,
    211

East Timor: genocide in, 166, 174;
    genocide in compared to others,
    176–183
Eckhardt, William, 98, 151
Ecuador, 76, 78
El Salvador, 57; death squads, 8, 29

Emergency Provisions Act (1973),
    199–200
Equatorial Guinea, 61
Escuela Superior de Guerra, 77, 80
Ethiopia, 61
Eurasia, 58
European Court of Human Rights,
    199, 237, 258
European Economic Community, 36–
    37
Evans, Peter, 134

Fairbanks, John King, 56
Faletto, Enzo, 134
Falk, Richard, 73–74, 79
Falkland Islands, 81
fear, 4, 9–11, 217
Federal Bureau of Investigation, 50
Fein, Helen, 166, 170
Filartiga v. Pena-Irela (1980), 258–259
Finer, S. E., 113, 115
Fitzgerald, Frances, 6
Fitzgibbon, Russell, 21
FMLN, 216
Ford, Gerald, 219
Franck, T., 209
Frank, Andre Gunder, 151
Freedom House, 19
FRETILIN, 172
Friedman, Milton, 38

Garner, Eric, 79
Gastil, Raymond, 20, 98, 113
Gelb, Leslie, 219
Gentili, Alberico, 238–240
geopolitical theory, 80–82
George, Alexander, 214
German Democratic Republic (GDR),
    122
Germany (1918–1919), 39, 165
Ghana, 150, 215
Gorman, Stephen, 78
Griffith, Ernst, 146
Grotius, (Hugo de Grot), 238, 240–
    241
Guatemala, 19, 52, 57, 81–82, 86
Guest, Iain, 97
Gurgel, Amaral, 75–76

Hague Conventions, 236, 253
Halliday, Fred: second Cold War concept, 100
Hammerskjold, Dag, 238
Heilbroner, Robert, 132, 134–135
Herman, Edward, 78, 97, 151, 172
Himmler, Heinrich, 55
Hitler, Adolf, 46
Holocaust, 165–169
Horowitz, Irving Louis, 167, 169, 194
humanitarian intervention, 249–252
Huntington, Samuel, 113
Hutus, 171, 175–176

Indonesia, 172
Inter-American Development Bank, 216
Irish Republican Army, 1, 190, 196
Italy, 265
Ivan the Terrible, 56

Jacobin Reign of Terror, 247
Japanese Red Army, 190
Jellicoe, Lord, 197–198
Jennings, Anthony, 201
Johansen, Robert C., 151
Johnson, Kenneth, 21
Johnson, Lyndon Baines, 209
Judges Rules (Britain), 197–198

Kampuchea (Cambodia), 61, 150; genocide in, 167–170, 174–175; genocide in compared to other genocides, 176–183
Kaplan, Stephen, 214–216
Kelley, Philip L., 77, 80
Kelman, Herbert, 88, 182
Kende, Istvan, 151
Kennedy, John F., 210
Kenya, 7
KGB, 219
Khrushchev, Nikita, 210
Kjellan, Rudolf, 80, 81
Ku Klux Klan, 53
Kuomintang, 56
Kuper, Leo, 166
Kurds, 166, 173, 176–181

League of Nations, 166, 170, 254–255
Lebanon, 237–238
Lemarchand, Rene, 171
Letelier v. Republic of Chile (1980), 258–259
Lieber, Francis, 236
Lipset, Seymour, 97, 112, 133–135, 137–138, 141, 146
Livingstone, Neil, 192–193
Lon Nol, 174
Lopez, George A., 74, 79
Louis XIV, 245
Lukes, S., 12

McCamant, John, 20
Mack, Andrew, 202
McKinley, R. D., 115
Mao Tse-tung, 53
Marchetti, Victor, 218
Marks, John, 218
Marx, Karl, 135, 145
Mayaguez, 215
de Meira Mattos, General Carlos, 77, 80
Michael's Law, 113
Miliband, Ralph, 138
militarism, 53; as a correlate of repression and state terror, 78, 79, 114, 119
Moore, R. Barrington, 134, 137
MOSSAD, 192

Nardin, Terry, 49
National Council for Civil Liberties (Britain), 196–198
National Liberation Front, 6
national security: definition, 76
Nazi, 4, 29, 30, 55, 165–167, 170
New International Economic Order (NIEO), 97, 148
Nicaragua, 150; mining of harbors, 216, 219
Nixon, Richard M., 210
NKUD, 50
Nordlinger, Erik, 115
Northern Ireland, 16; laws affecting terrorism in, 196–199

Nubians, 60
Nuremberg trials, 237

Odell, John, 128–129, 151
Official Secrets Act, 9
OGPU, 56
Okhrana, 56
Operation Phoenix, 6
Ottoman Empire: genocide of Arme-
    nians in, 166, 173, 176–183

Palestine Liberation Organization, 1
Paraguay, 57
Paris, Peace of, 251
Pasha, Enver, 173
People's Republic of China, 66, 209–
    210
Peru, 76, 78, 80–81
Phnom Penh, 174
Poland, 215–216
Police and Criminal Evidence Bill
    (Britain), 198
Pol Pot regime, 30; and genocide,
    167, 174, 176–183
Pope John Paul II, 48
Portuguese, 172
Powell, G. Bingham, 143
Premo, David, 88
Prevention of Terrorism Act (1974),
    196
Puffendorf, Samuel, 241–243
Pye, Lucien, 113, 133, 135

Qadhafi, Mu'ammar, 218

Randle, Michael, 78–79
Rapaport, David, 88
Ravenal, Earl, 151
Reagan, Ronald, 216
Red Cross (International), 171
Red Guards, 50
Republican Intelligence Service, 59
Richman, Sheldon, 151
Roosevelt, Franklin Delano, 216
Rwanda, 61, 167, 170–171, 176

Sandinistas, 216
SAVAK, 50

Schelling, Thomas, 213
Schneider, Rene, 218
Schoultz, Lars, 21, 131, 151
Scoble, H., p. 20
Secret Anti-Communist Alliance, 50
Shackleton, Lord, 197–198
Shah of Iran, 30
Shaka Zulu, 51
Sihanouk, Prince Norodom, 174
Sim, Joe, 197–198
Singer, J. David, 151
Sivard, Ruth, 100, 117, 120, 151
Skocpol, Theda, 65
Sloan, John, 82
South Africa, 13
Southern Cone, 76
Special Services, 57
state terrorism: definition, 3–6, 31–
    32, 45–46
Stalin, Josef, 53
Stohl, Michael, 2, 4, 46, 74, 79
Stormont Special Powers Act (Brit-
    ain), 199
Suárez, Francisco, 238–240
Sukarno, President, 47
SWAT, 54

Tannahill, Neal, 115
Textor, Johann Wolfgang, 238–242
Thatcher, Margaret, 9, 10
Thomas, Philip, 197–198
Tibetans, 166, 176ff.
Tilly, Charles, 51
Tokyo War Crimes Trial, 237
Travasso, Colonial Mario, 80
Trimberger, Ellen Kay, 65
Turner, Richard, 47
Tutsi, 171, 175, 176
Twa, 171

UDT, 177
Uganda, 10, 30, 60–61
UNITA, 219
United Kingdom, 13
United National Front, 174
United Nations, 167, 170; Charter,
    166; Convention Against the Tak-
    ing of Hostages, 257; Genocide

Convention (1948), 48, 169, 237, 256–257; Human Rights Commission, 61, 97; Security Council, 175; Universal Declaration of Human Rights, 256, 297
Uruguay, 57, 58, 76, 79–81, 85
Utrecht, Peace of, 246

de Vattel, Emmerick, 243–244
Velasco, General, 81
de Victoria, Francisco, 238
Videla, General Jorge, 89
Vietnam, 61, 174–175
Villegas, Osiris Guillermo, 77, 80–85

Wako, Amos, 97
Walsh, Dermot, 200
Walter, E. V., 51, 236
Waltz, Kenneth, 208
Warsaw Pact, 217
Weber, Max, 78, 79, 81, 112, 145
Weisband, W., 209
Westphalia, Peace of, 245–246
Wilkinson, Paul, 191, 193
Wiseberg, Laurie, 20
Wulf, Herbert, 151

Yuan, Shih-k'ai, 56

Zulu, Shaka, 51

Contributors

DAVID CARLETON is a doctoral candidate in Political Science at Purdue University. He has co-authored articles on human rights and U.S. foreign policy in the *Journal of Peace Research* and *Human Rights Quarterly*, and is currently researching the impact of economic stabilization on political repression in Latin America.

ROBERT A. FRIEDLANDER is Professor of Law at the Pettit College of Law of Ohio Northern University. He is currently Assistant Counsel to the Subcommittee on the Constitution of the Committee on the Judiciary of the United States Senate. He is the author and editor of seven books, including a four-volume documentary analysis of international terrorism. He has also published over 80 articles, book chapters, and review essays, focusing on such diverse topics as terrorism, human rights, international criminal law, and Middle East politics.

TED ROBERT GURR is Professor of Political Science and Director of the Center for Comparative Politics at the University of Colorado, Boulder. His twelve books and monographs on political conflict, governmental performance, and criminal justice include *Violence in America: Historical and Comparative Perspectives* (with Hugh Davis Graham, 1969, 1979), *Why Men Rebel* (winner of the Woodrow Wilson Prize as best book in political science of 1970), and *Rogues, Rebels, and Reforms: A Political History of Urban Crime and Conflict* (1976). His current work is concerned with the role of the state in conflict processes and trends in internal conflict, especially in highly stratified and segmented societies.

BARBARA HARFF is Visiting Assistant Professor of Political Science at the University of Colorado at Boulder. She holds a Ph.D from Northwestern University (1981) and has taught at La Trobe University in Melbourne, Australia, and at the University of Illinois, Chicago Circle. Her research interests are the international and comparative dimensions of massive human rights violations, especially the problem of genocide. Her monograph on "Genocide and Human

Rights: International Legal and Political Issues" was published in the Monograph Series in World Affairs, Graduate School of International Studies, University of Denver (1984). Other publications include a chapter in *The Age of Genocide*, edited by Michael N. Dobkowski and Isidor Wallimann.

GEORGE A. LOPEZ is Associate Professor of Government and International Studies and a Fellow at the Institute for International Peace Studies at the University of Notre Dame. He has published on problems of terrorism and international violence in *Chitty's Law Journal* and *Terrorism: An International Journal*. With Michael Stohl he has co-edited a number of books on the subject including *The State As Terrorist* (Greenwood, 1984).

CHRISTOPHER MITCHELL is Professor of International Relations at the City University in London and coordinator of the Conflict Management Research Group there. His main research interests and writings have centered on the nature of social and international conflict and ways of managing or resolving it without resort to violence. He is the author of *The Structure of International Conflict* and *Peacemaking and the Consultant's Role* as well as numerous journal articles. He is currently working on a study of how conflicts end, with particular emphasis on the difficult decisions that have to be made during processes of de-escalation and termination.

MICHAEL NICHOLSON was formerly Director of the Richardson Institute for Conflict and Peace Research in England, and is currently Visiting Professor of Political Science at Yale. His research interests are in conflict analysis and the philosophy of the social sciences, his most recent book being *The Scientific Analysis of Social Behaviour: A Defense of Empiricism in Social Science* (1983). The essay in this volume was written while a Fellow at the Netherlands Institute for Advanced Study.

MICHAEL STOHL is Professor of Political Science at Purdue University. He has published widely on problems of insurgent and state terrorism including articles in *Human Rights Quarterly, Journal of Peace Research* and *Chitty's Law Journal*. In addition he has edited *The Politics of Terrorism* and co-edited four other books.

GRANT WARDLAW is a Senior Criminologist with the Australian Institute of Criminology, Canberra, Australia. He is the author of *Political Terrorism: Theory, Tactics and Countermeasures* and numerous chapters and articles on terrorism, public order, and drug enforcement.

MILES WOLPIN is Professor of Political Science at the State University of New York at Potsdam. He holds degrees in Law and Political Science; has been a Fellow at the Peace Research Institute, Oslo; is a member of the Executive Committee of the Consortium for Peace Research, Education and Development (COPRED); and writes extensively on issues of militarism and social change in the Third World.